"This volume on human traffick... ...t line service providers, theorists, researchers, and passionate advocates for those who are moved by the scourge of modern-day slavery. It introduces and advances you to some of the deepest issues and questions that must be faced in order to offer a mature Christian response to this heartache. This brilliant work models how vastly different perspectives on this issue can sing together to create a song of shalom. This is a must read gift to the body of Christ."

Dan B. Allender, Ph.D., Professor of Counseling Psychology & Founding President, The Seattle School of Theology and Psychology Author, *The Wounded Heart, To Be Told* and other works

"Christians have been leaders, service providers, and financial supporters of the fight against sex trafficking going back the 19th century when it was called the white slave trade. This volume is an excellent collection of Christian thought on sex trafficking and the topics related to it."

Donna M. Hughes, Ph.D., Professor & Carlson Endowed Chair at the University of Rhode Island

"I am delighted to endorse this first volume of *Stopping the Traffick*. For more than a decade now the church has become aware of these issues largely through a plethora of media articles, documentaries and blogs. However, the content of many of these have presented a simplistic and often highly sensationalized overview and with sentimental responses to what is an incredibly complex environment of both the issues and responses. I believe this volume presents a unique profile of these challenges through the words of a broad spectrum of academics, activists and practitioners who have worked tirelessly with and for those who face the most vulnerable and exploitative environments in our world today. This volume asks and responds to the deep and often awkward questions that many people want to hear but struggle to bring into the light. It presents both an academic framework as well as a practical basis of case studies for many of these enabling the reader to gain a global perspective and understanding on the many cross-cutting issues that contribute to both the vulnerability and demand factors of human trafficking. I believe that knowledge equals responsibility—therefore, be prepared to be challenged beyond the words to action!"

Helen Sworn, International Director & Founder, Chab Dai, Cambodia

"Throughout history people of faith have played a vital role in justice movements and caring for the oppressed. This book is written specifically to engage people of Christian faith in not only recognizing the ongoing importance of that role but also the desperate need for thoughtful and practical approaches to complex issues.

You will find the authors represent a wide range of expertise and experience as well as a diversity of opinion. Coming from the perspective of a person of faith, but also as a leader of a non-faith-based organization I found myself agreeing with Christa Crawford who writes in her Introduction: "No one will concur with every perspective represented in this book. We don't want you to.""

There are thoughts and ideas expressed in *Stopping the Traffick* that had me enthusiastically nodding my head in agreement and others that I found troubling or disagreed with. Within the community of faith, as well as outside of it, and certainly within this book, there are a diversity of opinions and perspectives – if you have a firmly held view, you will likely find dissonance with some represented here, and hopefully find resonance with others – I know I did, and benefitted from it."

Rob Morris, President & Co-Founder, Love146

"This rich and comprehensive resource written by experts in the field will prove to be highly valuable to anyone caring for sexually exploited persons. The topics in this book are issues that must be discussed and thoughtfully engaged. I will highly recommend this book to students, organizations and anyone interested in this ministry. I will also keep it as an anchor resource on my desk."

Pamela MacRae, Ph.D., Associate Professor, Pastoral Studies Department, Moody
    Bible Institute, Director of "Ministry to Victims of Sexual Exploitation" major

"Stopping the Traffick is more than a timely address of the global epidemic of exploitation. Trafficking is one of these issues that is easy to address poorly. But Glenn Miles and his capable team of editors have achieved a benchmark of insight and credibility. Insight, because they've chosen to address sexual exploitation using over forty different professional voices, each writing in an area of expertise. And credibility, because they address trafficking as the *multiplex* problem it really is: from pimps to pornography, tourism to transgender communities, and theology to technology. Writers acknowledge the damage politics can do, yet the book refreshing rises above the political fray. In fact, many entries creatively appeal for a more compassionate Church to be involved. Most encouraging for me is the investigation into the wholesale neglect of boys (Chapter 4), a discussion long lost to politics and proportionality arguments.

From advocacy organizations to mission teams and academic classes, *Stopping the Traffick* is raw and engaging – as it must be – since it explores the complexity and urgency of global sexual exploitation. Here is a tool of training for the next generation of Christian response to sexual exploitation."

Andrew J. Schmutzer, Ph.D., Professor of Biblical Studies, Moody Bible Institute

"Stopping the Traffic is a timely response by reflective practitioners to the many questions the Church has of human sexual exploitation and trafficking but not sure where to look for 'biblical and theological' answers. While the readings remind us of the gross evil that lies at our doorstep and the mammoth challenges before us, it also directs us to hope—God and His people can and are already advocating to make a difference. This book should be in the bibliography of every advocacy training syllabus."

Rosalind Lim-Tan, Ph.D.
    Director, Holistic Child Development Institute, Penang, Malaysia

"All readers, whatever their cultural, socio-economic, religious or political views will find so much to grill their conscience in this book. Its extensiveness, the concrete research data, the social science, historical, and theological approach of its arguments will provoke one's spirit, soul, and mind. This book is a gift from God, the One who created all human beings-equal and free."

Nativity A. Petallar, Program Director, Holistic Child Development, Asia-Pacific Nazarene Theological Seminary, Manila, Philippines

Stopping the Traffick

A Christian Response to Sexual Exploitation and Trafficking

Series Preface

Regnum Studies in Mission are born from the lived experience of Christians and Christian communities in mission, especially but not solely in the fast growing churches among the poor of the world. These churches have more to tell than stories of growth. They are making significant impacts on their cultures in the cause of Christ. They are producing 'cultural products' which express the reality of Christian faith, hope and love in their societies.

Regnum Studies in Mission are the fruit often of rigorous research to the highest international standards and always of authentic Christian engagement in the transformation of people and societies. And these are for the world. The formation of Christian theology, missiology and practice in the twenty-first century will depend to a great extent on the active participation of growing churches contributing biblical and culturally appropriate expressions of Christian practice to inform World Christianity.

Series Editors

Julie C. Ma	Oxford Centre for Mission Studies, Oxford, UK
Wonsuk Ma	Oxford Centre for Mission Studies, Oxford, UK
Doug Petersen	Vanguard University, Costa Mesa, CA, USA
Terence Ranger	University of Oxford, Oxford, UK
C.B. Samuel	Emmanuel Hospital Association, Delhi, India
Chris Sugden	Anglican Mainstream, Oxford, UK

A full listing of titles in this series
appears at the end of this book

REGNUM STUDIES IN MISSION

Stopping the Traffick

A Christian Response to
Sexual Exploitation and Trafficking

Edited by
Glenn Miles and Christa Foster Crawford
with Tania DoCarmo and Gundelina Velazco

WIPF & STOCK · Eugene, Oregon

Wipf and Stock Publishers
199 W 8th Ave, Suite 3
Eugene, OR 97401

Stopping the Traffick
A Christian Response to Sexual Exploitation and Trafficking
By Miles, Glenn and Crawford, Christa Foster
Copyright©2014 Regnum Books International
ISBN 13: 978-1-4982-0078-3
Publication date 6/15/2014
Previously published by Regnum, 2014

regnum

This book is dedicated to the girls, boys, women, men and transgender people who are survivors of, or still experiencing sexual exploitation and trafficking, and to those who are bringing justice to the most vulnerable.

Contents

Foreword
  Glenn Miles   xv
Acknowledgements   xviii
List of Abbreviations   xix

**Introduction: Stopping the Traffick: How Should Christians
  Respond to Sexual Exploitation and Trafficking?**
  Christa Foster Crawford   1

Part 1
**What Can We Do about the Problems of Sexual Exploitation
  and Trafficking?**
  Introduction (Glenn Miles)   13
1. Is It Naive to Think Slavery and Exploitation Will Ever Come to an End?
   Key Issues (Kevin Bales)   14
2. How Can Donors Positively Engage in the Anti-Trafficking Movement?
   Key Issues (Jeremy Floyd)   19

Part 2
How Should We Make Sense of Sexual Exploitation?
  Introduction (Glenn Miles)   29
3. What Does the Bible Say about Being Involved in Justice for
   the Sexually Exploited?
   Biblical Mandate (Ian De Villiers)   31
   Case Study (Ian De Villiers)   38
4. How Should the Church Be Involved in Responding
   to Sexual Exploitation?
   Key Issues (Jim Martin)   41
   Case Study (Jim Martin)   47
5. Does Sex Matter to God? Why Should It Matter to Us as Christians?
   Theological Reflection (Dan Allender)   50
6. How Have We Messed Up Sex?
   Theological Reflection (Lisa L. Thompson)   55
7. Where is God When Sex Gets Messy?
   Theological Reflection (Andrew J. Schmutzer)   65
   Case Study (Andrew J. Schmutzer)   69
8. How Can We Survive in the Midst of the Mess?
   Theological Reflection (Bill Prevette)   71
   Case Study (Bill Prevette)   77
9. How Can We Get from Hostility to Hospitality When
   Dealing with Transgender and Other Sexual Minorities?
   Theological Reflection (Heike Lippmann)   79

Part 3
How Should We Respond to Demand?
    Introduction (Christa Foster Crawford and Glenn Miles)   87
10. Why Is Demand Important to Tackle and What Can the
    Church Do about it?
    Key Issues (Donna M. Hughes)   92
    Key Issues (Sven-Gunnar Lidén)   97
    Case Study (Sven-Gunnar Lidén)   103
11. Where Are the Men of the Church in Addressing Demand?
    Key Issues (Peter Grant)   105
12. How Can We Stop the Demand for Child Sex Tourism and
    Instead Create a Demand for Child Safe Tourism?
    Key Issues (Jesse Eaves and Tim Høiland)   111
    Case Study (Jesse Eaves and Tim Høiland)   116
13. Isn't It Time We See the Links between Pornography,
    Prostitution and Sex Trafficking?
    Key Issues (Nicole Garcia and Christa Foster Crawford)   118
14. How Can We Encourage Men in the Church to Challenge
    the Use of Pornography?
    Key Issues (Steve Siler and Tammy Stauffer)   123
15. Why Is Addressing Access of Youth to Pornography
    So Important to Tackling Demand?
    Key Issues (Christa Foster Crawford and Glenn Miles)   130
16. What Is Our Responsibility towards Pornographers?
    Are They Outside of God's Redemption?
    Key Issues (Craig Gross)   138
    Case Study (Craig Gross)   141
17. What Is Our Responsibility towards Pimps and Pedophiles?
    Are They Outside of God's Redemption?
    Case Study (Don Brewster)   143
18. Is There Hope for Men Who Visit Red-Light Districts?
    Key Issues (Christian Lenty)   147
    Case Study (Christian Lenty)   150
19. How Are We Doing Ourselves? What Can We Do about
    the Sexual Behavior of Expatriate Christian Men?
    Key Issues (Kenneth R. Taylor, Glenn Miles and Mark Ainsworth)   153

Part 4
How Can We Better Work with Boys and Men?
    Introduction (Glenn Miles and Christa Foster Crawford)   165
20. Why Do We Focus More on Girls Than Boys?
    Key Issues (Alastair Hilton)   169
    Key Issues (Doug Van Ramshorst)   174

21. What Are the Unique Challenges of Working with Boys and
    Young Men and How Can We Effectively Meet Their Needs?
    Key Issues (Alezandra Russell) 178
22. How Can We Effectively Work with Boys and Men in
    a Non-Judgmental and Supportive Way?
    Key Issues (Alastair Hilton) 184
    Advice from Practitioners (Jonathan W. Hancock) 193
23. How Should Christians and the Church Engage with Boys and Men?
    Advice from Practitioners (Doug Van Ramshorst) 197
    Advice from Practitioners (Jane Beal) 197
    Case Study (Derek Collard) 198
24. How Do We Deal With Being Considered "Pro-Gay" for Working
    with Men Involved in Commercial Sex and Being
    Considered "Anti-Gay" Because of Our Faith?
    Key Issues (Wendy Gritter) 201
    Case Study (Paul Goodell) 205
25. Should Christians and the Church Work with the LGBT
    Community and If So How?
    Key Issues (Carl Jylland-Halverson) 207
    Case Study (Carl Jylland-Halverson) 211

Part 5
How Can We Better Work with Transgender People?
Introduction (Glenn Miles) 215
26. What Is a Biblical Approach to the Transgender Community?
    Key Issues (Eric Mason) 218
27. How Can We Work More Effectively with Transgender People
    Who are Sexually Exploited?
    Key Issues (Jarrett Davis and Glenn Miles) 226
28. How Can the Church Effectively Minister to Transgender People
    Who are Sexually Exploited?
    Key Issues (Celeste McGee) 231
29. Why Does the Church Ignore Transgender People and How
    Can We Bridge the Gap?
    Key Issues (Duncan Craig) 238
    Case Study (Duncan Craig) 242

Part 6
How Should We Collaborate?
Introduction (Tania DoCarmo) 245
30. Why Is Networking Important?
    Key Issues (Brian Wilkinson) 248
31. What Are Some Existing Models of Collaboration?
    How Did They Develop? What Are Some of the Challenges?

       Case Study (Lauran Bethell)   252
       Case Study (Tania DoCarmo)   255
32. How Can Technology and the Internet Be Used
    to Enhance Collaboration?
       Key Issues (Christa Foster Crawford)   259
       Case Study (Tania DoCarmo)   263
       Case Study (Ané Auret)   264
33. What Are the Challenges of Partnership? How Do We Work with
    People/Organizations Who May Seem Controversial or Who May
    not Espouse Similar Christian Values (Without Compromising)?
       Key Issues (Helen Sworn)   268
       Case Study (Helen Sworn)   272
       Key Issues (Jennifer Roemhildt Tunehag)   273
       Case Study (Jennifer Roemhildt Tunehag)   278

Recommended Resources and Works Cited   281
Contributors   307

FOREWORD

In May 2009, Christian practitioners and others concerned about child sexual exploitation and trafficking came together for the second North American Asha Forum Consultation. The theme of the conference was "Beyond Awareness: Empowering a Response."

The conference was presented by Viva, the sponsor of the Asha Forum,[1] and Fuller Theological Seminary's Children at Risk Program.[2] Two of the editors of this book served on the conference steering committee: Christa Crawford (as Adjunct Assistant Professor of Children at Risk at Fuller) and Tania DoCarmo (representing Chab Dai, one of the conference sponsors).

In her opening remarks, Christa expressed the steering committee's passionate hope for the conference:

> By now, we have read the *Christianity Today* articles. We have seen the *Dateline* pieces. We have heard the Sunday sermons. We now know about all this darkness, but we still don't know what we could possibly do about it.
>
> This weekend, we will move Beyond Awareness and seek to equip and empower you with tools and resources to respond: in your church, in your community, maybe even around the world.
>
> This weekend, we will seek to go beyond good intentions to better practices. Beyond awareness to action. Beyond being overwhelmed by the darkness to learning how to bring points of light.

Love146 president Rob Morris reiterated the necessity for better responses in his opening keynote speech in which he described the tension between merely responding to the urgency of the need vs. the thoughtfulness it takes to create long-lasting and effective responses.

While these goals of the Asha Forum Consultation were crucial and compelling, unfortunately at the time there were not many resources available to equip practitioners to respond effectively, and even fewer that helped them thoughtfully consider how to create effective, lasting responses to the problems of sexual exploitation and trafficking.[3]

Realizing that many practitioners were struggling with the same questions and challenges in caring for people who are sexually exploited, I hoped that out

---

[1] Viva is a network of churches and community organizations that seeks lasting change in children's lives through the power of collective action. The Asha Forum's purpose is to inform, unite, equip and mobilize Christians worldwide in preventing all forms of child sexual abuse. www.viva.org

[2] http://www.fuller.edu/childrenatrisk/

[3] The few comprehensive peer-reviewed books targeted towards Christian practitioners at the time – and since then – consisted primarily of FAAST's *Hands that Heal Curriculum* (2007) and Phyllis Kilbourn and Marjorie McDermid's *Sexually Exploited Children: Working to Protect and Heal* (1998), both of which we commend to readers. In addition, some individuals and organizations had put out more informal practical manuals that were helpful to practitioners, but they were not widely known or easily obtained.

of the conference we could develop a compilation volume that would address the important questions that practitioners frequently ask themselves and that they are asked by others.

A working group formed during the conference came up with an initial set of questions that we thought practitioners, informed Christians and modern-day abolitionists would like answered. Some were theological, some were academic, but most were practical and the kind of questions that practitioners continually struggled to find answers to. This list was distributed to a range of people to verify that they were indeed what people wanted to know and for them to add more suggestions. We simultaneously invited people whom we thought were best qualified to answer each question to be contributors.

Although the book was birthed out of the Asha Forum we also wanted participation from other networks addressing similar issues. The International Christian Alliance on Prostitution (ICAP)[4] agreed to join us, which was a great gain because the questions practitioners need addressed did not relate only to children (which is the focus of Viva), but to all people who are affected (which is the scope of ICAP). We shared about the book at the 2011 ICAP Conference and were able to attract a number of contributors from that network as well. While many of the writers for this edited volume have come out of the Asha Forum and ICAP, we have also sought responses from people beyond these networks who are making important contributions to the thinking or doing pioneering work on the field.

In the process of adding contributors, we also had to keep adding to the list of questions as we realized more and more questions needed answering. Soon we had enough material for more than one volume but we didn't want to stop because we felt that people were eager to receive answers to the questions. Additionally, contributors told us how much they appreciated writing their answers because it gave them an opportunity to solidify thoughts that up until then they had found hard to put into words. This showed us how valuable it was to include as many questions as possible and we decided to turn the original book into a multi-volume project.

This first volume focuses on six key themes, from making sense of exploitation from a theological perspective, to understanding and addressing the role of demand, to better recognizing and reaching out to invisible groups, and more! We look forward to publishing additional volumes that address important questions about other issues including: How should we respond holistically? How do we address challenges in outreach? How should we ensure excellence in aftercare? How might we ensure safe and successful reintegration? How can we engage our brains as well as our hearts?

You can keep updated through our community on Freedom Collaborative[5] where you can also engage with the contributors about questions in this book and offer your own suggestions for future questions.

As editors we are proud to have such an amazing assortment of people contribute to this volume – people from a number of professional backgrounds:

---

[4] www.icapglobal.org
[5] http://freedomcollaborative.org

professors, doctors, nurses, lawyers, theologians, psychologists, sociologists. You only have to read the list of contributors to see a veritable "Who's Who" in the faith-based anti-trafficking community and beyond. Our contributors come from a range of church-manships from Quaker to Episcopalian to more charismatic. Some of the opinions represented may not suit every reader's taste but we wanted to ensure a wide range of voices could be heard. If you feel that there are other voices that need to be heard please let us know for future volumes.[6]

As you will see, these are difficult questions to answer. Our contributors have spent weeks and months refining their responses, and many years before then deliberating the issues in theory and in practice. Their answers embody the thoughtfulness that Rob Morris called us to engage in. But readers and the contributors alike may find that the answers given only lead to more questions! Nevertheless, it is our hope and prayer that those of us in the movement to abolish human trafficking will be inspired in reading this volume and encouraged by what *is* happening now and what we might be able to accomplish in the future – that people will see they are *not alone* but that the church *is* responding and they too can be part of what the body of Christ is doing to Stop the Traffick.

The book you are holding in your hands today seeks to realize the vision of that original Asha Forum Consultation by empowering the Christian response to sexual exploitation and trafficking with a tool that helps us to go beyond good intentions to better practice. It also seeks to fulfill Rob Morris' exhortation to think through the challenging questions of how to create long-lasting and effective change.

We hope and pray you will find this to be the case!

Glenn Miles

---

[6] http://freedomcollaborative.org

ACKNOWLEDGMENTS

We are grateful to the authors who have such extraordinary commitment to addressing these important issues that they have freely volunteered their time and hard work in writing essays and enduring the long and arduous editing process.

We also want to thank Steve Edwards,[1] Rachael Helsel and Shirley Love Rayburn for their contribution to this volume in contacting and following up with authors at different times over the past four years in the production of this volume. We also appreciate Priscilla Schafer for helping in the final stages of editing and collecting contributor biographies.

We are grateful to Patrick Knowles[2] who kindly developed the book cover.

Many thanks also go to Tony Gray of *Words by Design* for being our liaison person with *Regnum*, and Jessica Abel-Smith at *Oxford Centre for Mission Studies* for our liaison with them.

Finally, we could not have done any of this without the support of our spouses – Siobhan Miles, Mark Crawford, Genilson DoCarmo and Vincent Velazco – and their patience and love in this mammoth undertaking, especially in the final stages.

---

[1] http://en.gravatar.com/scorchingwords
[2] Patrick Knowles Design http://www.patrickknowlesdesign.com/cover_design.html

LIST OF ABBREVIATIONS

CST	Child Sex Tourism
ECPAT	End Child Prostitution, Child Pornography, and Trafficking of Children for Sexual Purposes
GRS	Gender Reassignment Surgery
LGBT	Lesbian, Gay, Bisexual, Transgender
MSM	Men who have Sex with Men
NGO	Non-Governmental Organization
STI	Sexually Transmitted Infection

INTRODUCTION

STOPPING THE TRAFFICK:
HOW SHOULD CHRISTIANS RESPOND TO SEXUAL
EXPLOITATION AND TRAFFICKING?

By Christa Foster Crawford

Stop the Traffick?

Isn't that an impossible and insurmountable goal?

And yet we as Christians do desire to stop trafficking and sexual exploitation – in our communities, in our own countries, in other nations where the issue is allowed to flourish, and ultimately – by God's grace – we'd like to see them eliminated completely.

So, how do we even begin addressing such an important – and yet overwhelming – task?

Thankfully Christians have a long history at the forefront of standing against injustice. Pioneers like Amy Carmichael, William Wilberforce, Catherine and William Booth and others stood up against sexual and other slavery, oppression and exploitation long before terms like "human trafficking" and "modern-day slavery" ever came into vogue. They were just doing what the people of God have been called upon to do since the days of the Prophets: Seek Justice. Defend the Needy. Free the Oppressed.

Standing up against sexual exploitation and trafficking is part of the "DNA" of who we are as the people of God, and it is something that God has consistently called his people to do, even to the present day.

So, once again, we wonder: How do we go about doing what we have been called to do?

Since the early 2000s a flood of awareness campaigns have awakened a new wave of Christians to contemporary injustices such as sexual exploitation, human trafficking and modern-day slavery. Many millions have been moved to compassion, and many thousands been moved to action. Ministries and faith-based organizations have raced to respond, compelled by concern that comes from the very heart of God. Some of those efforts continue today, leaders not only among faith-based efforts but also among governmental and other non-faith-based efforts. There is much to be celebrated.

But many others have themselves been stopped in their tracks in their sincere efforts to "Stop the Traffick." They've been stopped for many reasons: funding has dried up, visions have diffused, burning passion has led to just plain "burnout." After being inspired to care, mobilized to respond and readied to make a difference, many have become jaded and frustrated when their best efforts have barely made a dent in the overwhelming enormity of the problem and complexity of the response.

Again – desperately this time – we ask: How can we ever hope to stop the traffick, without the traffick running over us first?

Those who are still continuing to move forward know that the road is hard and the successes are few. They have discovered some of what does – and what does not – work, but they have had to do it the hard way of trial and error and costly mistakes. They know that the expenditure of limited time and money and human resources is worth everything when they see the difference it has made in the life of one person who was once entrapped and who is now on the path to freedom. But they also know that limited resources can always be used in more efficient ways. They have come to realize that "good intentions are not good enough" and that we must ensure that we are working in the most effective way possible. These enduring pioneers know that they need to know more to do their work better. But they too ask what all of us are asking:

Who can help us know how to stop the traffick in the most effective ways possible?

These questions and more are the reason we have written this book. This book asks – and seeks to give some answers – to the questions practitioners wrestle with most, questions such as:

- How can we make sense of sexual exploitation and trafficking?
- What can we do about the problem?
- How should we focus our response?
- How should we go about working with people who are exploited?
- How should we go about working with one another?
- How do we deal with the challenges?
- How can we do all of these things more effectively in order to finally stop the traffick?

In asking these questions, we realize that there are no easy answers.

Just as these questions represent difficult challenges, answering them presents hurdles as well.

First, there are many different perspectives to each question.

We have purposely asked people from a wide variety of positions and perspectives to address these questions. Most are practitioners who have been struggling with these issues on the ground as they try to help bring relief to actual victims. But some are also theologians, academics and others who have been thinking about these issues from a strategic level and can give a macro-view of the larger context in which these questions must be answered. It's crucial that both sides inform each other.

We've also brought together authors who are working in a variety of contexts. Many are working in Asia, but others are or have worked in Europe, the US and other parts of the globe. We have perspectives from developing countries and highly industrialized ones.

This book presents essays written by world-renowned experts like Kevin Bales and Donna Hughes and Dan Allender who have been working in the field for years and have large bodies of published works that are widely influential in their disciplines. We have much to learn from their expertise and are humbled that they have been willing to contribute to this volume.

But this book also includes essays that are just as important that were written by people who are only known by the communities in which they work. These are the "start-ups," courageous pioneers who have recognized hidden areas of darkness that the broader response has ignored. While the freedom movement in general (and Christians in particular) have focused on the forced trafficking of girls and more recently women, there are many more types of people who do not fit within our traditional categories of "victim" and therefore remain unseen in the shadows and marginalized. Such is the case with boys and men. Sometimes these invisible groups are the very groups that "good" Christians might ordinarily seek to avoid. Such is the case with transsexuals and the LGBT community. But, as the theological reflections in this book demonstrate, Jesus often came alongside the kind of people that others thought were "wrong" for him to mix with. Let us not forget how often Jesus spent time with sinners, and sexual sinners at that: adulterous women at wells, women of ill repute who poured perfume at his feet. He looked past the exteriors that drove the "righteous" away to see the true needs that lay underneath – needs that drew Jesus to them, and ultimately drew them to Jesus.

As you can already see, this is a book on a *Christian* response to sexual exploitation and trafficking. It's geared toward a Christian audience, and primarily written by Christian believers. But, we realize that there is no "one" Christian response to these issues. We have sought to reflect the unified diversity of the Body of Christ in this volume. Therefore, we have purposely asked people from a plurality of theological positions within the church to share with us how their faith impacts how they go about these issues, and perhaps as importantly, how these issues have challenged and matured them in their own faith. We have even sought contributions from a select few people who do not themselves identify with the Christian-based response, but who nevertheless see a key role for Christians to play in this issue. As we will see in the chapter in collaboration, we don't have to agree on every issue in order to agree to work together on an immense problem of common concern.

No one will concur with every perspective represented in this book. We don't want you to. Instead, we want you to be exposed to a wide variety of perspectives across the Body of Christ, to see how your faith leads you to respond. Some essays will discuss positions that you've never considered before. Perhaps these viewpoints will help you to see important things that you've missed and even be challenged to think differently, while still remaining true to your own orthodoxy. Other essays will confirm what you've already known and believed; perhaps they will ignite in you a renewed passion or help you to understand more deeply why you believe as you do and how you can share what works (and why it works) with others.

Second, straight-forward comprehensive answers don't yet exist because many of the questions are only recently starting to be asked.

In this volume, we spend most of the space discussing emerging issues, asking key questions about cutting-edge topics that weren't even on most people's agendas as recently as five years ago – topics such as addressing demand, working with men and boys and transgenders, maximizing effectiveness through evidence-based practice, and leveraging technology and the Internet for greater collaboration.

So, these essays are not definitive answers, but rather the stories and thought behind how we – as practitioners, academics, theologians and other strategic thinkers – have tried to wrestle with these important questions. Each of us may change our own minds later, as we learn more from the people we serve and from the organizations and individuals we serve alongside. But even though our thinking will evolve as our understanding increases, this book is meant to help you know the questions you yourself should be asking, and help you as you seek to find answers that work best in your own context.

In fact, we hope that this book will be far more than something you merely read once and then put on a shelf. We want it to be used. More than that we want it to be a *living, conversational book* you interact with individually and with others. We hope that you will read and discuss it with co-workers and colleagues in your location. *But we also want to hear from you!* Even with more than 40 contributors, there are still so many voices missing, including yours. How have *you* found success in answering the questions posed in this book? What have *you* learned that others can gain from? What are the particular challenges *you* continue to face?

We want this to be a book that evolves and improves through our collective experiences and understanding. To that end, we have set up a community where you can discuss the essays with the authors and each other, contribute additional perspectives on the questions asked in this volume, and even ask your own key questions and collaborate answers. Go to our location on Freedom Collaborative to join the conversation.[1]

Who Is This Book For?

If you have picked up this book, then this book is for you!

You may be a busy practitioner who is struggling to know how you can respond better. You know that God has called you to this work, you know that the injustice is clear and the needs even clearer. You've figured out some ways to respond but you still see what is missing and don't know what it will take to do better. You may feel all alone, wishing there was someone you could ask. But no one in your city knows what you are going through – or they're in the same position you are, also wishing there was someone who could help them figure out the answers.

While we've written this book for a broad audience, we've especially written it for you! All of us editors have been where you are – overwhelmed by the day-to-day needs and struggling to hang on in places where we also felt almost all alone. Thankfully over the last decade we've been able to meet

---

[1] www.freedomcollaborative.org

others who were asking the questions we too were wrestling with. We met them in chance meetings at conferences in other countries and while we were together only briefly we hung onto each other for dear life! When we returned home we knew that we were no longer alone but instead connected to a broader Body of believers to whom we could go for understanding, advice and support. Over the years, we've met many others through gatherings of practitioners such as Viva's Asha Forum, ICAP's global and regional conferences and CCTC's online conference.[2] We've been able to feel more empowered as we realize we are part of a much bigger community than just the small ones in our own locales. And while we alone may not know all of the answers, together we can ask – and begin to answer – the questions to help us better bring freedom and stop the traffick.

We invite you to become part of this community as well! While we may never have the chance to meet each other in person, we want to introduce you to some of the people who have made the biggest difference in the success of our own work. We want you to be able to listen in on the discussions in an ongoing global conversation about how we, as Christians and the church, can best respond to one of the most important issues of our time. While we won't be able to provide you with all of the answers, we hope to equip you to be able to think about ways you might apply what others have learned to your own contexts.

You may be someone who has only recently become aware of the tragedies of trafficking and sexual exploitation. You've heard God's prompting to get involved, but you have no idea how to even begin. You may be an individual, or you may be an entire congregation or mission organization. Either way you may be asking what can I do to respond? What does involvement even look like? What role am I supposed to play? This book seeks to expose you to a variety of responses. Not everyone is called to – or should – sell everything and move to the mission field to start a new work. If God is calling you to respond, it is because he has a specific role for you with your unique giftings to play!

As you will see throughout this book, that can be in a variety of different ways.

You may be called to contribute as a supporter who helps supply others with the money, prayer, technical support and other resources needed to get their job done. Whether you fill this overlooked but indispensable role as an individual or as a congregation or as a larger institutional donor, this book – especially the first chapter – will help you think about how *your* support can be directed for the maximum level of impact.

You may be called to become an advocate. Throughout this book we see the need for people to advocate – to speak out against these abuses and make our voices heard. This is needed at the governmental level to change official laws and policies. But it is also needed at the level of our own circle of influence where we can raise awareness of injustice and exploitation and challenge the

---

[2] See the Foreword for a history of how this book came about through two of these gatherings, and learn more about ICAP's and CCTC's conferences in Part 6, including how you can attend.

beliefs and attitudes behind them, including pornography and demand. The church as a whole has a mandate for advocacy: Speak out for those who are needy and oppressed, as Proverbs instructs. How will *you* make your collective and individual voice heard?

Or maybe you are being called to get involved at the grass-roots level responding to individual needs. If so, this book will help you learn where and how to begin. Each chapter contains an unparalleled wealth of resources and advice from leading experts and experienced practitioners – we only wish a book like this had existed when we first began. This book will expose you to a variety of unmet needs and innovative responses that may not be obvious at first. We hope you will be challenged to see how God might be calling *you* to creatively and with excellence serve those he puts in your care.

In whatever area God is calling you, we hope that this book will inform you of the principles required to respond well, and equip you with some of the resources that are available to respond effectively.

Finally, you may be a researcher or a professor; a denominational or mission leader; the head of an NGO, ministry or parachurch organization; the leader of a network or organization addressing injustice; or anyone else who has an influence on an entire generation of people who are being called to respond, and who in your position of influence can even impact the strategic direction of the movement itself. As the anti-trafficking movement has advanced rapidly in the last decade, we've been so busy doing the work that we haven't often had a chance to stop and think about how to do the work well. We have been so busy trying to pick up the shattered pieces of individual lives that we haven't had a chance to step back and take a look at the systemic brokenness in the collective whole.

But being able to see the big picture is essential for success. Practitioners need help to comprehend the broader context and to recognize strategic dynamics and trends. Conversely, macro-level players need to hear about the on-the-ground realities and real-life struggles to inform how they think strategically about solutions. This book offers both: smart, considered essays that introduce emerging issues and explore key thinking about new challenges, and case studies and other stories that demonstrate how well these theories have worked out in practice. We hope this book will help you as thought-leaders and organization heads with your thinking and planning. We also hope it will help inform and inspire you to lead the freedom movement forward in new and effective ways. We hope you will join one of our "Strategy Conversations" in Freedom Collaborative.[3]

We also hope you will widely share this book with people in your scope of influence. Although there are many books about trafficking that raise awareness for lay people, there are very few resources to equip and train those who are (or who are planning to be) practitioners. While this is not a step-by-step manual, our hope is that it will offer something even better: A framework for teaching people about the issues and an examination of how to approach these issues from a variety of theological, academic and professional

---

[3] www.freedomcollaborative.org

perspectives. If people are truly equipped with *how* to think about these enormous issues, hopefully the answers of *what* to do practically will be easier to both discern and accomplish.

Roadmap Forward

We know where we need to go: Stop exploitation. Move forward for freedom.

Now all we need to know is how do we get there?

This book is organized around six key questions:

- What can we do about the problems of sexual exploitation and trafficking?
- How should we make sense of sexual exploitation?
- How should we respond to demand?
- How can we better work with boys and men?
- How can we better work with transgender people?
- How should we collaborate?

We seek to explore answers to these questions (and related sub-questions) in a variety of ways. As already mentioned, we have asked people from different professions and perspectives to contribute. We've also asked authors to explain the macro-level thinking about the topics as well as describe the on-the-ground realities of attempting to address these questions in practice. Therefore, each of the sub-questions is examined at the big-picture level by one or more essays addressing Key Issues or Theological Reflections. Where possible, these are followed by one or more Case Studies that give flesh to the conceptual issues.

Each section within a chapter also contains Discussion Questions for further reflection and application. These questions can be considered alone or in groups by organizations who are working to address the issues. Finally, each chapter includes a list of Recommended Resources (listed at the end of the book). Not all of the resources will be helpful in every context, and not all the resources will be "acceptable" to every reader. As editors, we don't expressly condone or condemn every individual resource, but we want to provide direction for you as you seek to learn more, including from those who may have something valuable to provide even though we may not agree with them in every area.

So, how can we begin to stop the traffick? What are some of the key principles and aspects of a Christian response to sexual exploitation and trafficking?

Chapter 1 begins with an examination of what we can do about the problems of sexual exploitation and trafficking. Firstly, it asks whether we are naive to even think slavery and exploitation will ever come to an end. The chapter presents the case that large-scale change is possible because small-scale changes have already taken place. We can make a difference, by starting with ourselves. Secondly, the chapter asks what direction the anti-trafficking movement needs to take in order to make the most effective impact. Donors have a key role in shaping this direction, but first they must understand how to respond effectively. When churches, individuals and foundations fund efforts without thinking strategically about the best direction of focus and the need for impact-based and evidence-based practice, we are not doing the best we can about the problem of sexual exploitation and trafficking. This chapter seeks to help us to learn how to do better.

Chapter 2 looks at how we should make sense of sexual exploitation. The chapter begins with an examination of our call as Christians by asking: What does the Bible say about Christians being involved in justice for the sexually exploited and how should the church be involved in responding? But while the call to respond may be clear, these issues relating to sex and brokenness often raise murky and sometimes uncomfortable questions about core issues of faith. The remainder of the chapter consists of theological reflections by Christians from a variety of faith and professional perspectives who help us to struggle through key concerns such as: Does sex matter to God? Why should it matter to us as Christians? How have we messed up sex? Where is God when sex gets messy? The reflections also examine the role of faith for us as practitioners, both in terms of how our faith affects how we approach ministry to sexually broken and marginalized people, and in terms of how our faith can help us to survive in the midst of the mess.

Chapter 3 draws attention to an essential question that is only recently beginning to be asked and addressed: How should we respond to demand? First, the chapter looks at why it is important to tackle demand and how the church can make a difference through seeking to help change attitudes and actions of ourselves and others. Next the chapter explains why it is imperative to deal with pornography when addressing demand, including understanding the links that pornography has to prostitution, trafficking and overall dynamics of demand. It also explores how we can challenge the use of pornography by men in the church and protect youth from becoming a new generation of demand. Finally, the chapter looks at how Christians and the church can reach out to people who are ensnared by demand. Far from being outside of the scope of God's redemption, the people who are behind demand as producers and consumers are also beloved by God and worthy of care. We as Christians are called to go to the places where sinners hang out – in physical and virtual red-light districts, in brothels and bar-rooms, and, if we are honest, even in Christian organizations and ministries – to bring the message of hope and freedom to them so that those they exploit may also become free.

Chapters 4 and 5 shine a light on emerging responses to groups who have until now been hidden in the margins. These chapters discuss why we as a movement have focused more on girls and women and explain why we as Christians and the church should also be engaging with boys, men and transgendered people who can also be sexually exploited. These two chapters seek to answer the question of how we can better work with these invisible groups – including the unique challenges that arise – through examining key issues and theological perspectives, sharing lessons learned by pioneering ministries to these populations, and peering into case studies of how they have tried to apply these principles in practice.

Finally, *Chapter 6* recognizes that while we cannot stop trafficking and exploitation alone, together we can make a greater impact. The church worldwide is one of the greatest forces for good in the world, and also perhaps the largest network of people who are seeking to address all aspects of injustice, including the attitudes and sins that underlie the issues of exploitation and trafficking. But while we are one Body, it is not often that we are able to effectively come together as one mind to strategically address a common purpose. This chapter addresses key questions about collaboration, including its importance, its challenges, and how we can use technology and the Internet to do it better.

Disclaimers

As already mentioned, no one will agree with everything in this book. We have intentionally included a variety of perspectives. We hope that you will be able to take what works in your context, and even be able to learn something from the ideas and perspectives that you disagree with.

We also want to acknowledge that it is not possible to write about these issues in a way that will make everyone happy. Language is very important. When we fail to use words carefully, we will often fail to care. By using words such as "prostitute" or "sex tourist" we are defining a person merely by their behavior and sin, and implicitly condemning them to their fate, rather than recognizing that they are individuals created in the image of God, worthy of our concern and care. As well, words have political and other consequence. Words like "sex worker" are often used to promote prostitution as a desirable career for women. Many abolitionists avoid using such words to avoid condoning positions they hold untenable. The same is true of certain words involving the gay and lesbian community and transgendered people.

We have tried to be careful with the language we use in this book, but sometimes that goal conflicts with the demand for ease of reading and clarity of expression. In every instance, no matter the word that appears on the face of the page, the intent beneath it is to communicate nothing more or less than that we are all valued by God and worthy of his care, and that God does not want anyone to suffer from sexual exploitation or trafficking.

Concluding Thoughts

We are so thankful that you have picked up this book. We pray that it will equip you, inform you, challenge you and inspire you as you take up the call for freedom in whatever way God is leading you to *Stop the Traffick!*

PART 1

WHAT CAN WE DO ABOUT THE PROBLEMS OF SEXUAL EXPLOITATION AND TRAFFICKING?

Introduction, by Glenn Miles

Addressing the exploitation of children and vulnerable people has drawn the attention of many faith-based communities for millennia. In the past twenty years there has been a particular focus on sexual exploitation and slavery. In the beginning the response to the problem was mostly rescue only. Then responses began to include aftercare. But now we need a more holistic/multi-faceted response that goes beyond rescue and aftercare to include demand, prevention, education, reintegration and advocacy. While it is important that we cover the entire spectrum of response, for reasons of space this volume will focus mainly on responding demand and reaching out to "invisible" groups. Later volumes will address other types of responses.

This chapter explores two key questions:

- Is it naive to think slavery and exploitation will ever come to an end?
- How can donors positively engage in the anti-trafficking movement?

First, **Kevin Bales** encourages us that slavery can be eradicated in our lifetime. In contrast to the many men frequenting red-light areas that I have spoken to who say "Prostitution is the oldest profession" suggesting it will never end, Bales gives examples of times and places when slavery *has* been eradicated. He suggests that if it is has been possible in a small scale, it is possible on a larger scale. Many laws are now in place – they simply need implementation. Bales believes the universal move towards human rights for all can supersede what are seen as economic priorities. But we need to start with ourselves and what we teach our children in our actions.

Next, **Jeremy Floyd** follows on with a critical look from the donor's perspective at how donors can be most effective in their impact and scope, based on his own experience with the foundation Equitas. He explains the need for grassroots research and evidence-based practice, rather than responding to anecdotal and alarmist media stories or knee-jerk reactions which do not guarantee maximum effectiveness. Floyd describes a four-pronged approach to being a responsible donor: a commitment to focus, a commitment to learn, a commitment to networking and a commitment to improving through being willing to seek constructive criticism from those they serve.

CHAPTER 1: IS IT NAIVE TO THINK SLAVERY AND EXPLOITATION WILL EVER COME TO AN END?

Key Issues, by Kevin Bales

Is it naive to think slavery and exploitation will ever come to an end? The short answer to this question: "No."

Admittedly, slavery has been with us for a very long time. It is, in fact, prehistoric. Slavery is so old it existed before the invention of law and before the invention of money. So, if something has been with humans for every single day of their history, doesn't that make it permanent? Again, the answer is "no." While many cultures have had slavery and there has always been slavery somewhere on earth, being human doesn't require slavery. Many societies have existed and exist today without slavery. Though sometimes referred to as an "institution," slavery is not a social institution in the precise meaning of that phrase, which encompasses those key organized activities that are and have been present in all human societies and cultures, such as economic exchange or some form of family organization. Put simply, slavery is common throughout history and in evidence in most countries today, but it is not a universal attribute of human societies. Put another way, slavery cannot be assumed to be an innate characteristic or attribute of human beings.

Just because something isn't everywhere all the time doesn't necessarily mean that it can be brought to an end. And yet we know slavery can be eradicated. We know it because there are many communities and nations around the world that once had slavery and now do not. Some ended their slavery a very long time ago, like Switzerland. Other communities may have ended it more recently, such as the villages moving to freedom in Northern India. Whether long gone or just gone, slavery can end and be replaced with a way of living and working that makes slavery practically impossible.

So, if slavery is not a permanent and normal part of humanity, and if many communities have shown us the way to end slavery, what has to happen to bring it to an end? The answer to that question may be the missing link in the chain of events that will lead to eradication. It is an answer with several parts, and the first is not obvious, but it is exciting: slavery has been and *is* coming to an end.

Faith and religion (not always the same thing) played a key part in both sustaining and supporting slavery and then beginning its long downfall and eradication. From the time humans learned to write things down, a repeated theme was the religious justification of slavery. About 4000 years ago, when King Hammurabi had his new set of laws carved into stone, he made a point of explaining that God had given him the right to enslave by making him "the shepherd of the slaves." This paternalistic rationalization, that God (or the Market or DNA, etc.) has made some people superior and others inferior, some people within the curtain of grace and others forever outsiders, echoes throughout human history and into the present moment. From it grows great suffering, and slavery is its natural outcome.

Over the centuries many faith groups rejected this notion and deemed that slavery was against the law of nature and of God – but accepted slavery as inevitable and permanent. Greek and Roman philosophers, Essene mystics, and early Christians resigned themselves to a world where slavery was a fundamental part of life. And for most people throughout most of human history slavery was simply business, a productive activity akin to owning and using other livestock. But, all the while, the seed of liberation within each faith tradition was gestating within each faith tradition.

Within Christianity, as well as other faiths, lurked an explosive concept – that each person had worth and that we should treat others as we would want to be treated. Within Christianity it was an idea that was easy to conceal in the dense verbiage of religion controlled by a priestly class, but once the Bible was made widely available in the 17th century, its transcendent status and the power of Jesus' radical message began to spread. It was a truth and a key, unlocking the mind and opening a new understanding – that slavery wasn't just business as usual, it was a sin, a violation, an assault on the divine that existed in every person. Once unleashed, this truth proved unstoppable. From it grew the world's first human rights campaign in 1787, the first human rights laws, the invention of what we now call "non-governmental organizations," and a tradition of faith in action that went beyond immediate care for the needy to social justice. This truth created a radical and rapid redefinition of the ancient human activity of slavery and created the concept of "human rights."

My own faith community, the Religious Society of Friends (Quakers), were very much part of this early transformation, bucking a global economic, political and cultural slavery system thousands of years old and deeply powerful. Joining with others, they took great risks and sometimes paid the ultimate price, and legal slavery began to recede. Today, Quakers, in their own special brand of modesty, will sometimes pat themselves on the back and say, "Well, we're a bit muddled, *but didn't we do a good job on slavery*!" I don't join in, because we didn't. We started the work and then we didn't finish it, somehow letting it drift away when most legal slavery came to an end in the 19th century. Quakers are still working to "take away the occasion of all wars," to live in simplicity and with integrity, to find that of God in every person, but with slavery, we dropped the ball.

At the same time, it is a ball that kept rolling and rolling. We can see the end of slavery in its diminishing extent within the larger global population and economy. While a large number, today's 27 million slaves represent the smallest *proportion* of the global population to ever be enslaved. Likewise, the $30 to $40 billion in goods and services slaves produce each year is the smallest percentage of the world economy ever generated by slave labor. By comparison, Americans spend $41 billion per year on their pets. In global terms, slave output is a drop in the ocean. The same applies to the total number of slaveholders. While they may number in the low millions, for the most part they are isolated landowners and moneylenders, locally powerful but not part of a unified vested interest or organized industry supporting slavery. Economic historians tell us that when our anti-slavery movement began in 1787, slavery was equivalent in size and reach to the global automotive industry of today. We face a much reduced, splintered and marginalized slave industry.

Put simply, ending slavery threatens the livelihood of no country or industry. At the same time there are strong arguments that ending slavery is good for economies. While slaves may make money for slaveholders, they tend to be a drag on a community or country's economy. Slaves contribute little to national production; their work is concentrated on the lowest rung of the economic ladder, doing low-skill jobs that are dirty and dangerous. Economically, except for the criminals who profit, slaves are a waste. They add next to nothing to an economy and they buy nothing in a country's markets. Slaves are actually an untapped economic resource. For poor countries, when ex-slaves increase their earning and spending it is a small but important improvement in the national economy. At the international level if you compare countries on the strength of their economy and how many slaves they have, the picture is clear: the more slaves, the weaker the economy. This is not surprising because a "freedom dividend" comes with liberation. Freed slaves are more productive and consume more than they did in slavery, they are also likely to remove their children from the workplace and place them into schools. Increased productivity and consumption by adults coupled with education for children creates a virtuous cycle protecting them from re-enslavement.

All the economic reasons for ending slavery wouldn't count for much if there wasn't a desire to end slavery, but there is a growing consensus for change. No government or organized interest group is pressing the case that slavery is desirable or even acceptable. The world is united in its condemnation of slavery. The Universal Declaration of Human Rights simply underscores this, placing freedom from slavery at the top of the list of fundamental rights. The moral challenge today is not how to convince people that slavery is wrong, but how we can *act effectively* on our universally held belief in the absolute and essential equality of human dignity.

Legal frameworks back this up and are already in place. Laws against slavery are on the books in every country. Still, around the world some of these laws need updating and expanding, others need their penalties increased. And given the international nature of human trafficking, nearly all national laws need to be brought into harmony with each other. Actual eradication needs to concentrate on increasing the political will to enforce law, and not so much on campaigns to make new law. Probably the most important laws needing enactment are those appropriating the funds needed for eradication.

We also have strong examples of eradication. We know that when governments really get involved in collective international effort big changes can happen. In 1988 the Global Polio Eradication campaign began, with nearly every government in the world promising to take part. In that year, the crippling polio disease was active in one hundred twenty-five countries. By 2003, there were only six countries left with vestiges of active polio. As with many diseases, it will be difficult to wipe out the polio virus completely, but millions of children and adults have been saved. Slavery can also go from pernicious and pervasive to rare cases. Admittedly, like polio, the end of slavery probably doesn't mean its complete disappearance. Human beings are fallible, and sometimes from their own damage they damage others. Our aim in ending slavery is to make it unthinkable and subject to immediate and overwhelming response, just as we would respond to an outbreak of bubonic plague.

The history of our species, of the human climb into consciousness and wonder, may be shot through with slavery, but our creativity, our talent for wonder can also bring slavery to an end. For six thousand years we have loved and dreamed and built lives of security and beauty. We have also murdered, starved, and tortured, denying the common humanity of millions, enslaving or butchering them. Our vaunted civilization has been, and is today, nourished by the lives of slaves. We may not be able to stop the selfishness that wells up in each of us, or the grasping for power that seems so much a part of life. Our pride will make a stubborn opponent, as will our laziness and self-regard. But whatever our human failings, on one thing virtually every person agrees: slavery must end.

We will end slavery for our children. We love our children, yet we deliver them into a world that reeks with slavery. We teach them to respect others, to be tolerant and kind, but we feed them and ourselves with food grown by slaves and ignore their cries. Our children are not deaf to them; they see our inaction. We teach them the sin of slavery when we celebrate its small setbacks in history, then move on as if slavery is in the past. We will end slavery so that our children won't learn a lesson that has been passed down for hundreds of generations: that slaves don't matter, that humanity has done all it is going to do for slaves.

If we make the decision and apply ourselves, slavery could be gone in twenty-five years. We could decide now, and in our lifetimes achieve something that makes landing on the moon look like a minor historical footnote. We would want to end this crime even if it meant great sacrifice, but, in fact, ending slavery costs little. Whether it takes ten or twenty or even thirty billion dollars, the cost is a small fraction of what we spend on the most trivial of our entertainments. Share this cost among us all, citizens, businesses and governments over twenty-five years, and it is little more than pocket change.

We will end slavery because we know how. Whether the task is carrying one slave child to freedom or crafting policies that free thousands, we have successful examples before us. Slaves have been coming to freedom for hundreds of years. Today more slaves are being freed, and each liberation is a model for another. Freeing slaves can be hard work, but if you cut away the disguises the facts are simple: one person controls another through violence. Penetrate that violent control, and the slave comes free. Help that slave gain autonomy, and that person stays free. Although some of the fundamental systems of our economy are stacked against slaves, a revolution is not needed to free them, just a little bit of justice.

Today the importance of slaves is not economic; slaves are important to our moral universe. For all of our failings and challenges, there stands before us a gift of incomprehensible worth. Here is the end of suffering for millions. Here is the end of the common ugly sin we have carried for centuries. Here is the end of guilt and the damage we suffer when we pretend we have no guilt. Yet the best part of this gift is the part we cannot know. It is the new knowledge of our own power and the ability to dream as never before that we will earn through liberation. It is the new world that will be created when slavery is no more.

Discussion Questions

1. How do we deal with the mixed messages about slavery found in Scripture?
2. Slavery takes away freedom, which includes the freedom to pursue a spiritual path. How do we ensure we open the door to spiritual growth (even if it doesn't include our own faith tradition) for freed slaves?
3. Christians are often engaged in freeing and rescuing the enslaved – and expecting them to be grateful and malleable in return. When we do so are we helping them to freedom or just freedom on our terms?

CHAPTER 2: HOW CAN DONORS POSITIVELY ENGAGE IN THE ANTI-TRAFFICKING MOVEMENT?

Key Issues, by Jeremy Floyd

With the increasing international attention devoted to the crime of human trafficking, including media reports, advocacy efforts, campus activism and an expanding array of victim services and preventative efforts, it is no surprise that a growing number of donors are engaging in anti-trafficking causes. As a Program Officer for Equitas Group[1] I represent a specific group of donors, Christian family foundations, but I have also interacted with generous individuals and churches interested in making grants in this arena. In this essay I will draw on my experience and personal interactions to answer the question: How can donors positively engage in the anti-trafficking movement?

How and why donors choose to get involved in a particular issue and what sustains that involvement varies tremendously. As the saying about foundations goes: "When you've seen one foundation, well, you've seen one foundation." Philanthropic engagement in the anti-trafficking movement is significantly shaped by broader philosophical commitments, and these commitments present a donor with not only a number of opportunities but also a number of constraints. Such diversity means there cannot and should not be a one-size-fits all blueprint for "how a donor should address human trafficking." But there are important principles that should be considered by any donor.

Before suggesting general principles for how a donor might positively engage in the anti-trafficking movement, I will first explain the process of how Equitas became involved in the anti-trafficking movement in Southeast Asia, what lessons we have learned, and what principles have come to guide our engagement as we move forward. Perhaps our experience can be helpful for donors who have or who are considering entering into the anti-trafficking space.

Lessons Learned

Our overall approach as a philanthropic organization is distinguished by a commitment to go deep with selected issues in particular geographic locations.[2] For a number of years prior to founding Equitas Group in 2008, Lance Robinson had been involved in philanthropy by leading a general children-at-risk granting program spread over six geographic regions. Lance started

---

[1] www.equitasgroup.org

[2] This approach is known as "committing to your cause." See Leslie Crutchfield, John Kania and Mark Kramer, *Do More Than Give: The Six Practices of Donors Who Change the World* (San Francisco: Jossey-Bass, 2011), 19-36.

Equitas desiring a more specific and cohesive focus, and he initially chose to concentrate almost all grantmaking and advocacy efforts on two specific issues in two distinct locations. The hope was that such focus would generate higher impact and greater social change. The initial two directives addressed Child Domestic Servitude (or the Restavek system) in Haiti and Child Trafficking and Exploitation in Southeast Asia.

As our Southeast Asia initiative began, we set out to answer the question: As a major donor, how can we best address the issue of human trafficking? We spent an initial period of three or four months performing desk research, conducting interviews with various specialists, and took an initial field visit where we visited projects and dialogued with key experts in three Southeast Asian countries. We asked for their opinion on the best way a major donor could address the issue of human trafficking. Responses varied, but the best and most frequent advice we received was this:

> 1) Do not base your strategy on pop-level anti-trafficking books, hype, anecdote, sad stories or knee-jerk reactions. Be committed to evidence-based practice.

> 2) Consider gap areas. Trafficking is a complex phenomenon requiring a diverse response. Certain projects and organizations are more easily funded than others. Look for what is missing and do something about it.

As this initial phase ended we decided to concentrate primarily in Cambodia and gradually began making grants. As we continued ongoing desk research and quarterly field trips, we developed a diverse portfolio of grants with anti-trafficking projects spanning prevention, intervention and restoration. Within each of these areas we considered a variety of projects with all sizes of organizations, prioritizing developing relationships with grassroots organizations and funding gap areas.

Three important outcomes stand out as a result of our initial activity. First, we were able to *further understand* the nature of human trafficking and exploitation specific to Cambodia. While trafficking is a global problem, local manifestations vary. For example, in Cambodia, we learned that the trafficking victim is not predominantly the seven- or eight-year-old girl, but more likely to be between the ages of fourteen and seventeen. We also learned that the images of girls being chained to beds are extreme cases and not the norm. Finally, we learned that it is not just girls who are being exploited, but boys too. It is unfortunate that these manifestations are not always evident in the media and in many fundraising efforts because failure to acknowledge and grapple with local manifestations can lead to ill-informed and unbalanced interventions and philanthropic engagement.

Second, we were able to fund important projects that *filled gap areas* relating to exploitation of boys, the need for trained social workers, and the lack of quality research.

Boys: Very early on we had an opportunity to help launch what we are told was the first aftercare shelter for sexually abused boys in Cambodia. Additionally, we were among the first donors to support a new project aimed at providing specialist training for those working with sexually exploited boys. We are beginning to see some quality results from these projects and overall improvements in caring for exploited boys in Cambodia.

Social Workers: In 2011 we began supporting the efforts of the University of Washington to create a Social Work Department at the Royal University of Phnom Penh that offers an excellent bachelors degree in social work. This program promises to supply NGOs and government ministries with the quality social work staff they desperately need.[3]

Research: Many of the experts we interviewed pointed to the lack of quality research as a major gap area in the anti-trafficking movement.[4] We are currently supporting two research projects. The first focuses on "demand," and seeks to understand the mindset of men who pay for sexual services and use pornography. The second is a ten year longitudinal research project being conducted by the Chab Dai Coalition, and it aims to better understand the experiences of survivors on the path to reintegration, providing a much-needed look into what is and what is not working in aftercare programs.

Third, we were able to *sharpen our granting focus* by picking a specific entry point of engagement. We made over forty grants in the last three years and have been able to track activities and results from a number of different types of programs. All of this has confirmed what we anticipated: trafficking is complex, solutions are multi-faceted, and there are numerous opportunities and paths for donor engagement.

We've also been able to internally reflect on our values and passions as an organization, re-asking the question of how we can best address human trafficking.[5] Based our experiences, passions, and resources, we believe the best entry point for Equitas is the sector of child protection. Therefore, we are in the process of ironing out the details of a more specific and measurable strategy that will strengthen systems of protection for children who have been trafficked or who are vulnerable to being trafficked. Child protection itself is extremely complex and requires efforts at the individual, family, community and national level. But a narrow focus, even if complicated, provides us with a clearer entry point and rationale for what projects we will fund and which ones we will not.

---

[3] Most of the "social workers" on staff with the projects we support are not actually trained social workers. While some do receive on-the-job training, the widespread lack of skills is alarming, especially when one considers the extremely difficult task of caring for children who have experienced complex trauma.

[4] A good place to begin to understand the challenges facing human trafficking research projects is the Asia Foundation study, *Review of a Decade of Research on Trafficking in Persons, Cambodia* (The Asia Foundation, 2006). http://asiafoundation. org/resources/pdfs/CBTIPreview.pdf

[5] In addition to *Do More Than Give*, two other books have provided insight for us and are reflective of how we arrived at these decisions: Peter Frumkin, *The Essence of Strategic Giving: A Practical Guide for Donors and Fundraisers* (Chicago: University of Chicago Press, 2010) and Thomas Tierney and Joel Fleishmann, *Give Smart: Philanthropy That Gets Results* (New York: Public Affairs, 2011).

Four Commitments

Our activity over the last few years has provided us with the opportunity to learn and mature as an organization, and our experience has shaped how I respond to the question "How can donors positively engage in the anti-trafficking movement?" I would suggest that donors seeking to positively engage in the anti-trafficking movement exhibit the following four commitments: a commitment to *focus*, a commitment to *learn*, a commitment to *network*, and a commitment to *improve*. The presence of each of these commitments increases a donor's chances of achieving higher impact and positively affecting the anti-trafficking movement.

Commitment to Focus

The philanthropic model utilized by Equitas assumes that greater impact is achieved through a more specific focus. Not all donors will share this philosophy, and that is okay, but I believe it is something for all donors to consider. There are many benefits to a long-term commitment to fighting trafficking. If donors have previously been hesitant to focus more narrowly on specific causes, then perhaps engagement in the anti-trafficking movement provides an opportunity to try an alternative approach.

Since trafficking is a global problem and the response needed is so diverse, donors may not need to look beyond their current relationship circles and grantmaking activities and locales to discover how they could make a more meaningful commitment to fighting trafficking. In fact, they may determine that some of their work is already contributing to ending trafficking in some indirect way. In the least, donors will benefit by focusing on an entry point that both meets a social need *and* fits with the donor's passions. For us, our focus is in Southeast Asia and our entry point is child protection. For others it could be women's empowerment, community development, micro-enterprise or loans, education, leadership and organizational development or policy and legislation. Some donors prefer to support immediate relief efforts while taking on long-term challenges energizes others.

It may take time for a donor to determine its ideal entry point, but this should be no cause for concern, as long as they are moving in that direction. I believe that donors will increase their impact in the anti-trafficking community as they focus more specifically on distinct entry points and over time develop further clarity of what change they are seeking to accomplish within that area.

Commitment to Learn

A commitment to learning should be at the heart of all donors seeking to end trafficking. Fairly or unfairly, some donors have the unfortunate reputation within the anti-trafficking community of lacking an adequate understanding of the nature of human trafficking and the diverse response necessary to ending it. There is no end to the emotional (and often true) stories of those who have been victimized by traffickers and exploiters, and while these stories may seize donor attention to the existence of trafficking and inspire ongoing philanthropic engagement, research will likely demonstrate that they often are extreme or exceptional cases and not the norm.

Donors can commit to doing better and will increase our potential impact when we utilize quality anti-trafficking research and are acquainted with minimum standards of care. Paying attention to research provides a more nuanced picture of which populations are at risk, illuminates how trafficking is occurring in certain parts of the world and reveals significant gap areas in need of addressing. Being aware of minimum standards of care drives the entire anti-trafficking movement toward needed professionalization of services and prevents donors from funding organizations who are providing inadequate care.

Donors seeking to make an impact in the anti-trafficking movement must be committed to using reliable and substantive information to inform broader and sustained strategic activity. When we do, we will be on the path to positive engagement because we will be informed of the issues and be able to identify well-intentioned efforts to assist victims that are woefully inadequate and must either be significantly improved or outright avoided.

Commitment to Network

Probably one of the most common questions donors from my community ask of potential grantees is how they collaborate with others. It is a good question. The problem is we as donors too often do not collaborate very well ourselves. But if anti-trafficking donors want to increase our impact, we must make an unwavering commitment to networking. This undertaking requires intentional interaction with other donors, with researchers and with field workers. Equitas has benefitted from being a part of a new donor collaborative focused broadly on justice-based issues and more specifically on anti-trafficking work in Southeast Asia. We have been able to share knowledge, successes and failures and also to collaborate on specific granting projects. In addition to intentional networking with other donors, a donor's engagement and impact will be significantly improved when they are devoted to meaningful relationships with practitioners.

Like us, most of the donors from the community I represent do not have a permanent field presence. This presents challenges for accurately assessing field realities and cultural and contextual issues that have such an influence on programs and services being offered to survivors of trafficking. A donor may heed my advice about learning through reading research and understanding minimum standards, but without crucial field knowledge gained by an ongoing presence, he may fail to place research and minimum standards into proper perspective.

One way to overcome this challenge is for donors to maintain meaningful relationships with practitioners in their geographic areas of interest. Such relationships can provide the context for worthwhile dialogue and sensitive application of research recommendations and minimum standards. When we as donors commit to network in these ways, the anti-trafficking community can expect to benefit from improved knowledge, increased efficiency, higher quality programs, better accountability and, most importantly, the essential foundations of mutual trust.

Commitment to Improve

Donors want their potential grantees to exhibit a steadfast commitment to continual improvement, and we should hold that same expectation for donors engaging in the anti-trafficking arena. If donors and anti-trafficking organizations alike are committed to improvement, one area that must be addressed is shifting from the status quo focus on *activities* to a focus on *outcomes or change*. Organizations are often good at telling donors what they do (activities), but they struggle to adequately demonstrate how what they do contributes to positive outcomes or changes in the lives of whom they serve.

Donors often make granting decisions based on an assumption that an organization is carrying out a "right" set of activities. Who would argue that a victim of trafficking should not be in some way provided shelter, food, counseling and education? No one. But donors too often fail to follow up with their grantees to see what real and positive changes are happening as a result of these activities. We have to shift this emphasis if for no other reason than ensuring that the services provided survivors of trafficking are actually beneficial to them! How can we improve if we are not devoted to examining the impact of our work?

What is the role of the donor in this needed change? Donors should make it a priority to assist organizations in evaluating the change resulting from their projects or programs. This might incorporate capacity-building grants to provide organizations with a more rigorous monitoring and evaluation framework. Donors might fund independent, external evaluations on a periodic basis. Donors could also conduct a self-evaluation of the impact of their granting programs. All of these activities are achievable and need not be dismissed with a "what we do can't be measured" attitude. It is a difficult undertaking and requires the courage to be transparent, a willingness to adapt, and the ability to learn from failures. And here I would emphasize that trust in the grantor-grantee relationship is paramount. When anti-trafficking donors and organizations work together toward evaluating and refining services not on the presumed "rightness" of an activity, but on the changes such activity produces, a commitment to improve is most evident. What can be expected from a commitment to improve? Nothing more than better services and outcomes for survivors of trafficking.

Conclusion

I was very hesitant to agree to write this essay because we are such a young organization and it is often unwise to attempt to tell other donors what they should be doing. However, I am happy if our experience can assist others in considering how they can positively engage in the anti-trafficking movement. I am convinced we need more thoughtful, engaged and energetic donors in this fight. I am also convinced that as more donors exhibit the four commitments briefly highlighted here, the closer we will be to preventing and alleviating human trafficking.

Discussion Questions

1. As a donor – big or small – do you have a long-term commitment to fighting trafficking? What are some ways in which giving might be made more specific and impactful through increasing focus?
2. What are some ways in which you as a donor are learning about quality anti-trafficking research and minimum standards of care? How can informed donors help encourage improved care for victims?
3. How are you networking and collaborating with other donors, researchers and field workers? How can you increase your engagement and impact through sharing knowledge, successes and failures?
4. How can you develop meaningful relationships with practitioners to provide the context for worthwhile dialogue and sensitive application of research recommendations and minimum standards?
5. How can you encourage and equip the organizations you support to shift from an activities-based approach to an outcomes- or change-based approach? How can you assist organizations in evaluating the impact of their projects or programs (e.g. capacity-building grants for monitoring and evaluation, funding for external evaluations)?
6. As a donor how often do you examine the impact of your work, including self-evaluation of the impact of your own granting programs?

PART 2

HOW SHOULD WE MAKE SENSE OF SEXUAL EXPLOITATION?

Introduction, by Glenn Miles

As Christians we choose to use the Bible as a foundation for what we do. But we are also heavily influenced by a Christian culture that tends to see sex as an uncomfortable subject, especially when it comes to sexual abuse or exploitation. So we begin this book with a Biblical understanding of sex and the vulnerability of victims of sexual exploitation and trafficking and a strong sense that God is standing with us in bringing justice to those who experience injustice. We are also reminded that we can and often surprisingly do find God in the chaos and we can best begin the journey of healing for those we serve and for ourselves if we enter this space with humility.

This chapter explores several key questions:
- What does the Bible say about being involved in justice for the sexually exploited?
- How should the church be involved in responding to sexual exploitation?
- Does sex matter to God? Why should it matter to us as Christians?
- How have we messed up sex?
- Where is God when sex gets messy?
- How can we survive in the midst of the mess?
- How can we get from hostility to hospitality when dealing with transgender and other sexual minorities?

Ian de Villiers starts – where Biblical understanding should start – with the Genesis story of what God intended in the creation story and how it got messed up. De Villiers gives an overview of the Bible's redemptive story for both survivors and perpetrators that ends with a new heaven where there isn't a hint of immorality. He concludes by reminding us of how we can bring God's Kingdom now through churches becoming healing communities that eradicate loneliness and challenge oppression.

Jim Martin gives a recent historical overview of the church's response to this issue, celebrating how the faith-based community is now taking this issue seriously, albeit perhaps late. He describes how the church has found that by engaging in these issues of injustice in the darkest places of violent oppression and abuse that counter to expectation, the church "has most deeply experienced the presence and power of God." Martin encourages Christians to engage with Scriptures that call us to reach out to the exploited both in our local churches wherever they are and internationally. He also encourages NGOs to engage local churches in the issue.

Dan Allender reminds us that "God loves sex" and also that "Man is made in His image," male and female in complementarity, rather than dominance of one over the other. He reminds us that the evil one hates God so he tries to do everything he can to destroy God's image and so every person on earth is affected by this. Sex represents God's desire for us to experience true intimacy. Sexual redemption is something that all of us need to experience to one extent or another but change is possible for everyone thanks to a redeeming God and where there are those who are prepared to share the long journey of healing and restoring beauty.

Lisa Thompson gives a reality check of just how depraved the world has marred this beautiful sacred space of the image of God. God's intention for sex is desecrated through different forms of rape, mutilation of the body and pornography where the person photographed is objectified and even ceases to be recognized as a person. Thompson reminds us that God provides boundaries that are necessary for us to adhere to but that these boundaries provide freedom rather than the oppression we often anticipate. They help keep us from reducing sex to something to be used instead of something of beauty to be cherished.

Andrew Schmutzer reminds us that God does not leave man in his mess when he has "screwed up" sex. However, he also reveals how those who have experienced sexual abuse in its many forms may feel abandoned by God and in turn abandon God. Schmutzer describes how free will has led to us experiencing the consequences of our sin but he suggests that God nevertheless deeply grieves over this. He describes how the wounded lamb of God becomes deeply meaningful to the sexually violated. However, he reminds those of us working with the sexually exploited that "victory only" approaches are not helpful but that healing starts with listening and recognizing that stories will be messy and complex.

Bill Prevette talks about how working with some of the most marginalized in these very messy places can "do us in." He encourages us to consider how our work is shaped theologically, that is, how we as practitioners use the Bible to understand what we do. For example, when we talk of "Kingdom" we understand it to be "God's way of doing things." He suggests that the marginalized people we work with may themselves be "pointers" to the Kingdom but that the process of full understanding requires humility and not assuming we understand everything. We need to be people who can accept living in the chaos, whilst seeing glimpses of the Kingdom.

Finally, **Heike Lippmann** paints us an image of the kind of love we are to have when encountering people who are outside of the community because of sin. While she focuses on how we can respond to transgender and sexual minorities, her theological reflection on the father's love from Luke has application when working with anyone who is marginalized, including people who have experienced sexual exploitation.

CHAPTER 3: WHAT DOES THE BIBLE SAY ABOUT BEING INVOLVED IN JUSTICE FOR THE SEXUALLY EXPLOITED?

Biblical Mandate, by Ian De Villiers

Sexual exploitation and its often-related evils of trafficking and sexual abuse are generally and rightly seen as evils about which something must be done. There are a plethora of people, organizations, campaigns, networks and websites seeking to do just that. But action – even urgently needed action – needs to be anchored into understanding. Humanitarian and first aid workers know this well. The motto "first seek to do no harm" only exists because of the recognition that well-meaning and costly interventions can easily be damaging, not helping as intended.

In addition, the helpers themselves may be vulnerable and the beliefs that helpers hold can make a difference to both practice and outcomes. In particular, Christian responses can be strongly influenced by taboos and stereotypes. For example, Dr. Andrew Schmutzer points out that Christians can see abuse as being as too ugly or unbelievable for Christians to engage with.[1] In practice, there is widespread Christian discomfort when it comes to thinking about sex outside of marriage beyond simply seeing it as immoral: anybody involved is tainted at best, more likely stigmatized; open discussion is censured. The more socially conservative the community, the harder it is to talk about sex without stigma and judgment. But where victims of sexual exploitation may be coerced rather than forced, and where guilt and fear are common, judgmental attitudes cannot be helpful.[2]

So this Biblical reflection seeks to raise several questions and suggest pointers that can help our understanding of sexual exploitation, in the hope that it will aid informed choices in determining Christian responses to sexual exploitation. Before starting, a proviso: this is a brief article that can only touch on difficult issues about which much has been said and there is much more to work through. To begin with, there are the immediate questions about power and lust; but wider questions about community, belonging, healing and identity are also involved. These questions are relevant to perpetrators and exploiters, to communities (including faith communities) and wider societies, and to potential and actual victims.

---

[1] Andrew J. Schmutzer, "A Theology of Sexual Abuse: A Reflection on Creation and Devastation," *Journal of the Evangelical Theological Society* 51, no. 4 (December 2008): 788. http://www.etsjets.org/files/JETS-PDFs/21/21-4/JETS%2051-4%20785-812%20Schmutzer.pdf

[2] Terminology matters here, and is discussed elsewhere in this volume. I will not go specifically into terminology but the thinking in this chapter should help in reflecting on how to talk about victims of sexual exploitation.

Biblical Themes

There is no doubt that the Bible forbids exploitation and sexual immorality, and in particular the abuse of children. It is written throughout Scripture, from the giving of the law at the beginning of the Old Testament,[3] through Jesus' injunctions to care for the "least of these" and "these little ones,"[4] to the promise of a new heaven where there is not even a hint of immorality.[5] Exploitation, immorality and abuse are not things that can be condoned, let alone practiced by the people of God. However, we know that saying "No! Bad!" is not enough. Pedophilia, exploitation, trafficking all happen and the church has not always been a safe place. For the people of God to be salt and light, they need to be sharing these values and bringing safety to vulnerable people through practices based on those values. To bring healing and restoration will take more.

To start thinking about this, it is helpful to be asking "Who are we?" and "Who are they?" The Bible lays out themes to answer this in Genesis 1 to 4. These themes are then commented on and illustrated through the recounting of God's interventions in history through the Old and New Testaments before the final fulfillment of redemption and resurrection and re-creation.

In the creation passage, six critical themes emerge:

1. Man (that is, all human beings) is made in God's image. Intriguingly, Scripture uses the phrase in "our likeness." (Genesis 1:26) Schmutzer comments: "Humankind is not said to have the image of God, but each person is said to be in his or her psychosomatic whole the image of God."[6]

2. Human beings are made "male" and "female." Sex is built into the design. Genesis refers to biological sexual identity here, not to the more socially-constructed ideas of gender, with "men's roles" and "women's roles." Male and female are equally the image of God.

3. Sexuality ("they became one flesh") is intimately linked to loneliness. One person, alone, is somehow not enough. However, Adam's creation before Eve in Genesis 2 does not lesson the previous point about male and female being equally in the image of God.

4. As soon as sin and judgment arrived, sexual relations became complicated – from the idyll of no shame in the garden, to shame and the need to cover up.

5. Man is given to "rule" (Genesis 1:26, and the same word in Psalm 8) over God's creation, to subdue it. But man also now desires to rule over woman: "Your desire will be for your husband, and he will rule over you." (Genesis 3:16, NIV) By contrast, in the creation of woman the term "helper" is used. (Genesis 2) "Helper" is a word used of God in his relationship to Israel; inferiority is not implied.

---

[3] E.g. Numbers 18.
[4] Matthew 25:31-46; Matthew 18.
[5] Revelation 22:15.
[6] Schmutzer, "A Theology of Sexual Abuse," 792.

6. In Genesis 3, this rule is tarnished as it will require "painful toil" and "the sweat of your brow." In Genesis 4, Abel and Cain come to bloodshed over transactions of differing values in the first recorded exploitation of their possessions, their entitlements. Man's desires for more are already in conflict with his resources even whilst he attempts this rule.

We can draw some working conclusions from these themes, each of which is relevant in thinking Biblically about sexual exploitation:

*   Each human's worth is tied into God's valuing of that person. (As an example, see how God protects Cain after his punishment.)
*   Humans have a fundamental, created need for intimacy.
*   There is a hinted-at mirroring of a divine union that slowly will emerge in a Christian understanding of the God-community, the Three-in-One of the trinity.
*   Dominion has been given, but it can be turned to evil – seeking to be like God, seeking power over others.

It becomes clear that sexual exploitation is one of the ultimate ways in which the creation pattern is destroyed: from "helper" to "dominated," from intimacy to used. Relationship is broken; the image of God shattered. Healing and re-creation cannot come easily or lightly.

Examples from Scripture

From the expulsion from the garden through to re-creation in the New Testament, the Bible is a sad story of God's people not getting it right. Abuse, slavery, and the exploitation of women feature regularly.

Old Testament Examples

First, the whole story of the Exodus emphasizes God's concerns about exploitation (such as slavery and trafficking). God's people have become enslaved, forced into ever more impossible tasks, and God hears their cries ("I know all about their pain. And now I have come down to help them."[7]). It becomes the defining story of the people of Israel, of God's people. It also remains a centerpiece story in Christian teaching. First, Joseph, who was trafficked, enslaved and later redeemed, takes on Christ-like features. Second, the Passover is used to explain the sacrifice of the first-born son and gives us clues about the cost of freeing a people. Later on this was the story that the Christianized African slaves sang on their plantations; it resonates with exploited people. For the poor, the dream of the Promised Land still matters.

Second, alongside the freedom narrative, Exodus also recounts the giving of the law – instructions for living in redeemed community. Two facets emerge. One is God's continued compassion (and indeed passion) for those vulnerable to exploitation:

---

[7] Exodus 3:7 (The Message).

Don't abuse or take advantage of strangers; you, remember, were once strangers in Egypt. Don't mistreat widows or orphans. If you do and they cry out to me, you can be sure I'll take them most seriously; I'll show my anger and come raging among you with the sword, and your wives will end up widows and your children orphans.[8]

Two, this passage is located in the midst of other teachings related to poverty, usury and sexual conduct, with a hinge in Exodus 22:20 that states "anyone who sacrifices to a god other than God alone must be put to death," suggesting that we are thinking about idolatry. The usury instruction in Exodus 22:25–27 is particularly pertinent to bonded labor where poverty victims can never work hard enough to pay off their putative debts. Putting together the ideas in Exodus 22 reveals that sexual exploitation is a "perfect storm" where the three idols of money, sex and power converge. It is not new to this century; it is and always has been abhorred by the God who redeems.

Third, Deuteronomy provides much teaching about community and offers welcome antidotes to counter the above where immoral behavior begets God's punishment. In Deuteronomy, inclusivity begets God's blessing. It is not a meaningless inclusivity, as it includes regular storytelling and explanation of what it means to be the redeemed people of God (as well as extremely strongly worded cautions against inappropriate fascination with other gods or idols). This inclusive community life means a sharing of the sacred tithe with foreigners, orphans and widows;[9] it means a cancelling of debts to avoid poverty;[10] it means a generosity that protects the poor and vulnerable in the community;[11] it means liberation for slaves.[12] In Deuteronomy 22, we see that it also means that sexual ethics matter. Whilst the practice of proving a woman's virginity[13] may seem inappropriate to us now, the legislation does protect women. For example, the provision about a woman raped in the countryside[14] recognizes the greater power of the man and that legal protection is required. Deuteronomy also admonishes the community: "Don't ever forget that you were a slave in Egypt."[15] This theme and source of righteous behavior is always related to the vulnerable in the community (but not necessarily of the community). Finally, in Deuteronomy 26, worship and the giving of first-fruits is also related to those vulnerable being able to live well; and upon this is contingent the plea: "look down from heaven and bless your people."[16]

Sexual exploitation is a social and spiritual issue that these teachings in Exodus and Deuteronomy speak remarkably clearly to. The first response is about creating safe community; and the foundation is the memory of being freed. These remain critical foundations for building any Christian response.

---

[8] Exodus 22:21-24 (The Message).
[9] Deuteronomy 14:29.
[10] Deuteronomy 15:1-3.
[11] Deuteronomy 15:3,9-10.
[12] Deuteronomy 15:12.
[13] Deuteronomy 22:17.
[14] Deuteronomy 22:25-27.
[15] E.g. Deuteronomy 24:18, 22.
[16] Deuteronomy 26:15.

Unfortunately, the history of Israel from this point on suggests that these idealized instructions were rarely if ever achieved. The pinnacle of Israel's fame is ruined as David commits adultery with Bathsheba (exploiting his position of power, in this case, over her husband). God's patience with Israel is running out at the time of the Major Prophets. To choose just one, Ezekiel has graphic portrayals that describe Israel and Judah's sin in terms of a woman's lust and prostitution. [17] These passages are potentially problematic in reinforcing stereotypes about "the immoral woman" and so need to be carefully regarded as metaphors. But while Israel is portrayed as the loose woman, her "husbands" are as exploitive as any other exploiter. The codependency within an abusive relationship is recognizable by any relationship counselor.

New Testament Examples

The New Testament creates a bridge from the fallen world of sin and suffering to a new creation. Whilst the final fulfillment in Revelation is dealt with in an as-frustratingly-short passage as the Genesis creation passage, Jesus' teaching and then the story of the growth of the church (through the Epistles) is – again – about the theology and behaviors of a redeemed people. How does this new people live together, under God?

Tamar, Rahab, Ruth, Bathsheba. Matthew names just four women in Jesus' genealogy. Each of them is foreign, immoral, or both: a woman of the family who prostituted herself; a prostitute of some means – but foreign; a twice-married foreigner; a woman who colluded in adultery. The genealogy almost seems a joke, as Matthew meticulously constructs his generations of men in three sets of fourteen, demonstrating God's careful ordering – and then specifies five misunderstood women. While Matthew carries no implication that Mary was immoral, it is hard to imagine that her peers shared that view as they witnessed her inexplicable pregnancy.[18]

These five women stand as models of hope and redemption. Whilst sexual exploitation of males (boys and men) does occur, the great majority of this abuse is of females. In my own work I see time and time again that deeply entrenched gender discrimination remains a fundamental barrier to protecting women and girls. Here we do not have space to go much further into thinking about gender and the Bible, but there are many resources available elsewhere, including an article exploring Biblical foundations by Dr. Beth Grant.[19]

---

[17] See Ezekiel Chapters 16-23.

[18] The final part of Matthew's genealogy joke, of course, is his clarity that Joseph was only Mary's husband, not Jesus' father, as pointed out by Dr. Rowan Williams in *Christ on Trial: How the Gospel Unsettles Our Judgment* (Grand Rapids, MI: Wm. B. Eerdmans Publishing Co., 2003). The point is that for all the careful ordering of Israel's history, Jesus is an unexpected breaking-in of God, way beyond humanity's ability to construct its own salvation.

[19] Beth Grant, "A Theology of the Value of the Girl Child," Faith Alliance Against Slavery and Trafficking Website, http://storage.cloversites. com/faithallianceagainst

In Jesus' ministry he was labeled as the man who associated with sinners and prostitutes. Luke's gospel – the gospel of the outsiders – is particularly helpful. It is Luke who names the women and significant roles they played in Jesus' ministry[20] and it is again Luke who lays the emphasis on going out to the social outcastes, to bring them into the community of the King. Luke 14 and 15 are central in this. First, Jesus fills his guest list at the banquet with undesirables, and, second, follows up with teachings that are especially for "sinners" to tell them how committed he is to energetically seeking them out.[21]

Before these passages is the story in Luke 7:36-50 of the woman who anoints Jesus' feet at the house of Simon the Pharisee. This is a massively powerful story of redemption, as an immoral woman (often or usually thought to be a prostitute) is publicly forgiven. But much more than being forgiven, Jesus accepts her huge need for acceptance and forgiveness. How humiliating for Jesus to sit in respectable company with this woman crying over him, touching him, pouring oil over him. And yet Jesus shows no humiliation but instead identifies that the woman has come to him "loved much."[22] A degraded woman is sent by Jesus in *shalom*.[23] Her love is accepted, valued and publicly applauded. Jesus has no strait-laced comment or command. Her faith and her love matter. The *imago Dei* has been rediscovered and restored in her. And just in case we have missed the point, right at the end of his ministry, in Matthew 21:30-32, Jesus shocks his listeners, telling them that prostitutes will be more welcomed in God's kingdom than them!

Moving beyond the gospels, the Epistles address Christians who were trying to find ways to live together, including working through difficulties of sexual immorality. Jesus' endorsements of marriage had been strong – he had no compunction in recognizing God's joining together, patterned by Adam and Eve. But there is also in the Bible a curious silence that speaks to twenty-first century cultures, removing sex from its pedestal position. Much of the rhetoric around sex – the spoken and unspoken – arguably grants too much importance to sex. The church is organized around institutionalized sexual unions – the marrieds and the not-marrieds. More helpfully, perhaps, Paul's emphasis in 1 Thessalonians 4:3-8 is on good sexual ethics, in which "no one should wrong or take advantage of a brother or sister." The focus is the community relationships, not the marital relationships. This also makes sense of Paul's ambivalence toward marriage. This paper is about sexual exploitation, not about Christian attitudes to relationships and marriage. However, whilst sex and marriage are given inappropriate and unhelpful emphasis, it is questionable as to whether Christians are saying useful things to provide positive alternatives that work for people who have been abused, or who are potential or actual abusers, for whom a Biblical idea of intimacy and marriage has (so far)

---

slaveryandtrafficking/documents/A%20Theology%20of%20the%20value%20of%20the
%20girl%20child_2.pdf
[20] Luke 8:1-3.
[21] Luke 15:2.
[22] Luke 7:47.
[23] Luke 7:50.

not worked. But one of Jesus' few statements about heaven was that marriage will not exist in heaven.[24] Given Jesus' own lifelong singleness, this suggests that sex is not the big thing so often made out.

It may be that we need to think more about community instead. The doctrine of the Trinity is a hard one for us to really get to grips with – the Bible words that describe the relationship ("love," "honor," "glorify") feel distant. But that God exists in such relationships matters, because it speaks about interdependency and sharing that goes beyond marriage. Community (as in the Deuteronomy passages) matters, and this appears too to be all we are told of the redeemed community in heaven. This reflects much of the very practical teachings in the New Testament about the community,[25] about ensuring different roles for all,[26] and also Paul's teaching on marriage.[27] An alternative metaphor is the new temple,[28] a new community of "living stones."[29] These rich pictures are about living together in vibrant and strong relationships. It worked for Jesus, in a community of all sorts of people. Could a local church become an inclusive, healing community offered to those that need safety and healing? And could such a community stand as both a testimony against and an alternative for those who would abuse power?

Areas for Further Thought and Action

To draw these ideas together, here are four areas for potential thought and action:

First, stigmatizing of abusers or the abused, exploiters or the exploited, needs to cease. The existence of abuse and exploitation needs to be "normalized." Sexual exploitation happens, and it needs to be talked about and dealt with. For instance, the NIV translation of the Bible mentions the word "prostitute" 74 times. As the Bible proudly puts the immoral foreign women in the headlines of Jesus' genealogy, Christians need to find ways to be comfortable in engaging with what are too easily seen as "unspeakable" issues. As long as they are unspoken, license to exploit is granted, and victims' hurt is minimized.

Second, God has stinging accusations of those who collude in practices that grant one person power over another. This brings us to the critical need for churches to be engaged in challenging, at micro and macro levels, structural economic oppression and poverty. It must become a heartfelt concern of the non-poor amongst the Church.

Third, Christians need to find ways of practicing community that allow possible exploiters and perpetrators to find better ways to meet their loneliness and other needs and provide alternatives to the exploitative use of power over

---

[24] Matthew 22:30.

[25] E.g. in Colossians 3.

[26] 1 Timothy 5.

[27] 1 Corinthians 7.

[28] E.g. Ephesians 2:21.

[29] 1 Peter 2:5.

others. This is a huge topic that needs careful attention, with thought and respect paid not only to victims' needs but also to the whole areas of teaching and practice about fulfillment, relationships, commitment, justice and forgiveness.

Fourth, Christians need to create healing communities that respect those who are seeking freedom and restoration. But they need to do these in ways that are utterly non-stigmatizing, not patronizing, not controlling; all of these continue the hurt and injustice of previous exploitation. They also need to recognize the depth of the profound wounds of sexual exploitation. Wholeness after great disfigurement, as well as relational ability after abusive and exploitative relationship, are things that can only be achieved with great care. This can happen within the faith community's sacramental practices as well as social practices.

To conclude, I want to echo Schmutzer's clear call about addressing abuse:

> Like other social ills before, it is going to take time for the image-conscious expectations of church and various ministries to engage these dark realities at the level of victims' needs. Then we shall build healing communities for our sexually broken out in the open light of acceptance where the warm comfort of wholeness and safety can overshadow the painful traditions of silence and "victory."[30]

Case Study, by Ian de Villiers

CoVoice, Morang District, Nepal: Combatting Child Sexual Abuse And Sexual Exploitation Through A Local Church Network

This case study seeks to show how a small group of poor churches, being inspired by Biblical teaching about sexual exploitation, have been able to engage in sustained meaningful action.

CoVoice is a group of 17 churches based in the city of Biratnagar in south-eastern Nepal. Biratnagar is very close to the Indian border in Bihar, and has a relatively open border as well as many possibilities to simply walk from one country to the other. The border crossing is also relatively open, as Nepalis do not need visas to enter India. Statistics are available that show an official net movement of children into India through regulated border crossings.

CoVoice was initiated after CarNetNepal, the national network based in Kathmandu, identified Biratnagar as a key locus in trafficking. CarNetNepal's approach was to first engage church leaders in the issues through a workshop, and then to provide them with some appropriate tools with which to be able to address the problem. The main tool was a large flip chart that has the story of an abused daughter that can be worked through with literate and non-literate people at community gatherings (which obviously includes many children, particularly younger ones). Helpline cards then are given to each participant so that if they are concerned for themselves or someone else, they are able to get help.

---

[30] Schmutzer, "A Theology of Sexual Abuse," 812.

The big strength, however, is that because the pastor and members of a local church do these community events there is an immediate, relational connection into that local church. Whilst the congregations themselves are neither rich nor well-resourced (e.g. in training) they have what all churches have – people – and compassion on the vulnerable. One woman was enabled to leave a marriage where her daughter was being persistently raped. This was made possible because the church literally took her in, giving her accommodation and the means of support; they also chose that the stigma of leaving a marriage was less important than the child and mother's safety.

Several aspects of CoVoice's approach to addressing sexual exploitation seem to form a helpful model:

1. Their response to sexual exploitation came from a Biblically and socially informed appeal, laying out the facts and their Christian calling.
2. Despite deep taboos and discomfort with the issues, simple tools such as flipcharts and helpcards allows "baby steps" to take place while shared, practical responses are being worked out by the group.
3. A model of concentric circles of community allows a response by what is materially a poor church: vulnerable individuals are connected to caring congregations, congregations are linked together into the local network, then they are connected to local government and NGOs, and in turn resourced through national networks and NGOs that provide extra support as needed.
4. CoVoice enables the congregations to face outward: to their communities and the vulnerable within them, and to local duty-bearers (e.g. the police and secular NGOs) that have responsibilities when exploitation is discovered.
5. CoVoice is able to do meaningful prevention as it breaks the silence about taboo subjects. Sexual abuse is (tragically) ubiquitous but it is possible to do something meaningful about it.
6. CoVoice is increasingly less complicit in allowing deeply-embedded cultural beliefs (such as caste and gender discrimination) to persist as it models the presence of the kingdom of God.
7. CoVoice continually seeks new learning about the scale and scope of the issues in its locality and how to address them.

Discussion Questions

1. "Christians need to find ways to be comfortable in engaging with what are too easily seen as 'unspeakable' issues." What issues around sexual abuse are unspeakable for you, your church and social communities? How would you like that to change?
2. "Christians need to create healing communities." What are your best experiences of this? How does your Bible reading inform this, and how might you build on that in your church community?

3. The gospel is uncompromising both in its offer of forgiveness and restoration; but also in its condemnation of hurt caused to children. How can Christians maintain that balance for themselves in their role – and keep children safe at the same time?

4. There are no "quick fixes" for the people and systems that allow child abuse to happen. How can Christians equip themselves for patience and perseverance in ministry?

CHAPTER 4: HOW SHOULD THE CHURCH BE INVOLVED IN RESPONDING TO SEXUAL EXPLOITATION?

Key Issues,[1] by Jim Martin

Over the last several years much has been written on the subject of "justice." Much of this content has been produced by and for the church. Lately it seems the literature and websites of churches and ministries are seasoned with words like *justice, trafficking, slavery* and *abolition.* The last decade has seen several important books, both secular and church-related, dealing with such challenging subjects as commercial sexual exploitation and modern slavery. While it may be hard to pinpoint exactly how these difficult issues have found their way into the church's sphere of attention, we should certainly celebrate the arrival of more and more churches to these important challenges. We may protest that the church has shown up late; we may express concern that the church is sometimes clumsy in its efforts; but even so, let us celebrate that a discernible movement of God's spirit is taking shape capturing the attention of churches of all shapes and sizes as they begin to respond to the issue of sexual exploitation.

History of the Church's Response

Last century, at the close of World War Two, churches struggled to come to grips with issues like hunger, poverty and homelessness. The 1940s and 1950s saw a dramatic increase in the number of Christian humanitarian organizations.[2] Many of these were formed by faithful followers of Jesus who in their WWII service had seen a kind of poverty and suffering that previously had been unknown to them. The creation of these organizations was their courageous response to these needs and an expression of their willingness to explore what the Gospel of Jesus might have to say about such suffering. Now, more than fifty years later, it is difficult to find an evangelical church in the U. S. that does *not* have some sort of mercy program to address the issues of neighbors suffering for lack of basic needs.

While some Christian faith traditions have a long history of involvement in social justice, it is my conviction that we are now beginning to experience a similar maturing in my particular branch of the church (the Protestant evangelical church) with respect to issues of justice; this paper focuses on the

---

[1] The content of this essay has been expanded into a full-length book: Jim Martin, *The Just Church: Becoming a Risk-Taking, Justice-Seeking, Disciple-Making Congregation* (Carol Stream, IL: Tyndale Momentum, 2012). www. thejustchurch.com
[2] Elizabeth Ferris, "Faith-Based and Secular Humanitarian Organizations," *International Review of the Red Cross* 87, No. 858 (June 2005): 314.

response of this part of the church. I have spent the last decade of ministry involved in the church's response to issues of violent oppression – first as a pastor of a church deeply involved in the fight against unprosecuted sexual abuse of minors in a small community in Peru and most recently as the Vice President of Church Mobilization with International Justice Mission. From this perhaps unique vantage point, I can faithfully report that this growing movement is exciting and real. Though new and sometimes flawed, the church's engagement is as creative as it is courageous. Faithful followers of Jesus are taking significant risks to invest their time, talent and resources to join God's work of rescuing the oppressed, defending the orphan and pleading for the widow.[3]

The church's ultimate arrival (late though it may be) to this important social issue of our time likely comes as no great surprise. Because the suffering endured by victims of injustice in our world can be overwhelming to contemplate, affluent evangelicals the world over have often chosen to isolate themselves from such horrors and insulate themselves from the charged emotions that injustice-related suffering elicits. However, almost any exposure to the statistics and particularly the stories of the many victims of violent oppression around the world produces significant unrest for people of reasonably good heart. This turbulence of soul often leads to an energetic search for meaningful involvement in the issues. Certainly this has been motivation enough for many churches to take action.

Reasons for and Nature of Responding

Many churches are increasingly realizing that the Scriptures speak with surprising frequency about the issue of injustice. Indeed, a simple reading of the Old Testament alone reveals the fact that the issue of injustice is addressed with higher frequency than any other issue except, understandably, the issue of idolatry.[4] There is a growing awareness that God has always been deeply concerned for those on the margins of society, those whose lack of power and voice make them extraordinarily vulnerable. Further, people of faith are seeing once again that from God's perspective, God's people have always been his solution to the suffering of the world's vulnerable.

Both the compelling nature of the need, and the reality of God's call to engage are often reasons enough for churches to spring to action. I have been in contact with hundreds of churches where newfound passion has propelled congregations several steps down the road to direct engagement in the battle against injustice. But the issues of sexual exploitation and other forms of violent oppression are by nature so very dark, complex, confusing, chaotic and taboo that good intentions and passion only fuel involvement for a surprisingly short time. The inevitable loss of traction, feelings of disappointment and darkness can and often do thwart the plans of good-natured souls. In fact, what

---

[3] Isaiah 1:17.

[4] Christopher J.H. Wright, *The Mission of God: Unlocking the Bible's Grand Narrative* (Downers Grove, IL: InterVarsity Press, 2006).

churches often find as they engage the issue of oppression is that the faith they bring to the challenge is not rugged enough to survive the desperation they might feel as they get up close to the violence of injustice. The need to stay "in control," the need to be "safe," and the need for "success" begin to deflate the passion and hope they felt so clearly at the outset. This often results in waning commitment or a commitment to remain simply on the surface of the issue.

But for the churches that are able to move past these challenges into deep involvement, there are some surprises. While the statistics, the need and the call of God are often the primary motivation for my friends around the world who are taking risks to engage issues of violent oppression, there is a surprising benefit that few of us expected as we began this journey. What we've found is that the work of justice is some of the most fertile ground for discipleship that we've ever experienced. What we've found, counter-intuitively, is that the places of violent oppression and abuse that may seem utterly God-forsaken are in fact the places where we have most deeply experienced the presence and power of God. The call to the work of justice is therefore not God sending his church "out" to a place where God cannot be found. Rather, God is inviting us "in" to the place where he is already at work. Our good God is offering what many of us so deeply desire in our churches. In the work of justice, God is beckoning us to come and experience his profound love for us and for the vulnerable of this world. The call to fight against injustice is a call to deep discipleship.

Suggestions for Churches Wanting to Respond

What is most obvious after more than a decade of working with a wide variety of churches responding to God's call to "rescue the oppressed" is that there is no prescription for how to do it right. While there are many similarities in the processes that successful churches take, it will likely be no surprise that there is no clear *procedure,* no one-size-fits-all solution for mobilizing a congregation to meaningful action. In the absence of a blueprint, what I can offer is the outline of some decisions and steps that have been helpful as many churches have sought engagement in the fight against injustice.

Encounter

At International Justice Mission ("IJM") we are constantly guiding churches back to the need for a deep, ongoing encounter with the God of justice. Churches are often surprisingly ignorant of at least two things:

- The nature and extent of Biblical material calling the people of God to action for the sake of the vulnerable, and
- The nature and extent of injustice-related suffering in our world today.

This ignorance is surprisingly self-reinforcing: Churches do not see the world clearly because they are not hearing in the Scriptures the inexorable call to come out of isolation and engage the suffering of their neighbors. On the other hand, because they have so isolated themselves from the vulnerable of our world, today's Bible readers are simply unable to recognize that the suffering endured by a trafficking victim (for example) is actually spoken of in the Scriptures as something that concerns God and ought to concern God's people (see for example, Isaiah 1:17, Isaiah 58:6, Luke 4:18-19, Psalm 10). We encourage churches to form "Justice Learning Communities" that help educate their entire congregation about the Biblical mandate to do justice through the use of Sunday morning teaching, small group book studies and youth curriculum. Careful cultivation of an ongoing encounter with the God of justice helps reinforce solid foundational building blocks like sustainability, commitment, depth, humility and repentance. Practitioners will do well to limit their work with churches only to those who display the sort of humility that evidences itself in a willingness to learn.

Learning about the nature of injustice-related suffering in our world is often challenging because it requires something more of churches: courage. Privileged cultures around the world usually choose to isolate themselves from the suffering of the poor and vulnerable, once they have achieved a level of affluence that permits it. But Christians who take the scriptures seriously find in them a mandate. They find that like the Samaritan in Jesus' story, God is calling them to draw near to suffering, to see and to be moved with compassion. This first step is simple, but risky. It requires a willingness to learn about, pray for and engage (in small but significant ways) in the suffering of the world's vulnerable.

This is precisely why stories, carefully chosen and respectfully told by practitioners, are so helpful. It is most often through experiencing the story of a survivor's courageous battle against injustice, along with seeing what hope and success can look like, that the church's isolation is broken. Through appropriate stories, churches can begin to experience real compassion for those who are suffering.

Explore

As a deep encounter with the God of justice begins to shape the congregation, inevitably individuals emerge for whom learning is simply not enough and who will want to explore possibilities for engagement. At this point, many successful churches have formed smaller "Justice Task Forces" to begin exploring in three concentric circles: their church, their community and their international networks.

First, it is important that we begin this process of exploring opportunities for engagement at home. Given domestic violence and rape statistics, we should assume that *all* of our churches have victims of violent abuse already in their midst. Furthermore, human trafficking is a problem in the United States and other developed nations just as it is elsewhere around the world. Let us begin by ensuring that our own churches are true sanctuaries for these victims to receive the hope and healing the church can offer.

IJM also encourages churches explore their own congregations. We find that when churches begin to make justice a priority, new skills and even new congregants begin to surface. Some members who have been part of the church for a long time will step forward and offer skills and services that previously they had seen as irrelevant to the work of the church.

For example, for years I was on the pastoral staff of a medium-sized church in California. One Sunday after I presented our church's work with International Justice Mission to the congregation, a young professional came to talk with me. She was a Marriage and Family Therapist working for the county mental health services. Her caseload was so large that she was often tired and lacking energy for new relationships. Consequently, though she had attended Sunday services for several years, she had not become more deeply involved. But as a therapist, her interest was piqued when she discovered the church was involved in aftercare for victims of violent abuse. In one short conversation she related several skills she would like to offer as the church worked with these victims. I remember her excitement as she talked about the role of art therapy in the rehabilitation of trauma survivors, especially children. I had two simultaneous thoughts during our conversation: One, how thankful I was that there was such a talented professional in our church who was willing to offer her expertise where it was so deeply needed. The other thought was the embarrassed realization that I had never seen this woman in our church before. She had attended for several years but somehow the programming and opportunities we were offering weren't enticing enough to draw her out – until we started engaging with victims of oppression. I have a sense that there are many such young professionals in our churches today. They are likely not all therapists, but it would be wise for churches to spend time assessing their gifts, skills and networks in light of God's call to seek justice.

The second area for churches to explore is the possibilities for engagement in their own communities. Many churches have learned to perform a "justice audit" on their communities.[5] Churches are often surprised at how a few simple inquires in the community can quickly bring local justice issues to their attention. This of course puts the church at some risk. They may, in fact, discover an issue that they simply can't resist engaging.

Finally, churches can explore opportunities internationally. Many churches exist in healthy international networks. These networks are often capable of offering financial and human resources to places where they are needed. For example, a church in Florida may have a connection with a group of churches in Southeast Asia. These church networks often have undiscovered potential to deliver training and financial resources to places where they are desperately needed.

Engage

For many practitioners in the field, the idea of the Western church (as clumsy as it often is) engaging in meaningful international fieldwork can be a bit of a

---

[5] IJM's "Community Justice Assessment Tool" is a free resource that churches can use. https://secure3.convio.net/ijm/site/Ecommerce/901266949?VIEW_PRODUCT= true&product_id=1381&store_id=1101

hard sell. I have fought through the same skepticism myself. Many of us have seen enough Western church teams full of well-meaning white people in new safari outfits to know that not all teams offer a value-added contribution in the field. However, from the last ten years of experience I have to conclude that for churches willing to do the hard work of encountering God's call to justice and exploration of needs, arrival at meaningful engagement is possible – sometimes almost inevitable. Over the years, IJM has been profoundly surprised at what churches are capable of in the field. From starting brand-new aftercare homes to offering professional training on trauma care to starting new NGOs that pioneer economic self-sufficiency programs for trafficking victims, IJM has had the privilege of seeing the church meaningfully engage, finding traction and success.

Suggestions for Practitioners Working with Churches

In addition to churches needing to learn how best to respond to issues of violence, practitioners who are working at the grass-roots with victims of injustice need to learn how best to work with churches. Here are a few practical suggestions:

- *Exercise Discernment.* You don't have to work with every church that asks. If what they really want is a one-week tour and they have nothing to offer or are unwilling to learn, politely decline the relationship!
- *Plan Well.* Consider carefully how best to involve church groups in your work. Not all churches have the same capabilities. Fit the task with the talent of the church.
- *Challenge the Church to Stretch and Grow.* Creative and appropriate use of client stories and successful model church stories will cast larger vision for what is possible.
- *Think Bigger.* Most churches are capable of more than they think.
- *Help the Church Learn.* Provide resources, encourage them to explore the gifts and talents they possess.
- *Don't Be Afraid to Ask.* Specific projects often are very attractive to churches and provide a sense of connection and ownership that can motivate a congregation.

Conclusion

A significant shift is taking place in the global church. Among other things, this shift includes an openness to issues the Protestant evangelical church has previously ignored as irrelevant. This new interest in issues of justice in general, and in human trafficking in particular, is a very promising sign. There are human and professional resources in the church that could fuel the battle against human trafficking for years to come. So while it is certainly true that many churches have a lot to learn when it comes to engagement in issues such as human trafficking, the NGO community will do well to help churches learn and grow. The results are sure to offer surprising synergies, reveal new possibilities and meet the real needs of real victims the world over.

Case Study, by Jim Martin[6]

In the summer of 2007, 121 Community Church took a journey through the book of Amos led by their pastor, Ross Sawyers. At the conclusion of this study, Ross and the congregation felt God's call to them to respond and do something specific to engage in God's heart for justice and to join the fight against injustice. After a time of prayerfully seeking God's guidance concerning their role in His great work of justice, they formed the Amos Project – a mission effort specifically focused on addressing the problem of injustice in a way that glorifies God.

The church took a step of faith in committing significant funding to engage in a justice issue, but the details of such a project were yet to be worked out. In 2008, they created various teams to coordinate various aspects of the project including prayer, research and the engagement of the church body.

These teams spent months in research, prayer and discussion. They began by studying Scripture further and developing a firm theological foundation concerning how and why justice matters to God. Next they began to research the most serious injustices in the world today. As a church, they wanted to engage in addressing an injustice of the greatest magnitude. They also wanted to identify a particular area in the world and establish and maintain a long-term commitment to fighting against injustice in that region. Finally, after much prayer, fasting and discussion, the research and process teams narrowed the focus to children at risk. Various areas of focus emerged including the problem of child trafficking in Southeast Asia, specifically in the nation of Cambodia.

Next they contacted the International Justice Mission Church Mobilization department and invited Jim Martin, the Vice President of Church Mobilization, to visit their church. As they began to partner with IJM, IJM's former director of aftercare in Cambodia, Christa Hayden, also came to speak at the church about IJM and the problem of child trafficking in Cambodia. Christa and the 121 team have partnered together to see the fulfillment of God's call to the church to engage in fighting the problem of child trafficking in Cambodia and they are now doing so in a number of key ways.

Their church small groups, called Life Groups, have educated themselves about God's heart for justice and about the work of IJM Cambodia. Each group prays weekly for a specific IJM team member out in the field, for the nation of Cambodia and against the injustice of child trafficking. During Sunday services and nights of worship, they pray for God's work of justice among the victims of sex-trafficking in Cambodia.

---

[6] This case study comes from an interview with Rodney Howell, Missions Pastor, 121 Community Church on November 4, 2009. http://www.121cc.com/amos-project/

In addition, 121 is raising up a justice generation and educating their children and youth about these issues. Their youth group had a Cambodia night, which involved further education about the country and taking an offering to contribute to the cost of aftercare parcels for victims of child trafficking. Then they put together these parcels and prayed for each one and each victim that would receive it.

While exploring the injustice of child trafficking in Cambodia, 121 has also explored their local community and developed a ministry to help children at risk closer to home. This ministry includes providing for basic food and clothing needs, a mentoring program for vulnerable school children, and career advice and help in gaining work experience.

Rodney Howell, Missions Pastor at 121, noted how it was never difficult for the project team to find volunteers, in fact most of the team are volunteers rather than paid staff! He even saw members of the church who had previously struggled to get involved in various ministries volunteering the most time, effort and passion to the work of justice. It was as if they had just been waiting for an opportunity to serve in this way.

After months of education, exploration and engagement through prayer and giving, a team from 121 was able to visit Cambodia in 2009 and see firsthand the extent of the injustice of child trafficking and the response of God's people through organizations such as IJM and Agape, an aftercare partner. 121 returned from the trip passionate and ready to continue and develop the ways in which it engages in the fight against child trafficking in Cambodia. They have made a long-term commitment to help bring rescue and relief to the victims of violent oppression in this region.

Since that first summer Bible study on an Old Testament prophet, 121 has journeyed a long way into God's heart for justice. Rodney believes that the justice journey they have embarked upon really has been "God raising the value of what is in his word and putting it in our hearts, we were convicted and people were obedient in their response." He has seen the joy that comes in the realization that there are ways in which God's people can respond to huge problems of injustice. The problem of child trafficking is a truly horrific and grave injustice, but Rodney and the members of 121 Community Church can testify that this is not something we just have to accept. There are things you can do that affect real people and real lives.

Why not contact our Church Mobilization team churches@ijm.org to find out today about how your church can embark upon its own justice journey?

Discussion Questions

1. From your experience, what does it look like when churches neglect the Biblical mandate to seek justice? What are the consequences they experience themselves? What consequences are experienced by others?

2. From your experience, what does it look like when churches learn to engage injustice with both courage and humility? What are the benefits they experience themselves? What benefits are experienced by others?

3. Think about your own story – about your own journey toward the work of justice. What of this three-step process (Encounter, Explore, Engage) have you experienced?

4. What aspects of your story do you think might be helpful for churches to hear as they wrestle with the issue of biblical justice? Why?

5. This essay describes the work of justice as "fertile ground for discipleship," and the place where we "deeply experienced the presence and power of God." These are bold statements. How have you found this to be true? Are there ways you wish they were more frequently true for you?

6. As you think about your own context, is there a significant, value-add contribution you can imagine a church making? What would that look like? What steps could you take to cultivate a church relationship that might result in the meeting of that need?

CHAPTER 5: DOES SEX MATTER TO GOD? WHY SHOULD IT MATTER TO US AS CHRISTIANS?

Theological Reflection, by Dan Allender

Sex. The word warns, tantalizes, sells, allures, provokes. It circles in and through the core of our identity. It is the ground of heartache and hope, desire and despair for nearly every sentient human being on the earth. In fact, it is one of the key battlegrounds evil uses to turn the heart against the goodness of the creator, and foul the creation. To not think a great deal about sex – meaning, purpose, process; and its enemy – abuse, perversion, promiscuity, and misuse; is to allow the forces of darkness to do their bidding with anonymity and unchecked power.

There are a few assumptions underlying all that this brief article will say. First, God loves sex. He begins his magisterial proclamation of how the earth is made in the poetry of creation, and the pinnacle of the poem is the proclamation that male and female are made in the image of God.[1] Gender is the peak of God's revelatory work of creation. Male and female reveal something about God that bears the mark of creational glory. Sex is first gender, not genitality. Gender must be honored first and foremost as co-equal, each fully revelatory of God with no value of higher or lower, better or worse, good or bad implied.

Second, God loves story. The narrative of the second creation account in Genesis 2 tells the story of male and female's first meeting and the consequent commitment for every man to establish a radical new loyalty to his spouse that supersede all other bonds – tacit and oath bound, to enter the relational world of the other to grow their goodness and uniqueness, and then – and only then, to become one flesh. Sex is the denouement of the second creation account. The summary that sings of the glory of love, the joy of sex, and the wonder of God's creation: "Adam and his wife were both naked, and they felt no shame."[2]

Third, God's enemy – the evil one, hates God. It hates anything that reveals the character of God. It hates most virulently the image of God, maleness and femaleness. Most succinctly, evil hates the union of man and woman that comes from the joyful worship of the Creator through loyal love, truth, and delightful pleasure. Evil loves sex that is absent of loyalty; violates honor and truth; lacks pleasure and delight for one or both. Evil particularly celebrates sex that is shame-filled, power-distorted, degrading, and dignity assaulting.

Finally, evil marks every person on this earth with its hatred of sexuality. No one escapes its broad-brush of shame and degradation. It is endemic in every culture, family and relationship. No one is free from the foul haze that

---

[1] Genesis 1:26-28.
[2] Genesis 2:25 (NIV).

infiltrates every portion of the blue planet. It is naïve to think that some suffer sexual harm and others do not. The only way we can more faithfully and wisely engage the more severe forms of heartache and degradation is to more honestly enter the realm of how evil has intended harm for each person on the planet. Our focus will move to the key question of design. What is God's desire for our sexuality? And then by implication, why does the evil one spend such labor attempting to destroy the delight and joy of sex?

Why Does Sex Matter So Much to God?

Sex is meant by God to give us a profound taste of the goodness of God's character – a portrayal of God's delight in intimacy, pleasure and joy. Sex is an icon, a narrative that is meant to lead us to worship. Why does sex matter so much to God – sexual joy is meant to draw us into a stance of wonder and gratitude that calls us to delight in and celebrate God for his goodness.

God Has Written Sex as a Story

Sexual joy found both in the process of erotic play, arousal and foreplay, and the cumulative climax of orgasm overlaps the nature of narrative. There are considered to be four stages of the sexual process:

- Desire – an awareness of sexual arousal that is increased by anticipation and images of pleasure. The penis begins to move toward erection; the clitoris increases in size and capacity for arousal through vasco-dilation.
- Plateau – the penis and the clitoris have reached the capacity for orgasm through foreplay.
- Orgasm – the cumulative release of energy that briefly intensifies the sensations of pleasure through an increase in dopamine and serotonin, bio-chemicals that are most associated with pleasure and well-being.
- Decline – the return of the body to quiescence and rest.

The process is meant to be a story within a story. The larger story is the epic story of faithful, loyal honor and commitment to truth. Sex is designed to be a gift given and received, and returned endless between a man and a woman who pledge an oath of exclusive loyalty as God has done for us. As there are not to be competing gods or divided loyalties, there is to be no other who takes my heart or body – only my beloved.

And the larger story reveals that the one and true God seeks me and will redeem me irrespective of my flight or failure to obey, honor and serve. Sex is pursuit of the other in the face of uncertainty, danger and personal sacrifice. There are profound differences in the body and soul of a man that run counter to the way a woman has been written. The story of sex even before the fall of humankind into sin was designed to compel us to encounter difference, complexity, and the necessity for playful sacrifice.

Desire for a man is more often than not visually based, intense and sudden. For a woman, the desire stage of arousal is slower, relationally oriented on the quality of the care received well before the sexual encounter. Fast vs. slow; visual vs. relational.

Plateau phase for a man is rapid and usually achieved with little difficulty; for a woman reaching the plateau stage is easily disturbed by environmental, relational, and emotional factors. It is more fragile and takes more time and process. Rapid vs. slower; certain vs. fragile.

Orgasm for a man is singular, intense and brief; a woman's orgasm may be less or more intense, singular or multiple, briefer or longer. Simple vs. complex.

Decline for a man is usually rapid and complete; for a woman decline offer includes the desire for touch, conversation, and face-to-face intimacy. Disengaged vs. engaged.

At almost every part of the story there is apparent contradiction and complexity. It is no wonder men have taken the position for millennia that their sexuality is normative and a woman's is less sexual or more difficult. It is part of the tragedy of the fall that a man's story is normative, and a woman's body and narrative is viewed as deviant or at least deficient – to be under a man's authority or authorship, to determine her meaning.

God's design is that difference demands humility and openness to the other to learn and grow, to see and be in ways that are 'other' than we would have chosen on our own. Sacrifice leads to freedom and joy, not bondage and despair. To learn the ways of a stranger is to come home to be oneself. We cannot become who we are meant to be in God if we refuse the journey of reimagining redemption, and being reformed and remade in his image.

Sexual joy requires entering the particular journey and story of the one whom I have committed myself to in covenantal loyalty. She has been violated in some fashion prior to my engagement in her life. She has suffered culturally, familiarly, personally the hatred of the evil one against her gender. The same is fully true for the man. A wife must enter the dark and broken places of her husband's heart. Every person on the earth is naked and marred by shame.

To enter the grand story, we must humble ourselves by loving and serving the particular stories before us. I am married to one wife; my wife to one husband. I bring a story of past sexual brokenness to our marriage, including abuse, promiscuity and shame. And my wife must neither pretend it doesn't exist or was removed magically when I became a Christian or a more mature believer. On the other hand, she can't see me solely on the basis of brokenness even in the face of sin; but must believe all things are possibly redeemed and must join the arduous, daily journey of pursuing truth, goodness and beauty. And the same is true for my engagement with her brokenness and redemptive story.

It is one thing to know that sex matters to God. It is an entirely different matter to own up to our sexual story and the story of our spouse, and believe that the story of the gospel is also a story about our sexual redemption as a person, a couple, a family, a church, a nation, and a world.

Discussion Questions

This essay invites you to consider both why sex is so important to God and to God's enemy, the evil one. To make the best use of this essay it is advisable to do some journaling as you respond to these questions.

1. What was the primary message you learned about sex as a young person:

    from your Mom?
    from your Dad?
    from your siblings?
    from your peers?
    from your church?

2. What early sexual experience had the greatest effect on your life? Consider writing a 600-900 word narrative fully to engage the story. If you do this exercise be sure to include the setting or context of the harm, what relational factors let up to the situation, and a description of the characters that includes dialogue. Be sure to allow the plot to move forward to an ending that engages some of the effects of the experience. If this is a foreign idea or one you have never done before you might wish to look at *To Be Told* by Dan Allender.[3]

    Once the writing is finished make sure you provide yourself with good self-care and time to reflect on what you have written. If you are in a relationship with a wise and trusted counselor, it might be wise to have him or her read the story in order to begin reflecting on the implications of the story in your life.

    Address these questions:

    -   How did I come to see myself as a sexual being due to this experience?
    -   What accusations and judgments have I made about myself as a sexual being?
    -   How have I protected myself from engaging this and other stories?
    -   If I look into the face of God after reading this story, what do I see?

3. If you are married, please consider these questions:

    -   How do you deal with the difference in sexual responsiveness and desire in your marriage? Where has that been the basis of conflict? Deepened understanding?
    -   How well do you know the sexual story of your spouse? How well does your spouse know your own story? To what

---

[3] Dan B. Allender, *To Be Told: Know Your Story, Shape Your Future* (Colorado Springs: WaterBrook Press, 2005).

degree has shame kept you and your spouse from talking about sex in your relationship?

In no fashion am I suggesting every couple should share without reservation all the details of their sexual past. This would neither be edifying or honorable. However, unaddressed sexual stories inevitably show up in one form or another shaping our ability to enjoy and bless our sexuality.

Please consider what it cost personally and relationally to name and address these stories, at least with a trusted, well trained, and experienced therapist.

4. How has your sexual story influenced your calling and the way you work with others?

CHAPTER 6: HOW HAVE WE MESSED UP SEX?

Theological Reflection, by Lisa L. Thompson

Like smoke-filled air, bomb-shelled buildings, and bullet-riddled corpses, there are signs all around us indicating that the world is deeply entrenched in a war. This war pits license against liberty, appetite against fullness, objectification against personhood, autonomy against communion, and flesh against spirit. Its battles are played out on and in our bodies, against our sexuality. Most of us have been injured or maimed in the crossfire. The deep wounds of sexual abuse; the mass ruin of marriages; the slavish, unquenchable thirst of sex addiction; the relentless feelings of inadequacy and self-loathing created by confused views of our bodies; the life-long consequences of sexually transmitted infections: such things testify to our hearts that we have been wounded and that something on a larger scale has gone terribly awry.

While multitudes are casualties and suffer the disastrous consequences, few people seem aware of the ongoing hostilities. Perhaps that's because the geopolitical epicenter of this conflict is spiritual rather than temporal. Nevertheless, as I hope this article will show if we begin to look with spiritual eyes, we will see that indeed a war rages and that its effects are felt on earth as well as in heaven. *In this conflict, we face a cunning enemy seeking to destroy both our earthly lives and eternal souls, who in pursuit of that aim attempts to use our bodies and their sexuality as weapons against us.* The enemy's principal strategy involves tactical methods that invite and entice us to profane the body.

Profaning the Body

In modern society there is little respect for or acknowledgement of that which is sacred; this is especially true with respect to the human body. Examples abound. To begin, the body is ruthlessly objectified – by that I mean rendered a person-less thing. Through pornography, women most especially, are dissected by a camera lens into orifices, buttocks, genitalia, and breasts to be consumed by the masses. The personhood of the individuals used in pornography is largely – if not completely – irrelevant to pornography consumers. Further, contemporary pornography dehumanizes and degrades women through graphic depictions of abuse and humiliation so grotesque they almost defy description.

The body is relentlessly transmuted. From banned practices such as foot-binding, to modern-day "sexual reassignment" surgeries (i.e. sex change operations), cosmetic labiaplasties and serial plastic surgeries to reconfigure the body, humans increasingly treat their bodies as if they were something to be contorted into any form that cultural aesthetic dictates or the "owner" desires.

The body is violated. Rape is a unique form of such violation. Wendy Freed describes rape as an intrusion of "the most intimate and personal aspect of the self," and notes that the body, where one's self resides, is the place where the violation of rape occurs.[1] Consequently, a rape survivor can never entirely be free from the setting where the violation took place. In some cases, rape is so violent that fistulas (i.e. holes) in the urethra, vagina, or colon – occur, resulting in leakage of bodily fluids and feces. In many modern conflicts rape is used as a "weapon of war" whereby hundreds and thousands of women are savagely, systematically raped to instill terror, hopelessness, shame, and to "break" entire communities.

The body is aborted. A human embryo is initially enveloped in the body of its mother. By day twenty-two after conception the unborn child will have its own heartbeat and blood. By week eight – the time by which many women discover they are pregnant – every organ will be in place and fingerprints will have begun to form: the embryo will have its own unique body. Nevertheless, in abortion the sacred space of the womb is ruthlessly desecrated and the little embodied human is vacuumed out like a bit of debris.

The body is enslaved. Enticed by worldly promises of pleasure and emancipation from sexual norms, pornography users and sex addicts are deluded. Like robots set on "auto" they compulsively masturbate, seeking the next orgasm irrespective of how it is derived or who is hurt in the process.

Clearly, then, the human body is the subject of incredible violence, brutality and destruction, and it is especially profaned through its sexual capacities. Christopher West advises us that, "If we want to know what's most sacred in this world, all we need do is look for what is most violently profaned."[2] With this thought in mind it can be argued that the plague of profanity against the human body just described provides the *prima facie* evidence of the sacred importance of our bodies. Something about the sacredness of the body is at the heart of the war on our sexuality and kindles unbridled forces of evil to seek its annihilation. Why is that?

The Body: Sacred Space

Adam and Eve (as well as all of humankind that followed) were a mystical melding of soul, spirit and body different from other creatures in that thus created they reflected God's own image.[3] For human beings to be without any one of these three elements is to live outside the fullness of God's original design.

---

[1] Wendy Freed, "From Duty to Despair: Brothel Prostitution in Cambodia," in *Prostitution, Trafficking, and Traumatic Stress,* ed. Melissa Farley (Binghamton, New York: The Haworth Maltreatment & Trauma Press, 2003), 138.

[2] Christopher West, *Theology of the Body for Beginners: A Basic Introduction to Pope John Paul II's Sexual Revolution* (West Chester, PA: Ascension Press, 2004), 12.

[3] Lehman Strauss, *"Man A Trinity (Spirit, Soul, Body),"* Bible.org Website (June 14, 2004). https://bible.org/seriespage/man-trinity-spirit-soul-body

The body, while often vilified through the ages, is of vital importance to the three-fold amalgamation of a single person. Open the face-shield of a spacesuit and the astronaut will perish within moments. Similarly, destroy the human body and the essential space that our souls and spirits inhabit in the earthly realm ceases to exist. To be embodied is as essential to human life on earth as a spacesuit is to the life of an astronaut in outer space.

Biblical writers have used the term "temple" to express the idea of the body as a spiritual abode. In so doing, they elevated the concept of our bodies beyond something like a suit, capsule or tent to that of a sacred space. The Bible documents the critical importance of the "temple" to the Jewish and Christian faiths. In the Old Testament, the first temple of God – referred to as a tabernacle or the "Tent of Meeting" – was the physical place where God came to dwell among the people. Wherever the Tabernacle went the presence of God went also.

Generations later King Solomon built the temple in Jerusalem to replace the Tent of Meeting. Here, too, the presence of the Lord dwelled. Finally, in the person of Christ, God came to live as a human being, among human beings. As John 1:14 poetically expresses: "The Word became flesh and made his *dwelling* among us." Christ's human body was and is God's final temple.[4]

Thus, the human body is sacred space because it is filled and animated by an eternal spirit and divinely created soul. For those redeemed by Christ, the body's holiness is magnified by the indwelling of the Holy Spirit; the apostle Paul made this observation while admonishing Christians to live lives of sexual purity referring to the human body as the "temple of the Holy Spirit."[5] Further, Christ's coming in human flesh should banish any doubts as to the significance of the body. In sum, our bodies are the sanctuaries God erected for our souls and spirits that we might serve and worship him now and throughout eternity.

It is little wonder then, that the forces of hell are especially bent on desecrating our bodies. Satan is enraged by their glory, that they display God's image and facilitate our worship of the Almighty. Accordingly, Satan wages war against God and against us using our sexuality as one of his most potent weapons. As the commander of rebellion, he invites us to join forces with him. He invites us desecrate our bodily temples, luring us with promises of freedom and pleasure, all the while ensuring our bondage, discontent and even destruction. While none of us would run into a church and throw hand grenades, spray paint graffiti on the walls or spit on the altar, we do just that to our bodies when we join Satan's insurrection by participating in amoral sexual acts – acts that God has defined as out of bounds, as sinful.

But is God really and truly that concerned with our sexual conduct? Doesn't he have "more important" things on his mind? Shouldn't we be more worried about issues like global poverty, racial reconciliation or climate change?

---

[4] Revelation 21:22.

[5] 1 Corinthians 6:19 (NIV; all Scriptures in this essay are NIV unless otherwise noted).

God Cares about Sex

At this juncture, we are hopefully agreed that the body is a sacred space. Nevertheless, we live in a world that takes a radically different view. From the secular perspective, the body is private property; it is owned by the inhabitant and each individual makes the rules about what happens in his/her own "space." Accordingly, most people in modern society give little thought to the sacredness of the body or the implications for what this means about their sexuality. As a consequence, contemporary society claims the human body and its sexuality as moral-free zones.

From a Biblical perspective, however, it is abundantly clear that human conduct in sexual relations matters deeply to God. Setting out the rules for sex was something that God went to great lengths to do. For instance, in Leviticus 18 God gave Moses extensive ordinances for Israel regarding sexual behavior. Sex with close relatives including one's mother, stepmother, sisters, aunts, grandchildren and in-laws was forbidden, as was sex with a woman and her daughter, the wife of one's neighbor, animals, and between men. Even the native-born people of the land and the foreigners living among the Israelites were expected to follow these rules. Further, Leviticus 19:29 warned the Israelites not to "degrade your daughter by making her a prostitute, or the land will turn to prostitution and be filled with wickedness."

Matters of sexual morality are also of great importance in the New Testament. For instance, Matthew 14 relates that King Herod imprisoned and eventually beheaded John the Baptist because John confronted the king for having taken his brother's wife as his own.

Yes, God gave us sex, but He gave us sex with parameters. But why? If God made humankind and gave us the capacity to have and enjoy sex, why should there be any encumbrances regarding with whom or what we have sex? To explore the answers to this question, let's turn again to Eden.

The Bitter Fruit

In Genesis 3 we encounter the story of Adam and Eve and their rebellious act of eating fruit from the one tree in the garden that God forbade them to eat of (in fact, they weren't even supposed to touch it). Through post-modern eyes I imagine that Adam and Eve's transgression – eating the fruit – must seem a trivial violation. After all, it's not as if Adam and Eve plotted a hostile take-over of the garden, chopped down all the trees, plucked all the flowers, or even spoke insubordinately to the master gardener – God. They simply ate. At first blush, it hardly seems a criminal offense, much less a provocation for the "fall of man." And, yet, it was a grievous act, and one rooted in the same sins that drive so much of immorality today. Just what are those sins?

Appetite

First, let's consider appetite (a.k.a. lust). As the record tells us, Eve looked at the fruit the serpent offered her. It appealed to her eye: "the woman saw that the fruit of the tree was good for food and pleasing to the eye."[6] Further, as the serpent explained, by eating this fruit her eyes would be opened and she would become like God, knowing good and evil.

Then and there something monumental was triggered in Eve. As she considered the serpent's words, she began to believe she lacked something. This woman who lived in a paradise so sublime our minds can scarcely imagine it, and who literally walked with God, surrendered to the lie that the God who lovingly made her and fellowshipped with her was denying her something essential for her happiness and fulfillment.

Thus appetite was born. Not the kind of appetite one feels upon smelling the sweet aroma of grandma's bread baking in the oven, but the kind of ravenous, unrestrained craving that since that fateful day has forever changed the course of human events and been the cause of countless shipwrecked lives.

While numerous biblical examples illustrate the consequences of yielding to one's appetites, the account of King David certainly stands out. A man with many wives already, he lusted after Bathsheba, a married woman. Her marital status notwithstanding, he had sexual relations with her, and when she conceived, he ultimately executed a scheme to have her husband killed to cover up his offense. God was both incensed and incredulous at David's actions. Despite God's already lavish provisions for him, David acted rashly and murderously in order to get more.

Consider also the dire consequences of Esau's appetite (Genesis 25:29-34 and 27:1-40). He lost all the inheritance that was due him as firstborn son over a bowl of stew! Russell Moore has explained the problem this way: "From the tree in the garden to the wilderness beyond the Jordan to the present hour, the people of God are tempted to turn their digestive or reproductive tracts away from the mystery of Christ and toward the self as god."[7]

As Eve's offspring, we all have inherited the congenital spiritual defect that replaces hunger for God with a craving for alluring yet bitter "fruit." The quest to fulfill our lusts can consume our lives and can take many forms: the chase for recognition and respect, for fame, possessions, wealth, power, love or wisdom. For others, their answer to the hunger is one never-ending, compulsive pursuit of the so-called pleasures of the flesh – especially through seeking sexual gratification and breaking sexual norms. As Frederick Buechner has aptly observed, such "lust [i.e. appetite] is the craving for salt of a person who is dying of thirst."[8] In these pursuits we are sadly driven onward like automatons – almost mindless of our actions, yet still vaguely conscious of the aching emptiness in our spirits.

This is not to say that the hunger is not real. *It is very real.* Unfortunately, we feverishly work to fill spiritual hunger with things that never satisfy (e.g. more and more sex) when what we lack is God's *presence*. Since that day when

---

[6] Genesis 3:6.

[7] Russell D. Moore, "Love, Sex and Mammon: Hard Times, Hard Truths, and the Economics of the Christian Family," *Touchstone* (March 2009).

[8] Frederick Buechner, *Wishful Thinking: A Seeker's ABC* (New York: HarperCollins, 1993), 65.

humanity was banished from the garden, when we lost our intimate relationship where we walked with God, we have been stumbling around trying to fill that gaping hole in our hearts with anything we can find.

Isaiah 55:1-3 reminds us this is so. God beckons us to seek Him:

> "Come, all you who are thirsty, come to the waters;
> and you who have no money, come, buy and eat!
> Come, buy wine and milk without money and without cost.
> Why spend money on what is not bread, and your labor on what does not satisfy?
> Listen, listen to me, and eat what is good, and your soul will delight in the richest of fare.
> Give ear and come to me; hear me, that your soul may live."

Christ alone is the bread that satisfies the hunger.[9] He alone is the water that can quench the thirst.[10]

Ultimately, in eating the fruit, Eve and Adam signaled their mistrust in God. They did not believe in His provision or in His boundless love. Mistrust of God is the legacy they bestowed upon us all, and which drives us to do anything and everything besides heed his loving direction. Turning to Christopher West, we can see how foolish this distrust is:

> In essence, Christ's life proclaims: "You don't believe God loves you? Let me show you how much God loves you. You don't believe that God is 'gift'? This is my body *given* for you (Luke 22:19). You think God wants to keep you from life? I will bleed myself dry so that my life's blood can give you life to the full (John 10:10). You thought God was a tyrant, a slave-driver? I will take the form of a slave (Philippians 2:7); I will let you 'lord it over' me to demonstrate that God has no desire to 'lord it over' you (Matthew 20:28). You thought God would whip your back if you gave him the chance? I will let you whip my back to demonstrate that God has no desire to whip yours. I have not come to condemn you, but to save you (John 3:17). I have not come to enslave you, but to set you free (Galatians 5:1). Stop persisting in unbelief. Repent and believe the good news (Mark 1:15)."[11]

Autonomy

The events of the garden expose another important issue: our pursuit of autonomy. Without throwing a single spear or laying siege against the gates of heaven – with just one bite – Eve and Adam declared war against God. Why? They wanted independence.

Again, let's consider the fall. The serpent tempted Eve in part by explaining that if she ate the fruit she would become "like God." On the one hand, this sounds like a laudable desire. After all, in our daily lives as Christians, are we not working out our sanctification in order that we become more and more like Christ? Yet, on the other hand, Eve's desire was not about acquiring obedience

---

[9] John 6:26-27; John 6:48-51.

[10] John 7:37-39.

[11] Christopher West, *Theology of the Body for Beginners: A Basic Introduction to Pope John Paul II's Sexual Revolution* (West Chester, PA: Ascension Press, 2004), 43.

and humility – the hallmarks of Jesus Christ – but about her desire for personal power and control. By acting out on their desire to be "like God," by attempting to acquire forbidden knowledge and the requisite power that came with it, both she and Adam attempted to ascend to the throne of self-rule. It was an act of rebellion.

This was a war about governance – who would make the rules and who would be subject to them? Clearly, God – the eternal Supreme Being, the Creator of all things on heaven and earth – was and is the rule maker, the law giver. Further, as created beings who owed their very existence to God, Eve and Adam were subject to His laws, of which there was only one. Obedience to that rule was the one way in which God sought their loyalty and tested their love. Without this rule (i.e. not eating the fruit), God's relationship with Eve and Adam would have been as intimate as a relationship with a wind-up toy or a rag doll. Love is not real unless it is tested – unless the object of love can freely choose to love in return. Tragically for us all, Eve and Adam failed the test. Their disobedience, their attempt to usurp God's authority, their failure to love in return, won them the punishment issued to many an insurrectionist since: banishment.

So, here we are many millennia later, the exiled seed of insurrectionists each still attempting her or his own coup against God. Through our declarations of self-determination Satan enlists us as foot soldiers in his battle against the King of Heaven. We rail against God. We demand our freedom. We insist on making our own rules. We each in our hearts are a mini-Caesar or Genghis Khan claiming control of *our* destiny, *our* lives, *our* careers, *our* bodies, *our* sexuality.

As with the forbidden fruit, we suspect that the rules for sex are further proof that that God is holding out on us, that He is a miserly King. Yet, as the creator of sex, God was granting human beings the opportunity to comingle, to join – heart to heart, mind to mind, body to body – with another human being in an intimacy of relationship that mirrors that of his own triune self. Through the uniting of female and male in marriage and sexual intimacy, there is a joining of that which remains distinct but yet becomes a whole, just as in "the relationship between the three members of the Holy Trinity – Father, Son and Holy Spirit – [there] is simultaneous distinctiveness and complete unity."[12] Through the uniting of human "tabernacles" in a holy union, there is a way by which two human beings may join and enter the other's holiest space – the space where they alone and no other is present – and be "one flesh."[13] Thus, God created sex, in part, as a means by which two people could bond and commune with one another in a way that reflects His own nature.[14]

---

[12] Judith K. Balswick and Jack O. Balswick, *Authentic Human Sexuality: An Integrated Christian Approach* (Downers Grove, IL: InterVarsity Press, 2008), 75.

[13] Genesis 2:24.

[14] This illustrates the hollowness of masturbation which has rightly been called "self-abuse," since sex was created to bond one's self with another and one cannot bond with his/herself.

Sex also affords women and men the astounding opportunity to participate with God in new acts of creation – the bringing forth of another eternal being into the universe. Children are quite literally a physical embodiment of the "one flesh" union: a perpetuation of a union that fuses two but creates a unique one. Children are thus an enduring emblem of their parents' physical and spiritual union.[15]

Further, the rules for sex are there for our own protection. God warned Eve and Adam that if they ate of the tree of knowledge that they would die. Indeed, they did. Similarly, if we break God's rules for sex, there comes a harvest of heartbreak, suffering, hardship, and in some cases, premature death. God established sexual boundaries because He knows all too well our capacity to reduce all things to their utilitarian value. If there are no parameters on sex our selfish sexual desires ascend the throne of our hearts and we simply use others for their sexual value (e.g. their sexual assets) instead of loving them for who they are as persons and expressing that love in committed, giving, sacrificial sex. And, as in the garden many ages ago with its "one rule," the rules for sex are, in part, a test – a test to prove our obedience to and love for the God who made us and who has every right to make those rules.

Christians should care about the who, what, when, and why of sex because submission to God's ordinances for sexual behavior serves as a marker of our submission to and love for our Creator; protects us from spiritual, emotional and physical harm by others; inhibits us from abusing others; and when practiced within the sacred bonds of marriage, permits us to experience a oneness of being, a bonding of spirit with another human being capable of excelling all other human relationships and emulating that of the Trinity. Moreover, it may also produce children – an eternal physical and spiritual emblem of a one-flesh union.

The End of Exile

As this discussion has demonstrated, human sexuality matters deeply to God. After all, sex was his gift to us. Thankfully, God is not in heaven playing Grinch, wiling away his hours attempting to steal our sexual pleasure from us. That's Satan's job. It is Satan who has lured us with false promises of sexual pleasure and fulfillment if we pursue sex on his terms. It is Satan who masquerades as sexual liberator while he's busy taking captives. It is Satan, the original "con man," who convinces us to exchange the God-given sacred glory of our bodies for desecrated rubble and ruin. Satan sows lies and reaps the resulting harvest of disorder and confusion. Satan is the author of sexual anarchy and rebellion.

Praise God in Heaven that Satan's days are numbered! Praise God in heaven that we are not vanquished – that for all of us who call on Christ there is liberty, new life, and hope of the world to come!

---

[15] Sexual relationships between same sexes or with objects are not blessed with this potential for iconic preservation of their union, illustrating that they are outside God's created order.

In closing, I urge you to read John 20:10-16. This passage records the glorious scene where Mary Magdalene encounters the risen Christ. Friends, I think it is no coincidence that the risen Lord appeared to Mary Magdalene in a garden. Right then and there the story of redemption comes full circle. Mary Magdalene – like a metaphor for all daughters and sons of Eve – finds her Master and Redeemer in, of all places, a garden. It is a sign that through the power of Christ's resurrection the exile from Eden is finally over. The long search for fulfillment has ended; we can again walk in and be filled by the presence of the Lord.

Discussion Questions

1. In what ways are you a victim of Satan's war on human sexuality? In what ways have you joined him in sexual insurrection?

2. Reflect on Russell Moore's statement: "From the tree in the garden to the wilderness beyond the Jordan to the present hour, the people of God are tempted to turn their digestive or reproductive tracts away from the mystery of Christ and toward the self as god."[16] In what ways have you been tempted to turn your love of food, sex or pursuit of other desires into your god? In what ways are these temptations rooted in your personal mistrust of God?

3. In a discussion on freedom Frederick Buechner wrote, "To obey our strongest appetites for drink, sex, power, revenge, or whatever leaves us the freedom of an animal to take what we want when we want it, but not the freedom of a human being to be human."[17] In what ways do you see evidence of "the animal" in human society, in yourself? How might you find the power to live freely and fully human (see: Romans 8:5-8; Romans 12:1-2; 1 Corinthians 10:12-13; Galatians 5:16-26; Philippians 4:4-8; Colossians 3:1:17; Hebrews 10:19-25; and 1Peter 5:8-9).

4. Read John 3:16; John 13:34-35; John 15:9-15; 1 Corinthians 13:1-13, and 1 John 2:15-17. In light of these Scriptures, how is love different from lust? In your relationships with others and within the attitudes of your heart, do you display more love or lust?

5. Read Genesis 3:8-24 and reflect on Adam and Eve's banishment from the Garden of Eden. In what ways has your life reflected a similar exile from God's presence? Read John 20:10-18 and reflect on Jesus' appearance to Mary Magdalene. In your mind's eye imagine yourself in the garden on the day of Christ's resurrection.

---

[16] Moore, "Love, Sex and Mammon."

[17] Frederick Buechner, *Wishful Thinking: A Seeker's ABC* (New York: HarperCollins, 1993), 34.

What would you say to the Lord; what do you think He would say to you?

CHAPTER 7: WHERE IS GOD WHEN SEX GETS MESSY?

Theological Reflection, by Andrew J. Schmutzer

Sex is personal, but never private.[1] It is glorious in its intimacy, but costly in its brokenness.[2] Just who bears responsibility for this brokenness or who shares in the consequences? When sex is exploitative and betraying, has God fled the crime scene too? Is it simply best for Christians to appeal to mystery and then claim Romans 8:28: "We know that in all things God works for the good of those who love him?" As a theologian, I want to touch on some of these issues. But as a survivor of sexual abuse, I can't help but affirm that faith is typically a deep struggle for victims, if it survives at all. Sexual trauma in one's faith-journey complicates it, and many "abandon" God, as indeed, he seems to have abandoned them.

Eden Is Gone, But Not Its Design

As creation's artisan, God "forms"; as sustainer, he "breathes"; as provider, he "plants"; as cosmic king, he "blesses" man and woman as his earthly under-kings with reproduction and governance so that together they may "work and take care" of creation.[3] In short, only this kind of considerate king could observe that "it is not good for the man to be alone" (Genesis 2:18a).

Sexuality comes "on line" in the context of Eden's garden-sanctuary. God saw all that he made as "very good" (Genesis 1:31). But more than that; notice how God "allows himself to be affected, to be touched by each of his creatures. *He adopts the community of creation as his own milieu*" – 'I will make a helper suitable for him' (Genesis 2:18b; cf. Mark 10:5–9)."[4]

Human sexuality was made to operate within a vibrant relational ecosystem; one that was inter-dependent (Genesis 2:5, 19b; Genesis 5:2–3). This relational ecosystem formed bonds between God and humankind, male and female, humans and the ground, and humans and animals – bindings that will be shattered (cf. Genesis 3:14–19). The God of creation never fled his creatures, but tell that to the desperate prostitutes in Bogota who see no way out, or to the

---

[1] Andrew J. Schmutzer, "A Theology of Sexuality and Its Abuse: Creation, Evil, and the Relational Ecosystem," in *The Long Journey Home: Understanding and Ministering to the Sexually Abused*, ed. Andrew J. Schmutzer (Eugene, OR: Wipf and Stock, 2011), 105.

[2] "Sexuality," in Walter Brueggemann, *Reverberations of Faith: A Theological Handbook of Theological Themes* (Louisville, KY: Westminster John Knox, 2002), 195.

[3] See Psalms 8:3, Genesis 2:7, Genesis 2:8, Genesis 1:28, Genesis 2:15.

[4] Jürgen Moltmann, *God in Creation: An Ecological Doctrine of Creation* (London: SCM Press, 1985), 279 (emphasis added).

pimped children in Goa, sniffing glue to deaden their pain. Sex has become messy – the relational ecosystem, all the way around, has collapsed!

God is no Puppet-Master

Scripture teaches that "sex is a divinely willed characteristic of creation ... As a result, the Bible builds specific boundaries around the practice of sex."[5] Not so clear, however, is where God went when humans spoiled the relational ecosystem (Genesis 3:1–13). Does God care that sexuality is so broken? Where is God amid the utter brokenness of sex, as the world and its most vulnerable now know it? A puppeteer never releases the puppet; he merely cloaks his control. Not so with God. God's image bearers (Genesis 1:26) mistrusted their caring King (Genesis 3:5–6), and he's been actively involved in our healing ever since.

Jesus as Our Scarred-King

Humans crave autonomy and idolize self-determination, but then look condemningly around for God when things go awry. Just where is God then when sex becomes messy? Is he an aloof puppet-master or a doting daddy? Neither. The truth is, when it comes to sex, God did not coronate under-kings in his own image (Genesis 1:26–27; Psalms 8:5), grant them an embodied life that included sexuality – and then sabotage the Creation Mandate they were called to live out (Genesis 1:28). The messiness we find is the messiness we made. God is a God of order, but he is also a grieving-God.

The "pain" known to both woman (Genesis 3:16) and man (Genesis 3:17, "painful toil") surfaces again in the pain of God's "grieving" heart (Genesis 6:6) – in another context of exploitation! Where is God? – grieving with humankind's violent actions and deteriorating morals (Genesis 6:5), even as he works out the restoration for his broken creation: "We know that the whole creation has been groaning as in the pains of childbirth right up to the present time" (Romans 8:22). God did not create a world that exempted him.

Voluntary Suffering of the Lamb

The suffering God is also powerfully illustrated in Revelation, where we see the wounded Lamb standing "as slain" (Revelation 5:6). The eternal scarring of the Savior is extremely meaningful to the sexually violated. The theology of Christ's victory through sacrifice "emphasized the lasting benefits of his sacrificial death and resurrection."[6] As Kelly M. Kapic puts it:

The scandal of incarnation is the scandal of creation and the Creator. The God of Creation is the God of Recreation. The Triune God's commitment to his

---

[5] John N. Oswalt, *The Bible Among the Myths: Unique Revelation or Just Ancient Literature* (Grand Rapids, MI: Zondervan, 2009), 72.
[6] Robert H. Mounce, *The Book of Revelation* (Grand Rapids, MI: Eerdmans, 1977), 144, 146.

world is nowhere more clearly seen than in the incarnation ... The scandal of sin in the material and flesh of a created world could only be met and conquered by the scandal of the sinless Creator taking on this material and flesh in order to save the world.[7]

Ask again, "Where is God?" but ask in reverence for a Creator who began grieving long before he entered into broken creation itself, in order to redeem his creation. The answer is one of restoration: Immanuel – "God with us...reconciling to himself all things, whether on earth or in heaven, making peace by the blood of the cross" (Matthew 1:23; Colossians 1:20). The *imago dei* modeled the *mission dei*.

Responsibility and Sin's Continuum

To understand how why Jesus still referred to Eden's design for sexuality (Mark 10:5–9) is to understand how sexual violence *pulls apart*: person from integrated self, victim from family, believer from community, etc. This fracture of the relational ecosystem is also evident in modernity's pervasive "turn to the subject," insisting on dangerous notions like "my sex life" – an ethical oxymoron.

This fracture of sexual integration – even when harm was "unintentional" – illustrates the consequences experienced within sexual brokenness, whether harm was intended or not. Victims of rape, incest and molestation intuit this harm and may live with its effects for the rest of their lives.

The way the "messiness" of sexuality colonizes itself within the web of relationships is well illustrated in the recent sexual scandal surrounding the former Penn State football coach, Jerry Sandusky. A well-liked coach, who even developed a sports program for under-privileged children, in turn, used his community image and social standing to abuse boys. Though imperfect information may have been passed up several rungs in the chain of command, it was *motivated blindness* that kept people in the know from intervening. This is the dark side of loyalty, so well known among abused people.

How the Continuum Functions

Sexual violation is internal terrorism that sets in motion a complex sin-portfolio. This continuum functions as: cause à effect à further cause (cf. Tamar in 2 Samuel 13). Biblically speaking, sin naturally matures (Genesis 15:16; Romans 1:18–32). The Creator does not change the moral and physical principles that structure his creation; he preserves their outworking.

Thus the dynamic of intergenerational transmission reflects: (1) children impacted by their parents' sins, (2) creating conditions that negatively affect the options available to the children, (3) predisposing the children toward

---

[7] Kelly M. Kapic, "Christian Existence and the Incarnation: Humiliation of the Name," Evangelical Theological Society, Plenary Address (San Francisco, 2011), 9, fn.11.

certain choices (4) that contribute destructively to their present identities.[8] So, much of what makes sex messy is the toxic relational environment that envelops victims; an environment they now have to pull themselves out of. Sadly, toxic sexuality tends to live on through cultural practices and family beliefs. A staggering amount of perpetrators were victims themselves. A vast amount of incarcerated men were also sexually abused – by definition, one domino never falls in isolation.

Messy Responses, Too

Victims' stories are not easy to hear and the broken lives behind those stories don't form simple relationships either. Another messy aspect of sex is how others respond to victims. Healing is a journey, and this makes marriage, child-rearing and family life difficult for all. While a civilian would not dare tell a returning soldier with PTSD (post-traumatic stress disorder) to just "get on" with life, one of the most painful things I have experienced as a survivor of abuse is "random wisdom" from the non-abused.

Because people don't adequately understand sexual abuse, they are threatened by the messiness of abuse stories. As a result, they often say things precisely in order to distance themselves from the pain and mess that can accompany survivors. This is most painful when it comes from family members, trying to "fix" or "discipline" the survivor, who might have been abused in the same family. The faith community can also respond in a messy way.

The culture of "victory-only" spirituality that exists in many faith communities means, among other things, that those communities are a long way from understanding the *involuntary* suffering of many abuse stories. Many survivors have heard the flippant use of Romans 8:28 – translation: "Omelets come from broken eggs, so you are going to be such a tool for God!" This is messy theology that doesn't help anyone!

Concluding Thoughts

Addressing sexual violations is a messy obligation. Here are several reminders.

First: The story belongs to the survivor. Let the survivor define where God is at in his or her journey of healing. This is a tender time for victims, who are often "poached" by various social ideologies wanting their membership. Society, particularly in Western cultures, struggles far more with the apparent absence of God than God does showing up for human pain. God has been calling for the broken children of Adam and Eve ever since they rebelled (Genesis 3).

Second: The ethics of empathetic listening to the wounded will go far to bring healing. Victims may even test the love of their friends, but they still need to be heard. If their own father molested them, don't be surprised that

---

[8] Mark E. Biddle, *Missing the Mark: Sin and Its Consequences in Biblical Theology* (Nashville, TN: Abingdon, 2005), 120.

saying "Our Father" (Matthew 6:9–13) is distasteful, along with notions of God's "guardian angels." It is also in this context that any accompanying addictions must also be understood in their healing journey.

Third: Mature Christian leaders must acknowledge where metaphors for God have been crushed for victims, and help victims find new ones. This is part of discipleship. From the celebration of the Lord's Table to music used in church worship, leaders must be more intentional about connecting the messiness of abused men and women with Jesus' own suffering – they took his clothes, too! (John 19:23). Abuse defiles the victim's proper orientation to God. For the survivor, God himself has become lost among contaminating parties. Worship is destroyed for most victims because third parties are always wedge-shaped.[9]

Case Study, by Andrew J. Schmutzer

A woman in her mid-thirties came to talk with her pastor. She was full of anxiety and shame as she unpacked a story covering the last twenty years of her life. Presently, she is married, and has a four-year-old boy. Her presenting issues include: a non-existent sexual relationship with her husband (they sleep in two different rooms) and the fear that God has recently "left" her.

She was raised in a very strict Christian home. Her father sexually abused her from age ten to thirteen. Her teens and twenties were filled with drugs and alcohol. Some years later, she met a good man who helped her kick years of drug addiction and stay sober. Now, along with church involvement once again, she recently found out that her son was diagnosed with a congenital disorder directly related to her earlier years of drug use.

Since being sober she's been in and out of therapy to address her sexual abuse and now realizes that her drugs and drinking masked enormous pain and anger toward her father for sexually abusing her. Unfortunately, her healing has also surfaced the realization that she is disgusted with the thought of sex. After years of conjugal neglect, her husband is now embittered. Additionally, since her son's diagnosis, she is feeling very guilty for her past drug abuse but also increasingly angry with God for letting her abuse happen.

Key questions remain:
- Does she understand the pain that contributed to her substance abuse?
- Do all parties working with her understand how her father's incest not only destroyed his daughter's psyche but also his own marriage bed and her "bridging-metaphors" for father (i.e., Heavenly Father)?
- Do church leaders understand the objective reality of sin's fallout – she had no intention of harming an innocent person, but there is a messiness and permanent damage that is now spilling over in her "relational ecosystem."

---

[9] Cornelius Plantinga, Jr., *Not the Way It's Supposed to Be: A Breviary of Sin* (Grand Rapids, MI: Eerdmans, 1995), 44-45.

- Choices were made that have made sex messy in her life. What can healing possibly look for her?

Discussion Questions

1. How does the "relational ecosystem" function in various cultures (Western and two-thirds countries) to stifle the voices of victims and avoid needed interventions?
2. Though unpopular for theology and the social sciences to face, what are some complex ways in which victims actually participate in the moral chaos of their sexual victimization?
3. When so many different organizations, often with vastly different worldviews and social agendas, are trying to address trafficking, domestic violence and sexual abuse, what would it look like to learn to disagree at higher levels?
4. What are some key elements in a good model of cross-cultural intervention, especially when the social context is foreign, the history has not been experienced first hand, and faith commitments are expressed differently?
5. When it comes to understanding God and sexual trauma, there is a growing need for collaboration in "meaning-making" from an interdisciplinary and interdenominational perspective. What will make needed work and dialogue more of a reality?
6. What are the pros and cons of written, inter-faith and international policies that address such global crimes like trafficking, domestic violence and sexual abuse? Explain.
7. Because not all evil is equally devastating, what might a "taxonomy of evil" look like? Why might this be helpful for issues of ethics, intervention, funding and programs of healing?

CHAPTER 8
HOW CAN WE SURVIVE IN THE MIDST OF THE MESS?

Theological Reflection, by Bill Prevette

For those working with victims of trafficking, both ministry and life at the margins are often unpredictable. Organizations have to accept limits but there is no escape from living with mystery, uncertainty, and precariousness where we are cast upon God and looking for the coming of the Kingdom – as opposed to being sure that we "have it" or are "in" it. In this context, holistic ministry takes on a deeper meaning. Holism lives close to reality, works in the freedom of the Spirit, and holds to responsible relationships between persons where word, faith and life are closely, intimately and messily intertwined. In this chapter, I explore the question: How do those serving on the front-line of suffering with victims of trafficking make "theological" sense of the unpredictability and uncertainties of ministry?

Recently, I was asked to present a paper at a conference in the Republic of Moldova for organizational leaders ministering to people caught in trafficking. The organizers sent me a theme that reflects much personal experience in ministry:

> We hear repeatedly from the practitioners that the messiness and chaos of what we've "signed up for" can do us in, unless we have a clear understanding of who we are in the midst of it all, know how to balance out our lives – and ultimately leave the outcomes up to God.

As activists, practitioners, caregivers, and human beings responding to those impacted by the scourge of human trafficking, we find ourselves often in the depths of our personal emotional, spiritual and professional reserves. To begin, I pose two questions:

- How is our particular work or intervention shaped theologically?
- What is it about our specific practice that points us to God in Christ?

Clarifying the Term "Theology"

This chapter offers both a theological and practical reflection concerning "holistic mission in light of the Kingdom of God." Two disclaimers are needed.

Firstly, theology is *not* the domain of academics locked away in libraries or research centers. Theology is to *think, act*, and *speak* for God; it is ever in the making. Theology requires imagination, experiment, decision and action. In that sense, everyone who speaks of and acts for God is doing theology at some level. Practitioners are effective "operative theologians." They live and work close to human pain and suffering and bring God's grace to bear on chaotic situations. When we speak of the "Kingdom of God," we understand this as the term repeatedly used by Jesus to describe his "way of doing things."

Secondly, the term "holistic" has become something of a "buzz word" in contemporary mission practice. The term "holistic" is often assumed to mean the integration of physical, mental, emotional, psycho-social, and spiritual well-being. Holistic outcomes are described as redeeming whole persons and communities. "Holistic" can become a propagandist term if not tried and tested theologically.

We will examine the intersection of the Kingdom of God, holistic mission, and the realities of serving those at risk from trafficking. It is my contention that "holistic mission" must be grounded in a local context and make room for human suffering as well as human flourishing.[1]

Have We "Arrived" in the Kingdom of God?

Due to limits of space, I cite a familiar text for an initial reflection. In Matthew, we follow Jesus making his way to Jerusalem after Peter's confession at Philippi:

> At that time the disciples came to Jesus and asked, "Who is the greatest in the kingdom of heaven?" He called a little child and had him stand among them. And he said: "*I tell you the truth, unless you change and become like little children, you will never enter the kingdom of heaven.* Therefore, whoever humbles himself like this child is the greatest in the kingdom of heaven."[2]

Do we recognize the theological argument in this passage? The disciples ask "*who will be the greatest*" in the coming Kingdom of God? They assume they are already "*in*" the Kingdom where they seek power, status and rank. Can we see ourselves in this narrative? Have we wondered what place we have in the Kingdom? Jesus turns their argument upside down and calls for a radical change (*metanoia*) in how they perceive His Kingdom. He seems to be saying they have "*yet to enter*" the Kingdom. They are on the way but have not arrived, and are possibly in danger of missing it![3]

We might read this passage and immediately assume that "to be like a child" means to be "simple, carefree, child-like." However, we do not know much about the child that Jesus placed in the midst of the disciples. She could have been a sick child, a happy child, or even an abused child. We know that "normal" children in first century Palestine were not given much attention in rabbinical theological discourse.

---

[1] A selected bibliography on "Holistic Mission" is included at the end of the chapter.

[2] Matthew 18:1-4 (emphasis added).

[3] In this reflection on Matthew 18, I am drawing from insights gleaned from the Child Theology Movement and my on-going work with Dr. Haddon Willmer and Dr. Keith White; see www.childtheology.org for papers and discussions.

Remaining Open to Theological Pointers

Could Jesus' placement of the child in this text serve as a "theological pointer"? The child seems to point to something the disciples *have yet* to understand and grasp about the Kingdom. Like the disciples in this story, we assume we have certain truths and assurances in God. But could it be that those we serve – the lowly, the broken, the abused, those that we see as recipients of our ministry – could they too serve as pointers to something we *have yet* to understand in the Kingdom of God?

Change in this text is connected with the word "humble." To be humble is to be meek, and aware that we are deeply dependent on God. Humility is not generated or given to us but rather by being brought down, and standing before the future, the amazing generous grace of God *comes to us.*

In other translations "unless you change" is translated as "be converted," "turn around," "return to square one," and "begin again." As we begin each day, we do well to remind ourselves that we are at the mercy of the living God: "There is no creature hidden from His sight, but all things are naked and open to the eyes of Him to whom we must give account."[4]

Much of our language, speech, practice and action for God assume that we know the Kingdom of God and are *in line* with it. Activist caregivers claim to represent and present a confident Biblical Christianity. But are our versions confident enough to imagine the massive and rich contemporary Christian world as a circle of disciples who struggle with what the Kingdom of God is and so argue about who will be greatest?[5] Are we confident enough to imagine ourselves as longing to bring the goodness of the Kingdom, while at the same time acknowledging our tendency to miss the target?

Awareness of Injustice and Evangelical Response

I imagine we have all asked the question, "How long oh Lord must these 'afflicted ones' suffer?" Like the Psalmist, we struggle to understand why the wicked seem to prosper (Psalm 73:3-11). Over the last thirty years, there has been a growing emphasis in Evangelical Christian mission on holism, justice and serving the poor. The Christian response to human trafficking has followed a similar pattern.[6]

There is much to celebrate in the promise of the Gospel; it offers us hope, faith and love. God is constantly disturbing and surprising us. People of faith can offer "treasure in earthly vessels" to those they serve.[7] Yet, ministry with

---

[4] Hebrews 4:13.

[5] Haddon Willmer, e-mail message to author, March, 2010 (referring to the scope and scale of global movements that portend to "reach all the people of the world" with the Gospel).

[6] There are scores of faith-based agencies working to combat human trafficking. A good list of resources and agencies is found at: http://www.salvationarmyusa.org/ (follow the link to human trafficking).

[7] 2 Corinthians 4:7.

the abused and exploited and those who are the victims of trafficking can also lead to anxiety, disappointment and even resentment in caregivers. What follows are several proposals for those working with mystery, uncertainty, precariousness; who are willing to embrace pain, promise and puzzlement in their ministry.

Faulty Vision in Our Vocational Fulfillment

Shortly after ten aid workers were killed in Afghanistan on August 6, 2010, Ajith Fernando wrote "To Serve Is to Suffer." His words help us in confronting pain and puzzlement:

> Vocational fulfillment in the kingdom of God has a distinct character, different from vocational fulfillment in society. Jesus said, "My food is to do the will of him who sent me and to accomplish his work" (John 4:34). If we are doing God's will, we assume we will be happy and fulfilled. But for Jesus, and for us, doing God's will includes the cross. The cross must be an essential element in our definition of vocational fulfillment. Paul's theology emphasized the need to endure frustration patiently as we live in a fallen world awaiting redemption. Paul said that we groan in this frustration (Romans 8:18-27).[8]

When we have a faulty understanding of fulfillment in our vocation we can become deeply frustrated. This is seen in projects and with caregivers who experience "unrealized horizons of expectation." In these situations frenetic activity can act as a "cover" for unresolved anxiety. The current emphasis on efficiency and measurable results makes frustration even harder to endure. Biblical fulfillment includes both joy and pain; the cross is both vertical and horizontal.

Thanks be to God, many Christian organizations can demonstrate *in a measure* what God has "already accomplished in Christ" in redeeming the humanity and spiritual lives of those rescued from trafficking. This should not be trivialized. But our engagement with women, youth or children reveals an important theological reality that "The already in the Kingdom and in Jesus is not simply the holistic transformation of the world or humanity ... the already in Christ includes [much] pain and suffering."[9]

Human existence, and especially traumatic human situations, are "neither perfectly consistent (as rational control-needy people usually demand them to be), nor incoherent chaos (what cynics, agnostics, and unaware people expect them to be); instead, *human life has a cruciform pattern*. It is a 'coincidence of opposites' a collision of cross-purposes. We are all filled with contradictions needing to be reconciled."[10]

---

[8] Ajith Fernando, "To Serve Is to Suffer," *The Global Conversation* (blog), *Christianity Today*, August 2010. www.christianitytoday.com/globalconversation /august2010/
[9] Haddon Willmer, review of *Mission as Transformation: A Theology of the Whole Gospel*, by Vinay Samuel and Chris Sugden, eds., *Transformation* 18, no. 3 (July 2001): 194-96.
[10] Richard Rohr, *Everything Belongs: The Gift of Contemplative Prayer* (New York: Crossroad Publishing Company, 2003), 178.

An Invitation into "Sacred Space"[11]

As we work, we learn to pray that our illusions will fall away. Indeed, God does erode them, but in serving others or leading our organizations we can become trapped in normalcy, that is, "just the way things are in our lives. Our work revolves around solving problems, explaining things and taking sides."[12]

Working with abused or traumatized people requires that we allow ourselves to be drawn into a *sacred space*. This is sometimes called *"liminality."*[13] Holistic spiritual, social and human transformation occurs when we move beyond the status quo into areas where we lack managerial competency. Here we find ourselves with arms outstretched, our palms turned to heaven, openly embracing difficult questions.

If we are not prepared to accept temporary chaos, and to hold to the necessary anxiety that chaos entails, then difficulty arises in moving to deeper levels of faith, and of prayer, and in our relationship with God. It is important to accept this reality both for oneself and to create and nurture ministries and organizations that make sacred space possible, where degrees of uncertainty are accepted while holding to faith and hope.

When we are led out of normalcy and the status quo into sacred space it may often feel like suffering. These are times for letting go of what we were "used to" and moving into a new life in the Spirit. The regularity of our lives needs at times to be interrupted, and the systems we are clinging to for control need to be deconstructed. But we are resistant as it is easier to stay in our "comfort zone." Very few people want to have their lives or work deconstructed.[14]

Do We Expect Certitude or Fidelity?

We face a dilemma in ministry because we have a hunger for certitude! But the gospel is not so much about certitude as it is about fidelity, that is, the faithfulness of God towards us. In our effort to control, we try to translate fidelity into certitude because fidelity is an open, relational category and certitude is a flat, mechanical category. "We must acknowledge our thirst for certitude and recognize that if we had all certitudes in the world, it would not make the quality of our life any better. Fidelity is like having a teenager in the house, we never get it settled for more than 3 minutes, and we have to keep negotiating."[15]

---

[11] I have drawn from Rohr, *Everything Belongs*, Chapter 6 "Return to the Sacred" and Rohr's lectures in this section.

[12] Rohr, *Everything Belongs*, 154.

[13] Liminality (from the Latin word *līmen*, meaning "a threshold") is a psychological, neurological, or metaphysical subjective state, conscious or unconscious, of being on the "threshold" of or between two different existential planes, as defined in neurological psychology (a "liminal state") and in the anthropological theories of ritual by such writers as Arnold Van Gennen and Victor Turner.

[14] Rohr, *Everything Belongs*, 156-8.

[15] Walter Brueggemann, "Nineteen Theses: Overcoming the Dominant Script of Our Age" (paper presented at the Emergent Church and Theology, Minneapolis, MN, 2005).

We do not usually ask God to pull down or shake our support "systems" which can be religious, organizational or personal, but interventions in human trafficking require fidelity and tax our reserves. Those working with dysfunction, addiction or trauma are by fiat deeply engaged with dissonance, paradox and contradiction, which are relational categories not mechanistic ones.

Holistic Mission and the Disturbance of God

Christ-centered care for the poor and marginalized should represent a meaningful integration between what is "*from above*" (God's eternal purposes) with that which is "*below*" (human concerns for life in this present world). Much of the evangelical literature and language about holistic change tends to leave "spirituality" or salvation in Christ, which engages with eternal life with God, on one side.[16] On the other side is the validity of caring for the human community, addressing hunger, abuse, trauma, and the need for family, or what some describe as "Samaritan theology," in helping people make it through another day on earth. I refer to this as a "two-sided" approach to holistic mission. Can we work towards a more meaningful integration of eternal and human concerns?

God does not remain "bracketed" on His side of the equation in holistic mission. God, in His freedom, goes beyond our predictions and our reasonable expectations. The cross "articulates God's odd freedom, His strange justice, and His peculiar power."[17] God surprises and disturbs; this is one of Barth's points in his exposition of Romans 12:1-2:

> Once again we are confronted with this sidedness of the whole course of our human existence.... our life and will and acts are brought into question. For the freedom of God, the "Other sidedness" of His mercies, means that there is a relationship between God and man, that there is a dissolution of human "this sidedness" and that a radical assault is being made upon every contrasted, second, other thing.[18]

At this point, exploited women and youth provide another theological clue. Those engaged in ministry, advocacy, and intervention must do the best they can, taking reasonable action, thinking creatively, and at times taking risks in caring for the whole person. Moreover, they must remain open to what we cannot plan or predict of God in advance.

Brueggemann argues that the categories of the enlightenment tempted theologians and Christians to "out-science" science and they built systems concerned with establishing "proof" and "evidence that demand a verdict" and left little room for "uncertainty."

[16] Language for eternity with God is various; the point is that for salvation to mean anything worthwhile it must take into account the demands of God on the human situation. If left to assumptions and no critical evaluation, then the message of God in Christ is bracketed, not informing the totality of faith-based action and intervention.

[17] Walter Brueggemann, *The Prophetic Imagination*, 2nd ed. (Minneapolis, MN: Fortress Press, 2001), 99.

[18] Karl Barth, *The Epistle to the Romans,* trans. E. C. Hoskyns, 6th ed. (Oxford: Oxford University Press, 1968), 427.

People who have been traumatized are experts at upsetting established theories, organized programs and their methodical caregivers; they constantly surprise, challenge and disturb, and in so doing they speak (or shout) the language of God. Holistic mission and care entails openness to the prodding and judgment of God, and sensitivity to the experiences and pain of those who have been abused and are living in a fallen world. God is not limited by "holistic" agendas; most people who have been severely traumatized will always carry the scars of their experience.[19] In my view, any account of holism must take into account God's freedom and disturbance, God's "gift of pain."[20]

In conclusion, we ask how the term "holism" accounts for the death, burial and resurrection of God in Christ. In the crucifixion of Jesus we experience "the ultimate act of criticism in which Jesus announces the end of the world of death ... and takes the death into his own person. The criticism consists not in standing *over against* but in *standing with*; the ultimate criticism is not one of triumphant indignation but one of passion and compassion that completely and irresistibly undermines the world of competence and competition."[21]

Case Study, by Bill Prevette

Embracing Uncertainty and Unpredictable Realities in the Kingdom of God

Ellie's experience is a distressing case of trafficking, one of the few that falls in the stereotypical Hollywood portrayal of trafficking. She had already been out of her home country several times, working in restaurants. Her first jobs were decent work, and her skills in cooking paid off. She was a strong believer, she grew up in a pastor's home.

When a friend told her he had another job, she thought it would be like the past. Instead, she was drugged and forced to prostitute herself. When she cried

---

[19] Here I take some issue with those who predict that children can be "completely restored to wholeness." All children (and human beings) carry signs of both wholeness and brokenness; sin is a present reality, and any "holistic" agenda that does not reckon with sin falls short in describing the life in the Kingdom. The balance, in my thinking, is found in the walk of faith that places trust in God's sustaining love and His unlimited freedom.

[20] Philip Yancy and Paul Brand, *Pain: The Gift Nobody Wants* (New York: Harper Collins, 1999). In interviews with NGO personnel, narratives of sacrifice, pain and disappointment are often mentioned together with the power of faith to sustain them in especially difficult circumstances or in accounts of working with especially difficult children. I suggest that these accounts of disappointment and frustration should be included as "holistic outcomes." For a piercing study concerning the Christian faith and the problem of evil and pain see Ulrich Simon's *A Theology of Auschwitz* (Atlanta: John Knox Press, 1979).

[21] Brueggemann, *The Prophetic Imagination,* 94-5.

out, "No, I'm a virgin!" the traffickers laughed and said, "Good, we'll get more money."

After two months of this hell, she managed to escape. Her emotions, her psyche and her faith were in shatters. How could God allow this? Why did she, a Christian, have her life destroyed? She had always wanted to grow up, find a nice husband, get married, have children and serve God. And to add to her nightmare, many in her church and home village judged her, thinking she was a "bad girl," spreading untrue rumors about her.

Ellie found a community of grace and love at Christian home in the capital city. Physical and emotional healing was able to start, albeit slowly. She found a place where she was safe to share her anger, her doubts and her pain. Restoration comes with unconditional love, not pity; with acceptance, not rejection. And after months, she is beginning to see a future. She is learning that perhaps God can redeem what happened to her. She is beginning to think she could go back to school and learn how to help other broken girls with similar questions and experiences.

Discussion Questions

1. How does Ellie's story act as a theological "pointer" for those who have become overly confident in their approach to God, his Kingdom and promises?

2. What would you want Ellie to know about your expectations of God? How would you help her find balance in puzzlement, promise and pain?

3. What would "sacred space" look like to Ellie and how would you go about trying to create that for her and others?

4. What would be your response to someone who told Ellie that she must "recommit her life to Christ and go back to church" if she wanted to go forward?

5. Ellie is a living example of God's "gift of pain." How does her story help you to integrate what is from above (eternal and transcendent) with what is from below (of this earth)?

CHAPTER 9: HOW CAN WE GET FROM HOSTILITY TO HOSPITALITY WHEN DEALING WITH TRANSGENDER AND OTHER SEXUAL MINORITIES?

Theological Reflection, by Heike Lippmann

The "More Than Gender" report by Love146[1] on the sexual exploitation of transgender people in Phnom Penh, Cambodia showed that transgender people seek and express their identity within a context that excludes and discriminates them. The issues related to identity formation are complex. When we ask the question "Who am I?" we mostly answer it in relation to people, place, purpose and possessions. These relations are somewhat corrupted even to the point of exploitation being accepted as a part of an assumed social identity, as we have seen in the report.

Unfortunately the concept of sin has often been misused and misinterpreted. It has been reduced to certain "sinful" deeds and used like a label that excludes people from community. However, it is helpful to look at it as a condition that affects all human beings and the reality we live in. A better understanding of sin can contribute to a more welcoming attitude towards those who are excluded from society and, sadly, from church life.

The Human Dilemma

Human beings were created in God's image with the purpose of being in relationship with God and with each other.[2] But being God's human counterpart didn't seem to be enough for them. They wanted to be more and that resulted in being less of what they were supposed to be. Sin corrupted their relationship with God and with each other. Wolfhart Pannenberg, a German theologian, describes the consequences: "In their remoteness from God they are also robbed of their own identity."[3]

Scripture describes the first attack on the first humans in Genesis 3. The Catholic Theologian Gisbert Greshake wrote about the nature of this attack and the following thoughts are based on his interpretation.[4] The aim of the attack was to destroy Adam and Eve's trust in God's goodness. After their creation

---

[1] Jarrett Davis and Glenn Miles, "More Than Gender: A Baseline Study of Transgendered Males in the Sex Industry in Phnom Penh, Cambodia" (Phnom Penh: Love 146, October 2013).

[2] Genesis 1:27.

[3] Wolfhart Pannenberg, *Systematische Theologie Band 2 – Eine trinitarische Theologie* (Goettingen: Vandenhoeck & Ruprecht, 1991), 207.

[4] Gisbert Greshake, *Der dreieine Gott* (Freiburg: Herder, 2007), 326-28.

they were placed in a garden that was supposed to be their home where they could find life to the full as a gift from God. They were told that they shouldn't eat from one particular tree. With this request God was saying, "You can put your mind at rest. Trust me." But this is exactly where mistrust began: "Maybe God isn't good. Maybe we won't find life to the full and real happiness when we are faithful to him. Maybe he denies us what is best for us. Maybe he only wants to keep us down." Fear entered their lives – fear that they would miss out if they received their lives solely out of their relationship with God. God became a rival who restricted them and whom they had to stand up against.

Scripture says that the sinner desires to be like God, which means he wants to be like the "rival God" that was introduced by the tempter. This reveals a corrupt understanding of who God is. Adam and Eve didn't see themselves placed before a Trinitarian God who gives himself to his creatures in love. They saw a God who is selfish. Against him or without him they had to acquire as much life as possible. The consequence is that men took the place that belonged to the relational God and what was promised them as gain led into the exact opposite.

God – as Trinity – is community, and being created in his image means to be made for relationship with him and with each other. By its nature sin turns this into its opposite: self-isolation and self-centeredness. It is the refusal to find life in community with God and with each other. God-given freedom is turned into autonomy that aims to find happiness, satisfaction and identity without "the other." Ironically, striving for autonomy is an attempt on one's own life because we can only be fully human in community with God and with one another. The kind of life that is acquired otherwise turns out to be "not enough" because something finite (career, relationship, possessions, etc.) cannot fulfill the deepest longing for love, life and happiness. Therefore, sin is ultimately a lie. Instead of life, the sinner puts himself into the sphere of death. Death in Scripture is more than just physical death. Death is the realm of futility, hopelessness, emptiness and nothingness, with physical death as the obvious sign that in the end striving for life without "the other" was for nothing.

Relationships Gone Bad

Sin leads to isolation and the destruction and/or loss of relationship. This means that sin is not only a private matter but it also affects the way people live together in society. Slander, betrayal, disloyalty, rivalry, corruption and exploitation are a few obvious symptoms of this. The intensification of negative behaviors and attitudes lead to societies where true community is unattainable. Mistrust and the fear that "there won't be enough for me" and that "I miss out if I don't fight for myself and only myself" aren't ingredients for a society where people can thrive.

As previously mentioned, transgender people's social identity was at least partly formed by the shaping forces of exclusion and discrimination. Their difference from others was heightened by the reaction of family and society reinforcing the sense of difference and separateness from society as a whole. This is a reflection of the "communal" structures of sin at work. It seems that transgender and the rest of society effectively chime the same note: that difference must lead to exclusion. In other words, society says, "You are different which means you are separate from us." By living out their difference transgenders say, "We are different which means we are separate from you." This seems to be the nature of how their social identity is shaped. It is almost like a double-declaration of exclusion. This doesn't mean that both sides suffer the same. Transgender people are the ones who are exposed to violence and discrimination because it suits society for transgender to be separate, whereas transgender have to live with their identity no matter how it is formed.

A Different Kind of Love

Jesus' ministry as it is portrayed in the New Testament was a ministry of hospitality. He was sent to extend God's unconditioned and unconditional grace and love to all people, no matter what their background or social status was. There is no story about Jesus and transgender people. However, there are many stories, especially in Luke's Gospel, that present Jesus interacting with the "untouchables" of his time who were pushed to the margins of society, and the effect that interaction had on their lives.

The Gospel of Luke even allows us a glimpse into the heart of Jesus' mission: the love and grace of God, the father. To emphasize this Luke provides three parables: the lost sheep,[5] the lost coin[6] and the return of the prodigal son.[7] When Jesus was criticized for welcoming sinners and eating with them[8] he responded with these stories. The focus here will be on the third story since it reflects the divide that is evident within Jesus' audience at the time. Furthermore it reveals that the Father doesn't simply bridge the gap between them but offers a new foundation for their relationship with him and with one another.

In *Exclusion and Embrace*, Miroslav Volf worked on a "theology of embrace"[9] and his reading of the story at the social level provides helpful insights in this regard. He sees both sons as governed by the same kind of logic, which is in sharp contrast to their father's.

The Sons' Logic

When the younger son who had run away from home considers his return to the father, he realizes the damage he had done. He states twice that he is no longer worthy to be called a son.[10] As Volf explains, "he has been shaped by the

---

[5] Luke 15:3-7.
[6] Luke 15:8-10.
[7] Luke 15:11-32.
[8] Luke 15:2.
[9] Miroslav Volf, *Exclusion and Embrace: A Theological Exploration of Identity, Otherness, and Reconciliation* (Nashville: Abington Press, 1996), 156.
[10] Luke 15:18,21.

history of the departure, which cannot be erased."[11] Therefore his request is to be made like a hired man. In his opinion "the history of betrayal will have changed his identity and reconfigured obligations and expectations."[12]

The older son distanced himself when he heard about the return of his brother.[13] After his brother had left he excluded him and did not keep him in his heart. Now, after his return, he was not willing to welcome him back. In his opinion some basic rules had been broken:

> "The one who works (v.29) deserves more recognition than the one who squanders; celebrating the squanderer is squandering. The one who obeys where obedience is due (v.29) deserves more honor than the one who irresponsibly breaks commands; honoring the irresponsible is irresponsible. The one who remains faithful should be treated better than the one who excludes the others; preference for the excluding one is tacit exclusion of the faithful one."[14]

According to this logic it would pervert justice to receive the younger brother back as a son and not just as a hired hand. And here the two brothers reach the same conclusion: The older one demands what the younger one expected.

The Father's Logic

What distinguishes the father's logic from the sons' logic is that it is not built around "either strict adherence to the rules or disorder and disintegration; either you are 'in' or you are 'out,' depending on whether you have or have not broken a rule. He rejected this alternative because his behavior was governed by the one fundamental 'rule': relationship has priority over all rules. Before any rule can apply, he *is* the father to his sons and his sons *are* brothers to one another."[15]

This does not mean that moral performance and the quality of behavior are irrelevant. Although they might affect the relationship, relationship is not rooted in them. Repentance, confession and consequences for one's actions have their place *in* the relationship, but are not prerequisites *for* it. The father's will to embrace both his sons is grounded in his indestructible love and his commitment to his sons and not in rules.

Jesus embodied this unconditioned and unconditional love and grace of God towards all people. His words and actions were guided by the same indestructible love that flows from the heart of the father. He is a father to all people and his love and acceptance create a new foundation for their relationships to one another. In his household everybody is welcome. Just like the father's embrace in the story is not rooted in the moral performance of his sons, Jesus' loving engagement with the ostracized of his time is not rooted in

---

[11] Volf, *Exclusion and Embrace,* 159.
[12] Volf, *Exclusion and Embrace*, 159.
[13] Luke 15:28.
[14] Volf, *Exclusion and Embrace*, 162.
[15] Volf, *Exclusion and Embrace*, 164.

their status in society or their past actions. Jesus' mission is fueled by this indestructible love.

What Does This Leave Us With?

We touched briefly on the destructive nature of sin and contrasted it with God's love that has the power to restore what is broken. As Followers of Jesus we've tasted this love, depend on it and are called to extend it to others.

However, welcoming people who are different into our communities might ultimately mean the loss of the community as we knew it, or at least of some aspects that were dear to its members. Every new member brings something that changes and challenges existing community structures and relationships. We form a new community with them. This means gain and loss at the same time for all involved. Being hospitable comes with a cost.

There is a need for people who are free and humble enough to make space in their hearts for what is other, for people who extend God's hospitality by engaging in other people's lives, for people who are willing to journey with others and in doing so learn to become accepting and welcoming. A loving community that embraces what is "other" might even have the potential to transform society. The presence of such a community within society is a prophetic presence, an expression of God's hospitality towards his creation. Jesus leaves us with no alternative but to love with an unrestrained creative love.

Discussion Questions

1. In what way does this approach to "sin and the grace of God" challenge your understanding of community?
2. What would such a community look like?
3. What kind of action/ministry would reflect the "unrestrained creative love" of God for all people?

PART 3

HOW SHOULD WE RESPOND TO DEMAND?

Introduction,
by Christa Foster Crawford and Glenn Miles

Sometimes we get so busy dealing with the effects and impact of the sex industry that we don't adequately address the cause.

Alternatively we seek to address the cause, but we only deal with one side of the issue. We easily forget that the sex trade is a business that has more than one set of causes. On one side is the supply – the exploited victims – and on the other side is the demand – the clients, who are usually male. We must recognize, understand and deal with demand, not only supply.

Often when demand *is* addressed it focuses mainly on the prosecution of those who sexually exploit young girls. The exploitation of other vulnerable groups such as boys, adult women and men, and transgendered people is only beginning to be more broadly realized, and often laws and legal frameworks – especially in the global South – make it difficult to prosecute people who sexually exploit these victims.

Meanwhile, the HIV agenda over the past few years has done a disservice to this issue because it usually only promotes the use of condoms to reduce the harms of commercial sex, without also challenging why the use of other people in commercial sex is harmful at both the individual and societal level. Consequently few materials have been developed to challenge men to consider the disadvantages of engaging in prostitution in the first place.

There are a few budding efforts to raise awareness about the need to stop demand. In the UK, beer mats/coasters featuring a semi-erotic picture and a telephone number were distributed to pubs/bars.[1] When men called the number, they received an automated message that challenged men about the use of prostitutes! In Cambodia, posters entitled "What Men Should Consider"[2] have been used to challenge men to become consciously aware of the underlying dynamics and process that leads them to engage in commercial sex and to actually think about the negative consequences that result. This is a small beginning, but many more materials need to be developed to help men understand that sex is not a right but a privilege that requires consent. This has further been additionally challenging because the abolition movement has been primarily driven by female feminists, when men prefer to listen to men.

So how should we respond to demand? There are three important aspects to this question.

First, we must understand why it is important to tackle demand. This requires us to explore the many factors that are drivers behind demand. For instance, negative cultural attitudes about men and sex, myths of male entitlement to sex and the idea that "boys will be boys," to name only a few.

---

[1] A few organizations have used this concept to prevent harm against women including OXCAT (www.oxcat.org.uk), Restored (www.restoredrelationships.org) and others.

[2] http://gmmiles.co.uk/wp-content/uploads/2013/05/Man-Eg.pdf

Also to be considered are the ways in which men from a wide range of cultures do not respect and value women and children and see their own needs as superseding those of others.

Second, we must recognize the importance of addressing pornography when tackling demand. This is important in two ways. One is the connection between pornography, commercial sex and sexual exploitation in terms of harm. Two is the way in which pornography fuels demand. Far from being harmless, pornography is known to be addictive and can also have insidious effects on the expectations and sexual demands of users, leading to increased demand. Understanding the dangers is especially crucial when it comes to young people who are being exposed to pornography in a way that has never existed before because of the pervasive ease of access through the Internet, "smart" mobile phones and other technology.

Third, we must consider how we as Christians and the church should reach out to the people who are caught up in the web of demand – both perpetrators like pornographers, pimps and pedophiles – as well as users and buyers of sex, including men within the church who can also be prone to fall short of the glory of God.

Where is the church in all this? Largely it is silent and when it does speak it is often puritanical which is unhelpful to young people who need boundaries but not straight jackets. Meanwhile some men are recognizing their role in behaving differently and being role models to others inside and outside of the church. Some organizations are focusing on legal reform, working with government departments of justice and interior, strengthening the ability of the police to take appropriate action and prosecution of pedophiles. Others are working towards criminalization of the buyers of sex rather than the prostituted people themselves. Some are focusing on using the media to challenge tourists and expatriates who frequent red-lights areas in developing countries. But a small number of organizations are starting to challenge men on the street to think and behave in a different way, to challenge pimps and pornographers, and to challenge the sex industry at different levels.

In seeking to answer the overall question of how to respond to demand, this chapter explores the following issues:

- Why is it important to tackle demand?
    - Why is demand important to tackle and what can the church do about it?
    - Where are the men of the church in addressing demand?
    - How can we stop the demand for child sex tourism and instead create a demand for child safe tourism?
- Why is it important to deal with pornography when tackling demand?
    - Isn't it time we see the links between pornography, prostitution and sex trafficking?
    - How can we encourage men in the church to challenge the use of pornography?
    - Why is addressing access of youth to pornography so important to tackling demand?

- How can Christians and the church reach out to people who are caught up in demand? Are they outside of God's redemption?
    - What is our responsibility towards pornographers? Are they outside of God's redemption?
    - What is our responsibility towards pimps and pedophiles? Are they outside of God's redemption?
    - Is there hope for men who visit red-light districts?
    - How are we doing ourselves? What can we do about the sexual behavior of expatriate Christian men?

The first set of essays address the question: Why is it important to tackle demand?

To begin with, **Donna M. Hughes** explains the dynamics of demand when it comes to sex trafficking, detailing the role of the four players who make up demand: the men who purchase commercial sex, the exploiters who profit from the sale, the destination countries whose laws, policies and practices support demand, and the culture that tolerates and even supports sexual exploitation. Hughes reports that although in the past little attention has been paid to demand, in recent years there has been a growing abolitionist movement that seeks to address demand through enacting laws and policies that hold perpetrators accountable. She also highlights the important role that churches and faith communities can play in helping to reduce demand by advocating for changes in the culture and the law.

Next, **Sven-Gunnar Lindén** takes a look at the buyers of sex. He describes how peer pressure and intimacy issues are often part of the problem. Although there is a promise of excitement in prostitution, men are often left with a feeling of shame and emptiness. Next he explores ways in which the church can tackle demand through addressing visibility, reducing accessibility, helping men find a way out, and finally, through changing attitudes. Specifically, he suggests lobbying governments to do legal reform, whereby rather than legalizing prostitution, efforts are made to recognize the wrong behavior of buyers of sex and to prosecute their actions. He also gives examples of how the church can help to challenge the media and sex industry. Finally he explains how the church can help men to believe that they can change their behavior. It is only when attitudes towards women in prostitution change that behavior will change.

Peter Grant takes this position on attitude-change to the next level. He highlights the attitudes and dynamics behind demand, such as the power differential between men and women and the way in which this is exaggerated through men engaging in prostitution and perpetrating domestic violence. He then reminds us that Scripture paints a different picture: God hears the cry of the oppressed. As well, Jesus humbled himself and therefore expects men to lay down the power they have. Rather than dominate, men are encouraged to provide respect towards women and speak out when they see or hear something that diminishes women. Grant gives a number of practical suggestions of how men can change the prevailing culture by standing up against it.

Finally, **Jesse Eaves and Tim Høiland** explore how Christians can advocate against the demand for child sex tourism and create a demand for child safe tourism. First, they describe how advocacy has been used successfully to change US laws to better protect children from child sex tourists. Next, they tell us about the importance of spreading the word about laws against child sex tourism, as illustrated by a multi-country advocacy campaign to deter offenders. Finally, they provide a case study that demonstrates how speaking out can result in relief for exploited children, followed by resources that can help equip others to speak out and make a difference as well.

*

The next set of essays address the question: Why is it important to deal with pornography when tackling demand?

First, **Nicole Garcia and Christa Foster Crawford** explain the links between demand and pornography, including possible correlations between pornography use and use of prostitution. They underscore the need for any attempt to address demand to also address pornography. They also review the connection between supply and pornography, specifically the use of pornography by pimps and traffickers for "grooming" people into prostitution, and by customers for "training" in how to perform. Further, they demonstrate how pornography can be both a tool for trafficking (used as blackmail) and a purpose of trafficking (by relying on trafficking for actors).

Second, **Steve Siler and Tammy Stauffer** explore how we can we encourage men in the church to challenge the use of pornography. But first, they remind us that we need to look at people as "made in the image of God" rather than the destructive way in which pornography degrades a person into something to be used. Siler and Stauffer say that we must react proactively to the pornification of our cultures. They encourage us to use our own brokenness to cry out to God for healing and restoration of ourselves and others. They challenge the notions that "boys will be boys" and that "men shouldn't share their weaknesses" and encourage confession to each other to bring about healing in the church and restoration of men to their right position in the church.

Third, **Christa Foster Crawford and Glenn Miles** examine why we must address the access of young people to pornography when it comes to tackling demand. Not only is pornography harmful to children, it also creates attitudes and leads to actions that perpetuate demand. Therefore, if generations of young people continue to be exposed to pornography in increasing measure it will be impossible to ever see an end to demand. Crawford and Miles also explain the harmful effects of pornography on children's views of sexuality and the changes that it causes to their developing brains. Finally, they give advice on how to teach youth about healthy sexuality and provide principles and resources for keeping children safe from online threats and pornography.

*

The final set of essays address the question: How can Christians and the church reach out to people who are caught up in demand? Are they outside of God's redemption?

To start, **Craig Gross** shares from his experience reaching out to people in the pornography industry. He challenges the often-accepted view in the church that you "believe," then you "behave" and then you can "belong." He flips this on its head and says that, like Jesus, we should first accept and welcome people and then when they feel part of an accepting community (the church) their behavior will change. He challenges the church to reach out to those in the pornography industry – from pornographers to producers to actors. Why? Because Jesus loves them! We can learn much from the story of the way Jesus spoke to the Samaritan women.

Next, **Don Brewster** exhorts that our responsibility to love extends even to pimps and pedophiles. From a practical as well as a Biblical perspective on the redeemed life of Paul, Brewster shares about how he himself was challenged to do something more than assist with victims. He describes a well-known location where child sexual exploitation was occurring and tells the story of how he and others came to passionately take up the challenge of finding a way of reaching out to the pimps and pedophiles there.

Christian Lenty shows us that we must also reach out to the buyers of sex. First, he challenges us not to call men who frequent red-light districts "sexpats" or "sex tourists" because by doing so we are unhelpfully labeling them instead of seeing them as people who can change. Lenty encourages us to look beyond our preconceptions and see them as people in need of God's love. He suggests that rather than criticize, we need to carefully listen to their stories without judgment. He explores some of the different ways that he understands the reasons men are in red-light areas based on his extensive time speaking to them on the streets of Bangkok. He concludes that there is no place that God's light can't reach.

Lastly, **Ken Taylor, Glenn Miles and Mark Ainsworth** reveal that people who are caught up in demand are not just those who are outside of the church, but those within the church can be ensnared as well. They describe a recent study of expatriate Christian men in Cambodia showing that even though these men came to serve, the highly sexualized environment in which they work put them seriously at risk of compromise that would not only negatively affect their ministry, but also harm the very people they are seeking to serve. The authors challenge expatriate men working in these sexualized cultures to maintain their sexual integrity through being aware of the risks these environments create. Men are encouraged to look at the factors that make them more vulnerable on a personal and contextual level and to take necessary means protect themselves, including building supportive relationships with other men. Organizations and churches are also encouraged to take steps to protect the men who serve with them before compromise occurs and families, communities and organizations are affected.

CHAPTER 10: WHY IS DEMAND IMPORTANT TO TACKLE AND WHAT CAN THE CHURCH DO ABOUT IT?

Key Issues, by Donna M. Hughes

The Demand: Where Sex Trafficking Begins

In light of shared moral responsibility to help the millions of people who are bought, sold, transported and held against their will in slave-like condition, a conference entitled "A Call to Action: Joining the Fight Against Trafficking in Persons" was held at the Pontifical regorian University in Rome on June 17, 2004. The event was part of the twentieth anniversary celebration of full diplomatic relations between the United States and the Holy See, and their shared work to promote human dignity, liberty, justice and peace. The following is the text of my speech.

The Trafficking Process: The Dynamics of Supply and Demand

The transnational sex trafficking of women and children is based on a balance between the supply of victims from sending countries and the demand for victims in receiving countries. Sending countries are those from which victims can be relatively easily recruited, usually with false promises of jobs. Receiving or destination countries are those with sex industries that create the demand for victims. Where prostitution is flourishing, pimps cannot recruit enough local women to fill up the brothels, so they have to bring in victims from other places.

Until recently, the supply side of trafficking and the conditions in sending countries have received most of the attention of researchers, NGOs and policy makers, and little attention was paid to the demand side of trafficking.

The trafficking process begins with the demand for women to be used in prostitution. It begins when pimps place orders for women. Interviews I have done with pimps and police from organized crime units say that when pimps need new women and girls, they contact someone who can deliver them. This is what initiates the chain of events of sex trafficking.

The crucial factor in determining where trafficking will occur is the presence and activity of traffickers, pimps and collaborating officials running criminal operations. Poverty, unemployment and lack of opportunities are compelling factors that facilitate the ease with which traffickers recruit women, but they are not the cause of trafficking. Many regions of the world are poor and chaotic, but not every region becomes a center for the recruitment or exploitation of women and children. Trafficking occurs because criminals take advantage of poverty, unemployment and a desire for better opportunities.

Corruption of government officials and police is necessary for trafficking and exploitation of large numbers of women and children. In sending countries, large-scale operations require the collaboration of officials to obtain travel documents and facilitate the exit of women from the country.

In destination countries, corruption is an enabler for prostitution and trafficking. The operation of brothels requires the collaboration of officials and police, who must be willing to ignore or work with pimps and traffickers. Prostitution operations depend on attracting men. Pimps and brothel owners have to advertise to men that women and children are available for commercial sex acts. Officials have to ignore this blatant advertising.

Components of the Demand

There are four components that make-up the demand: (1) the men who buy commercial sex acts, (2) the exploiters who make up the sex industry, (3) the states that are destination countries, and (4) the culture that tolerates or promotes sexual exploitation.

The Men

The men, the buyers of commercial sex acts, are the ultimate consumers of trafficked and prostituted women and children. They use them for entertainment, sexual gratification and acts of violence. It is men who create the demand, and women and children who are the supply.

I recently completed a report for the US Department of State Trafficking in Persons Office on the demand side of sex trafficking that focuses on the men who purchase sex acts. Typically, when prostitution and sex trafficking are discussed, the focus is on the women. The men who purchase the sex acts are faceless and nameless.

Research on men who purchase sex acts has found that many of the assumptions we make about them are myths. Seldom are the men lonely or have sexually unsatisfying relationships. In fact, men who purchase sex acts are more likely to have more sexual partners than those who do not purchase sex acts. They often report that they are satisfied with their wives or partners. They say that they are searching for more – sex acts that their wives will not do or excitement that comes with the hunt for a woman they can buy for a short time. They are seeking sex without relationship responsibilities. A significant number of men say that the sex and interaction with the prostitute were unrewarding and they did not get what they were seeking; yet they compulsively repeat the act of buying sex. Researchers conclude that men are purchasing sex acts to meet emotional needs, not physical needs.

Men who purchase sex acts do not respect women, nor do they want to respect women. They are seeking control and sex in contexts in which they are not required to be polite or nice, and where they can humiliate, degrade, and hurt the woman or child, if they want.

The Exploiters

The exploiters, including traffickers, pimps, brothel owners, organized crime members, and corrupt officials make-up what is known as the sex industry. They make money from the sale of sex as a commodity. Traffickers and organized crime groups are the perpetrators that have received most of the attention in discussions about the sex trafficking.

The State

By tolerating or legalizing prostitution, the state, at least passively, is contributing to the demand for victims. The more states regulate prostitution and derive tax revenue from it, the more actively they become part of the demand for victims.

If we consider that the demand is the driving force of trafficking, then it is important to analyze the destination countries' laws and policies. Officials in destination countries do not want to admit responsibility for the problem of sex trafficking or be held accountable for creating the demand. At this point to a great extent, the wealthier destination countries control the debate on how trafficking and prostitution will be addressed. Sending countries are usually poorer, less powerful and more likely to be influenced by corrupt officials and/or organized crime groups. They lack the power and the political will to insist that destination countries stop their demand for women for prostitution.

In destination countries, strategies are devised to protect the sex industries that generate hundreds of millions of dollars per year for the state where prostitution is legal, or for organized crime groups and corrupt officials where the sex industry is illegal.

In the destination countries, exploiters exert pressure on the lawmakers and officials to create conditions that allow them to operate. They use power and influence to shape laws and polices that maintain the flow of women to their sex industries. They do this through the normalization of prostitution and the corruption of civil society.

There has been a global movement to normalize and legalize the flow of foreign women into sex industries. It involves a shift from opposing the exploitation of women in prostitution to only opposing the worst violence and criminality. It involves redefining prostitution as "sex work," a form of labor for poor women, and redefining the transnational movement of women for prostitution as labor migration, called "migrant sex work." It involves legalizing prostitution, and changing the migration laws to allow a flow of women for prostitution from sending regions to sex industry centers. The normalization of prostitution is often recommended as a way to solve the problem of trafficking.

States protect their sex industries by preventing resistance to the flow of women to destination countries by silencing the voice of civil society. In many sending countries, civil society is weak and undeveloped. Governments of destination countries fund non-governmental organizations in sending countries to promote the destination country's views on prostitution and trafficking. Authentic voices of citizens who do not want their daughters and sisters to become "sex workers" in other countries are replaced by the voice of the destination country, which says that prostitution is good work for women. The result is a corruption of civil society.

In a number of countries, the largest anti-trafficking organizations are funded by states that have legalized prostitution. These funded NGOs often support legalized prostitution. They only speak about "forced prostitution" and movement of women by force, fraud, or coercion. They remain silent as thousands of victims leave their communities for "sex work" in destination countries. Effectively, these NGOs have abandoned the women and girls to the pimps and men who purchase sex acts.

When prostitution is illegal, but thriving, government officials often look jealously at the money being made by criminals, and think they are not getting their share. In countries that are considering the legalization of prostitution, the estimated amount of the future tax revenue is often used to argue for legalization.

Germany legalized brothels and prostitution in 2002. German lawmakers thought they were going to get hundreds of millions of Euros in tax revenue. But the newly redefined "business owners" and "freelance staff" in brothels have not been turned into taxpayers. The Federal Audit Office estimates that the government has lost hundreds of millions of euros in unpaid tax revenue from the sex industry. Recently, lawmakers started to look for ways to increase collection of taxes from prostitutes. The state seems to be taking on the role of pimp by harassing prostitutes for not giving them enough money.

Although legalization has resulted in big legal profits for a few, other expected benefits have not materialized. Organized crime groups continue to traffic women and children and run illegal prostitution operations alongside the legal businesses. Legalization has not reduced prostitution or trafficking; in fact, both activities increase as a result of men being able to legally buy sex acts and cities attracting foreign male sex tourists.

The promised benefits of legalization for women have not materialized in Germany or the Netherlands. In Germany, legalization was supposed to enable women to get health insurance and retirement benefits, and enable them to join unions, but few women have signed up for benefits or for unions. The reason has to do with the basic nature of prostitution. It is not work; it is not a job like any other. It is abuse and exploitation that women only engage in if forced to or when they have no other options. Even where prostitution is legal, a significant proportion of the women in brothels are trafficked. Women and children controlled by criminals cannot register with an authority or join a union. Women who are making a more or less free choice to be in prostitution do so out of immediate necessity – debt, unemployment, and poverty. They consider resorting to prostitution as a temporary means of making money, and assume as soon as a debt is paid or a certain sum of money is earned for poverty-stricken families, they will go home. They seldom tell friends or relatives how they earn money. They do not want to register with authorities and create a permanent record of being a prostitute.

The Culture

The culture, in particular mass media, is playing a large role in normalizing prostitution by portraying prostitution as glamorous or a way to quickly make a lot of money. Within academia, "sex workers" are represented as being empowered, independent, liberated women.

To counter these harmful messages, there is an important role for churches to play in describing the harm of prostitution to women, children, families, and communities. In the United States, the Evangelical Christian churches are increasingly involved in the human rights struggle against sex trafficking and exploitation.

Faith communities, from the grassroots to the leadership, need to use their voice of authority to combat the increasing sexual exploitation of victims and its normalization.

Abolitionist Movement

There is a growing abolitionist movement around the world that seeks to provide assistance to victims and hold perpetrators accountable.

In Sweden, beginning in 1999, the purchasing of sexual services became a crime. The new law was passed as part of a new Violence Against Women Act that broadened the activities that qualified as criminal acts of violence. With this new approach, prostitution is considered to be one of the most serious expressions of the oppression of and discrimination against women. The focus of the law is on "the demand" or the behavior of the purchasers of sex acts not the women.

The US government has adopted an abolitionist approach at the federal level. In 2003, President George W. Bush issued a National Security Presidential Directive. It was the first US opinion on the link between prostitution and trafficking: "Prostitution and related activities, which are inherently harmful and dehumanizing, contribute to the phenomenon of trafficking in persons..."[1] This policy statement is important because it connects trafficking to prostitution and states that prostitution is harmful. This policy goes against attempts to delink prostitution and trafficking and redefine prostitution as a form of work for women.

As a result of this abolitionist approach, more attention is being focused on the demand side of sex trafficking. Destination countries, particularly those that legalize prostitution, are coming under new scrutiny.

Conclusion

I believe that only by going to the root causes, which are corruption and the demand in destination countries, will we end the trafficking of women and children.

---

[1] Office of the Press Secretary, The White House, "Trafficking in Persons National Security Presidential Directive" (February 25, 2003).

We need to urge all governments, NGOs, and faith communities to focus on reducing the demand for victims of sex trafficking and prostitution. All the components of the demand need to be penalized – the men who purchase sex acts, the traffickers, the pimps, and others who profit, states that fund deceptive messages and act as pimp, and the culture that lies about the nature of prostitution.

We could greatly reduce the number of victims, if the demand for them was penalized. If there were no men seeking to buy sex acts, no women and children would be bought and sold. If there were no brothels waiting for victims, no victims would be recruited. If there were no states that profited from the sex trade, there would be no regulations that facilitated the flow of women from poor towns to wealthier sex industry centers. If there were no false messages about prostitution, no women or girls would be deceived into thinking prostitution is a glamorous or legitimate job.

Discussion Questions

1. How does the complicity of government officials with criminal operations impact the ability to address demand?
2. What are the false assumptions and myths that men make about prostitution in your context? How can these myths be dispelled?
3. How does the culture of the media in your context normalize prostitution and how can this be addressed?
4. How would the penalization of demand work in your context? How could you contribute to the process make it possible?

Key Issues, by Sven-Gunnar Lidén

> I will not punish your daughters when they turn to prostitution, nor your daughters-in-law when they commit adultery, because the men themselves consort with harlots and sacrifice with shrine prostitutes – a people without understanding will come to ruin!
>
> Hosea 4:14 (NIV)

Why Is It Important to Tackle Demand?

Normally when talking about prostitution the focus is on the person selling her or his body. As in Hosea, the person in prostitution is the one punished and there is little to no understanding about the men who are the buyers. However, it is just as important to recognize the role of the buyer. Without a demand for prostitution, the problem would not exist.

International law calls on countries to "discourage the demand that fosters all forms of exploitation of persons, especially women and children that leads to trafficking" through legislation, education, social measures, cultural measures and other means.[2]

Churches can play a vital role in such efforts to address demand. But first, we must understand about demand.

Who Are the Buyers?

We know that the majority of persons buying sex in the world are male, although there are a small number of women. In Sweden, for example, police estimate the proportion is around 97% men to 3% women.

Research has shown that there are two major categories of sex buyers.[3] The first group is sensation-seekers who are looking for fun and an extra thrill without any obligation. The second group is men who have a crisis of intimacy. These men have relational problems and are in need of someone to relate to.

The Way In

There are many ways that men become buyers of sex. Some stumble into it by chance. One man in Sweden told me: "I walked the streets. She looked at me. She approached me and I felt elected." This man felt chosen by the woman in prostitution. It is important to note this person's failure to take responsibility for his actions.

More often men become buyers of sex in a group situation. A study of men in Scotland revealed the following:

> Interviewees spoke about intense pressure from other men to use prostitutes. "There was pressure to go along with the guys. It was a common experience for young guys, for their 16th or 18th birthday." One of our interviewees said that he visited the Amsterdam legal prostitution zone with his friends as a "rite of passage." One of this young man's friends chose not to buy sex and as a result was harassed and teased by the rest of the group. "There was an atmosphere of all the lads egging each other on," another man told us. "One in particular was a virgin and seemed like he didn't want to do it but all the guys pushed him into it and he did it."[4]

---

[2] United Nations Convention against Transnational Organized Crime, Protocol to Prevent, Suppress and Punish Trafficking in Persons, Especially Women and Children, Article 9.

[3] Sven-Gunnar Lidén, "DEMAND From a Sociological Point of View," in *EBF Anti-Trafficking Resource Book 3: Demand,* ed. European Baptist Federation Anti-Trafficking Working Group (Hungarian Baptist Aid, 2009), 22.

[4] Jan Macleod, Melissa Farley, Lynn Anderson and Jacqueline Golding, *Challenging Men's Demand for Prostitution in Scotland: A Research Report Based on Interviews with 110 Men Who Bought Women in Prostitution* (Glasgow, Scotland: Women's Support Project, 2008),10.

Interestingly, some research indicates that if a man had not paid for sex by the age of twenty-five he was less likely to do so in the future.[5]

Wanting Out

Regardless of how they become sex buyers, many men want out. In a survey done in the 1990s in the city of Gothenburg, Sweden, a majority of the forty sex buyers questioned answered that they would like help to be able to stop buying sexual services.[6]

Prostitution creates men who feel guilty and ashamed of themselves. In a study of sex buyers in Scotland, 59% reported feeling some degree of guilt or shame, with 25% expressing significant guilt and shame about their prostitution use.[7] The men also reported that after the purchase of sex they experienced negative emotions 41% of the time, including feeling regretful, disappointed, dirty or guilty.[8] Several men indicated "ambivalence about purchased sex, saying that while they forged ahead and bought women in prostitution, they put it out of their minds afterwards."[9] The men also reported feelings of emptiness after buying sex.

There are often similarities between buyers and sellers of sexual services. Often they seek out each other not out of lust, but to deaden the pain of earlier losses. Both groups act destructively because of frozen inner trauma. Both need help. The men need help just as the women do. These male sex buyers carry inside them a force that is destructive both for themselves and their environment.

What Can the Church Do to Tackle Demand?

So, what can the church do to help men stop being buyers of sex?

There are a number of things that the church can do to tackle demand, including:

- Address visibility
- Reduce accessibility
- Help men find a way out
- Change attitudes

---

[5] T.M. Groom and R. Nandwani, "Characteristics of Men Who Pay for Sex: A UK Sexual Health Clinic Survey," *Sexually Transmitted Infections* 82, no. 5 (2006): 364-367.

[6] Emma Ohlsson, Susanne Sterba and Anika Ulff, *Uppbrottsprocessen – en dragkamp. En studie om män som har slutat köpa sexuella tjänster* [The Breakup Process - A Tug of War. A Study of Men Who Have Stopped Buying Sexual Services] (Gothenburg, Sweden: University of Gothenburg, 2002).

[7] Macleod et al., *Challenging Men's Demand for Prostitution in Scotland*, 26.

[8] Macleod et al., *Challenging Men's Demand for Prostitution in Scotland*, 18.

[9] Macleod et al., *Challenging Men's Demand for Prostitution in Scotland*, 18.

Address Visibility

Today it is absolutely impossible to protect anyone from being exposed to nudity or sex. Just walking along the street or watching TV, which should be harmless activities that everyone does, exposes us to nude pictures and sexual content. The message is "Sex is for you!" and the image is of the available woman.

Making the sexual visible is a way to get most men triggered and interested and ready to act. Legalized prostitution needs to be visible because the "product" needs to be sold. Prostitution is widely advertised and mainstreamed on the Internet, in newspapers and through street advertising. Pornography can be seen as a "window" for prostitution. There is a statistically significant association between sex buyers' use of pornography and the frequency of their use of women in prostitution.[10] The more the church can participate in pushing pornography and prostitution out of mainstream world, the more it will prevent the creation of sex buyers.

Churches can also help stop the advertising of sexual exploitation. In many places, ads in local papers are the most common way that sex buyers arrange for prostitution. In Spain, people challenged these ads and were able to have them removed. Churches can lead efforts in their own cities to encourage people to stop buying newspapers as long such ads are in it.

Reduce Accessibility

How easy it is to get a woman. Image a man who went to a pub, got himself a couple of pints and took a walk. In the quarter next to the pub there is a red-light district and he goes there out of curiosity and suddenly decides to buy sex. This is what happened when a friend of mine first got involved in prostitution.

Accessibility is a very important issue for the topic of demand. When Sweden changed its laws to get rid of street prostitution it made buying sex less accessible. Now a man really has to look for a woman in prostitution to find one. And demand has decreased from 13% to 7% in 10 years.[11]

The Internet has made it even easier to access pornography or arrange for prostitution, anonymously and without even leaving one's home. Prostitution and pornography on the Internet are on the increase and the sex industry has engaged in a lobbying effort that is pushing this as a "normal" thing to watch and buy. It's about making it available to create an increase in demand for sex they can profit on.

But such lobbying does not have to go unanswered. Churches can start campaigns against the sale of sex on the Internet. They can encourage boycotts

---

[10] See the essay by Nicole Garcia and Christa Foster Crawford later in this chapter for a discussion of the research.

[11] Jari Kuosmanen, Tio år med lagen. Om förhållningssätt till och erfarenheter av prostitution i Sverige [Study of prostitution in Sweden], in *Prostitutionen i Norden – Forskningsrapport,* ed. Charlotta Holmström and May-Len Skilbrei (Denmark: TemaNord, 2008).

or lobby for changes in laws. There are many ways that churches can take action to reduce the accessibility of prostitution wherever it takes place.

Help Men Find a Way Out

Just as there are many ways into buying sex, there are also a variety of ways out. Many sex buyers live in a lie, are ashamed that they are buying sex and are afraid of the addiction it has created. They spend a lot of time trying to get money to buy sex and trying to keep it a secret. Many say that they are relieved when they finally get a chance to stop.

In addition to guilt and shame, some men feel ambivalence about buying sex. For men who had left the business of buying sex in Sweden, they reported that doubt about the purchase was the first and most important step in leaving.[12] The reasons for their doubt included negative experiences or disappointments, divorce, fear of diseases or being addicted. It was very important to the men that someone gave support to their feelings of doubt. Providing this support is one thing that churches can do. Men who have started to doubt have bad consciences already and need support to leave, not judgmental attitudes or punishment.

Another thing that can help men want to leave is the stigma and illegality of prostitution. The Swedish men reported that the view of sex buyers in society and fear of public exposure was an important part of the doubt that led to a decision to stop buying sex. Another way to prevent men from buying another person is to make laws that charge the men. In Scotland a number of men were skeptical about there being any effective deterrent, yet at the same time they acknowledged that the possibility of criminalization deterred them.[13] Churches can help ensure that laws against purchasing sex are enacted and actually enforced.

Helping men take responsibility for their actions can also be effective. The sex buyers live in a "push" and "pull" situation, when buying women in prostitution still has a great attraction but the situation is also full of guilt. The turning point comes when they start to take responsibility for their action. From that day on they can build a new life and fill the emptiness in life with something else. Churches can provide support groups and counseling where these changes can take place.

In order for men to be able to leave, they must first be reached. Organizations such as Project KAST[14] in Gothenburg, Sweden, and MST Project[15] in Thailand and Cambodia are doing the important work of outreach to sex buyers. For instance, KAST spreads leaflets in the streets, places advertisements in papers and also publishes interviews addressing the sex buyers in newspapers. In five years, they have made 1000 contacts and 350

---

[12] Ohlsson et al., *Uppbrottsprocessen – en dragkamp* [The Breakup Process – A Tug of War].

[13] Macleod et al., *Challenging Men's Demand for Prostitution in Scotland*, 27.

[14] Swedish acronym for "Buyers of Sexual Services."

[15] See the essay by Christian Lenty in this chapter.

men have been in the counseling program. The project has functioned well. KAST social workers say that nine out of ten people who come to KAST change their lives. This is true because those who come for help dare to see their own pain. "It is not enough to hunt the sex buyers with the law; we can also help them get out of it," says Maia Gustafsson, one of the counselors. Churches can help men find a way out by starting an outreach to sex buyers in their own cities, or by partnering with existing ministries to provide assistance with outreach teams, prayer or financial and other support.

Change Attitudes

A final way to reduce demand is to change the attitudes of men who buy sex.

A study of sex buyers in Scotland revealed that prostitution was the first sexual experience for 17% of those interviewed.[16] Unfortunately, the sex that men learn in pornography and prostitution – disconnected and unemotional – is the opposite of the sex that most women are interested in. A good way to prevent demand for women in prostitution is for churches to help men to gain self-confidence and skills to handle normal relationships, as well as to learn about healthy sexuality.

Empathy is another attitude to address. Lack of empathy for the women in prostitution is at the core of men's justification for their behavior. The sex buyer only thinks of himself. The woman is an object there to please him and his wishes, and he uses the power of money and force to make her do so. But he fools himself that she likes it or that he is doing her a favor by giving her money, love or something else. This perception is something that can be addressed by focusing on the issue of empathy. By being in touch with the experience of these women, the ways of sex buyers can change. They begin to see the person in prostitution for who she is: another human being who deserves to be treated with respect and dignity. One man described how he changed his perspective towards women who sell sex: "My opinions changed – I stopped doing it [paying for sex] when I started to drive a group of girls. I made friends with them and saw them as people. Before, when I was paying for sex, I didn't think about them at all."[17]

Having empathy makes buyers less likely to believe they have a right to harm or humiliate women in prostitution because the women they have purchased in the past are no longer anonymous fantasies but real people. Churches can help men understand the Biblical value of women and overcome the negative stereotypes, myths and misconceptions that support the buying of sex.

One effective tool for changing attitudes is "John's Schools." In several cities in the United States, men who are arrested for soliciting a woman in prostitution can be sentenced to attend John's School. At these sessions, they

---

[16] Macleod et al., *Challenging Men's Demand for Prostitution in Scotland*, 10.

[17] Maddy Coy, Miranda Horvath and Liz Kelly, *It's Just Like Going to the Supermarket: Men Buying Sex in East London* (London: Child and Woman Abuse Studies Unit, London Metropolitan University, 2007).

are introduced to women who have come out of prostitution and hear their stories of violence and abuse. Being exposed to the "real story" of women's lives has shown to be a good way to change men's behavior. These John's Schools are effective deterrents and can successfully reduce demand. Churches can help establish John's Schools in cities where they do not yet exist. In addition, they can informally incorporate the teaching about the reality of prostitution into their teaching and programming in order to help prevent men from buying sex in the first place.

Conclusion

Demand must be tackled in order to end prostitution and other forms of sexual exploitation. Churches can play in important role in addressing demand by learning more about the role and dynamics of demand, engaging in actions to reduce demand in their society, and helping individual sex buyers to find a way out.

Case Study, by Sven-Gunnar Lidén

Hans Hernberg is a deacon in a church in Stockholm who provides counseling to men who are sex addicted, including pornography addicts, men who buy sex in prostitution and others. As an expert on addiction he sees common features behind it all and believes that people can change.

He has found that all kinds of sex addiction normally start with the use of pornography. It starts with curiosity and enters into an addiction, with men getting hooked on it against their will. From there it continues into sex clubs and then prostitution. And it leads into shame and self-condemnation. Behind it all is crisis in relationship; "intimacy" has been changed into "intensity." Problems from early relations with parents, sisters, lovers, etc. need to be addressed.

The men whom Hernberg counsels have sought help because of their pain and fear of consequences. Confession is important in the therapy. A real confession to a priest where everything can be named and told to someone who will keep the secret is a cleansing moment. It provides the opportunity to begin the more honest work of dealing with the triggers. This is also a first step of taking responsibility. Because denial of responsibility is a part of the problem, even some forms of prayer can support the addiction. For example, praying that "it is in God's hands what is happening" takes away personal responsibility once again.

The therapy starts with writing down one's history, using the thematic of harm, fear and secrets in their different relationships. This will expose what kind of triggers steer the behavior – what triggers them to go to action and makes the behavior seem automatic and hard to control. The therapy emphasizes cognitively changing the behavior. The goal in counseling is to understand the issue of choice where the individual is given responsibility for his choice. While sex buyers can be irresponsible and hide their shame behind a more easily described addiction, the therapy helps them to be able to confront their fear in relationships and to learn how to manage them in a constructive way to create good relationships.

Discussion Questions

1. What are your feelings towards people involved in prostitution? What does the Bible have to say about how to treat those involved?
2. What is the overall view in your city about buying sex? Is there a red-light district in your city?
3. How are men being socialized about how to view women in your context?
4. What myths have you heard about men's sexual behavior?
5. What can you do about addressing visibility? Reducing accessibility? Helping men find a way out? Changing attitudes?
6. Who in your city can offer help to those who want to stop buying sex?
7. As a church, who can you cooperate with in this area?
8. Does your church have a men's group or want to start one? What can men learn about the equality of women in these groups? Equality is one way to fight demand!
9. Churches may want to share the stories of men who have come out of buying sex as a witness of the successful impact of the church. However, addicted people are often without boundaries and can easily expose their sin openly in a way that becomes negative to them. How can we balance the individual person's need for integrity with the church's need for witness?

CHAPTER 11: WHERE ARE THE MEN
OF THE CHURCH IN ADDRESSING DEMAND?

Key Issues, by Peter Grant

Pornography is one of the biggest businesses on the Internet, with an estimated four million pornographic websites. Over one million women and girls worldwide are estimated to be enduring forced commercial sexual exploitation. What is behind all of this demand?

Understanding the Demand

This demand flows primarily from the beliefs and attitudes of men towards women. Where women are not seen as equal to men, where they are not valued equally as human beings, and where they are treated as possessions to be owned and used by men, then abuse will necessarily follow. To end the reality of violence against women, it is the attitudes and actions of men that have to change.

A minority of men choose to dominate women in relationships, abusing power and generating a cycle of violence. Many regard prostitution as harmless, regardless of the fact that women are often trafficked into prostitution against their will and primarily for the profit of criminal gangs. Many more of us see sex as entitlement in our relationships and take advantage of the availability of pornography to objectify women and satisfy our sexual desires without committing ourselves to the costly joy of a long-term relationship with a real human being.

How Should the Church Respond?

Where does God fit into this? The Bible makes it clear that God hears the cries of the oppressed and intervenes on their behalf. To the extent that we harm or damage a woman that he has created and loves, then we will face his wrath and judgment. Jesus, however, showed us a better way to live based on respect, mutual submission and service.

The heart of the gospel is the laying down of power. Christian men should be part of the solution, not part of the problem; but churches – and Christian men in particular – have often been silent on these issues. To challenge this silence we have founded "Restored," an international Christian alliance of men and women working together to transform relationships and end violence against women.[1] Within Restored we are calling on men to sign up with our

---

[1] www.restoredrelationships.org

men's campaign "First Man Standing" and to be willing to be the first man in their family, sports club or church to stand up and speak out against violence against women.

We want to inspire men to be great friends, lovers, neighbors, brothers and sons, and to be wonderful fathers to their own daughters and sons. We are looking for men of courage, willing to challenge attitudes and actions towards women in themselves – and in others – when they see something going wrong.

In particular we are asking men to:

- **Respect all women** everywhere and demonstrate love and support for the women and children in their family;
- **Challenge other men** by speaking out to their friends and colleagues about ending violence and negative attitudes towards women; and
- **Join the cause** and make a pledge never to commit, condone or remain silent about men's violence against women in all its forms.

Each of these actions is explored in more detail below.

Respect All Women

The Bible encourages us to treat "younger women as sisters, with absolute purity."[2] Most men would not want their sisters or daughters appearing in pornographic magazines, but all women are someone's daughters. There is so much to enjoy about being male and female, and in having both male and female friends, without having to abuse women and girls. Some societies react by separating men and women so that there is almost no social contact. But this is often another way of saying that all relationships between men and women have to be sexual. We should stand against this; respecting and enjoying the richness and depth that the two sexes, and our various interactions, give to our lives.

Over 2000 years ago Jesus modeled a life of respect for women. He treated them as equals, gave responsibilities to them and was even financially supported by women. Throughout the New Testament we see women like Phoebe, Junia, Mary and Priscilla sharing responsibility for the growth of the Church. All of this was totally radical in a culture where women were defined by the men in their lives; their fathers, husbands or sons.

Turn the clock forward to today. So have we moved forward from that place? Is there respect for all women in all walks of life? Are women equal to men in our modern society? It could appear the answer is yes. In many societies, women are able to vote, own property and stay in employment when they are married. In reality however, the answer is no, women are not always respected. Often their opinions and input into conversations are undermined and ignored purely because they are female. They are the subject of thousands of jokes and put-downs.

Prostitution is rarely spoken of in our churches and pornography is regarded as a purity issue for men without seeing that it also involves abuse and objectification of women. The regular diet of topless and sexually provocative

---

[2] 1 Timothy 5:2 (NIV).

photos in films and magazines objectify women in a way that affects us all – the women who are photographed, the men who look at them, and our societies as a whole. The photos and accompanying commentary seep into minds and relationships, affecting our view of what is normal, making people less satisfied with the real-life person that they live with. They suggest to violent men that society agrees that it is acceptable to degrade and abuse women. It is not.

We believe it is the responsibility of all men to challenge this, by respecting women; showing that women are valuable through our actions and words. Men and women are equal in God's eyes, and we must see change. Here are some ways that can happen:

- If you are married or have a partner, then love her, treat her as an equal, share responsibility for housework and childcare and don't value your priorities or work more highly than hers.
- If you have children, challenge stereotypes and language they may pick up that undermines and puts down girls. Instead bring them up – whether they are boys or girls – to know that it is who you are, not what gender you are that matters. Most importantly, fully respect and value their mother.
- Help and encourage all the women in your family to achieve and value themselves. Recognize the difficulties they may face, purely because they are female, and support them emotionally and practically in moving forward.
- In your workplace take time to hear and engage with the ideas of women, consider whether in the past you have disregarded their input because they are female and make a conscious decision to change that.
- In your church, consider the implications of the teachings often given that put women down and insist they are less important and less valuable than men. Tell the women in your church that they are valuable and develop ways with other men to support women in the church, maybe through doing childcare for women's events or encouraging specific women you know who are struggling to feel valuable

As men stand up and through their actions and words show that they fully respect all women, we will change lives and transform culture.

Challenge Other Men

We create the culture around us and we can change it. The second part of First Man Standing is to challenge the attitudes of your friends towards sexist jokes, prostitution, pornography and stag nights which involve degrading women. It is hard not to be seen as a killjoy and to suffer verbal abuse ourselves, but given what's at stake, it's worth it. People need to hear that there is another view out there. Young men need good role models of positive attitudes and relationships as demonstrated by older men.

Challenging people changes culture. We can all recall people who have challenged us. Sometimes we don't appreciate it at the time, but we can be thankful for everyone who has helped us to make better decisions or to change bad habits. To challenge other men requires courage. But isn't that what we are here for?

Under First Man Standing, we hope for two main kinds of challenge between men. Firstly, we all need to be encouraged. We want to see men grow in their capacity to be good friends, good fathers, good boyfriends and good husbands. How can you encourage other men in their relationships? Here are some ideas:

- Be a positive role model. Sons copy their fathers. If you love your wife and children, your sons will learn what it means to be a good husband. You may not realize how many other people also look to you as a role model.
- Be a good friend. Many men are desperate for friendship. Be willing to pay the price of giving time to other men and encouraging them.
- Provide advice and challenge men to do better. We all need help in building good relationships. If you see someone who needs help in relating to their children, or to other adults, then talk to them and give them examples from your own experience.
- Provide positive feedback. When you see someone doing something well, give them positive feedback.
- Talk about the benefits of good relationships. Church leaders and others who have a public platform will have particular opportunities in this area.
- Tell other men about First Man Standing and get them involved!

Secondly, we can challenge men to change. The Bible says: "Among you there must not be even a hint of sexual immorality … nor should there be obscenity… or coarse joking."[3] Evil flourishes when good people remain silent. Our societies have become more and more sexualized and much abuse of women goes on unchallenged. The attitudes and actions of many men need to change. You can help by doing some of the following:

- Challenge the work obsession of many men that leaves them with no time for people and relationships.
- Challenge negative behavior that you see in other men that is destructive to their relationships.
- Find a way of challenging sexist remarks and jokes.
- Stand up against the display of pornography and other material that objectifies women.
- Be willing to be different in a group of men and stand against a culture that supports lap dancing, use of prostitutes, pornography and other abuse of women.
- Organize stag nights that do not involve the abuse or objectification of women.
- Challenge other men who speak about the abuse of women, whether by themselves or by others.

---

[3] Ephesians 5:3-4 (NIV).

Male accountability groups and individual one-to-one friendships provide excellent opportunities to challenge other men. Why not discuss these issues in your men's group or amongst your friends and agree what actions you can take in your own context.

Join The Cause, Starting Where We Are

The final part of First Man Standing is to join the cause and make a pledge never to commit, condone or remain silent about men's violence against women in all its forms.

We can start at home in our own relationships. In Ephesians, Paul writes: "Husbands, love your wives, just as Christ loved the church and gave himself up for her."[4] What does it mean to love your partner as Christ loved the church? It means giving time to listen. Putting her needs before your own. Praying regularly for her and your children. Being encouraging. Not manipulating situations to get sex. Sharing financial responsibility. Recognizing that relationships are tough and that we all need support and encouragement to make them work.

It is not just our relationships with our partners that can be deepened. We need to be good fathers, sons, brothers and neighbors. Our children need fathers who are there and who provide care, support and a positive role model as they grow up. Many men find it hard to make good friends with either men or women, and we need to work at this too, since we all need those with whom we can be completely open and honest.

You can sign up to First Man Standing at www.restoredrelationships.org/firstmanstanding. For those who sign up we will send out more ideas and details of how you can practically work through the implications of First Man Standing and send you a regular e-newsletter to keep you in touch with how the campaign is developing.

Conclusion

It is amazing how one man, standing out against the prevailing culture, can change it. Most men don't want to be involved in anything that hurts women. Speaking up about the issues and explaining the impact of people's attitudes and actions really can change the culture of your workplace and family. As many men stand up in this way, first a nation and then the world can be changed. We can make a difference in reducing pornography, prostitution and violence against women. Let's do it.

---

[4] Ephesians 5:25.

Discussion Questions

1. How did Jesus model masculinity? What can men learn from him?
2. What attitudes and actions do you and your friends have that need to be challenged? Are you willing to change? Are you willing to challenge your friends?
3. How do these attitudes and actions lead to a demand for prostitution, pornography and other forms of sexual exploitation?
4. How can our conversations make exploitation and trafficking seem acceptable or unacceptable?
5. What can you do to get involved in ending demand?
6. What would it mean for you to be a "First Man Standing"?

Chapter 12: How Can We Stop the Demand for Child Sex Tourism and Instead Create a Demand for Child Safe Tourism?

Key Issues, by Jesse Eaves and Tim Høiland

Today, there are an estimated 20.9 million victims of forced labor in the world.[1] Current estimates say that there are millions[2] of children who fall victim to sexual and labor exploitation through trafficking, being sold for sexual purposes, being used in child pornography, as well as through child sex tourism (defined as "the commercial sexual exploitation of children by men or women who travel from one place to another, usually from a richer country to one that is less developed, and there engage in sexual acts with children, defined as anyone aged under 18").[3] What's more, children often become part of the larger tourism industry through forced begging, selling souvenirs, or even the growing issue of "orphanage tourism."[4] As followers of Christ, we are called to seek justice for the oppressed.[5] How can Christians effectively heed that call to combat heinous offenses such as child sex tourism and create a demand for child safe tourism?

In reality, there are many ways to put up an effective fight against those who would exploit a child at home or abroad. The fight against child sex tourism (CST) and the larger issue of child trafficking is typified by what are known as "The Four Ps": Prevention, Protection, Prosecution and Partnership.[6] The sale and exploitation of children (including CST) is a result of both supply-side factors (relating to the victim) and demand-side factors (relating to the perpetrator). Typical responses focus primarily on protecting children and preventing vulnerability on the supply side. For instance, combating poverty,

---

[1] International Labour Office, *ILO Global Estimate of Forced Labor: Results and Methodology* (Geneva: ILO, 2012), 13.

[2] It is impossible to know for certain the exact numbers because of the clandestine nature of exploitation. Since perpetrators and victims do not stand up to be counted, estimates can only be surmised from law enforcement data such as arrests and convictions and estimates by such groups as the International Labour Organization and UNICEF. See, for example, UNICEF Website. http://www.unicef.org/protection/57929_57979.html

[3] ECPAT, "CSEC Terminology," ECPAT Website. http://www.ecpat.com/EI/Csec_cst.asp

[4] See, for example, Child Safe Tourism Website. http://www.childsafetourism.org and "Children Are Not Tourist Attractions" http://www.thinkchildsafe.org/thinkbefore visiting/index.html

[5] Isaiah 1:17.

[6] See US State Department, *Trafficking in Persons Report 2010*, 15.

providing access to education and strengthening communities are just a few of the many possible ways to foster prevention of CST in countries around the world from a supply-side perspective.

However, in order to be truly effective, demand-side factors must be addressed as well. In this article we will examine ways to address the Four Ps from the perspective of demand. Specifically, we argue that Christians must work to prevent vulnerability, protect exploited children, prosecute perpetrators, and form public and private sector partnerships to create effective public policies and use our power as consumers to change the marketplace to be "Child Safe." In short, the most effective way for Christians to fight the exploitation of children is to take part in direct advocacy with their government, their communities and even the companies they do business with. This includes a unique role for faith communities to advocate on behalf of – and in unison with – vulnerable children around the world.

This article will examine two cases in which advocacy has been successfully used to challenge the demand for child sex tourism: advocacy for revision of US laws to better prosecute child sex tourists and a multi-country advocacy campaign to deter offenders. It will also demonstrate how each of us can contribute to make all tourism safe for children.

Advocacy for Revision of Laws

In order for the law to effectively address demand, it must accurately adapt to evolving patterns of child sex tourism. When it fails to do so, perpetrators will go free and demand will not be challenged.

This was the case with US law prior to 2003. In order to gain a conviction, prosecutors had to prove that a perpetrator traveled to another country with the *intent* to sexually abuse children. This was a standard that was very difficult to prove. Moreover, it did not address all of the forms of CST that were taking place.

There are two types of child sex offenders: "preferential" and "situational." Preferential offenders demonstrate a deliberate pattern of intentionally and habitually seeking sex with children. Situational offenders include tourists who may not normally engage in illicit activity but do so in environments where such opportunities are more readily available to them and they end up asking the question "why not?"[7] Throughout the 1990s, efforts to tackle the problem of child sex tourism were focused almost entirely on preferential offenders. Previous US law was usually sufficient to cover the acts of preferential offenders who often would have traveled to a foreign country with the intent to engage in sex with children.

However, in reality, not all offenders have that intent, and not all who engage in sex with a child in a foreign country have actually traveled there for the purpose of engaging in sex with a child. Law enforcement officers and organizations working with children in various countries around the world

---

[7] Julia O'Connell Davidson, "Child Sex Tourism: An Anomalous Form of Movement?" *Journal of Contemporary European Studies* 12, no.1 (April 2004): 33.

increasingly saw that most abuses were committed by situational offenders.[8] But, for the most part, the acts of situational offenders were not covered by existing US law.

The realization by law enforcement, prosecutors and child rights organizations that the majority of offenders were slipping through the cracks exposed the need for a new law. In response, American advocates (including many people of faith) lobbied the US Congress to pass the 2003 PROTECT Act. This law strengthened provisions against child sex tourism by penalizing any US citizen or legal resident "who travels in foreign commerce...and engages in any illicit sexual conduct with another person."[9] In short, the prosecution no longer must prove that the defendant traveled with the intent to purchase sex with children. Further, the definition now allows for the prosecution of all people who have sex with children, regardless of whether a monetary transaction occurred. This means that situational offenders can now be prosecuted more easily. In fact, while only 12 people had been arrested for CST prior to the Act, within the first five years after its passage, 67 people had been arrested and 47 of them were convicted.[10]

The 2003 PROTECT Act built upon the good elements of previous legislation, but the addition of a broader range of offenses closed the loopholes that had allowed previous offenders to get away with their crimes. These are improvements that would not have occurred without individuals and organizations voicing the need for change. However, it was the partnerships that resulted from this new policy that had the biggest impact on children.

Advocacy Campaign to Deter Offenders

While advocacy from many organizations and individuals is essential for passage of improved laws, new laws alone are not enough. It is also imperative to spread the word about their existence so that situational offenders might be deterred from acting in the first place. The Child Sex Tourism Prevention Project was one such effort.

From 2003 to 2007, the US State Department, the US Department of Health and Human Services and the US Immigration and Customs Enforcement (ICE) partnered with the Christian organization World Vision in implementing a multi-pronged strategy of awareness, education and deterrence. The primary objectives of the project were to deter US citizens from sexually exploiting children while traveling abroad. The project was implemented in the US as well as Brazil, Cambodia, Costa Rica, Mexico and Thailand – countries with a

---

[8] Based on anecdotal evidence and observations in the field by World Vision, ECPAT and other NGOs, and based on the sheer volume of tourists traveling in at-risk areas, the majority of offenders appear to be "situational" offenders.

[9] US PROTECT ACT of 2003, 18 U.S. Code Section 2423(c).

[10] The Protection Project, *International Child Sex Tourism: Scope of the Problem and Comparative Case Studies* (The Protection Project, Johns Hopkins University, January 2007), 24; US Immigration and Customs Enforcement, "Operation Predator: Targeting Child Exploitation and Sexual Crimes" Fact Sheet (November 20, 2008), 2.

high volume of American tourists and booming tourism industries in general. Many child sex tourists from wealthier nations often travel to poorer countries due to ease of travel, lax law enforcement and dated legal systems.[16]

As a result, the first part of the project was a strategic media campaign focused on alerting American travelers to a simple truth: If you abuse a child in another country, you will go to jail in your own country. That message was reinforced through various forms of media strategically placed to dissuade sex tourists at each step of their process of taking a trip. Internet pop-up ads, posters and video public service announcements (PSAs) displayed in airports, ads placed in in-flight magazines, in-flight video PSAs,[17] posters in arrival immigration areas, billboards in heavily-visited tourist areas, and even messages on the back sides of the helmets of motorcycle taxi drivers – all of these served to both deter situational offenders and educate the broader public and urge them to take action.

The second and third prongs of the project were related to training, education and awareness. It is no secret that child sex tourists and others who exploit children do not like attention and therefore do not stand to be counted. Therefore, US Immigration and Customs Enforcement agents provided training to local law enforcement in the five focus countries and also to World Vision staff (as well as other NGOs) in how to identify potential child sex tourists, how to report and investigate them, and how to provide the right kind of information and evidence that could help investigators and prosecutors.

The final piece of the project was related to the education of individuals and communities both in the US and in the five participating countries. Awareness training in vulnerable communities was coupled with initiatives aimed at increasing the income and stability of at-risk families. Furthermore, Americans wanting to take action were given advocacy tools with which to raise their voice and act, primarily through reporting suspicious behavior through a special website.[18] Finally, the partnership set up an advocacy website to engage and educate the American public on the issue to help create a "culture of zero-tolerance" on this issue.[20] In fact, the website included a way to report suspected child sex tourists directly to ICE, and from 2004 through 2007 over 3,300 tips were logged through the website.[21]

---

[16] Catherine Beaulieu, "Extraterritorial Laws: Why They Are Not Working and How They Can Be Strengthened," in *Creating A United Front Against Child Exploitation*, ECPAT International (Bangkok: ECPAT International, June 2009), 6; US State Department, *Trafficking in Persons Report 2008*, 25.

[17] The focus was on airlines flying to the countries where the project was implemented. Participating airlines included United Airlines, US Airlines, TACA and President Airlines. CNN Airport network played the video PSA during peak international departure hours in over 30 airports across the US.

[18] Formerly, www.stopchildtourism.org; later changed to http://www.childsafetourism.org/actions/report-abuse/.

[20] World Vision US, *Child Sex Tourism Prevention Project: Final Report* (Washington D.C.: World Vision US, February 2007), 5.

[21] World Vision US, *Child Sex Tourism Prevention Project*, 9.

Conclusion

There is still more to be done and there are a number of issues yet to be addressed to improve the global response to the exploitation of children, particularly in the tourism industry.[22] For instance, US law currently defines a sex tourist as someone who travels to another country. In reality, anecdotal research from organizations like World Vision and ECPAT[23] has found that child sex tourists can be (and often are) from the same country as their victims.[24] Governments in both sending and destination countries must change policies and definitions to reflect the current situation and to provide the best tools to combat child sex tourism and other forms of child exploitation. However, those changes are unlikely to occur without the voices of concerned and informed citizens.

While this essay focuses specifically on child sex tourism, it is important to advocate for governments, companies, and individuals to continue to strengthen all policies and practices related to the protection of children. Laws and conventions such as the UN Palermo Protocol,[25] the US PROTECT Act, the US Trafficking Victims Protection Act, and private sector initiatives such as *"The Code of Conduct for the Protection of Children from Sexual Exploitation in Travel and Tourism"*[26] all gained attention and eventual implementation because everyday people voiced their support. It is the voices of concerned citizens that help to strengthen specific policies on child sex tourism, human trafficking and all forms of exploitation – not only of children, but also of women and men. It is also the voices of concerned citizens that demand every year that governments create and fund invaluable programs that work to reduce victim vulnerability around the world. It is the voices (and wallets) of concerned consumers that encourage and reward companies that implement policies that respect the rights of children.

There is a direct role everyone can play in combating these heinous offences committed against children. But as experience has shown time and again, we must be vocal and speak as communities united in the fight for justice. Whether it is a matter of calling or emailing your governmental representatives or

---

[22] See Catherine Beaulieu, "Extraterritorial Laws" and Amy Fraley, "Child Sex Tourism Legislation Under the Protect Act: Does it Really Protect?" *St. John's Law Review*, 79 (2005): 445-83.

[23] Catherine Beaulieu, "Extraterritorial Laws," 6.

[24] One reason for this is in the rise in HIV/AIDS rates in developing countries, coupled with misinformation about the spread of the disease. This has led to an increase in local men traveling to another town or region to have sex with virgins, whom they believe will be more likely to be HIV/AIDS-free and even, somehow, able to cure them of their illness. (See Benjamin Skinner, *A Crime So Monstrous: Face-To-Face with Modern Day Slavery* (New York: Free Press, 2009), 4. See also Christine Roche, "High Rates of HIV Infection Documented Among Young Nepalese Girls Sex-Trafficked to India," *Harvard Science* (Harvard School of Public Health, October 14, 2007).

[25] United Nations Protocol to Prevent, Suppress, and Punish Trafficking in Persons, Especially Women and Children.

[26] www.thecode.org

reporting someone you have reason to believe is engaged in the exploitation of a child, it is ultimately our responsibility to stand up as faith communities and fulfill our calling to "defend the rights of the poor and the needy."[27]

Case Study, by Jesse Eaves and Tim Høiland

Imagine yourself travelling in a foreign country and a child begging on the street asks you for help. He doesn't ask for money. He asks you to help him. What would you do?

In 2011, a woman in Santo Domingo, Dominican Republic found herself in that exact situation. Three Haitian boys (aged 8-9) approached her asking for money. The woman started talking to the boys and before long, their story came out. The boys were forced to beg every day beginning at 5 a.m. when a van dropped them off at key tourist hot spots. If they did not bring back at least US$8 at the end of the day, they were beaten or denied food. The boys said there were more children like them and asked for help. The woman took the boys to the police.

Based on information the boys provided, the police, in partnership with the child welfare agency (the National Council for Children, aka CONANI) and the International Organization on Migration (IOM), staged a raid on the house where the other children and their captors were located. The police expected to find maybe 5 children and were shocked to find 44 children including 10 infants who were all used for forced begging.[28]

On June 4, 2012, the Dominican Republic took an important step forward in the fight against human trafficking. After a year of investigation and court proceedings, the court convicted two men of forced child begging, the first conviction of its kind in the country's history.[29] The men had trafficked the young children from their homes in Haiti, telling the parents that the children would attend school and get jobs in Santo Domingo or Miami. Instead, the children had been forced to beg and when they were not on the streets they were crowded into a one-room apartment with no kitchen and no bathroom, forced to sleep under the table and under the bed.

The partnership of IOM, CONANI, law enforcement, prosecutors and even the U.S. Embassy was crucial to providing the technical capacity and political motivation to bring this case forward, prosecute the perpetrators, protect the survivors, reunite them with their families and see good policies become good

---

[27] Proverbs 31:9 (NIV).

[28] "Haitian Migrants Exploited, Forced to Beg," *The Seattle Times,* February 23, 2011. http://seattletimes.com/html/nationworld/2014312783_apcbdominicanhaitihumantraffic king.html

[29] US State Department, *Trafficking in Persons Report 2008*, 154.

practice.[30] However, it was all started by the bravery of three children willing to speak up and one woman willing to listen and take action.

So what can you do?

While the focus on children in the tourist industry often rests on sexual exploitation, as a tourist travelling abroad, you are much more likely to encounter other forms of child exploitation such as forced begging. According to a recent survey, 76% of Australian travellers were aware of child exploitation connected to the tourist industry.[31] Yet the study also found that while most tourists wanted to help they were confused or unsure of what action to take.[32] It is crucial for everyone – particularly those called by faith to seek justice – to educate themselves on what child exploitation looks like it and what to do if they find it. It's only through people like us having the courage to speak out that vulnerable children can find the justice and opportunities they deserve.

Discussion Questions

1. What can you do to combat the demand for child exploitation? What choices can you make before, during and after you travel that will help protect children? For practical ideas, visit the Child Safe Tourism website (www.childsafetourism.org).

2. What are your elected officials (both local and national) doing to combat child exploitation? Call them, write them, email them and ask. See the World Vision Advocate Network website for advice in getting started (http://www.worldvision.org/get-involved/advocate).

3. How can you support companies in the service industry that have taken a stand against child sex tourism in their businesses? To learn more, visit The Code website (www.thecode.org).

---

[30] Jessica Bousquette and Jesse Eaves, "We Are Working With Our Bare Hands: Strengthening USAID's Response to Human Trafficking" (Washington D.C.: World Vision US, December 2012), 5.

[31] Arnie Matthews, *The Child Safe Traveller* (Sydney: World Vision Australia, University of Western Sydney, November 2013), 2.

[32] Matthews, *The Child Safe Traveller*, 3.

CHAPTER 13: ISN'T IT TIME WE SEE THE LINKS BETWEEN PORNOGRAPHY, PROSTITUTION AND SEX TRAFFICKING?

Key Issues, by Nicole Garcia and Christa Foster Crawford

Pornography, prostitution and sex trafficking share some connections. Because of this, any attempts to address prostitution and trafficking must also tackle pornography. This is true whether we are looking at addressing the supply or demand side of the issue.

Supply-Side Connections

While pornography, prostitution and trafficking are different aspects of the sex industry, they are also related. Some experts would even argue that pornography is integral to prostitution.[1]

First, many people who are in prostitution or who have been trafficked have been subjects of pornography. In one study of people in prostitution in nine countries, almost half (49%) reported that pornography was made of them.[2]

Second, pornography can be used for "seasoning" or "training" into prostitution. "New research provides evidence that johns show pornography to prostituted women to illustrate the sexual activity they want to participate in or observe. Other research demonstrates that pimps and traffickers use pornography to instruct and desensitize their victims."[3] In the nine-country study, 47% of those interviewed were "upset by attempts to coerce them into imitating pornography."[4]

Third, pimps and traffickers can use pornography as a tool for trafficking into prostitution. Sometimes traffickers will take pictures or videos of their victim while she or he is nude or engaged in sexual acts. The trafficker will

---

[1] Melissa Farley, Ann Cotton, Jacqueline Lynne, Sybille Zumbeck, Frida Spiwak, Maria E. Reyes, Dinorah Alvarez and Ufuk Sezgin, "Prostitution and Trafficking in 9 Countries: Update on Violence and Posttraumatic Stress Disorder," *Journal of Trauma Practice* 2, no. 3/4 (2003): 44.

[2] Farley et al., "Prostitution and Trafficking in 9 Countries: Update on Violence and Posttraumatic Stress Disorder," 44.

[3] Robert W. Peters, Laura J. Lederer and Shane Kelly, "The Slave and the Porn Star: Sexual Trafficking and Pornography," *The Protection Project Journal of Human Rights and Civil Society* 5 (Fall 2012): 8-9.

[4] Farley et al., "Prostitution and Trafficking in 9 Countries: Update on Violence and Posttraumatic Stress Disorder," 44.

then threaten to show the pictures or videos to the victim's family unless the victim agrees to engage in prostitution. For some, the enduring threat of harm from the pornography can be fatal. In a visit to Costa Rica, author Victor Malarek heard the following from a woman in a bar, who was hoping to sell sex that night:

> This girl I knew was videotaped and then she found out it was on the Internet. She went to a café for Internet and found herself. She ran screaming from the place. She begged people if there was anything to remove this from the Internet and was told it was there forever. The next day, she was found dead. She cut her wrists.[5]

Finally, pornography can be the purpose of trafficking. According to expert Donna Hughes, "production of pornography and Internet sex shows are markets which often rely on trafficked victims."[6] In some cases, pornographers force victims of trafficking to make pornography or perform live Internet sex. But coercion is also common in the pornography industry as a whole:

> Less extreme forms of coercion involving the production of pornography may occur with greater regularity. Often, women involved in the production of so-called mainstream hardcore pornography are pressured by their agents, directors, and fellow performers to engage in sexual activity that they do not want to participate in, such as anal sex. This pressure can cross into sexual assault, but in some circumstances it can also be a form of human trafficking.[7]

Because of these supply-side connections, it is essential to tackle pornography if we are ever to address prostitution and trafficking.

Demand-Side Connections

It is also necessary to tackle pornography in order to stop the demand for prostitution (and secondarily for victims of trafficking).

According to some experts, pornography fuels demand for prostitution and/or trafficking.[8] But even if direct causation is difficult to establish, there are proven connections between prostitution and pornography. As discussed below, some research indicates that men who purchase sex may be more likely to use pornography, and the use of pornography can lead men to seek out prostitution.

First, studies have shown a correlation in usage of prostitution and pornography. Stack, Wasserman and Kern (2004) found that men who had paid for sex were almost four times more likely to use pornography.[9] Similarly, Monto and McRee (2005) found that men who had been arrested for trying to

---

[5] Victor Malarek, *The Johns: Sex for Sale and the Men Who Buy It* (New York: Arcade Publishing, 2009), 146.

[6] Donna M. Hughes, *The Demand for Victims of Sex Trafficking* (2005), 25.

[7] Peters, Lederer and Kelly, "The Slave and the Porn Star: Sexual Trafficking and Pornography," 7.

[8] Peters, Lederer and Kelly, "The Slave and the Porn Star: Sexual Trafficking and Pornography," 8.

[9] Steven Stack, Ira Wasserman and Roger Kern, "Adult Social Bonds and Use of Internet Pornography," *Social Science Quarterly* 85, no. 1 (2004): 83.

patronize a street prostitute were much more likely to participate in other aspects of the sex industry, including using pornography.[10] Their study, which compared the behavior of more than 1600 "offenders" with that of men in two "nationally representative samples of U.S. households," found that 66.1% of the offenders had purchased an X-rated film in the last year compared to 24.0% and 36.2% of men in the comparison groups.[11] Farley, Bindel and Golding (2009) studied 103 men in London who had purchased sex and found that 58% used pornographic videos at least once a month and that 51% used pornography on the Internet at least once a month (in fact, 20% viewed Internet pornography once a week and 15% did so more than once a week).[12] On the other hand, Tewksbury and Golder (2005) found in their study of more than 1300 offenders that 25% had never used pornography, and that "90% of the respondents who did report using pornography claimed to do so less than once a month."[13]

Second, some studies suggest that the use of pornography can lead to the use of prostitution. Macleod, Farley, Anderson and Golding (2008) found that among men who had paid for sex, the more pornography they used, the more likely they were like to seek out a prostitute.[14] Their study of 110 men in Scotland who had purchased sex found "a statistically significant association between these punters' pornography use and the frequency of their use of women in prostitution."[15] The study reports:

> We compared men who were high frequency users of prostitutes (once a month or more) to those who were low frequency users (once or twice, ever) with respect to their use of print, video, and Internet pornography. Those who were most frequent users of pornography were also the most frequent users of women in prostitution $(r = .26, p = .006)$.[16]

The study recognized two possible explanations for the connection: "One interpretation of this finding is that more frequent use of pornography supports and stimulates men in their use of women in prostitution. It is also possible that men who are infrequent pornography users may be less likely to use women in prostitution."[17]

---

[10] Martin A. Monto and Nick McRee, "A Comparison of Male Customers of Female Street Prostitutes with National Samples of Men" *International Journal of Offender Therapy and Comparative Criminology* 49, no. 5 (2005).

[11] Monto and McRee, "A Comparison of Male Customers of Female Street Prostitutes with National Samples of Men," 11.

[12] Melissa Farley, Julie Bindel and Jacqueline M. Golding, *Men Who Buy Sex, Who They Buy and What They Know* (London: Eaves, 2009), 21.

[13] Richard Tewksbury and Seana Golder, "Why Do Johns Use Pornography? Predicting Consumption of Pornography by Clients of Street Level Prostitutes," *The Southwest Journal of Criminal Justice* 2, no. 2 (2005): 107.

[14] Jan Macleod, Melissa Farley, Lynn Anderson and Jacqueline Golding, *Challenging Men's Demand for Prostitution in Scotland: A Research Report Based on Interviews with 110 Men Who Bought Women in Prostitution* (Glasgow, Scotland: Women's Support Project, 2008), 16.

[15] Macleod et al., *Challenging Men's Demand for Prostitution in Scotland*, 16.

[16] Macleod et al., *Challenging Men's Demand for Prostitution in Scotland*, 16.

[17] Macleod et al., *Challenging Men's Demand for Prostitution in Scotland*, 16.

Interviews with men who have purchased sex reveal that some men engage in prostitution in order to act out what they have seen in pornography. In the words of one man: "Many times in my life I start out watching porn, next thing I know I am in my car looking for the real thing."[18] A man in the Scotland study explained how pornography and prostitution are connected: "Some guys watch a lot of pornography and expect their partners to perform certain acts. They'll either pressure their partner to a certain point or then go and get what they want."[19] Another man in the 2009 London study said, "the more I've watched pornography, the more specific my wants have become. Watching pornography has shaped my sexual desires. I watch pornography and I discover 'hey, that really turns me on' and I want to recreate what I've seen in porn."[20] Often men seek to recreate those acts through prostitution: "79% of the punters told us that it was easier for them to ask a prostitute to perform certain sex acts than to ask their regular partner."[21] These accounts show that pornography may not pull the trigger in making a person go out and purchase sex but it does seem to be a contributing factor as it does normalize such behavior[22] and acts as a permission-giver.[23]

There is also a scientific reason behind the connection of seeing an act in pornography and seeking to act it out (for instance through prostitution). Advances in neuroscience allow us to observe the effect of pornography on the brain:

> Pornography, by offering an endless harem of sexual objects, hyperactivates the appetitive system. Porn viewers develop new maps in their brains, based on the photos and videos they see. Because it is a use-it-or-lose-it brain, when we develop a map area, we long to keep it activated. Just as our muscles become impatient for exercise if we've been sitting all day, so too do our senses hunger to be stimulated.[24]

The result can be addiction. Mental health experts on pornography and sexual addition describe an escalating cycle that begins with use of pornography, graduates to the use of more explicit material and desensitization, and culminates in the acting out of the pornography through the use of prostitution or other forms of commercial sex.[25]

---

[18] Malarek, *The Johns*, 194.

[19] Macleod et al., *Challenging Men's Demand for Prostitution in Scotland*, 24.

[20] Farley et al., *Men Who Buy Sex*, 22.

[21] Macleod et al., *Challenging Men's Demand for Prostitution in Scotland*, 24.

[22] Mary Eberstadt and Mary Ann Layden, *The Social Costs of Pornography: A Statement of Findings and Recommendations* (Princeton, NJ: The Witherspoon Institute, 2010).

[23] Max Taylor, Ethel Quayle, and Gemma Holland, "Child Pornography: The Internet and Offending," *Isuma-Canadian Journal of Policy Research* 2, no. 2 (2001).

[24] Norman Doidge, *The Brain That Changes Itself: Stories of Personal Triumph from the Frontiers of Brain Science* (New York: Penguin Group, 2007), 108.

[25] See Victor B. Cline, *Pornography's Effects on Adults and Children* (New York: Morality in Media, 2001), http:// www.scribd.com/bluptr/d/20282510-Dr-Victor-Cline-Pornography-s-Effects-on-Adults-and-Children and Patrick J. Carnes, *Don't Call It Love: Recovery from Sexual Addiction* (New York: Bantam Books, 1992), 23–24.

To date, social science research about the demand side of prostitution has been limited, and there is insufficient data to conclusively show a causal connection between pornography use and the use of prostitution.[26] But it is clear from neuroscience and psychology that pornography gives users an appetite for something they want to act on, and social science research shows that prostitution is a common place for the acting out of such sexual desires. It is also clear that men who engage in prostitution have an increased prevalence of using pornography. Despite all that remains unknown, one thing is certain: We must continue to understand and address the role of pornography if we ever hope to address demand.

Discussion Questions

1. What are your thoughts on the connection between pornography, prostitution and sex trafficking?
2. When looking at the issue of sex trafficking, how important do you think it is to address pornography when working with policy makers?
3. When creating awareness, how can this information help you?
4. Pornography usage is increasing and youth are being exposed to it at earlier and earlier ages. How do you think this might affect the issue of sex trafficking in future years? Do you think it will affect it at all?
5. With this information in mind, what do you believe to be the biggest hurdle in fighting sex trafficking? Has it changed your perception?

---

[26] The studies discussed vary on numbers and there are no truly representative samples in any study available that would give numbers that can be used to make any generalizations. Also, the studies by Tewksbury and Golder (2005) and Monto and McRee (2005) both had samples of men who were arrested for patronizing street prostitution; men who purchase prostitutes via indoor prostitution are not as likely to be arrested. Furthermore, prostitution is occurring more and more indoors than it is outdoors, thus making it even clearer that those studies do not have representative samples. Also, it can be assumed that men who purchase prostitution indoors may have more access to the Internet, which is how they were able to gain access and information to indoor prostitution.

CHAPTER 14: HOW CAN WE ENCOURAGE MEN IN THE CHURCH TO CHALLENGE THE USE OF PORNOGRAPHY?

Key Issues, by Steve Siler and Tammy Stauffer

When a man calls himself a follower of Christ and recognizes that every person portrayed in a pornographic image is Somebody's daughter or son – created in the image of God – he can no longer be complacent, or worse, objectify others to gratify his own selfish desires.

As Christians we believe that God our Father created each and every human being and loves them as his own child; we believe in the inherent value and dignity of every woman, every man and every child. And in order to effectively preach and live the gospel in our time – and lead and mentor our families and communities – we must respond proactively to the pornification of our culture.

Why We Need to Respond

It should go without saying that pornography is responsible for the increased demand in sex-trafficked persons, sexual harassment, abuse and violence. As believers, God calls us to live out the truth that the objectification of women and children through pornography is dehumanizing and lethal to individuals, marriages and families. We are also called to categorically reject the increasing acceptance of pornography into mainstream culture.

Far beyond even these critical truths, it follows that a same realization must inevitably energize any serious follower of Christ not only to be open to transformation in his or her own heart, but also to seek to raise the awareness and sensitivity of those in his or her sphere of influence. Men are being called to protect and become advocates for women, children and victims instead of turning a blind eye or living the life and lies of one who uses those already oppressed (see Proverbs 14:31).

For Christian men, the challenge to stand for sexual wholeness in this culture is the greatest adventure of our time. This is an adventure that can fulfill a man's need to be significant. And it is clear as we look at the brokenness and pain left in the wake of the multi-billion dollar pornography industry and the sex trafficking trade that there is much work to be done.

Preparing to Respond

Examine Our Own Hearts

No man, however, can or should tackle these dark issues before he becomes aware of the brokenness in his own heart and soul, and is willing to come before His Heavenly Father as a child. Michael Cusick boldly and graciously addresses this brokenness in his book *Surfing for God*: "Only when we recognize the deeper rupture in our soul will we feel compelled to seek God with a passion that wells up from deep inside."[1] Through this recognition and vulnerable statement the words of Psalm 34:18 become palpable: "The LORD is close to the brokenhearted and saves those who are crushed in spirit."[2]

This brokenness in men ironically creates and sustains the weakness, wounding and similar brokenness in the children and women who are being used, abused and trafficked into the sex industry. When we begin to experience personal healing in our hearts the great adventure of becoming godly leaders in our families, our churches and our communities can truly begin. We believe a call to become an advocate for those being oppressed is part of this healing journey, and promises to bring freedom for victims and victimizers alike.

We also must shine the light of truth on these problems – confessing our sins, asking for forgiveness and educating ourselves to the full extent of what the Bible has to say about these issues. We must go into the world armed with God's word knowing that "our struggle is not against flesh and blood, but against the rulers, against the authorities, against the powers of this dark world and against the spiritual forces of evil in the heavenly realms."[3] Only then will we be ready to challenge the societal norms of pornography, prostitution and sexual violence against women and children.

Confess to One Another

Another critical step in this process is that men must come clean about their own sexual sin to one another. It still amazes us to know there are men sitting beside one another in the same pews Sunday after Sunday suffering in silence because they have accepted the lie that having a problem with an issue such as pornography is not socially acceptable to talk about; let alone if it has progressed to the point of visiting strip clubs or engaging in prostitution.

Until we confess our sins to one another there can be no honest dialogue in the church, and without that we leave each other to struggle against this cunning and relentless enemy alone. That is a fight that few men can win without help.

Conventional wisdom says that guys don't talk about their feelings. Over and over I (Steve) have heard that as an excuse for why one can't talk to men about the issue of pornography. And I've found from personal experience when speaking to groups of men that that is simply nonsense. True, they may be used to doing it in a more off-color way. But I've found it is actually quite simple to get guys to talk seriously about pornography.

I start by giving them something I call the Ephesians 5:3 quiz (see below). Ephesians 5:3 says: "among you there must not be even a hint of sexual

---

[1] Michael John Cusick, *Surfing for God: Discovering the Divine Desire Beneath Sexual Struggle* (Nashville, TN: Thomas Nelson, 2012), 40.
[2] All Scriptures in this essay are from the NIV.
[3] Ephesians 6:12.

immorality." Assuming that a score of zero would be considered living up to the Biblical standard, I can tell you without exaggeration that I have never met a man who passed this quiz. *Everybody* fails! The last time I gave this quiz in a church one man raised his hand and asked, "Why is 'No' even on here?" Most men answer "Yes" to between 15 and 20 of the 22 questions.

Ephesians 5:3 Quiz

Have you ever...?

• Had a sexual thought about a woman, other than your wife, at church?	YES	NO
• Lusted after another man's wife in your heart?	YES	NO
• Undressed a woman with your eyes in person?	YES	NO
• Undressed a woman with your eyes while watching TV or a movie?	YES	NO
• Undressed a woman with your eyes while looking at a magazine?	YES	NO
• Rented or gone to an R-rated movie in hopes of seeing nudity or sex?	YES	NO
• Looked at a naked woman online accidentally?	YES	NO
• Looked at a naked woman online on purpose?	YES	NO
• Talked "dirty" about a woman to yourself under your breath?	YES	NO
• Listened to, or told, a "dirty" joke or story about a woman?	YES	NO
• Looked at a "swimsuit" issue?	YES	NO
• Looked at a scantily clad woman on a billboard?	YES	NO
• Looked at a scantily clad woman on a bus stop sign or bus placard?	YES	NO
• Been inside a strip club?	YES	NO
• Watched a suggestive TV commercial (cheerleaders, lingerie, perfume)?	YES	NO
• Visually locked on to a body part as a woman walked by at the mall or past your car?	YES	NO
• Looked at a Playboy or other "men's" magazine?	YES	NO
• Watched risqué cable TV after your wife went to bed?	YES	NO
• Recorded something with sexual content off of the cable to watch "later"?	YES	NO
• Masturbated to thoughts of other women (real or imagined)?	YES	NO
• Masturbated with a magazine?	YES	NO
• Masturbated to something on the TV?	YES	NO

© www.musicforthesoul.org

After I've given them the quiz I ask them to pair off with someone in the room they do not know and tell them how they did. The lively conversation that ensues – a reflection of how relieved they are to have their secret out in the open – causes such a din that I have to shout to get their attention.

Once I get them to quiet down and we've established that everybody in the room has fallen short of this standard and is guilty of sexual sin then I tell them the good news:

Jesus died for this sin *too*!

Of course this should be obvious. Even though we are church-going men, we're sinners. And Jesus is the source of our forgiveness and redemption.

So what are we so afraid of? Why do we continue to go around acting like sexual sin is something we can't talk about in the church? I believe that this needless shame – built on centuries of bad theology that told us the body is evil – is what has led to a generation of men who are afraid to stand up and take on the pornography-filled culture and sexual perversions of this world.

Of course there are the cultural stereotypes too, the whole "boys will be boys" mindset; and these types of attitudes certainly can encourage bad behavior in many men. But that's not why they don't speak out on pornography. They don't speak out on pornography because too often they are ignored or worse yet shunned by the very people who should be walking along side of them on this journey. It is so important that men make this confession to one another as men, and that we accept our brothers who do.[4]

Live for Significance

Once a man has come clean then he no longer has to live in *fear*. Shame no longer rules his actions. With the fear issue out of the way then we can begin to talk about what men really long for in their lives.

We believe that all men long for significance; to be a part of something big, something important – something that they can leave behind that says to the world: "I was here. I made a difference."

Far too many men are under-employed, working in jobs that do not challenge them or give them the opportunity to achieve anything they deem significant. They are leading, in these modern times, the lives of "quiet desperation" of which Thoreau wrote so many years ago.

Men are hungry for significance.

What opportunities do the problems of pornography, prostitution and sexual abuse provide to answer that call for significance? To answer that question we must first pose some others:

What man doesn't want to protect his family?

What man wouldn't like to be respected as a community leader?

What man doesn't want to leave behind a world somehow better than how he found it?

The time has come for a countermeasure that will awaken the hearts of people everywhere starting with each man, and empower a movement to create

---

[4] The issue of coming clean to our wives is just as important. No man should expect his wife to be initially happy about this revelation, however the truth will eventually come out and it's much better that your wife hear it from you than for you to be "busted." Regardless how she learns about it this it will feel like betrayal to your wife because it is. When sharing the information admit your wrongdoing, apologize, offer to get counseling help, and then give her sufficient time to process. Do not ask for forgiveness right away. Honor her by allowing her time to work through her feelings. Whatever you do, don't be defensive. In addition, be aware that the spectrum of pornography viewing can range all the way from occasional, casual use to the level of full-blown, uncontrollable addiction. If you fall into the latter category long-term professional counseling will be necessary.

a world where pornography and its related activities are considered morally and culturally unacceptable.

How We Can Respond

Begin a Conversation

"She's Somebody's Daughter" – three words to encourage our culture to honor women for who they were created to be, and reject the mindset that makes light of and profits from the degradation of women for sexual pleasure by calling it entertainment. *She's Somebody's Daughter*[5] is an initiative that exists to begin a conversation on the issues of pornography, prostitution – any sexual abuse – toward the end that we become a world that honors the value and dignity of every woman as Somebody's daughter.

Raising public awareness and bringing the truth of the social and human costs of pornography and its related activities to light is the goal. By humanizing the issue in a way that challenges people to consider the girl being victimized and the girl behind the camera, we believe we can change the cultural tide.

This is a conversation that will resonate with Christians and non-Christians alike, with victims and victimizers alike. We believe that God can and will exponentially increase awareness and create a new kind of culture – one that honors women – for generations to come.

Mentor Our Children

This leads to the responsibility we have to mentor our children – the leaders of the next generation. In the church we tell our kids that the truth will set them free. Then we steadfastly shy away from telling the truth about the culture in which they are growing up. Our teenagers deserve better. In this media-drenched sexualized society they are fighting an unprecedented battle against enormous odds. Our girls struggle with body image issues and eating disorders, and our young men are learning that objectification, and even violence towards women, are the norm.

The culture and our media are not afraid to talk about sex or to make a profit from exploiting women, men, and children; neither should we succumb to the silence, fearful to speak truth and shed light on these issues. We teach our kids safety skills such as to hold hands and look both ways before they cross the street. This is just as critical and necessary if they are to live safe and productive lives. We need to equip our children and stand with them. There are many good online resources available for families, such as Enough is Enough.[6]

---

[5] www.shessomebodysdaughter.org
[6] www.enough.org

Take a Stand

When men have worked their way through brokenness, been willing to confess sexual sins to each another, and taken steps to protect their families, then the adventurous journey can really begin, as they go to their churches and communities to let their voices be heard. This can easily feel like a full-time job because once the blinders are off one instantly sees just how precipitous our slide has been in the last several years.

In order to bring this full circle, as we believe God is calling us to do, allow us to challenge men by offering one more step on this journey. Let us address the concept of the users becoming the advocates and heroes, ushering in forgiveness and grace to these issues. Imagine if men were to sincerely and courageously offer a corporate request for forgiveness from women for the exploitation and objectification many women have been subjected to. What power might a corporate confession such as this tender in the hearts and lives of our daughters and sons who are being sexually abused every day? To the hearers of this message, offering grace and forgiveness, blessing and honor?

As godly men, start looking beyond your own comforts and self-gratifications and begin to pave the way for abundant life and eternal healing to be brought to the broken-hearted – reflecting the love of Christ. This is the kind of movement we are being called into as, together, we stand up against the injustices happening to those we have been entrusted to protect.

Make a Difference

There are many practical ways to take action to begin to make a difference. We are called to "be the light of the world,"[7] and there are many opportunities available for those who will stand for the integrity and value of all people in the face of pornography and sexual exploitation:

- Begin in your own home by making sure there is strong pornography-blocking and accountability software on your all computers, and parental controls on all television sets.
- Start programs in your church that provide awareness, education and counseling around the issues of pornography abuse and body image issues for both adults and teens. Make these programs *ongoing.* Pornography is a 24/7/365 business. The church's response needs to be as well.
- Start an accountability group.
- Reach out to the single-moms in your community and offer to mentor their sons on this issue.
- Host an event in your church or at a local community center celebrating the achievements of young women in your community that are *non-appearance* related (academics, art, music, athletics, science, public service, etc.)

---

[7] Matthew 5:14.

- Hold a silent prayer vigil outside a local adult bookstore. Buy lunch for the employees. Tell them that you love them and explain to them – without arguing – why you are doing what you are doing.
- Find out what the local obscenity laws are in your community. Meet with local politicians. Respectfully ask them to enforce the laws that are on the books.
- Go online and research organizations that are working to prevent pornography and sex trafficking. Support one either through volunteering or giving financially, or both!

These are the kinds of actions that empower and bless individuals and energize communities. And these are only a few examples. There are countless opportunities. The point is this: each one of us can make a difference if we choose to do *something*.

Conclusion

We can no longer pretend that going to church on Sunday morning and watching the Victoria's Secret fashion show on Tuesday night is alright. Viewing pornography is adultery. In Matthew 5:28 Jesus says, "anyone who lusts after a woman has already committed adultery with her in his heart." We cannot pretend that this is okay with God. And we cannot pretend that pornography is not advancing and extending its tentacles into more and more areas in our lives.

It is time, men, to shine the light of truth in your own lives, to mentor your children, protect your families and heal your communities. You can view women and children differently. You can become the man, healed and whole, that God created you to be. It is your responsibility as men to turn from being blind users to being godly heroes, and, if you are willing, to begin the great adventure of our time.

Discussion Questions

1. In what ways has exposure to pornography affected your view of sex and/or women in general?
2. How openly and often does your church speak about this issue? What resources are in place for those who struggle?
3. Before attempting to tackle a global issue like human trafficking, what might it look like for your church to first hold a forgiveness/healing service for men and women (the user and the abused)?
4. What is one way you can respond to this issue today, first in your own home, and then in your church?

CHAPTER 15: WHY IS ADDRESSING ACCESS OF YOUTH TO PORNOGRAPHY SO IMPORTANT TO TACKLING DEMAND?

Key Issues, by Christa Foster Crawford and Glenn Miles[1]

As we have seen elsewhere in this chapter, it is essential to deal with pornography when tackling demand. The need to do so is even more urgent when it comes to children and youth who have unfettered access to pornography and therefore unlimited exposure to its harms.

As important as it is to protect children for their own sake, it is also vital to address the access of young people to pornography if we ever hope to stop demand. Other essays in this chapter have discussed ways in which Christians and the church can help end demand through changing attitudes and other means. By faith, we hope to make an impact on demand so that in generations to come, exploitation and trafficking will no longer be issues. How long will that take if the rate of demand remains constant? One generation? Two? More? And yet because of rapid changes in Internet and communications technology, more and more children are being exposed to pornography than ever before in history. How many generations will it take to address demand if the rate of pornography use increases exponentially? I fear that even by faith we could not stop that tide, unless we begin to do something to prevent the exposure of young people to pornography.

An Evolving Threat

Pornography is not a new problem, but modern technology has changed its nature and reach. In the past pornography was available only in printed form to those adults who sought it out, usually for a price. Now it is freely available, even to children, at the click of a mouse. The pervasiveness of online pornography extends to all corners of the globe; even children in developing countries or remote villages can gain access through increasingly available "smart" mobile phones.

Not only is Internet pornography more accessible, it is also aggressive. Only last week my 13-year-old son and I were playing a family-friendly game that he had downloaded onto his mobile phone. We had been playing together in the car in offline mode but when we entered our driveway the phone picked up our

[1] We are grateful to Ysrael Diloy of Stairway Foundation for his hard work on an earlier version of this essay.

Wi-Fi connection and an option box appeared. While I ordinarily avoid clicking, I didn't know how to navigate his phone and ended up doing so by mistake. I was assaulted by the graphic depiction that appeared – this was no "innocent" soft-porn image! And yet how many unsuspecting people – including innocent children – make the same mistake? Gaming companies seeking revenues are banking on it being the norm rather than the exception, even in games marketed to children and youth.

But it doesn't stop there. Pornography is not the only online threat that children face. The anonymity of the Internet makes children feel safer than they really are. This false sense of safety, coupled with changing modes of interacting with one another (screen-to-screen rather than face-to-face), has created new ways in which children can be harmed – and even cause harm to themselves or each other – via technology.

The posting or texting of nude and compromising images of oneself or others is a rising concern. "Sexting," cyber-bullying and related practices take place not only by adults, but also by young people whose sense of judgment is not fully developed, and who are not fully aware of the permanent nature and potentially damaging consequences of their actions. They often do not realize that once the images are out there, they are out there *forever*, and therefore accessible to anyone. What was done to have fun in the moment can cause trauma that lasts for a lifetime, or worse. In some cases, young people whose pictures were posted without permission have even taken their own lives out of shame.

Furthermore, old-fashioned predators use newly popular online media to groom and exploit their victims. Social media, online games and other applications encourage children to post personal information, giving pedophiles the very information they need to build intimacy and gain access. Once a connection has been established, predators may exploit children virtually (though sexually-explicit conversations or the use of a webcam) or in person (through meetings arranged through online conversations, often where the predator was posing as a fellow child.) Predators also use child pornography to groom children into believing that it is normal for adults to have sex with children.

Finally, pornography is a problem that is exacerbated by the Internet, but not limited by it. Even offline forms of pornography such as DVDs are finding wider distribution among children, especially in developing countries where pirated videos are for sale cheaply and without any restriction on who buys them. Moreover, in the shops where these DVDs are sold, hard-core and soft-core versions are often mixed together and children as well as adults may be seen rummaging through the selection with little if any understanding of the dangers posed. Once purchased, DVDs are easily shared. For example, children exchange pornography DVDs for minimal "rent" in some school playgrounds in Cambodia. Furthermore, in some parts of the world pornographic DVDs are shown publically on buses or in waiting areas, even when children are present.

Understanding the Nature of Harm

So why does access of young people to pornography matter? Is it true that pornography, especially in "softer" forms, is really "no big deal" as some would have us believe?

Studies show that pornography can cause documented harm, not just to children but also to adults. These findings are being confirmed by advances in neuroscience that can actually show how pornography changes our brains, which in turn impacts our behavior.

Pornography harms people in a myriad of ways. This is even more so the case with children and young people because of their incomplete stage of development. Repeated exposure to pornography can cause damage to every part of a child's being, including mental and emotional development, emotional health and relationships, views about themselves and others, attitudes about sex and sexuality, and even neurophysiology. While all of these areas are important, this essay will focus on the last two effects because of their direct relationship to demand.

Effects on Views of Sex and Sexuality

Pornography shapes how children think about sex. But it does so in a way that distorts developing values and perceptions about human sexuality. Far from being a good method of teaching children about sex as some may claim, pornography "teaches without supervision or guidance, inundating children's minds with graphic messages about their bodies, their own sexuality, and those of adults and children around them."[2]

The messages that pornography imparts are false. It teaches about body parts and sexual acts, rather than integrated beings and relational intimacy. It teaches dehumanization and self-gratification rather than that the inherent value of others and self-sacrificial love. Children who learn about sex from pornography will be led to believe that sex is an entitlement, in which the man is dominant and the woman is there only to satisfy his needs. They may learn a variety of sexual positions, but what will they comprehend about the unique beauty of true commitment and love?

Effects on the Brain

Not only does pornography change how we think about sex, pornography *also changes the brain itself.* This is an important realization when it comes to adults (and understanding addiction to pornography), but it is an even more critical fact when it comes to children whose brains are still developing and won't be completely developed until their early twenties.

---

[2] Gary R. Brooks, *The Centerfold Syndrome: How Men Can Overcome Objectification and Achieve Intimacy with Women* (San Francisco: Jossey-Bass, 1995).

New developments in neuroscience reveal exactly how pornography changes our brain. Morgan Bennett's article, "The New Narcotic," clearly distills the findings of science into laymen's terms.

First, pornography affects the brain in the same way as other addictions.[3] Bennett explains the process as follows:

> While the term "drug addiction" typically has been reserved for chemical substances physically ingested (or inhaled or injected) into the body, internet pornography – taken in through the eyes – affects the brain chemically and physically in a manner similar to that of illegal chemical substances. William M. Struthers, Professor of Psychology at Wheaton College, explains in his book *Wired for Intimacy: How Pornography Hijacks the Male Brain* that pornography works "through the same neural circuit, has the same effects with respect to tolerance and withdrawal, and has every other hallmark of an addiction." This is because the same parts of the brain react to both illegal substances and sexual arousal. Dopamine, the chemical triggered by sexual arousal and orgasm, is also the chemical that triggers addiction pathways in the brain.[4]

Second, pornography changes the actual wiring of the brain. Again, Bennett explains:

> [Neuroscientist Donald L. Hilton] argues that sexual images are "unique among natural rewards" because sexual rewards, unlike food or other natural rewards, cause "persistent change in synaptic plasticity." In other words, internet pornography does *more* than just spike the level of dopamine in the brain for a pleasure sensation. It literally *changes the physical matter* within the brain so that new neurological pathways require pornographic material in order to trigger the desired reward sensation.[5]

The reason that pornography changes the brain is because of a phenomenon called "neuroplasticity," which Bennett explains through an analogy:

> Think of the brain as a forest where trails are worn down by hikers who walk along the same path over and over again, day after day. The exposure to pornographic images creates similar neural pathways that, over time, become more and more "well-paved" as they are repeatedly traveled with each exposure to pornography. Those neurological pathways eventually become the trail in the brain's forest by which sexual interactions are routed. Thus, a pornography user has "unknowingly created a neurological circuit" that makes his or her default

---

[3] In fact, pornography affects the brain in *worse* ways than other addictions. Because it simultaneously stimulates and relaxes the brain unlike other drugs that do only one or the other, pornography "is a type of polydrug that triggers both types of addictive brain chemicals in one punch, enhancing its addictive propensity as well as its power to instigate a pattern of increasing tolerance. Tolerance in pornography's case requires not necessarily greater quantities of pornography but more novel pornographic content like more taboo sexual acts, child pornography, or sadomasochistic pornography." Morgan Bennett, "The New Narcotic," *Public Discourse* (The Witherspoon Institute, October 9, 2013).

[4] Morgan Bennett, "The New Narcotic."

[5] Morgan Bennett, "The New Narcotic," citing Donald L. Hilton, Jr., "Pornography Addiction: A Supranormal Stimulus Considered in the Context of Neuroplasticity," *Socioaffective Neuroscience & Psychology* 3 (2013).

perspective toward sexual matters ruled by the norms and expectations of pornography.

These "brain trails" are able to be initiated and "paved" because of the plasticity of brain tissue. Norman Doidge, MD – a psychiatrist, psychoanalyst, and author of the New York Times and international bestseller, *The Brain That Changes Itself* – explores the impact of neuroplasticity on sexual attraction in an essay in *The Social Costs of Pornography*. Dr. Doidge notes that brain tissue involved with sexual preferences (i.e., what "turns us on") is especially malleable. Thus, outside stimuli – like pornographic images – that link previously unrelated things (e.g., physical torture and sexual arousal) can cause previously unrelated neurons within the brain to learn to "fire" in tandem so that the next time around, physical torture actually does trigger sexual arousal in the brain. This in-tandem firing of neurons creates "links" or associations that result in powerful new brain pathways that remain even after the instigating outside stimuli are taken away.[6]

Thus neuroplasticity is not only important to understand in terms of the process of addiction, it is also vital to understand in terms of how profoundly pornography affects and harms children.

Finally, pornography's re-wiring of the brain has lifelong effects:

Another aspect of pornography addiction that surpasses the addictive and harmful characteristics of chemical substance abuse is its permanence. While substances can be metabolized out of the body, pornographic images cannot be metabolized out of the brain because pornographic images are stored in the brain's memory. While substance abusers may cause permanent harm to their bodies or brains from drug use, the substance itself does not remain in the body after it has metabolized out of the body. But with pornography, there is no timeframe of abstinence that can erase the pornographic "reels" of images in the brain that can continue to fuel the addictive cycle.[7]

This means that the pornography viewed by children will, in a very real sense, stay with them for the rest of their lives. Even as the specific images fade over time, their impact will become ingrained. What better reason is there to protect children from harm?

Stopping the Tide of Demand

We must protect children from the harm of pornography for their own sake. But we must also protect children for the sake of stopping demand.

Demand is built upon unhealthy attitudes about sex and gender. Pornography amplifies these attitudes and rehearses them in graphic detail. Not only that, the harmful attitudes instilled by pornography are actually installed through permanent pathways in their brains.

Neuroplasticity means that pornography not only influences *what* children think about sex now, but it also determines *how* they are able to think about sex for the rest of their lives. This has profound impacts, not only on the child's own health, development and relationships, but also when it comes to the wider issue of demand. We are unwittingly programing an entire generation to have

---

[6] Morgan Bennett, "The New Narcotic."
[7] Morgan Bennett, "The New Narcotic."

brains that are permanently rewired to have views about sex and sexuality that are the very same attitudes that underlie demand and exploitation.

Furthermore, it is not just attitudes underlying demand that are at issue. Pornography can also generate demand for actual sex and exploitation. Although the porn industry might tell us otherwise, people who watch pornography – including violent forms – want to try out what they see.[8] Pornography shapes people's expectations for sex and what they expect from their partner (and, for some, what they expect from prostitution). What was "normal" for them ten years ago is different than now. What is normal in a few years time may be very different than what it is normal for them now. Will it be more violent? More selfish? More bizarre? It is yet to be seen.

But one thing is clear: Unless we stop the tide of demand through protecting children from pornography, exploitation will continue to occur for generations to come.

Protecting Children from Harm

So how do we protect children and young people from the harms of pornography and online threats? What is the best way to do so without scaring them and causing further damage?

Teach Healthy Sexuality

First, we must teach children about healthy sexuality. Parents need to talk to children about pornography but first they need to talk to them about sex. They should not just leave it to others, and they should certainly not leave it to pornography, which is where children will learn from if no one else teaches them.

The best place for children to learn about sex is the home, but this is not always possible. If parents don't feel comfortable talking to their children about sex or if children are embarrassed to hear it from their parents then realistically teachers and youth leaders may be the best people to talk to children about what is good healthy sex, about the dangers of pornography and about the things they can do to protect themselves against sexual abuse, exploitation and trafficking.

There are a number of resources that can be used to teach children. Programs such as "Good Touch, Bad Touch"[9] developed by Love146/Chab Dai provide information in a narrative style to girls and boys to protect them from sexual abuse. Stairway Foundation uses a series of animated videos to teach children and young people about the risks of incest/sexual abuse, pedophilia

---

[8] See, for example, Graham Fordham, *"Wise" Before Their Time: Young People, Gender-Based Violence and Pornography in Kandal Stung District* (Phnom Penh: World Vision Cambodia, 2005) and Deirdre O'Shea, *A Preliminary Study into the Accessibility by Minors of Pornography in Cambodia: Briefing Paper No. 1* (Phnom Penh: Child Welfare Group, 2003).

[9] www.good-touch-bad-touch-asia.org

and sex trafficking as well as how to protect themselves.[10] In the US, "Tell Your Friends"[11] developed by Fair Girls covers topics such as human trafficking, pimp culture, the use of language and victim blaming. "My Life, My Choice" is a more in depth curriculum for at-risk girls developed by Justice Resource Institute.[12]

When teaching children about sexuality, we must rid ourselves of misassumptions about vulnerability that are based on faulty views about gender. Girls look at porn. Boys are sexually abused. Both girls and boys can be sexually exploited, pimped and trafficked. Both boys and girls need protection and care. It is also good for boys and girls to learn together and to hear each other's perspectives in a safe way, led by trainers who have been adequately briefed in child protection.

Parents and others must also be aware of what messages they are teaching children about sex and sexuality, especially the ones communicated without using words.

Picture this: A mother comes into her son's bedroom and he quickly switches the screen to what looks like homework. But the mother is not fooled; she saw enough of the previous screen to know he has been looking at porn. She leaves the room upset and her son is left alone in shame. When the mother tells her husband what happened he smiles wryly and says, "Don't worry about it. Boys will be boys!" Rather than talking to his son he silently condones it (perhaps conveniently forgetting the way in which porn negatively affected him in his youth).

Now picture a similar scene, but this time it is the father who catches his daughter viewing porn (as more and more girls are doing). The father is upset and goes to his wife. How will they react in this situation? Most likely the wife will not say, "Don't worry about it. Girls will be girls!" Instead, as concerned parents they will likely sit down and work out how they are going to talk to their daughter and try to discern why she feels the need to look at pornography. Hopefully they will seek to create an environment where uncomfortable questions can be asked without the fear of judgment or shame. Ideally they will seek to impart Biblical views about gender and sexuality, model godly male-female relationships, and instill healthy views about body image and self-esteem.

Such a response is needed for both boys and girls, but unspoken assumptions about gender and sexuality often speak louder than the words we actually say.

Teach Young People to Be Safe

Second, we must teach children and young people how to be safe. We have seen how changes in technology have increased vulnerability to pornography and online threats. Do we unplug children from the Internet? No, we must remember that the increasing reach of the Internet can be a good thing,

---

[10] www.stairwayfoundation.org
[11] www.fairgirls.org
[12] www.jri.org

empowering more and more people, including young people, to have better access to good information and resources. But unfortunately those same highways for good can also lead to bad.

So how do we keep young people safe online? There are a number of tools available, including online safety tips and Internet filtering software. A few of these tools are listed in the Recommended Resources but there are many others out there, and more are being developed all the time.

But even the best tool will not have optimal effectiveness if we have not first prepared ourselves. We must be willing to talk to children at their own level, and not in a way that causes them to feel fear, punishment or shame. We must also not be afraid of honestly talking to them about the threats. The threats will not go away simply because we are embarrassed to talk about them. In fact, Stairway Foundation, which has trained hundreds of children to be safe online, has found that most often young people are more concerned about what their parents' reactions will be than they are bothered about the content of online-safety material itself.

Conclusion

While pornography and online threats pose very real risks to children and raise very sobering implications for the perpetuation of demand, there is hope for the future. By recognizing the importance of these issues, addressing the underlying dynamics, and availing ourselves of effective tools, we can begin to make a difference in the next generation – one child at a time.

Discussion Questions

1. What are the particular harms that can happen to children who watch porn and how are these compounded by age?
2. What are the realistic ways that we can protect children from these effects without inciting or alarming them?
3. What action can you take in your organization to ensure that children are protected as much as possible and encouraged to make the right choices?

CHAPTER 16: WHAT IS OUR RESPONSIBILITY TOWARDS PORNOGRAPHERS? ARE THEY OUTSIDE OF GOD'S REDEMPTION?

Key Issues, by Craig Gross

For a long time Christians have been taught a three-step approach to God. It starts with belief. Essentially, if you believe the right things, it will lead to a change in behavior. When you have changed your behavior, you will be accepted by the church. Believe, Behave, Belong.

If you believe this way, you will behave this way, and if you behave this way, you can belong here. This is preached, modeled and affirmed in thousands of churches across America.

It's time to flip this. The Jesus of Scripture reached out and loved people regardless of where they were. It is essential to show people that they can belong in your world even if they don't act, think, behave or believe like you.

Imagine a church or community where Jesus was communicated in such a way that everyone belonged. They were included. And from this feeling of belonging, over time the message of Jesus made an impact on their belief. And from that newfound fullness of God, their behavior changed.

If this practice won out over religious dogma, rooted in rules and regulations, more people would find hope in the authentic Christ.

The bottom line is this: as the chasm between the real Jesus and the counterfeit Jesus gets wider, Jesus becomes more and more irrelevant.

The results are in. Those outside of the church with limited or no faith are jaded. Those within faith circles who look down on them are judgmental.

The jaded and the judgmental. Both need to be reconnected to a simple truth: Jesus loves them. Regardless of how they got to this place, both are disconnected from the full purpose they were created to complete.

Reaching Out over the Internet

Eleven years ago, I started a formal outreach called XXXchurch.com. The letters "XXX" freaked the church people out and the word "church" freaked the porn people out. The two words blended the seedy and the sacred.

Today, XXXchurch.com is the largest anti-porn website on the Internet. More than 70 million visitors have logged on since its inception. XXXchurch.com averages half a million visitors a month. A half million a month is a lot for a Christian site. I think some of those hits are people searching for naked nuns. It could have even been a pastor or two wanting to get a glimpse of the former church secretary named Jessica Hahn. I have heard it all.

For the person who is addicted to viewing porn, XXXchurch offers some answers. For the person who is performing, it offers some alternatives. Regardless, XXXchurch is expressing its voice of hope. I want to connect both with people who are in the industry and those messed up by the industry.

It's a tough road that sometimes leads me to do crazy stuff in order to build a platform to communicate that there is hope.

Porn is addictive and destructive, and prolonged exposure costs most people more than they were willing to pay. But at the same time I am an advocate for free speech and freedom of expression, which has made me a target of organized religion and at the same time embraced (with a few exceptions) by the porn industry.

Despite my willingness to speak against the effects of porn, most people in the porn industry casually embrace who I am and ignore why I do it. In the religious world it is the opposite. Many in the church world despise who I am and ignore what I do. It's strange, or at least ironic. Scroll through the contacts on my phone and you'll find some of the top names in the adult industry. You won't find many church folks – not an indictment, just a reflection of the life I live.

These people have become my friends. The closest to me of all these is Ron Jeremy, the adult-film actor. I love this guy. Then there are Matthew, the gay-porn-convention promoter, Eddie, my porn-producer buddy, or the countless number of porn stars we have gotten to know over the last seven years. I don't like what they do for a living. But the message of Jesus unites; it does not divide.

I can't list all the names of the people who, off the record, in a moment of authenticity, told me they wanted out. Sure, the industry would say, "Go ahead and get out." But the reality is in many cases the families of the performers disowned them when they started doing porn. The families say, "You have no one, and it's your fault." The porn industry says, "You have no one, and it's your fault." They have been abandoned by two groups that despised each other, yet both agree: "It is the performer's fault."

So what is our responsibility to pornographers? In a word: Love.

Are they outside of God's redemption? Not anymore so than your everyday-types-of-gluttony sinners found at every church. Our job as Christ-followers is to love them, regardless of whether they say sorry or not.

The world divides.

Jesus unites.

The world expects differences to get in the way of friendships. Religion, and even more specifically the Christian institution called "church," is known for thinking it is right and everyone else is wrong. The church expects people who do not prescribe to their tenets to somehow find their way into the sanctuary. They expect the pornographers of this world to come inside, but only once they figure out they're "lost."

Not the case with Jesus. He said, "I have come for the sick. The healthy do not need a doctor."[1]

Reaching Out at the Well

The Scriptures describe an awkward encounter that Jesus intentionally set in motion.[2] On his way to Galilee, he took the disciples on a life-lesson leisure stroll to Samaria. Understand that from a geographic standpoint, it was a tad bit out of the way. Jesus was traveling from Judea to Galilee, which was miles to the north. The established route between these two cities ran to the east along the Jordan River. But Jesus did not take the established route. He needed to go to Samaria even though it was out of the way.

On a much larger scale, it would be like me trying to get from Los Angeles to Miami via Minnesota. Obviously it was not that many miles, but in these days and culturally speaking, it was way out of the way. But that is how we connect and authentically love the outcasts like Christ did: We go out of our way.

Samaria was a land of outcasts, it was the ghetto where "Gentile Dogs of People" lived. In the culture of the day Samaritans were considered the lowest of the low. They were despised, considered dirty and unacceptable to any good Jewish person. By going through Samaria, Jesus was painting a picture not only of his willingness to go to those considered the least, but also of his willingness to love them regardless of what religion dictated.

Those with Jesus grumbled and wondered why their leader was taking them to Samaria. Why would anyone go the outcasts? The same reason Jesus did: To love those deemed unlovely.

Once they arrived, Jesus sent the disciples to get some food. Then, unconventional in method, Jesus approached a woman at the well ... alone. Shattering the religious rules, he spoke to her. She was alone, an outcast. Obliterating the customs and manners of the day, Jesus spoke life to her. He asked her for some water. Her response was critical and inquisitive. She wanted to know why a Jew would ask a Samarian for a drink of water – Jews shunned the outcast Samaritans. To a Jew, they were the lowest on life's ladder and the least likely to be loved.

But not to Jesus.

He invited the woman's lover to get a drink of life too. Through the conversation, her pain and her issues with rejection, abandonment and trust were all exposed. Jesus knew she had been divorced five times and she was with her sixth lover. Still, he offered unconditional love. She wanted a drink for her thirst and exhaustion. He offered her a drink for eternity.

He loved.

When I read this story, I am astounded. I see in Jesus everything I want to be. I see his willingness to break the mold in order to enact the miraculous.

---

[1] See Mark 2:17 (paraphrase).
[2] John 4.

Jesus was willing to go to the depraved of society to love. Consider the relational patterns in this woman's life:

- Samaritans were culturally and socially the lowest.
- A Samaritan woman was deemed lower.
- A divorced Samaritan woman lower still.
- A two-time divorced Samaritan woman, lower.
- But a three-time divorced Samaritan woman was even lower.
- A five-time divorced Samaritan woman? She was an absolute sociological train wreck.
- Now take that same woman and shack her up with a lover? It can't get any lower than this outcast.

And yet Jesus chose this woman to illustrate that his love has no boundaries. And he used the simplicity of a drink of water to do so.

So, what is our responsibility towards pornographers?

Perhaps Scripture is telling us we too need to take the time to go to the out-of-the-way and despised places, and take the risk of offering living water in Jesus' name, even to those who least "deserve" it.

Case Study, by Craig Gross

"Jenna Presley" was a rising star in the world of pornography when we first met her at a porn convention in 2005. She was young, beautiful and was taking the adult film industry by storm, making a name for herself almost immediately. That's who she was when she happened upon the XXXchurch booth at this porn show and met one of our volunteers, a woman named Rachel.

Rachel approached Jenna – and all the other people at the porn convention – in the same way that Jesus approached the Samaritan woman at the well. Non-threatening, relational, letting them talk and just listening.

When we go to these shows, we bring special New Testaments that have the phrase *Jesus Loves Porn Stars* emblazoned on the cover, and we always do our best to get them in the hands of those who work in the adult industry, just as a reminder that Jesus loves them, too, and there's nothing they can do to stop that.

Rachel handed Jenna one of these and the two of them just got to talking. Not about Jenna's profession or her life choices; just about "girl stuff" – a fifteen-minute conversation about makeup and clothes and doing hair and all the surface-obsessed, how-do-I-look topics that women in the porn industry care deeply about.

At no point did Rachel try to convince Jenna that she was a sinner, that she was living a life of debauchery and depravity, that she needed to "get right with God." Rachel just met her where she was. And gave her a drink.

The convention wrapped up and everyone went their separate ways. We came back the next year and Rachel ran into Jenna again. They talked again. They laughed again. They said goodbye again.

The same thing happened the next year. And the next. And the next.

This went on for seven years. Seven years of running into each other at this porn show; seven years of gabbing about makeup and clothes.

Seven years of Rachel treating Jenna like a person, not a product.

Until one day, we got an unexpected email in our XXXchurch inbox. An email from Jenna, who told us her real name was Brittni, and that she had left the porn industry because she had given her life to Christ.

Jesus met her in a real, amazing way, and she just wanted to let us know that we had a part in it. Because of the way Rachel had treated her, Brittni had begun to get a grasp of what the unconditional love of Jesus looked like. Everyone in Brittni's world as a porn star gave her attention because they wanted something from her – usually to use her body to make money for themselves.

But Rachel and the rest of our team didn't look at her that way. She was just a woman who deserved to be loved in spite of her outcast status. And Brittni is now serving the Lord – and going back to porn conventions with the XXXchurch.com team, too!

Discussion Questions

1. Who would be considered the "lowest of the low" in your neighborhood? In your city? In your state? In the country? How would Jesus treat them?

2. Are there any "woman-at-the-well" types of people in your world that you feel a responsibility to reach out to? Who are they? In what concrete ways can you present Jesus to them?

3. Do you struggle with pornography? If so, what's your responsibility to those who produce porn? To others who struggle with it?

4. What do you make of the case study presented above? How do you feel about the concept of presenting Jesus in small, ordinary, seemingly innocuous conversations with people?

5. If you, like Craig, scrolled through the contacts on your phone, how many outcasts would you find represented there? How do you feel about this?

CHAPTER 17: WHAT IS OUR RESPONSIBILITY TOWARDS PIMPS AND PEDOPHILES? ARE THEY OUTSIDE OF GOD'S REDEMPTION?

Case Study, by Don Brewster

Is there hope for pimps and pedophiles? The word on the street is "No! Once a pedophile, always a pedophile, there's no cure." There is no word on the street concerning the pimps, so we'll assume it's the same: "There's no hope." Beyond the streets there is very little research in this area, and in this writer's opinion what does exist can be little more than anecdotal considering the clandestine nature of that which is being researched.

Of course as Christians we know hope is not the issue, hope abounds. The first epistle of Peter – a letter of hope in the face of hopelessness – confirms this truth. Peter writes of "a living hope through the resurrection of Jesus Christ from the dead."[1] And that hope is available to all, regardless of where we have been or what we have done. So the question should not be about hope, but instead help: Is there help for pimps and pedophiles? More to the point: What are Christians doing to help the various perpetrators of sexual exploitation and trafficking? It seems far too little.

Taking it further, it is more than offering help, but offering it Biblically, in a Christ-like way, that results in a life transformed. The difficulty is not found in understanding the methodology, but rather in finding those willing to follow it. Looking through the gospels and the book of Acts we find Jesus' example of a life-transforming process that changed the world: Relationship. Jesus loved enough to build relationships with a rag-tag group of twelve, knowing full well that not all of them would be changed. It was a difficult three years for Jesus as seen in His ministering to thousands, fighting a small but vocal minority opposition, and being frustrated by the lack of progress in the twelve (as evidenced His response to Peter's request to explain a parable – "Are you still so dull?"[2]).

Still, Peter is a shining example of the result of Jesus' perseverance in building a life-transforming relationship. Peter went from being an instrument of Satan tempting Jesus away from the Father's plan,[3] to a coward denying he knew Jesus,[4] to the man chosen by Jesus to lead His newfound church,[5] to the man through whom God wrote His plan of sanctification,[6] to the man crucified

---

[1] 1 Peter 1:3 (NIV).
[2] Matthew 15:16 (NIV).
[3] Matthew 16:23.
[4] Matthew 26:69-75.
[5] John 21:15-17.
[6] 2 Peter 1:1-11.

for refusing to deny Jesus.[7] A transformation founded on faith and built on a process of sanctification, both coming through a relationship.

Now the question changes again: Who has enough faith and love to befriend the various perpetrators of sexual exploitation, and even more so of child sex trafficking? I can say my own initial answer to that question was a resounding, "No! I am called to care for rescued girls and to prevent the trafficking of others, not to be a buddy to those who hurt them." I had never considered the pimps and pedophiles as the "least of these"; it was more convenient to define that category myself than to look to God for the answer. Still he gave me the answer when we began a ministry in Svay Pak, Cambodia.

An Experience in Process

Svay Pak, Cambodia is infamous worldwide as a center for child sex trafficking. Although great amounts of time and money have been spent trying to rid this small village of its great evil, success has been short lived. Educational and economic development efforts, while beneficial, do not defeat evil, as evidenced by our own experience in the West. Periodically Cambodian law enforcement supported by Western NGOs would sweep into the village rescuing girls, arresting perpetrators and closing brothels. But not long after these successes the evil would reappear smarter, more clandestine and just as pervasive. It was in response to this situation that Agape International Missions (AIM) was called to begin ministry within the village of Svay Pak. Jesus said, "the gates of Hades will not overcome it [His church]."[8] And it seemed if any place on earth was protected by the gates of Hades it was Svay Pak.

The ministry opened in September 2007 in a former brothel, now called Rahab's House, a place of safety and hope. The initial ministry was a kids' club led by the staff of AIM's aftercare center and staffed by girls volunteering from the center to bring the love of Jesus to children in a village that many had been trafficked through, and in a building in which a few had been raped of their virginity. Over the next eighteen months the ministry expanded rapidly as the love and hope of Jesus was shared through church ministries consisting of the kids' club, healthcare, education, discipleship and small business development. Rahab's House now consisted of three paid staff members, a ten-member church leadership team, and a thirty-one-member fulltime volunteer staff, all from Svay Pak. Through their efforts lives were being changed and thirteen girls had been rescued from sex trafficking; however, the one segment of the community not touched by the ministry was the perpetrators.

The question now became how would this ministry reach the traffickers, pimps and brothel owners with the love and hope of Jesus? What could open the door for building those life-changing relationships? Where would they be willing to come and give the staff an opportunity to love them? The answer: a gym – the Lord's Gym. It would be a place for them to hang out and do

---

[7] According to early church tradition.
[8] Matthew 16:18 (NIV).

something they enjoyed, and a place where they could be loved unconditionally. In March 2009, the Lord's Gym, Svay Pak opened.

The opening of the gym drew more than 100 men, but it settled down to approximately forty active participants, almost all of them involved in the sex trafficking of girls. Since the gym's opening, the staff of Rahab's House has worked six days a week at the gym, loving and praying for men whose actions repulsed them; building relationships that allowed them to speak into their lives about the sin in their actions, and the hope of salvation found in Jesus. Over time, half of these perpetrators began regularly attending church, and three young men have chosen to stop their involvement in human trafficking. This decision was based upon four factors: One, someone had shown them over time that he loved them regardless of their actions. Two, this same someone, in love, shared the truth about the sin in their lives. Three, this same someone shared the truth about the hope available to them. Four, this same someone opened the door to the work of the Holy Spirit in their lives. A look at the life of one of these young men will provide greater insight into the process of life transformation.

A Life Changed

Let's call him Peter. This is his story as he shared it with me.

Peter is a young man who has lived his entire life in Svay Pak. As far as he knows his family has always been involved in child sex trafficking, including trafficking his two younger sisters, both under ten years of age.

At age thirteen Peter began using drugs. At age fourteen, after years of watching the pornography used to train young trafficked girls, he began to rape girls in the village, including daily raping his own sisters. Temporary relief was afforded his sisters when Peter reached age sixteen and he became a freelance child sex trafficker. (His sisters have been rescued through the efforts of the Rahab's House staff and are now safe and doing well in one of AIM's aftercare centers.)

Child sex trafficking is a very lucrative business, with very little risk in a village like Svay Pak where it receives the protection of very powerful men within Cambodia. Peter would make trips into Vietnam, sometimes with a small advance ($200) from a brothel owner. The primary purpose of the money was to pay off border guards if caught crossing the border with undocumented girls. Peter never had to use the money for that purpose; he knew many paths to avoid the guards. Once in Vietnam he would acquire the girls in one of three ways: (1) steal them – kidnapping; (2) trick their families by offering good employment for the girl in Cambodia; or (3) buy the girl from the family. (He only bought virgins, paying $1,000 for a "pretty" virgin, and $500 for an "ugly" virgin.) Once back in Svay Pak Peter would sell the girls to a brothel owner or another trafficker. He would be paid $2,000 for a pretty virgin, $1,000 for an ugly virgin, and would negotiate a price for the other girls; the younger and pretty they were the more money he could get. An average trafficking run would net Peter $4,000 to $7,000.

This was Peter's life before the Lord's Gym.

When the gym opened Peter was faithful participant whenever he was in town. And every day the pastor of Rahab's House would spend time with him, encouraging him in his workout, praying for him, explaining why the child sex trafficking happening in Svay Pak was wrong, and over time telling him about Jesus and inviting him to church. He always declined. Then came the day his sisters were rescued and it was evident to Peter that the pastor knew exactly what he had been doing. Yet, when he showed up at the gym there was the pastor waiting for him, encouraging him in his workout, praying for him, explaining why the child sex trafficking happening in Svay Pak was wrong, telling him about Jesus and inviting him to church. This time Peter accepted the invitation.

Over the next two months Peter attended church service as faithfully as he came to the gym, not missing a single Sunday. After service on that eighth Sunday he came to the pastor and told him he was giving up drugs and trafficking and would not be hurting girls anymore either. He said, "I'm beginning to think you might be right about that stuff being wrong pastor. Anyways I want to know more about Jesus, and if I ever did get caught trafficking I might have to go to jail." After a month had gone by and Peter had been faithful to his word, the pastor helped find him a job on a construction crew – $50 a month.

At the time of this writing another four months have gone by and Peter remains good to his word. His boss on the construction crew says he is doing a great job and is happy to have him. It is early in the process, too early to claim victory; however, there is substantial evidence that the life transformation process is in motion.

Discussion Questions

1. How do I feel about loving people who hurt children? How can I open my heart to be a conduit of Christ's love for the perpetrators?
2. Where is sex trafficking happening in my community? Who can help us identify these places?
3. What are ways we can meet perpetrators' felt needs and build a love relationship through which Jesus can bring transformation?
4. Who are the people already serving in the places where sex trafficking is happening, and how can we partner with them?
5. God is asking, "Whom shall I send?" Who among us will respond as Isaiah did: "Here I am, send me!"?

CHAPTER 18: IS THERE HOPE FOR MEN WHO VISIT RED-LIGHT DISTRICTS?

Key Issues, by Christian Lenty

We need to begin to alter our perception of the men who visit overseas red-light districts. Our first question is, should we even call these men "sex tourists"? Is it possible that by calling them sex tourists that we are automatically stereotyping them, which then releases us from the responsibility of caring for them? At MST Project, an outreach to men who travel to red-light districts looking for sex, we choose to look past the stereotype and see the individual standing before us and to see these men for where they can be, not for where they are.

Men choose to engage in the sex industry for a variety of reasons, some more common than others. From our experience talking to men who have come from overseas to red-light districts in Thailand and Cambodia, we have found that there are a number of men who are choosing to engage in the sex industry because there is a deeper root cause that has led them to that point in their life; in essence, it is a coping mechanism. Some of these men have experienced some form of physical or sexual abuse from a relative or from someone else. Others are dealing with emotional abuse or pain, for instance from the separation of divorce (either from their own marriage or as children of divorce), low self-esteem, or wrong perceptions of what a healthy relationship is. Such men are looking to the sex industry as a way to find identity, love, value and self-esteem. In addition, some men are driven by peer pressure.

To reach out to these men, we need to look into the deeper issues that bring them to the red-light district. Sometimes the deeper issues are not found in an analytical viewpoint but in the ability to look beyond what you see and take a glance into his past twenty or thirty years ago that have brought him to where he is today.

Let's look at some of the common reasons that we have found of why men come to red-light districts, and the hope that God offers in light of those reasons.

Need for Intimacy

There are some men that we have found whose desire for intimacy is rooted in the lack of intimacy that they have with their wife or in a relationship from the past. They are at a point where they have been married ten or fifteen years or longer and yet they have "fallen out" of love. They are no longer in a marriage with a partner; they are in a house with a roommate. They no longer find it easy to share hopes and dreams but to argue about little things. They no longer have a desire to walk a journey with its ups and downs but to leave when the going gets rough. We believe that men in these situations begin to look for what they have lost, which is the intimacy that they had with their wife, and they believe that they can find this with a woman halfway across the world. Yet it is a search for intimacy that they can never find in a one-night encounter.

For example, once when we were talking with a man who was visiting a red-light district overseas, he answered each one of our questions we asked with full honesty. When we finally asked him our last question, "What is your reason for coming to this area tonight?" he looked at us, glanced across the road then at his feet, and said, "To tell you the truth, I came here looking for something that I know I am not going to find here: companionship."

The good news is that men in red-light districts do not have to be alone. We can share with them the hope that comes from a God who knows them, created them, loves them and accepts them, no matter where they are, and no matter what they have done.

Need to Find Value and Identity

There are some men who grow up with such low self-esteem as a result of parents, friends or experiences that they are unable to integrate fully into society and develop normal healthy relationships. Therefore they are trying to find who they are as a person by seeking out someone who will tell them what they long to hear. But what they are hearing is not the truth. What they hear is what their money is able to buy. Therefore their value is found only as long as they have the money to fulfill their emotional longing for value and identity. Yet when their encounter is over, the beer bottles are empty, and the woman is gone they find themselves empty once again and wondering who they are. The never-ending and never-satisfying cycle of longing to find value and love continues only to never be fulfilled.

An example of this can be found in the story of a man we met from Ireland. The man told us that he has a Thai wife/girlfriend who had come out of the sex industry. He also told us that he has a wife and two children in Ireland. He has been separated from his wife for seven years, though she refuses to get a divorce because she doesn't want their marriage to end. He has not talked to his daughter for quite some time. After listening to him tell his story we asked him, "If you could hit the restart button on your life and undo a lot of the things you've done, would you?" Without hesitation, he said yes. We told him that it was possible through Jesus Christ and entering into relationship with him. We asked the man if he loved his Thai wife/girlfriend and he said no. Then he asked, "What IS love? I don't even know what it is?"

We told him that love is a commitment and that love is a choice to stay devoted to one person, even when feelings don't seem to be there at times.

Even in the midst of immorality and depravity, True Love cannot be denied nor hidden.

Hurts and Pains

It is fair to say that all people have hurts and pains in their lives, and to a certain extent these hurts and pains affect our behavior. They can ruin our esteem or determine our friendships. But some people let hurts and pains control their lives. Some men who have been hurt end up engaging in activities that only end up hurting others. The result is a cycle in which those who have been hurt bring others into their circle of pain. Is this right? No. But for some men who have been so hurt by emotional, physical or sexual pain or abuse, they know of no other way to cope with their pain besides seeking out sexual services.

Once during our outreach in Thailand, we met an expatriate man who asked us if we were Christians. We told him that we were and he shared with us his life story of how his wife back home left him, how he misses his son, how coming to Thailand was a choice he wished he could take back, and how he longed to return home. He then looked at us and said, "Can you save my soul?" We responded by saying that we could not save his soul but that God could! As we proceeded to share about God and our own personal walk, the man would interject how he doubted that there was a God, or that God could love him, or that God even knows that he exists. However, we continued to share our story, and finally the man said that he just wanted peace – peace in his life. As he shared, we sensed that here was a man who had lost that which was dear to him – his wife and family – and that he had come to the red-light district to deal with the hurt and pain that accompanies that kind of loss.

Is it right that he is in a red-light district? No.

Is it right that he chooses to engage in this lifestyle? No.

But after hearing his story it is easy to understand why he made the decisions he did.

Loving a man in a red-light district does not mean that we condone his behavior. Rather, loving him – in the midst of all of life's messiness – enables us to talk with him, not at him, and to extend grace and love at a time when he least expects it.

Sex = Love Myth

We live in a world that is overtly sexualized in all aspects of society. It is a society that tends to equate sex with love when in fact nothing can be further from the truth. Sex is the act of love between a husband and a wife within the Biblical definition of marriage as ordained by God. Yet we have gone so far from that truth that men now tell women that if they love them, they must have sex with them. And some women believe that if a man has sex with her then he must love her. Yet not only do these thoughts permeate our everyday society but they are also the reason why some men seek to go to red-light districts. Men who cannot find love within normal healthy relationships with their wife now seek to find "love" – even a love of fantasy proportions – through an encounter with a random woman.

We once were engaged in a conversation with a man who said that he and the rest of the men in red-light areas only went there because humans get horny. We asked him what he thought love was, and he responded that love was a hormonal emotion. We shared with him the truth that humans can live without sex but we all need love. He told us that no it was the other way around.

There is a general confusion today about what love truly means and many men and women are in a constant and futile attempt to find "love" in all of its false forms.

What better place is there then than a red-light district to share the true meaning of love, and the radical love that Christ has for each person who is there.

Conclusion

After talking to these men and hearing their stories and some of the reasons why they have come to the red-light areas, it begins to become clear that they are not all sex tourists. They are not all the sex addicts that some would think they are. They are fathers and sons, brothers and friends, and we must look at them as such. It is because of stories like these that we persevere in red-light district throughout red-light district – because these men are worthy of God's love, God's redemption and God's restoration.

In closing, we choose to see a person, not a perpetrator. We choose to see a man, not a client. We choose to see someone to love, not someone to hate.

We love these men because God first loved us. God has not forgotten about these men and neither will we because the Father's love is available to all, at all times, and in all places.

We must also begin to open our arms instead of pointing our fingers, and to firmly hold onto the belief that there is no place too deep where the hand of God cannot reach down to rescue someone, anyone.

Case Study, by Christian Lenty

Here are some stories of the men that the MST Project outreach teams have met.

- One night we met a Western man in Patpong, one of the well-known red-light districts in Bangkok, who said he was down there for the women. He told us that the previous night he finally experienced what he thought and believed was true love for the first time in his life. Some people might hear his comments and be disgusted at his thoughts, but we ask ourselves, "What kind of life has he lived where he has never experienced love for 65 years?"
- We met an Australian man in another red-light district in Thailand. He looked like your typical tough guy; tall and strong. When he spoke, he spoke with the typical bravado tough-guy speech. He said that he had

been sleeping around since his youth and felt that he was "God's gift to women." However, after thirty minutes, he got past the bravado and allowed us to see into his heart, where real vulnerability was hiding. His wife had kicked him out of the house because of his sexual addiction and she wasn't willing to take him back. He really wanted to be back with his wife but he didn't know what to do or how to overcome his addiction. Although he seemed like the stereotypical "sex tourist," in reality he was a man who wanted to be restored to his wife. By overlooking the stereotype we were able to get to a vulnerable place in his heart.

- One night in Phnom Penh, Cambodia, we met a man who told us that he had grown up with an abusive father who would always yell at him. This continued even as the man grew into adulthood and to this day he does not have a good-standing relationship with his father. From our conversation and what this man told us about what he was looking for, we can understand how growing up in a home environment like that would lead him to a place like a red-light district seeking acceptance and value – two things he lacked growing up.

- Another man we met told us how he had lost his wife and family through divorce and shared with us the hurt and pain that he was feeling. At one point he asked us, "Can you save my soul?" After speaking with us for a while, he let us pray for him. In the middle of the prayer we looked up and saw that he was crying. Here we were in a red-light district with music blaring, drunk men everywhere, women soliciting customers – and in the middle of it all was a grown man crying as we prayed over him. That moment will forever be confirmation to us that there is a tremendous need here, and we have a responsibility to meet that need. We saw into this man's need by seeing what God sees in the middle of a red-light district. He sees the immorality and the sin, but he also sees the hearts of men and the many hurts that they have.

Discussion Questions

1. Do you think that grace pertains to men in red-light districts? If so, how? If not, why?
2. What, if anything, do you think could inspire these men to seek change? How can you help bring that about?
3. Do you think it is best to portray judgment or love towards these men? Which would you respond to best?
4. Do you think that judgment could encourage increased negative behavior by causing the man to feel ostracized from general society?
5. How can we offer men something more meaningful and long-term than what they could find in a red-light district?

6. Do you agree with the perspective that some men frequent red-light districts as a remedy to the hurts and pains in their life? If not, why?

CHAPTER 19: HOW ARE WE DOING OURSELVES? WHAT CAN WE DO ABOUT THE SEXUAL BEHAVIOR OF EXPATRIATE CHRISTIAN MEN?

Key Issues, by Kenneth R. Taylor, Glenn Miles and Mark Ainsworth

Conservative Christians generally agree with the Bible's advice to flee sexual immorality and to abstain from sexual behavior outside of marriage. Consequently, viewing pornography and purchasing sexual services from persons working in prostitution and erotic massage are deemed by most Christians to constitute sexual misconduct. However, a number of recent surveys have called attention to the significant dissonance existing between what Christians profess and what they practice. Christians – even ones who believe that sexual immorality is wrong – are not immune to being caught up in the web of demand. Vulnerability to sexual misconduct is particularly relevant to Christians fighting sexual trafficking and exploitation because it may affect their capacity to help the victims of these practices.

This essay discusses the results of a survey that was conducted in 2013 of the sexual beliefs and behaviors of expatriate Christian men in Cambodia.[1] The purpose of the survey was to identify their views about sexual temptation, to measure their vulnerability to locally pervasive forms of sexual misconduct, and to assess their coping strategies. Our hope was that through this inquiry, churches and Christian organizations would consider the need for tailored support services to support the sexual integrity of Christians fighting sexual trafficking and exploitation.

Rates of Pornography Use among Christians in the United States

Since the advent of cybersex, a number of surveys have been conducted regarding Christians' use of pornography. While there is some skepticism as to the scientific accuracy of these figures,[2] what is clear is that pornography is a struggle for many men in the church.

In 2005, *Christianity Today* reported that 57% of pastors surveyed said that "addiction to pornography is the most sexually damaging issue to their

---

[1] Kenneth R. Taylor and Glenn Miles, "Survey of Expatriate Christian Men Living in Cambodia Regarding Views and Practices of Pornography, Erotic Massage, and Prostitution," *Social Work & Christianity: An International Journal,* forthcoming.

[2] See, for example, Daniel Weiss, "All Men Look at Pornography, Right?" Rock Website, April 3, 2011.

congregation."[3] A brief run-down of the numbers show how prevalent pornography usage appears to be: Barna Group reports that 12% of Christian respondents admitted to pornography use in the past week,[4] ChristiaNet.com polls indicate that 50% of all Christian men are addicted to pornography,[5] and 63% of the men who attended Focus on the Family's "Men, Romance & Integrity Seminars" admitted to struggling with pornography in the past year.[6]

Church leaders are also at risk. In a 2001 *Christianity Today* survey, 51% of pastors indicated that Internet pornography was a possible temptation, 43% admitted visiting a pornographic site at least one time, and 37% said viewing pornography was a current struggle.[7] In another survey, 30% of pastors admitted viewing Internet pornography in the previous 30 days.[8]

Study of Pornography Use among Expatriate Christians in Cambodia

We wanted to see if these same dynamics applied to expatriate Christian workers in Cambodia, a highly sexualized context where opportunities for sexual misconduct abound.

Background

Cambodia has a fairly large expatriate Christian mission and NGO community that is there mostly to contribute to the wellbeing of local communities. It is generally motivated by high moral standards and many are active in fighting sexual trafficking and exploitation.

Our survey was designed to assess whether the men in this community were experiencing similar challenges to sexual integrity as those in other parts of the world. Based on anecdotal evidence and experience working in other contexts, our working hypothesis was that the incidence of sexual misconduct would be in line with the findings in the US.

In the event we determined this to be the case, we further wanted to develop preventative and remedial programs to support struggling individuals. Indeed, the ultimate purpose of the survey was not academic, but rather to encourage expatriate Christian men to think about their behavior and consider how they could protect themselves or receive appropriate help if necessary. With that goal in mind, and given the ethical implications of such a survey, we also provided a counseling contact at the end of the questionnaire.

---

[3] Christianity Today, "Christians and Sex Leadership Journal Survey" (March 2005).

[4] Barna Group, "Young Adults and Liberals Struggle with Morality" (August 25, 2008).

[5] ChristiaNet, Inc., "ChristiaNet Poll Finds That Evangelicals Are Addicted to Porn," *Market Wired* (August 7, 2006).

[6] Donald R. Barbera, *The 80% Solution: Christians Doing the Right Thing* (Bloomington: Xlibris Corporation, 2012), Chapter 12.

[7] Christianity Today, "The Leadership Survey on Pastors and Internet Pornography," *Leadership Journal* 22, no.1 (Winter 2001).

[8] Mark Bergin, "Porn Again," *World Magazine* (April 23, 2005).

Goals and Methodology

We primarily wanted to test for the prevalence of sex addiction among our respondents.[9] We also asked about two behaviors that are particularly pervasive in Cambodia:

- Viewing pornography, especially on the Internet where it is anonymous and easily accessible, and
- Buying sexual services from persons working in prostitution and erotic massage.

The questionnaire consisted of 25 questions, which are described below.

We conducted the survey in 2013, using the electronic and confidential survey tool, Survey Monkey. We disseminated the survey through the electronic mailing lists of three of the primary communication modes for reaching expatriate Christians in Cambodia.[10]

We received 100 responses to the survey. Of those, 11 surveys were not valid and were discarded. An additional 7 were from respondents who were not Christians; these surveys were disregarded because this subgroup was too small for its answers to be compared with the Christian subgroup.

How Are We Doing Ourselves?

The remaining 82 responses were analyzed and help us to see a picture of how Christian expatriate men in Cambodia are doing in response to sexual temptation.

Results about Pornography

The questionnaire asked the following questions about attitudes towards and use of pornography:

- What is your view of porn?
- How often do you view porn?

Attitudes towards pornography were widely disapproving as almost 93% thought it was always negative. Only 6% replied that it may be acceptable for relieving tension and one respondent saw it as something positive.

Nevertheless, even though an overwhelming majority (93%) disapproved of pornography, only a minority (45%) said they totally abstained from it. Viewed

---

[9] We acknowledge the negative connotations that the term "sex addiction" has, particularly among Christians, as a shaming label, an imprecise and arbitrary term, an absolver of responsibility, a rationalization of a spiritual problem, and a label denying grace. While we appreciate these objections, we consider the term useful in exploring unwanted sexual behavior.

[10] ICF InfoFlow (the International Christian Fellowship's website used by a wide range of Christians to access advertisements on jobs, trainings, events, goods and services), Men's Prayer Breakfast (which many Christian men in Cambodia are recipients of) and Chab Dai (which includes leaders of 52 faith-based NGOs in Cambodia working on the issues of trafficking).

another way, this means that more than half of the respondents *did* view pornography. About 1 in 3 (33%) acknowledged occasional indulgence and 19% viewed it on a regular basis. Even among those who have a categorical negative attitude toward pornography, about 16% still regularly viewed it.

The persistence and the frequency of this dissonance suggest that the coping strategies of more than half of the Christian expatriate men who responded have been ineffective. It is possible that they are trapped in the dynamic that Patrick Carnes calls the "Addiction Cycle."[11]

Results about Prostitution

The questionnaire also asked the following questions about attitudes towards and use of prostitution:

- What is your view on prostitution?
- Why do you think men use prostitutes?
- Have you had a "traditional massage" where the masseur touched you sexually?
- How did you respond when you were touched?
- Do you feel that "erotic massage" is the same as prostitution?
- Have you ever had sexual intercourse with a prostitute?

When asked about whether they approved or disapproved of prostitution, 85% of respondents reported disapproval, 6% neutral and 1% were positive (7% did not respond). Somewhat surprisingly, the percentage that reported disapproval of prostitution (85%) was slightly lower than the percentage that reported disapproval of pornography (93%).

As well, only 50% of the respondents thought that prostitution and erotic massage were equivalent; 20% saw them as categorically different, 19% said it depended, and 30% (24 respondents) gave no answer.

When asked whether they had ever had actual intercourse with a prostitute, 1 in 10 respondents answered "Yes" (15% did not give an answer). Exactly the same number of respondents acknowledged visiting a masseur for erotic purposes.

We also asked respondents if during a "traditional" massage (not intended to involve sexual services), the masseur had ever touched them sexually. Of the 72 participants who responded to this question more than 1 in 3 (36%) had been touched sexually during the massage. Of those 26 respondents, only 8 told the masseur to stop. The majority ignored it (12 respondents) and 6 respondents even encouraged it.

---

[11] Patrick Carnes, *Facing the Shadow* (Carefree: Gentle Path Press, 2005), 2-29. Briefly, the "Addiction Cycle" is a pattern in which one tries to avoid the unwanted behavior by willpower, followed by temptation, leading to fantasizing, then to "playing around the edges" and finally resulting in acting out. This is followed by feelings of shame and despair, which eventually gives way to new internal promises to not do it again.

Results about Sex Addiction

Finally, we asked respondents questions about sex addiction, based on the PATHOS screening test[12] that comprises these questions:

- Preoccupied: Do you often find yourself preoccupied with sexual thoughts?
- Ashamed: Do you hide some of your sexual behavior from others?
- Treatment: Have you ever sought therapy for sexual behavior you did not like?
- Hurt others: Has anyone been hurt emotionally because of your behavior?
- Out of control: Do you feel controlled by your sexual desire?
- Sad: When you have sex, do you feel depressed afterwards?

We embedded five of the six PATHOS questions in our survey. One question: "Has anyone close to you been harmed emotionally by your sexual behavior?" was inadvertently omitted from the questionnaire.

Overall, 56% of respondents reported that they were preoccupied by sexual thoughts, 53% reported hiding some of their sexual behavior from others, 49% felt depressed or discouraged about some aspect of their sexual behavior and 22% have felt controlled by their sexual desire. Yet only 19% of respondents have ever sought counseling/therapy for sexual behavior they did not like.

According the PATHOS screening test, a "yes" to any 2 questions indicates a possible sex addiction and a "yes" to 3 or more indicates sex addiction. Of the respondents in our study, 35% answered "yes" to 3 or more questions. Another 22% answered "yes" to 2 or more questions. This means that sex addiction is indicated in more than 1 out of 3 of the Christian expatriate men who responded to our survey, and more than 1 in 4 of them show indicators of possible sex addiction.

These results are somewhat lower than most surveys of the Christian population conducted in the United States. However, the accidental omission of one of the PATHOS questions undoubtedly produced a lower percentage than would otherwise have occurred. Although we cannot pinpoint the level of sex addiction in this survey, based on prevalence probability calculations for three alternative scenarios we believe that the percentage would be somewhere between 45% and 65% indicating sex addiction, with the sexual behavior of another 25-30% also of some concern.[13]

---

[12] Patrick J. Carnes, et al., "PATHOS: A Brief Screening Application for Assessing Sexual Addiction," *Journal of Addiction Medicine* 6, no. 1 (2012): 32-34.

[13] Please refer to the actual study for an explanation of the methodology. Kenneth R. Taylor and Glenn Miles, "Survey of Expatriate Christian Men Living in Cambodia Regarding Views and Practices of Pornography, Erotic Massage, and Prostitution," *Social Work & Christianity: An International Journal,* forthcoming.

Conclusions of the Study

These results indicate that in spite of their belief that pornography, prostitution and erotic massage constitute sexual immorality that the Bible heeds them to avoid, a significant percentage of Christian expatriate men in Cambodia truly struggle with sexual integrity.[14] Many even find themselves trapped in the cycle of sex addiction.

This of course has many negative effects on the men, their families and their work or ministry. But many conceal their struggle due to awareness of the dissonance between what they believe and what they do, their tendency towards being socialized to avoid discussing sexual topics, and the shame or fear of judgment they may experience when they do fall into sin. This only reinforces the development of an unhealthy, addictive cycle and possibly even sex addiction.

It matters, then, to know whether the strategies these men have found to cope with this struggle suffice or whether they are in dire need of external help.

What Can We Do about the Sexual Behavior of Expatriate Christian Men?

When asked about possible solutions, 65% of respondents felt that the church should directly address pornography and prostitution among its members. The two leading specific recommendations were:

- Provide counseling and support groups for at-risk individuals (52%), and
- Have more frank sermons and discussions about sexuality in church (40%).

When asked to expand, respondents suggested programs addressing the problem more directly, such as professional counseling, positive non-shaming support groups, forums for open discussions on sexual realities, good books and literature, and strong mentoring and discipleship relationships. Accountability groups, on the other hand, were heavily criticized on the grounds that they are not always safe because they may be judgmental, shaming or non confidential. They were also said to often be superficial, vague and to drift toward irrelevance and finally to extinction. Others stated that it

---

[14]One limit of this study is that it was not able to distinguish men who are working in anti-trafficking from those not in this field. It might have been helpful to learn whether expatriate Christians who are partly or fully involved in anti-trafficking ministry also experience this dissonance, whether they perceive this as affecting their field work, and whether they would be willing to seek and/or offer support towards attaining sexual integrity. However, given the limited size of the subgroup, such differentiation would have compromised the confidential nature of the answers given and therefore reduced respondent openness. Future research on this issue with a focus on Christians in anti-trafficking could both strengthen field work and provide an opportunity to brainstorm on appropriate, feasible solutions tailored to the needs of both expatriate Christians and those at home.

might be preferable to have support groups that are not oriented on a single issue.

Coping Strategies Used by Christian Men

A recent Barna study showed that a majority of Christians, as opposed to non-Christians, actually do try to resist temptations. The strategies included praying and asking God for strength (18%), using reason to weigh the options (12%), choosing to just say "no" (10%), and avoiding tempting situations altogether (10%).[15] However, both this study and the previously mentioned 2001 *Christianity Today* survey found that responses were mostly individualistic and that mechanisms of accountability were rarely used.[16]

There is a consensus among practitioners (and our respondents largely agreed) that support outside the individual is a good idea. However, in our sample, only a minority were inclined to seek it. Of the men who meet the criteria for sex addiction, only 34% were interested in help outside themselves. Of the categories acknowledging one or two indicators, only 20% would utilize a support group. Presumably, this means they are currently depending on prayer, Bible study, willpower, and possibly one-on-one accountability.

Obstacles to Solutions

We have identified four main obstacles that may prevent Christian men struggling with sexual integrity from seeking external help.

1. Resistance To Support Groups. According to research[17] the most commonly stated reasons for not attending a support group are:
- Their emphasis on spirituality and religion,
- The underlying concept of powerlessness versus the culture's emphasis on self-reliance,
- The idea that groups are only for people whose addiction is worse than one's own,
- Their focus on negative aspects of behavior rather than on growth orientation,
- Fear of becoming dependent on the group,
- Fear of receiving bad advice from group members,
- Doubts regarding the groups' effectiveness, and
- Personal aversion to "opening up" to strangers.

Among Christians, we have frequently heard the following reasons given:
- Lack of specification of Jesus Christ as the higher power,

---

[15] Barna Group, "New Research Explores the Changing Shape of Temptation" (January 4, 2013).

[16] Christianity Today, "The Leadership Survey on Pastors and Internet Pornography."

[17] Alexandre B. Laudet, "Attitudes and Beliefs About 12-Step Groups Among Addiction Treatment Clients and Clinicians: Toward Identifying Obstacles to Participation," *Substance Use Misuse* 38, no. 14 (2003): 2017-47.

- The sufficiency of Scripture in dealing with chronic sin, and
- The impacts on one's faith of being subjected to labeling as an addict.

2. The Tendency To Conceal Personal Weaknesses. The results of our survey revealed that several respondents thought that support groups would be good for others, but not for themselves. A telling anecdote is that while some respondents stated that they would utilize either therapy or group support, only one has contacted the follow-up resource provided at the end of the questionnaire. Furthermore, according to our survey less than 20% of respondents have ever sought counseling or therapy for their unwanted sexual behavior.

3. Lack of Change Readiness. Respondents must first be ready to change. Alexandre Laudet explains that the path toward change readiness "involves a fairly long initial stage in which denial about addiction needs to be broken down. Individuals who do not believe they have a problem or who believe that their problem is not severe enough to require help are unlikely to engage in support.... Denial of a problem or of a problem's severity is a major barrier to seeking and obtaining help."[18]

4. Treatment Dogma. Finally, many pastors are reluctant to preach on sexual temptation and misconduct or do so in such a way that they appear insensitive to the real-life anguish that people face. This is especially true of those who sit in church who struggle with same-sex attraction. Without realizing it, pastors often convey the message that sexual misconduct is in a special shame category that should only be referred to in vague terms. All of this discomfort has the effect of deterring congregants from engaging in honest dialogue, either in a group or in one-to-one relationships.

Perhaps the biggest divide in the Christian community is the holistic versus exclusively spiritual approach to healing. Whereas, in recent years, more and more Christian pastors and leaders are accepting the idea that there may be more to the story as to why a particular believer struggles with sexual misconduct than simply that he/she is spiritually deficient, there remains a great many who prescribe exclusively spiritual remedies.

It should be clear to the reader that the authors of this study believe that spiritual recommendations such as Bible study and memorization, prayer, contemplation, discipleship, and regular fellowship with other believers are all very positive and healthy practices. However, we have come to view humans as body, soul, mind and spirit, with the implication that practitioners of other disciplines may also have important insights about and contributions to soul healing. Of particular note in the area of addictions are the remarkable discoveries involving the brain's function, both in the genesis of addiction and in its treatment. As Daniel Amen, a brain researcher and Christian, has said: "Living with a healthy brain gives people the opportunity to be and act healthy; living with a damaged brain often leads to great struggle."[19]

---

[18] Laudet, "Attitudes and Beliefs About 12-Step Groups", 2028.

[19] Daniel G. Amen, *Healing the Hardware of the Soul: How Making the Brain-Soul Connection Can Optimize Your Life, Love, and Spiritual Growth* (New York: Free Press, 2002), 16.

Recommendations for Church and Missions Leaders

Church leaders and mission leaders must see the results of this survey and its implications as a serious issue. Following are some recommendations for how they along with Christian social workers can help support Christian expatriate men to avoid sexual misconduct:

- Provide training that adopts a Biblical approach to the prevention of sexual misconduct. This training should be provided to expatriate Christian men, preferably beginning when they first arrive on the field. Such training can take place through men's support groups that also discuss sexual issues. Similar programs should be developed in other contexts.

- Appreciate that different men require different approaches, but also appreciate the value that many have found in support programs while considering how to tailor services.

- Encourage leaders of Christian organizations abroad to take this issue seriously, but in a preventive rather than punitive manner. Help should be sought from professional counselors and experienced leaders early in crisis management situations when one of its members is found to have violated standards of appropriate sexual behavior. From these consulting relationships, better guidelines may be developed as to appropriate response protocols.

- Include questions in application forms and orientation packages for new workers about previous emotional and sexual histories that may require further consideration before acceptance, depending on the resources available on the field and the extent of the problem.

- Install Covenant Eyes or similar accountability software onto all computers, laptops and smart phones supplied by Christian organizations to their staff so as to reduce access to pornography. This also implies that staff be notified and requires their full collaboration.

- Provide a list of "safe" massage establishments and guidelines to minimize the risks in utilizing these services, such as always being accompanied by a spouse or, if unmarried, by an accountability partner.

- Provide general accountability guidelines that not only help "avoid the appearance of evil" but that also help keep men safe in practical ways. Consideration can be given about what standards to set with regard to being alone with a person of the opposite sex, etc. But at a minimum, ministries that work with prostituted and sexually exploited people should have strict prohibitions against both male and female staff doing outreach alone. Organizations should also have "protection policies" that protect children and adult beneficiaries from harm and that prevent the staff and organization from actual and alleged misbehavior.

Conclusion

Research reveals a dissonance among expatriate Christian men working in missions and development NGOs in Cambodia between their stated views and their actual practices on the issue of sexual misconduct. While there was almost universal disapproval of pornography (93%), less than half of the respondents totally abstained from viewing it (46%). Instead, about 1 in 3 indulged occasionally and about 20% did so on some regular basis. Similarly, while 85% of respondents disapproved of prostitution, just over 1 in 10 have in fact had intercourse with a prostitute, and 1 in 10 respondents have visited a masseur for erotic purposes. Roughly half have hid some of their sexual behavior from others (53%) or felt depressed or discouraged about some aspect of their sexual behavior (49%).

A significant portion of expatriate Christian men are also affected by sex addiction. At a minimum, sexual addiction was indicated in more than 1 out of 3 respondents, and possible sex addiction was indicated in more than 1 in 4. However, these results are projected to be much higher were respondents to be asked all six of the questions used to screen for sex addiction.

These troubling results suggest that individualistic, exclusively Bible-centered coping strategies may not suffice to prevent undesired behavior. Given the prevailing view among counseling practitioners and researchers that seeking external help is effective, especially in the early stages, we strongly recommend the establishment of support services through churches and Christian organizations with the active participation of professional counselors who adopt a holistic approach.

The oft-quoted phrase, "physician, heal thyself"[20] is a word to the wise, derived from Jesus' injunction to "take the plank out of [our] own eye"[21] as we are in the business of trying to help others. Addressing this issue "with gentleness and respect, keeping a clear conscience" is of the utmost importance as the expatriate Christian community's presence in Cambodia is motivated by a desire to share "the hope that [it has]."[22]

Discussion Questions

1. In your own organization/church how do you encourage transparency and accountability among men?
2. If you are a man working to address sexual exploitation, which other man/men do you feel comfortable to open up to and how do you keep the focus on sexual issues?
3. If you are a woman, how can you support men in your organization and church to be accountable without creating inappropriate guilt and shame?

---

[20] Luke 4:23 (KJV).
[21] Matthew 7:5 (NIV).
[22] 1 Peter 3:15-16 (NIV).

PART 4

HOW CAN WE BETTER WORK WITH BOYS AND MEN?

Introduction, by Glenn Miles
and Christa Foster Crawford

In Cambodia there is an old proverb that says: "Girls are like a piece of white linen. If they are dropped in the mud they are stained forever." By contrast boys are depicted as a piece of gold: "If they are dropped in the mud then they are easily washed clean." Whilst this appears to give a positive view of boys, it is actually negative because it implies that if boys are abused/exploited then they should easily be able to recover. This differential of the perceptions of boys and girls are common around the world. Boys are often depicted as tough and resilient. Girls are depicted as weak and vulnerable. Of course, the truth is girls can be and are resilient and boys can be and are vulnerable.

These misperceptions about male vulnerability have impacted the anti-trafficking movement. From popular depictions in the media to *de facto* policies of police and other government agencies tasked with fighting trafficking, gender seems to be the defining factor, not exploitation: Young girls are victims, young boys go unnoticed; adult women can sometimes be victims, but teenage boys and grown men almost never are. We need to recognize and address our hidden misperceptions in order to be able to make visible the vulnerabilities and needs of boys and men who are sexually exploited and trafficked and begin to respond to them.

For some Christians, the reason they have been slow to respond is the concern of being seen as "pro-gay" by reaching out to men who have sex with men (MSM). Despite the fact that many males in prostitution do not in fact self-identify as gay, this remains a barrier for some ministries to get involved, and for some donors to support needed efforts to protect vulnerable people. Recently, a friend who works with exploited sexual minorities was asked by a potential faith-based donor about their position on gay marriage. The friend was understandably exasperated that their funding could be affected by their opinion on something that had nothing at all to do with what they were doing. Humility and listening are skills we all need to aspire to at whatever level we are working in the abolition movement.

How then can we better work with boys and men? This chapter explores six key questions:

- Why do we focus more on girls than boys?
- What are the unique challenges of working with boys and young men and how can we effectively meet their needs?
- How can we effectively work with boys and men in a non-judgmental and supportive way?
- How should Christians and the church engage with boys and men?
- How do we deal with being considered "pro-gay" for working with men involved in commercial sex and being considered "anti-gay" because of our faith?

- Should Christians and the church work with the LGBT community and if so how?

First, **Alastair Hilton** discusses some of the reasons why the focus has been more on girls. Despite evidence that boys do indeed experience sexual abuse and exploitation with serious consequences, it challenges the very premises of "our collective understandings of sexual violence – that men and boys are the victimizers and women and girls are the victims." Social mythologies, shame and reluctance to report abuse, constricting expectations of masculinity, and the failure of social and legal services are all reasons why we have failed to focus on men and boys as we should. Hilton then describes steps we can take towards positive change, including examining our own unhelpful beliefs and assumptions. Finally, he contends that recognizing the vulnerabilities of males "does not detract from the experiences of women and girls but rather improves our understanding of how power and control has the potential to be abused in all settings."

Doug Van Ramshorst then illustrates the dynamics of why we focus on girls from the first essay with humorous depictions of just how challenging it is for us to see that men can also be in need, and just how difficult it is for many people to understand why anyone would even want to reach out to men in prostitution. Yet Van Ramshorst also gives us a sober reminder that the forces of harm that threaten females in prostitution are the same ones that menace males as well, and when we fail to see the possibility of men as victims their voices will be silenced from calling out for the help they need and they will be marginalized from even the limited assistance that is available.

Second, **Alexandra Russell** discusses the challenges faced when we do recognize the vulnerability of boys and men and attempt to reach out to them. She describes five key problematic issues her organization encounters in providing services: family and cultural obligation, limited education, gender stereotypes, personal self-worth, and homelessness. She also shares how they have tried to navigate these challenges to more effectively meet the needs of the boys in their care. She concludes with a story of success in the life of one of the young men they have served, but also a warning that our failure to address the above challenges threatens the ability of the people in our care to continue to succeed.

Third, in answer to how we can work with males in a non-judgmental and supportive way, **Alastair Hilton** describes the importance of being honest with ourselves and facing the prejudices that we often hold. This kind of reflection can be done individually or in a group. He reminds us that listening to the boys and men themselves is vital if we are to understand their world. He suggests that we need to recognize that boys are vulnerable but also endorse their resilience in spite of what has happened to them. Creating a network of supportive people will facilitate healing as will trying to understand the cultural and contextual factors that led to the abuse in the first place. Hilton also stresses the importance of finding out from the boys themselves what they say they need for recovery to take place. Finally, he makes recommendations for good practice and shares lessons learned from a variety of settings, including England, Cambodia, Hong Kong and the United States.

Jonathan Hancock gives additional practical advice for how we can overcome the barriers that keep us from working with men in prostitution in a compassionate and non-judgmental way, beginning with picturing them as members of our own family and imagining that we are helping Jesus when we are helping them. He also encourages us to learn about their needs through studying the issues and listening to their stories. Finally, Hancock reminds us to pray for wisdom for how to respond and for our own hearts to be able to reflect the heart of God.

The fourth question, how we should engage with boys and men, is addressed through practical advice and a case study. **Doug Van Ramshorst** recommends starting small and being consistent, which builds trust. He maintains that listening is key to understanding and meeting their needs. **Jane Beal** advises us to have compassion and empathy, to understand holistic needs, and to provide mentorship, modeling and accountability. As well, the church must be authentic and transparent in order to be a place where broken people can come for help. Finally, **Derek Collard** describes how he was personally called to do something about reaching out to men who sell sex in massage parlors in Cambodia. He also shares stories of how one ministry has been able to care for these men by asking them what their needs are and then providing training and other resources to help meet those needs.

The next two pieces address the question of how we deal with being considered "pro-gay" for working with men involved in commercial sex and being considered "anti-gay" because of our faith. To begin, **Wendy Gritter** takes on the challenges of working in an environment where there appears to be polarization of the so-called "gay agenda." Once again we are reminded to listen to each other and learn to be respectful of opinions that may be different from our own cultural norms. Not surprisingly, perspectives inside and outside the faith-based community differ, so people of faith come to divergent perspectives on the question of what faithful discipleship for a gender or sexual minority looks like. Gritter suggests that "acknowledging this diversity does not mean that one must consider all views equally valid," however, it does require what she describes as "a posture of humility."

Next, **Paul Goodell** provides us with a case study that demonstrates how one Christian organization working with MSM has been able to affirm an orthodox Christian stance on sexuality while still maintaining a positive relationship with the local LGBT community. The key they discovered is love. Goodell explains: "Positions and points of view can be argued with, but genuinely loving actions committed consistently over many years cannot be."

Finally, **Carl Jylland-Halverson** addresses the question of whether Christians and the church should work with the LGBT community. While Christians should not compromise their values when working with others, Jylland-Halverson warns that "Christians ministering to people who are at risk of human trafficking limit their own entry into communities of people who need their help when they exclude members of the LGBT community from assisting in these efforts." He then shares ways in which Christians and the church can work with the LGBT community in caring for MSM. Like previous contributors, Jylland-Halverson recommends respect and humility. He also encourages bridge building – choosing consciously to find commonality between Christian and LGBT communities – and provides some principles for effective partnership. He illustrates how this has been done effectively with two case studies of working across perceived barriers in the very different contexts of Chicago and Mumbai.

CHAPTER 20
WHY DO WE FOCUS MORE ON GIRLS THAN BOYS?

Key Issues, by Alastair Hilton

As our knowledge of the sexual abuse and exploitation of children and young people grows, so we become more aware of the significant gaps in knowledge and resources that restrict our efforts to prevent, protect and provide sensitive services for *all* victims and survivors. In recent years – locally and globally – activists, practitioners, academics and policy makers have paid increasing attention to the issue of the sexual abuse, exploitation and rape of boys and men.

Wherever this occurs, whatever the identity of the abusers, relating to familial child abuse, sexual exploitation or situations where men and boys are raped as a weapon of war (such as those reported in conflict zones such as the Congo) it largely remains a taboo subject shrouded in secrecy.

Its existence challenges the basic premises and foundations of thought that have formed the backbone of our collective understandings of sexual violence – that men and boys are the victimizers and women and girls are the victims, sometimes described as the "feminization of victimization." This dynamic contributes significantly to rendering male survivors silent and restricts the ability of potential helpers to recognize the issue and respond appropriately.

The Evidence about Male Abuse and Exploitation

Increasing global research suggests that the sexual abuse of boys can no longer be denied and points out the long-term consequences of its occurrence. A 2002 World Health Organization report on violence and health observes that although acts of sexual violence are experienced predominantly by women and girls, the rape of boys and men by men is a significant problem in a variety of settings, as is the coercion of young men into sex by older women.[1] Additionally, the first *Study on Global Violence* by the United Nations estimated that some 150 million girls (14 percent) and 70 million boys (7 percent) are sexually abused each year around the world. The report also cites a study of mainly developed countries showing that 36 percent of women and 29 percent of men in the sample group reported sexual abuse in childhood.[2]

Lifetime impacts of abuse are similar to those experienced by women and girls, including post-traumatic stress disorder, depression, low self-esteem,

---

[1] World Health Organization, *World Report on Violence and Health* (Geneva: WHO, 2002).

[2] Paulo Sergio Pinhiero, *United Nations Study on Global Violence* (Geneva: United Nations, 2006).

relationship difficulties, suicide attempts and alcohol and drug misuse. Non-consensual sex involving young people in developing countries is an important yet under-researched subject with considerable public health implications;[3] growing evidence indicates that it also plays a significant role in the spread of the HIV/AIDS pandemic.[4]

One of the most insightful contributions to this issue was provided by the International Save the Children Alliance based on reports from thirteen countries in the Americas, Asia, Africa and Europe.[5] It is one of the few studies available that details abuse issues in relation to both girls *and* boys, providing stark evidence of the reality of child sexual abuse in the twenty-first century. These and other studies reveal what survivors, many activists and some practitioners have known for a long time – that the sexual abuse of boys and men is a significant problem but also one that is largely hidden and misunderstood, resulting in poor service provision and inadequate responses at individual, family, community, organizational and societal levels.

So Why Do We Focus More on Girls Than Boys?

Despite increasing awareness, what we do know about the sexual abuse of boys is still fairly limited, leading to poor planning, training, responses and coordination of services in both developed and developing nations. As one Cambodian boy fortunate enough to survive a long period of abuse and exploitation remarked: "We males are like females; we have pain and shame, so why do people treat us like this? Being born as a male is very difficult…when you have problems, no one helps…why do they help only girls?"

Until recently the prevalence, dynamics and effects of sexual abuse of boys have been largely concealed from social consciousness. This concealment is enforced by perpetrators, but it also exists at every level of society through social and cultural mythologies that act as barriers to disclosure and effectively collude with the abusers to ensure silence. Boys are often compared to girls and suffer in that comparison. These social mythologies guide and inform social responses, or lack thereof, to the sexual abuse of males; they support the claims and counter claims of perpetrators and often become an internalized part of the child's identity.[6]

---

[3] Shireen J. Jejeebhoy et al., "Non-Consensual Sexual Experiences of Young People in Developing Countries: An Overview," in *Sex without Consent: Young People in Developing Countries,* ed. Shireen J. Jejeebhoy et al. (London-New York: Zed Books, 2005).
[4] World Health Organization, *World Report on Violence and Health.*
[5] Save the Children Norway, *10 Essential Learning Points: Listen and Speak Out against Sexual Abuse of Girls and Boys* (Save the Children Norway, 2005).
[5] Matthew Parynik Mendel, *The Male Survivor: The Impact of Sexual Abuse* (Thousand Oaks: Sage Publications, 1995).
[6] Josef Spiegel, *Sexual Abuse of Males: The SAM Model of Theory and Practice* (New York: Brunner-Routledge, 2003).

There are no simple explanations, but certainly, boys' reluctance to report abuse and a failure of society to recognize and respond contributes significantly. Whilst the prevalence of all forms of abuse of boys is far higher than we care to recognize, statistics do little to reflect either the extent of the problem or the difficulties boys face in disclosing sexual abuse, often with tragic consequences. Other numerous studies confirm a tendency towards under reporting about and by male survivors.[7]

For individual boys, factors inhibiting reporting include powerful social and cultural definitions and expectations of masculinity, namely: the male ethic of self-reliance, notions of youthful sexuality (where sexual assault is often perceived as a "rite of passage"), and if they do report, more freedom to lose compared to girls. The stigma and shame of abuse, implications for perceptions of a boy's sexuality being questioned, and negative social responses combine with other factors to render most boys silent. Experience and anecdotal accounts also reveal that fear of the consequences of disclosure as well as not knowing who is safe to tell contribute significantly.

Research exploring social responses towards abused boys in many settings reveals that they are far less likely to be believed and that the severity of abuse is often minimized, whilst legal services are less likely to follow up prosecutions where boys are concerned. Boys are also less likely to be offered counseling support and when they are, duration is shorter.[8]

In essence even if we do recognize the abuse of males, we struggle to know how to help. Professionals also express feeling as isolated as the boys they are trying to support – for many, quality training, support and consultation are nonexistent. The same patterns are repeated within families where parents and siblings also struggle to believe, understand and support; consequently boys are often blamed for their abuse. Assumptions about the sexual abuse of boys being a "homosexual" problem (and not one of abuse) also casts its shadow across the issue.

Effects are minimized across cultures where parents and caregivers focus more attention on girls but also seem to be less concerned for boys.[9] For some this may be related to the manifestation of strong beliefs in the notion of and loss of virginity, honor and reputation in relation to girls. As in most cultures, what is often applied to one gender is denied to the other. Whilst this view is often unhelpful to girls, resulting in discrimination and lack of consideration of their needs, it excludes boys from the equation altogether. They become an "invisible population."

There also exists little understanding of the developmental and behavioral differences between girls and boys prior to and following abuse, and those boys externalizing their pain are often seen as problematic, bad, and in need of punishment rather than empathy and support.

---

[7] See, for example, Josef Spiegel, *Sexual Abuse of Males.*

[8] See, for example, Mike Lew, *Victims No Longer*, 2nd ed. (New York: Quill/Harper Collins, 2004) and Adrienne Crowder, *Opening the Door* (New York: Brunner Mazel, 1995).

[9] Josef Spiegel, *Sexual Abuse of Males.*

Society's response to the abuse of boys is also caught up in what we understand by masculinity. Boys are trapped in a media-maintained male stereotype and are expected to be self-reliant, devoid of fear, power-seeking and controlled. Toughness is the price they pay for being male. In various cultures these core messages are manifested in different ways. For example, in Cambodia a well-known song carries the message that it is "better to bleed than cry." Whatever your cultural background, I am certain this is something we can all relate to. At every turn throughout childhood, both male and female children are programmed to live up to expectations that limit their possibilities of expression, which can be harmful for both genders.

In developed countries, dramatic social changes – manifest in the restructuring of the family, shifting employment patterns and the achievements of women – have had little significant impact on the behavior of men and how they behave as role models. Boys still grow up believing that they will be "king of the castle" and that expressing their vulnerability is taboo. The men they see around them are not radically different to the men their fathers would have seen. They still expect to hold authority in the family, they still expect to be the main breadwinners, and they still do little housework and spend far less time with their children than their wives do.

Faced with traditional expectations of being a man, it is no small wonder boys are virtually silent when it comes to disclosing even minor forms of abuse. Symptoms like depression, aggressive acting out, an inability to trust and low self-esteem – together with the developmental delays experienced by most abused children – are familiar to many practitioners working with girls and boys, though less is known or understood about the particular impact on boys.

Taking Steps towards Positive Change

In any setting, whatever the specific cultural and social influences, if we are serious about addressing the issue of sexual abuse and exploitation of boys it is essential to critically explore the issue utilizing an inclusive ecological framework of analysis, one that begins by exploring our individual and collective beliefs and perspectives related to the sexual abuse and exploitation of boys.

In order to facilitate change we need to consider the origins of these ideas and how they are manifested within and across relationships and domains – for individuals, families and communities, within and across cultures. What are these core beliefs? Are they accurate and helpful, or based on social mythologies resulting in discrimination and silence? How are they maintained and what influence do they have on our personal and professional lives? If we extend this analysis to organizational and social responses and policies, we begin to see that solutions may require a radical rethink.

We also need to apply this analysis to our ideas about boys, men, masculinity and sexuality, as well as to our views of childhood and children, and the differences we perceive in relation to male and female identity. Consideration of what constitutes power and consent within relationships can also inform and enable a greater understanding of boys' abuse. This can help us to both understand the problems and begin considering the required solutions.

Reflection has to take place on how these ideas in turn influence, and/or are influenced by, academic thinking (and consequently the development of organizational, donor, and social and welfare policies) that reveal and enable – or continue to hamper and hide – the issue of boys' abuse. The relationship is complex; it is not always linear or easy to unravel and make sense of. It requires us to retain openness to new ideas and to embrace the realities of the world in which we live.

Whilst acknowledging that responses to and services for women and girls are far from adequate in many settings, one may ask how is it possible that the progress and achievements for women and girls have left men and boys largely excluded? In my experience, in many cases it is unfortunate to observe that in relation to social, welfare, NGO and donor policies, the term "gender" has morphed into something meaning "women's issues" alone, with the effect of largely excluding men and boys.

We know where we stand with that. Women are the oppressed; men the oppressors and abusers. Support for "women and children" has therefore in many settings come to mean women and girls, as numerous influential reports almost completely ignore the victimization of males. They fail to take into account the fact that although men abuse women and girls they also abuse boys and other men. As well, the sexual abuse of children by women is another area needing greater exploration. Where children are concerned, what many current "gender perspectives" fail to take into account (despite good intentions) is that *all* children have less power than all adults, irrespective of their gender. Such perspectives are divisive and discriminatory.

An alternative is to consider that the acceptance that boys and men can be and are abused in fact seeks to enhance and strengthen so-called "gender perspectives," not betray or dismantle them. Recognition of the abuse of boys and men does not detract from the experiences of women and girls but rather improves our understanding of how power and control has the potential to be abused in all settings. Any perspectives that effectively deny or minimize the existence of oppression and abuse of *any* group or individual need to embrace new realities and change.

Obviously greater recognition of the abuse of boys will have profound resource implications, but it is vital they do not remain neglected or considered as competition for existing and scarce resources. Until adequate, appropriate, effective and sensitive services are provided for all, boys will continue to be overlooked as victims of sexual abuse and exploitation. Only when more men and boys are empowered and enabled to speak out and risk the stigmatization that female survivors have experienced for centuries, and only we listen to the reality of their lives, will we begin to challenge the myths, secrecy and homophobic attitudes that surround the suffering that belies boy's silences.

In conclusion, let us consider the crucial question: "How would things be different if we acknowledged male victims?" Psychologist Frederick Mathews' excellent research explains the importance of beginning with us as adults:

We would recognize that regardless of our own theoretical starting points male victims have their own voice, their own meanings for their experiences; if we remain ignorant of, overlook, or fail to explore their stories, we will miss much of what we need to engage them in therapy and healing....

We would recognize that solving the complex problem of violence in society will never be achieved until *all* the stories and voices of victims of violence are heard... until men and women of goodwill begin to work side by side, and until the means of our collective struggle toward peace reflect respect, compassion and inclusion as our minimum standard....

Perhaps the greatest responsibility for the plight of boys and young men lies with adults. *We* are the ones who conduct single gender and biased research. *We* are the ones who present to the media more political opinions about male victimization than provide objective, empirically based information. *We* are the ones who help maintain biased stereotypes about boys and men and keep them trapped in their silence. *We* are the ones who help reinforce in the public mind an image of strong and resilient male victims who are, in truth, human beings suffering in much pain, isolation and loneliness....

It is up to us to speak against abuse and injustice, and for compassion and inclusion... we cannot pretend to be a community in search of justice whilst tolerating a double standard, allowing a divisive discourse around violence and abuse, leaving male victims outside our compassion and caring concern.

Eventually all victims, male and female will see our hypocrisy. If we do not speak for all children, male or female, then we ultimately speak for none.[10]

Key Issues, by Doug Van Ramshorst

In the shadows, behind a line-of-sight-obscuring pile of rocks we see a mustachioed man in black, frustrated, untangling a mass of knotty ropes. A dame saunters closer and closer to the aforementioned pile of rocks. The mustachioed man looks up from his readied rope with a sneer. He is covered in sweat. A crippled cigarette elevates to a forty-five degree angle as he rubs his gloved hands together, smiling a toothy smirk, exhaling a smoky cloud of pure evil.

He leaps, she screams. She slaps, he laughs. He throws her over his shoulder; she beats his back and kicks her legs. The villain struggles to get his ensnared beauty to the tracks. Throwing her down between the rails, he puts his limited knowledge of knot making to work. As the steam whistle blows, the scoundrel stands erect, twists his mustache into two perfect, bullhorn points, lets out a dastardly cackle, covers the lower half of his face with his cloak and makes a hasty retreat into the brush.

The damsel squirms and screams. She sees the plumes of smoke exploding from the locomotive, barreling closer and closer to her, but the ropes are just too tight. The whistle becomes a constant shriek. The ground quakes with the force, as twenty thousand tons of machinery grow uncomfortably close.

---

[10] Frederick Mathews, "Implications," in *A View From Inside The Box III: "Invisible Boys"* (Survivors West Yorkshire, 2009) 53.

At the last moment, a silver streak cuts the blue sky in twain. A glowing silhouette of masculinity touches down just inches from the dame. As the halo-esque glow dissipates, our hero's clean-cut, strong jaw line widens to reveal the world's most perfect smile. She faints. The hero works with great speed to loosen the maiden's limbs and torso. Not a drop of perspiration travels from his well-groomed pompadour to his brow. Not a speck of dirt or coal dust sullies his white spandex/lycra poly blend jumpsuit. In seconds she is free. He cradles her limp body like Michelangelo's Pietà and leaps into the air, completely free of gravitational limitations, just as the locomotive passes, cutting the ropes into pieces.

So… what the heck does this have to do with our civilization's overwhelmingly uneven focus on female victims of sexual exploitation as opposed to the boys and men that fall victim to the same devious acts? Simply put, I believe we use an antiquated and oversimplified paradigm to view this very complicated issue.

The victim in this trite story is the stereotypical damsel in distress. I could have used any number of damsels in any number of distressing situations. Any Disney film where the female lead needs the help of some handsome prince, every Mario Brothers game, in which the princess is always *frustratingly* in another castle, any sitcom featuring a smarmy husband and a simple, but pretty wife – all reinforce the idea that women need rescuing. All of these antiquated gender-role-strengthening stories pile up in our minds and manifest themselves in our behavior.

As our lives have unfolded, we have taken a variety of strange turns and ended up in ministries serving women and men involved in sexual exploitation. *Good for us.* Unfortunately we have brought with us the pattern of *men rescuing and women needing to be rescued.* I am aware that practitioners are primarily women in the field within which we work, but our culture is masculine and societal influences seep into the ways we work and the motivations we have for doing said work.

How many times have you brought up your work with an individual only to be greeted with a "Pretty Woman" reference? How many times have you seen a person's interest dwindle when you mention that maybe the work we do isn't as easy as swooping into the rough neighborhoods our clients are from, taking them shopping, giving them a few elocution pointers and welcoming them into their new lives?

Now imagine how that conversation would go if you worked with men. At Emmaus, we work exclusively with men involved in survival prostitution. When talking to folks about our clients, especially to those outside the urban ministry realm, the conversation and corresponding interest looks something like this.

Hello, I work for a ministry called Emmaus. (Subject's interest peaks)

We are an ecumenical ministry. (Subject is a bit less interested, but still engaged)

We are based in Chicago. (The subject is now looking at his or her shoes, but is still cordial)

We work with individuals involved in survival prostitution. (The subject gets confused... I explain that we prefer not to call our clients "prostitutes" for a variety of reasons... the subject nods his or her head. Interest increases a bit, because ministry to *prostitutes* is *different*)

Most of the individuals we work with struggle with a few... or all of the following obstacles: severe mental illness, deteriorated physical health, disjointed family backgrounds, chronic homelessness and extensive criminal records. (Interest dwindles to the point where the subject is looking around the room and may even rub the back of their head or sigh)

Oh and by the way, I say... the individuals involved in survival prostitution that we work with are men. (Conversation just flat-lined. After five minutes of attempted resuscitation, the crash cart is unplugged and the time of death is announced)

In the opening knight-in-shining-armor story, what would change if the damsel was not a damsel at all, but a man? More importantly, what if the new damsel looked a lot like our villain?

Would the hero still be willing to risk his life to untie some dude? Probably, he is a hero after all. But, would he actively go looking for men that give an impression that they themselves are villains, and safely shove them out from under falling pianos? If a ship sank and the hero could either save one woman or a group of five men, what do you think he would he do?

The villains we rescue our men from are the product of the same brokenness as the villains exploiting girls and women through prostitution. But he is, in most cases a man exploiting another man. In the mind of most people, prostitution among homosexuals is "ickier" than prostitution among heterosexuals. But there is nothing redeeming about prostitution in either realm. It is all born out of suffering and it all ends in suffering. So no matter what the orientation, all is tainted. God sees all forms of prostitution as brokenness, and therefore all those involved in the sex trade, regardless of gender, need our attention.

What about the train? The metaphorical train our men face is the same metaphorical train, hurdling down the tracks to destroy females. The train represents outside forces, things we cannot control. The victim's past, systematic injustice, racial prejudice, poverty and poor health – these factors are all barreling towards persons involved in prostitution and will kill them if something doesn't change. It may be said that boys and men have more of a *choice* in the matter. *They got themselves into the situation, they can get themselves out.* But if their histories carry the same baggage, what makes it easier for a man to pull himself out than a woman? There are some obvious answers to this.

Certainly, the demand for women is higher. Women are more often controlled by pimps, tricks and traffickers. Often times, women are at a physical disadvantage to their controllers. And, maybe, women are more likely to accept help.

Gender role stereotypes that make men the heroes and women the damsels in distress also work against those that reach out to men, because it may feel emasculating to ask for help. Men involved in prostitution generally have to hit rock bottom before they reach out for help. These men are discriminated against everywhere they go. Harassed by police, targeted in jail, seen as a blight on the gay community, met with apprehensive and hesitantly (*if at all*) open arms at church, beat up in the shelters, excommunicated by families... I could go on, but I think you get the point. Our guys have been burned and they need a safe place to go when they are ready for a change.

If the general public is shocked to find out that there is an organization working exclusively with men involved in prostitution, it is safe to assume that the men being victimized are also a bit surprised when they hear of our existence. This being said, be assured that an information deficit is serious a factor in our work.

Discussion Questions

1. Is there more of a focus on girls than boys in your area? What about of women over men? How about boys over men?
2. Why do you think there is often more a focus on the needs of females over the needs of males? Do you agree with any of the reasons given by the authors? Why? Do you disagree with any of the reasons? Why?
3. Are there any myths or preconceptions about males and masculinity in your context? Are there any myths or preconceptions about the abuse and exploitation of males in your context? Have those attitudes changed? What do you think can help them change?
4. What do you think can be done to put more focus on the needs of males without taking away needed attention and resources from the needs of females?
5. Are there any particular cultural reasons in your country that make it difficult for the church to reach out to young men as victims?

CHAPTER 21: WHAT ARE THE UNIQUE CHALLENGES OF WORKING WITH BOYS AND YOUNG MEN AND HOW CAN WE EFFECTIVELY MEET THEIR NEEDS?

Key Issues, by Alezandra Russell

Four years ago I noticed a need while walking through the red-light district of Chiang Mai, Thailand. While the global community drew attention to women and girls who were victims of trafficking and exploitation, few were identifying that an entire gender was also at risk – males. At the time there was a dearth of services by community-based and government-run organizations to young males in the sex industry. Fast-forward four years; there now exists a grassroots organization, Urban Light, which is committed to empowering young males who are victims of trafficking and exploitation.

Urban Light has spent the first few years working to understand the target population being served, assessing *their* needs, *their* vision and how Urban Light can best support *their* journey beyond the bars. Our strategy for how we can best provide services has been to learn directly from our clients through individual needs-assessments. We have tailored our menu of services keeping our client in mind, recognizing that each person possesses very different needs and are at very different points on their journey of rehabilitation.

Effectively meeting the needs of the boys and young men we serve is a daily challenge as Urban Light navigates with limited resources, limited in-country support and limited funding. The core services offered at Urban Light – education, housing, health-care, outreach and prevention – have infused this at-risk community of young males working in the sex-trade with once absent resources that now create an opportunity to move beyond the red-light district of Chiang Mai. However, in more than four years of providing services to young males, Urban Light has encountered challenges in five key areas: (1) family and cultural obligation, (2) limited education, (3) gender stereotypes, (4) personal self-worth and (5) homelessness and alternative housing. These five challenges must be addressed and be made a priority if there is to be a shift in the lives of our participants.

Challenge #1: Family and Cultural Obligation

The young men Urban Light serves come from villages located in remote areas throughout Thailand, Burma and Laos. Currently eighty percent of our participants are ethnic minorities who have been raised within a traditional hilltribe community inside of Thailand, while twenty percent are Tai-Yai or other ethnic groups whose families have migrated from Burma and settled in Thailand. The personal journeys of our youth tend to follow a very common theme: extreme poverty, limited access to education and employment opportunities within their villages, younger siblings to care for, and a cultural expectation to provide financially for elders and parents. This dynamic is described by researcher Peter Jackson:

> "Most [sex] workers belong to the poorer rural classes where children by 15-16 years of age must shoulder a full adult work load and where their inescapable and lifelong obligation to parents is a fundamental cultural characteristic."[1]

This dynamic relates to females as well as males. In the communities where Urban Light participants come from the burden falls on males. It is this cultural pressure coupled with the lack of opportunity that allows the sex trade to flourish and the ethnic minority groups of Thailand and its neighbors to be marginalized.

If mapped out, the common migration trends of young people who leave their hilltribe communities would illustrate the final destination most often being the urban cities and beach-towns of Bangkok, Pattaya, Phuket and Chiang Mai. The financial-lore of these few cities are what propels and fuels this great migration for many of our young men. There is a collective image that in these cities one can find financial freedom to support families back home. However, the unfamiliarity of urban life places this migrating group at risk of the temptations of their new environment – drugs, alcohols, sex work, etc. Without community advocates or community involvement, new challenges arise for this often young, defenseless and vulnerable population of young men.

Challenge #2: Limited Education

A recent study conducted by Love146 and Urban Light of males in the sex industry in Chiang Mai, Thailand, revealed that of the 50 young males interviewed, 80 percent had only a ninth grade education or less, while 1 in 5 had received no formal education at all.[2] Urban Light participants have often shared that access to education was always a desire, however the expectation to support the family financially did not allow for such a privilege. Despite education being free there are hidden costs associated with learning (such as uniforms, transportation and materials) that prevent our youth from accessing an education. Researcher Matt Grieger stated it best: "in most cases, the young man decided to drop out of school because he knew it was a hardship for his family to pay for his education."[3]

---

[1] Peter Jackson and Gerard Sullivan, eds., *Lady Boys, Tom Boys, Rent Boys: Male and Female Homosexualities in Contemporary Thailand* (Binghamton, NY: Haworth Press, Inc., 1999).

[2] Jarrett Davis, Elliot Glotfelty and Glenn Miles, *Boys for Baht? An Exploratory Study on the Vulnerability of Male Entertainment Workers in Chiang Mai, Thailand* (Love146 and Urban Light, 2013), 22.

[3] Matthew T. Grieger, "Challenging Conventional Wisdom: Sex Work, Exploitation, and Labor Among Young Akha Men in Thailand" (master's thesis, George Washington University, 2012), 76.

For the boys who come from extreme poverty, the more expensive education is to their family (both in terms of direct costs and opportunity costs), the less of an option it is for them. Therefore many boys arrive in these thriving and overwhelming cities with little education, limited command of the Thai language and extremely low self-esteem as a result. Grieger explains the impact:

> "As important as Thai language is, its transformative impact should not be overstated. Even if one of my respondents becomes fluent in Thai but still has only a sixth or ninth grade education, this still represents an enormous barrier to employment."[4]

Providing free education and alternative learning programs tangibly empowers our male participants to access employment opportunities beyond sex work. Urban Light has found that the young males who received alternative education and language training were able to secure jobs within the hotel and restaurant industry as well as in large international chains such as the 7/11 convenience stores.

Challenge #3: Gender Stereotypes

When I first traveled to Thailand in 2009 to study the situation of trafficking and exploitation, I followed an international assumption that only young women and girls were affected as indicated by the available research at the time. As recently as the 2013, the US Trafficking in Persons Report for Thailand stated that "women and children from Thailand are subjected to sex trafficking,"[5] making no mention of males or the commercial sexual exploitation of boys (CSEB). This sentence echoes the global dialogue that paints all victims of trafficking as "women and children," leaving males excluded entirely from the radar of the international community. As ECPAT points out, "The little notice given to boys primarily identifies them as exploiters, pimps and buyers of sex, or as active and willing participants in sex work, not as victims or survivors of exploitation."[6]

The notion that boys are not the abused but the abuser is an example of the critical overarching stereotypes Urban Light must battle and aim to change. According to the book *Abused Boys: The Neglected Victims of Sexual Abuse*, "Researchers have noted sexual activities involving adults and boys get reported less often than sexual behaviors involving adults and girls. They have speculated that this is because people see sexual activities with girls as more serious and more abusive than the same activity with boys."[7]

---

[4] Matthew T. Grieger, "Challenging Conventional Wisdom", 83.
[5] US State Department, *Trafficking in Persons Report 2013*, 6.
[6] ECPAT-USA, "And Boys Too: An ECPAT-USA Discussion Paper about the Lack of Recognition of the Commercial Sexual Exploitation of Boys in the United States" (ECPAT-USA, 2013), 2.
[7] Mic Hunter, *Abused Boys: The Neglected Victims of Sexual Abuse* (New York: Fawcett Columbine, 1990), 5.

It is sadly not uncommon from individuals to make judgments such as, "But they don't *look* like they have been abused," insinuating that because there is no *visible* abuse or because boys are meant to be "tough" that the abuse is therefore made-up or somehow non-existent. This is clearly prejudicial and harmful to the males who see themselves as victims. Grieger states:

> "The more the stereotype of an 'acceptable' victim is propagated, the more difficult it is to recognize the exploitation of those who do not fit this archetype. By creating an echo chamber featuring a narrow construct of a victim, those who do not fit the mold are marginalized."[8]

To address this global stereotype that is placed on our youth it must become a collective priority to challenge these beliefs. Urban Light focuses a great deal of time and effort on life-skills workshops that address gender stereotypes, prejudices and how to challenge what culture and society has pre-determined us to be. The sad reality is that a global culture has deemed boys and men incapable of being victims of exploitation and abuse and it is only when this can be an acknowledged that the proper steps towards healing can take place.

Challenge #4: Personal Self-Worth

The Thai paradigm prematurely scripts the destiny for many of the hilltribe and ethnic-minority males that Urban Light serves, proclaiming this population to be "trash," "throw-aways" and "delinquents." These repetitive forms of marginalization experienced by the young men seep deep into their self-assessment and self-worth producing deep-rooted challenges. The Love146/Urban Light study confirms this. Of the 50 males interviewed, 4 out of 5 reported some negative feelings towards themselves such as shame and guilt. This self-loathing is for many of our boys what keeps them returning to the red-light district and the reasons that alcohol and drug use become normal coping mechanisms. Urban Light participants will often come to the center with signs of that self-harm and self-mutilation have become issues within their lives, for instance cutting themselves on purpose in order to release anger, aggression, sadness and depression.

To combat the darkness and depression that can quickly and suddenly overcome our clients, it is imperative that *each* young man feels validated and heard. Ways to promote validation and well-being include one-on-one meetings between a staff member and the participant; creative therapy through various forms of programming such as art, baking, sports, guitar lessons and group activities; and constant "check-ins" that involve calling, texting and going to the places our clients tends to frequent such as bars, Internet cafés, friends' homes, etc.

---

[8] Matthew T. Grieger, "Challenging Conventional Wisdom", 119.

Challenge #5: Homelessness and Alternative Housing

The consequence of under-reporting of the commercial sexual exploitation of boys in Thailand is that services and needs go unnoticed and funding un-administered. The most common need our clients share with our Urban Light team involves access to housing. However, the most significant challenge that comes with providing housing to our participants is that many of them have been living on their own for years, "surviving" on their own and shy away from any forms of rules or regulations. Previous participants of our Transitional Housing Program were diligent about showing up to the Center everyday, participating in activities and being respectful and responsible. However, once they entered the housing program a significant shift occurred – either they soared at the freedom or they were unprepared for the responsibility.

Housing – a basic human need – became anything but a basic fix. I would advise any organization looking into providing housing to create a very detailed list of rules and timelines, and to initiate all participants with a probationary period and in-depth orientation. This can then be followed with regularly *un*scheduled room checks. Some young men will grab onto this opportunity and lives will be dramatically altered, while others will simply not be ready for this responsibility and will need to be removed from housing until ready. Programming for all the boys in the program can include life-skills and other training to help them learn the "soft skills" needed for successful independent living, even before they are individually ready for it.

Facing the Challenges

During Urban Light's infancy our aim was always to provide basic services to all at-risk young males we encountered during our outreach efforts. Immediately following our founding, Chai[9] appeared at our Urban Light Youth Center. Because he was a young, ethnic-minority male from northern Thailand who was the eldest of four and the only son, we immediately knew the demands posed on him. He shared common themes – poverty, being new to an urban city, homelessness, drug abuse and working in the boy bars of Chiang Mai. Following an application, in-take and one-on-one meeting our Urban Light team knew the steps that were required should an alternative life be possible.

Three months after Chai first came to the Center our staff had already placed him in our transitional housing program. Soon after that we enrolled him in an intensive English course at a language school, helped him obtain a passport, and watched him take driving lessons and eventually earn a driver's license. Eventually he started working at Urban Light as a youth leader. All of these steps were part of a master plan that had been created for Chai with *his* input and the guidance and support of the Urban Light team. Together they planned, envisioned and challenged self-doubts, fears and possible options.

---

[9] Not his real name.

Presently Chai is succeeding at everything placed along his path, however the days of Chai falling into a deep depression are not entirely gone nor can we expect them to be. Depression and desperation still creep up, paralyzing him from seeing all his accomplishments. Often this is triggered by family pressure and demands, especially when he returns to his home to see the money and possessions his peers have accumulated by working in the sex trade. The overall success and shift that took place in Chai's life was a joint effort, one that involved both his commitment and the commitment of the Urban Light team.

By organizations recognizing and meeting these challenges, our hope is this can be the story of countess young men throughout the world.

Discussion Questions

1. How do family, cultural or other obligations in your context create vulnerability to exploitation? How can those dynamics be addressed? How can we respectfully challenge religious and cultural perspectives such as fatalism that stand in the way of empowerment?

2. Are there barriers to education in your community? What is the nature of those barriers (legal, economic, access, other)? How can poor families be supported so that they can afford the opportunity and direct costs of sending their children to school? How can your organization help provide alternatives if access to formal education is unavailable?

3. What gender stereotypes about males are prevalent in your context? How do those stereotypes affect males' perception of their own abuse and exploitation? How do stereotypes prevent them from receiving services? Does your organization create a safe space for them to talk about their victimization/exploitation? What are the different needs of males, females, LGBT people, etc. and how can your organization tailor services to each group?

4. In what ways do your participants face challenges about personal self-worth? How does poor self-worth affect their behavior and increase their vulnerabilities? What are some ways your organization can promote well-being? What services are available to address issues such as self-harm and substantive abuse?

5. What housing and other practical needs exist in your context? Are adequate and accessible government resources available? What are the gaps and barriers to access? How can your organization help address these needs? What challenges do you face in addressing them?

CHAPTER 22: HOW CAN WE EFFECTIVELY WORK WITH BOYS AND MEN IN A NON-JUDGMENTAL AND SUPPORTIVE WAY?

Key Issues, by Alastair Hilton

This article shares advice, good practices and lessons learned from a variety of practice settings, including England, Cambodia, Hong Kong and the United States.

Preparing The Ground

Before we begin to start working with boys, whatever our setting or role (e.g. caregiver, teacher, community or social worker, counselor, psychologist, pastor) there are several fundamental things we need to do to prepare the ground.

1. Reflect, Share and Learn

We must begin by being honest about any potential barriers to engaging with and working effectively with boys. Reflect on your thoughts, feelings and attitudes towards and about boys, irrespective of whether they have experienced abuse. Possible reflection questions include:

- My hopes and fears are…
- The things I like/dislike about boys are…
- When working with boys I find it difficult/easy when…
- The things that I find that make it easier to work with boys are when they…
- The things that I find that make it harder to work with boys are when they…
- I find it easier to work with boys when… I say or do…
- Things that my organization does well when working with boys are…
- Things that my organization could do better when working with boys are…
- One thing I know is helpful for working with boys is …
- Questions I have about boys are…
- What learning needs do I have?
- What resources do we need to meet those needs?

Reflection can be done individually or in a group. If done in a group, allow space for male and female groups to work both separately *and* together, as same-gender groups often reveal important and specific concerns.

After reflection, develop an action plan to meet identified needs. Also continue to reflect and evaluate as you progress in your work: highlight strengths, seek new knowledge and skills, share what works with others and build on those things.

2. Listen to Boys and Learn More about Social, Relational, Cultural, Biological and Developmental Issues and Influences

Make time to find out more about boys and young men. Learn about specific developmental issues relating to boys and their influence on behavior at different ages and stages of life. This can help avoid potential conflicts as we come to understand that much of boys' behavior that we struggle with occurs simply because they are built that way.

Also take time to learn more about boys, gender perspectives and masculinities and what their world is like to live in. You can do this by reading and accessing useful resources and by being creative in your time with them. Build on the relationships you already have to create space and opportunities for boys to tell you how it is for them. Above all, be prepared to listen.

3. Remember the "Whole Person" and Work from Strength-Based Perspectives

It is vital to remember that before boys and young men were abused, they were and still are boys. Avoid labeling them as potential troublemakers, or as risky and dangerous, just because they have been victimized. They may have problems and present challenges, but like all survivors they also have an amazing capacity for strength, creativity, protectiveness and resilience given the right environment, opportunities and support.

In our research with Cambodian boys, many shared that they wanted help but they also wanted to avoid being labeled as just "victims" or as potential abusers.[1] Male survivors need understanding, opportunities to build safe relationships, get on with their lives and have fun with their friends and families too. Also remember to be open to cultural and ethnic differences and influences for boys as well as yourself.

4. Build Partnerships and Support Structures

For many survivors their abuse often takes place in isolation. Recovery needs to take place with the help of others. The same is true of helpers, caregivers and supporters, whether they be professional paid workers, volunteers or family. Effective supervision, support and forums for sharing, learning and offloading should not be considered a luxury – they are a vital prerequisite. Network,

---

[1] Based on interviews by the author; see also chapter 3 of Alastair Hilton et al., *"I Thought It Could Never Happen to Boys"* (Phnom Penh: World Vision, Hagar and Social Services of Cambodia, 2008).

make links with others and make self-care a priority. Survivors will also benefit from this – they need examples of people around them who also know how to care for themselves.

5. Learn about Specific Sexual Abuse Dynamics, Impacts and Effects Related to Boys and, Crucially, What Boys Need from Helpers and Supporters

It remains a vital cornerstone of our work to understand how abuse takes place and what the implications are for boys and those around them. We must explore social and cultural factors alongside bio-psychosocial factors, including those specific to boys. A great deal of information can also be gleaned from the recommended resources at the end of this article.

In order to learn from boys themselves, we must listen to them – and provide opportunities for them to share in safe and enabling environments. Child participation and involvement is crucial, whether that be one-to-one, in small groups or in more formal (but child-friendly) research projects. Any efforts to support a child following abuse should be based on a sound foundation of local and culturally-appropriate knowledge and skills to avoid the potentially damaging effects of well-meaning but inappropriate interventions.

What Do Boys Say They Need from Us?

In our Cambodia study, we took great efforts to discover and elicit from the boys what they considered to be important features of individual helpers, supporters and services and essential elements for their recovery. These elements (summarized in the diagram opposite "Essential Elements of Recovery"[2]) should act as the foundation stones of our work.

We also worked closely with colleagues and projects assisting boys and young male survivors of sexual abuse in the United Kingdom and Hong Kong, asking what they considered to be the most important things boys needed from helpers and elements of beneficial approaches. As seen in the table below (p.188), the similarities are striking; boys and young men from very different countries, cultures and social backgrounds often identified similar, if not identical, needs.

The information revealed from this international research is extremely valuable. Practitioners must reflect upon how to apply these findings in practice, whether it be face-to-face counseling, group work or the environment and set up of your agency. For example, in relation to the need for "choice and empowerment," agencies should ask whether and how boys are encouraged to express their own ideas and choices? (e.g. Do they have a choice of a male or female counselor? Can they choose a venue or time for counseling that suits them?) When victims are abused they are disempowered and deprived of choices, so it is vital that choice is considered a cornerstone of their recovery.

---

[2] Source: Alastair Hilton et al., *"I Thought It Could Never Happen to Boys"* (Phnom Penh: World Vision, Hagar and Social Services of Cambodia, 2008).

Essential Elements
of
Recovery

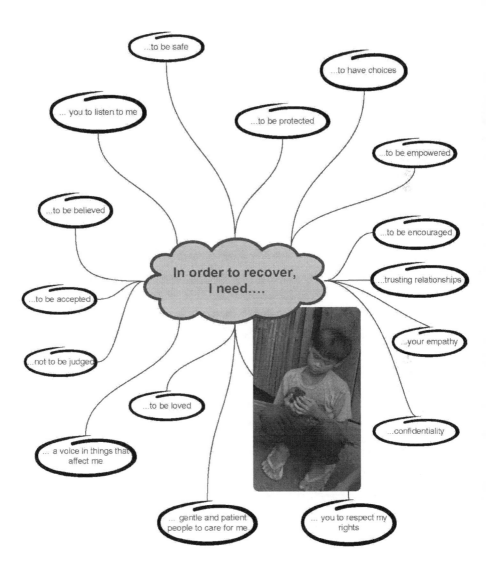

What Male Survivors Say They Need From Helpers, Supporters and Services		
Hong Kong	**Cambodia**	**UK**
Safety and acceptance	Safety	Safety & security
Confidentiality	Confidentiality	Confidentiality
Someone to trust and listen	Empathy	Compassion & empathy
Easy access to services without others knowing	Not to be judged or blamed	Anonymity
Not to judge what we say	To be believed	To be believed, listened to and not condemned for their actions before they seek help
Accept the boy as a whole	To be loved	
Counselling and therapy	Staff not to use harsh words or violence	
Confidential street-based counselling and life skills	Protection from abuse	Not to be judged
Help to deal with fear	Staff to have skills in psychology and counselling	Highlight acceptance and hope
Education, because some boys may not realise that what happened is abuse	Encouragement	A friendly welcome from all staff
	Trust	Trust & trusting relationships
Disseminate information about the issue/service widely	Help with education and finding jobs	Professionals and others to be aware, approachable and well trained
Use media to talk about prevention and helping victims	Activities and sports	Choices
	A calm, safe place to stay, free of violence and bullying	Want to feel less isolated
Helpline and online services for those who dare not see a counsellor in person	Parents and staff to be patient and gentle	Boys need to feel that they are not alone and that their fears and experiences are going to be taken seriously
	Respect for our rights	
Practical assistance	Someone to ask about our feelings and listen	Community styles are best rather than traditional health settings
Involve survivors who have recovered to share their experiences	Broadcast widely about this problem	
	Friends, fun and laughter	Drop-in services
A place to feel relaxed which helps me express myself without limitation	Help with our health	Not to be passed on all the time to other services
	Groups with a facilitator	Services available when they are needed—in a crisis
Medical and nutritional help and guidelines		Help us have a greater sense of self worth
More documentation of people's experiences to break the silence		Services that promote independence and personal empowerment
		Support groups to reduce isolation

The insights from this research should be applied to *all* aspects of our work if we are to be truly survivor- and boy-focused. You could begin by sharing these ideas with boys and asking which ones they consider to be important, asking them for additional ideas. This will not only help them feel empowered and part of the process but may also help them realize that they are not alone. Better still, in your own setting, carry out sensitive and ethically-based research with boys to find out what they need and rigorously evaluate the services you already provide, ensuring a commitment to implementing "lessons learned."

Other Key Issues and Pointers for Good Practice

Research indicates that the mental health and other health needs of young men and boys are often hidden, ignored or misunderstood by those around them. Their behavior is often seen as anti-social and "bad" resulting in punishment, rather than as a distress signal leading to help. The truth is many do not know how to act any differently. Cries for help may be present (such as drug and alcohol use, aggressive outbursts, problems with school, or increasing self-harm and suicide rates) but these signs are often ignored – or in many cases, boys are blamed for anti-social behavior, pushed away or punished.

This section will look at recommendations for more effectively understanding – and meeting – the needs of boys and young men.

Develop a Deeper Understanding and Appreciation of Gender Roles and Help-Seeking Behavior

In most societies, to a greater or lesser degree, young men are taught from an early age to hide their thoughts, feelings, vulnerabilities and needs. For many who have grown up believing that males are protectors of themselves and others, being seen as vulnerable is unacceptable in their eyes. They are scared of being seen as weak because they may be teased, mocked, belittled and feminized. Being seen as a victim completely turns their world upside down and they may go to great lengths to conceal their experiences. One boy remarked, "You can be dying inside but no one must know." Boys also learn from an early age to seek the acceptance and approval of other men and boys, so they spend a lot of energy and time on living up to expectations of themselves and others about what a "real man" is. So much of what we teach boys is simply not good for them, and does little to prepare them for when things go wrong.

This conflict between trying to "Act like a man!" and how they really feel inside can act as a significant barrier to both asking for and accepting help. Potential helpers may at times also perhaps unwittingly collude with these gender stereotypes and either pay little attention to or get irritated by certain behaviors, such as expressions of vulnerability and perceived weakness. For many boys and men the reality of "How I feel" (confused, frightened, vulnerable and despairing) and "How I am supposed to act" (confident, fearless, invincible and hopeful) are very different for boys and we need to remember this. The boys' family, peers and other helpers – also influenced by these gender expectations – can either be a considerable and valuable source of help or a problem. Numerous research and experiences from many diverse settings indicates that the social responses towards boys and men experiencing sexual abuse are often hostile, distrusting and blaming.[3] One boy in the Cambodian study, frustrated by unhelpful responses of others, said: "Boys can't cry out. If we cry, they say we are weak... but they don't know how much hurt we have."

Boys in many settings and from different backgrounds need help to learn to identify their emotions, express them and manage them so they can then understand their experiences more. Much of "gender socialization" is not good for their health and mental health – it teaches boys that they have to be tough and strong, but does very little to help them overcome problems in safe ways. They are taught to be independent and not rely on others for sources of support. This can isolate them and have potentially hazardous consequences.

For a boy or man "not to know" can be seen and experienced as a failure and betrayal of masculinity. Therefore we need to avoid colluding with these attitudes and redefine help- seeking as a sign of strength where possible. Helpers often say "boys won't do that" but there needs to be a "can do" mentality for boys to benefit fully from what is on offer and reach their full potential.

Lesson from Practice – What Helps Boys and Men Access Support?

Research and experience in the UK in relation to health and mental health services shows that several key factors can encourage males to use services.[4] First, the provision of services must recognize and accommodate the help-seeking dynamics of boys. For instance, confidentiality and privacy must be highlighted (e.g. help lines, private waiting area, ease of access, or off-hour appointments when there may be fewer women and children around).

Second, emergency access should be made available. Because boys and men often leave things to the last moment and ask for help in a crisis, services need to be able to respond in those circumstances. In many cases, merely offering a waiting list or referral will be insufficient and the boy may never return. Strive to set up a system where initial appointments or drop-in services are easily accessible at the times when most needed.

Another helpful lesson learned is that males will often access services when they have more information about who they are going to see, what the service offers and what the motivations are of those offering the support. Too many barriers (both external and internal) to help-seeking discourage males from approaching a service. Make efforts to share easily-accessible information about what you do, who you are and why you are doing it.

---

[3] See, for example, Josef Spiegel, *Sexual Abuse of Males: The SAM Model of Theory and Practice* (New York: Brunner-Routledge, 2003), 54.

[4] Based on the author's experience and research over the years; see also the work of the UK organization: Working with Men. http://www.workingwithmen.org

Lesson from Practice – The "Visibility" of the Issue Can Be Crucial

Several years ago I was involved in setting up a service for male survivors in the UK. We followed a deliberate strategy of high-profile publicity, backed up by training and preparation for the potential response. The publicity included the placement of bright, colorful posters relating to the service in specially-selected venues, including doctors' surgeries, where staff were trained how to respond to initial inquiries.

One doctor told me that in twenty years he had *never* had a male disclose abuse. He was astonished to discover that within a very short period of time men were disclosing at a rate of several each week. Most were not seeking medication or referrals but simply felt relieved that there was simply someone to listen and believe. For many the visibility of the posters (and therefore the issue) helped them feel less isolated and able to talk.

Good Practice – Be Creative and View Boys Positively

Overcome resistance to work with boys and young men and be creative in your approach. Regard boys and young men positively, not as a problem. If you see them as a problem they will walk away and you have lost your opportunity. Work from established relationships and seek to deepen them. Work in new environments where boys and young men spend their time. This may mean establishing outreach projects, so be creative and willing to try new things. Provide accessible support on their terms and in ways in which they will be prepared to engage, not just in ways that adults think best.

Good Practice – Use Energy, Humor and Activities

Many boys and young men hide behind jokes and humor to conceal their difficulties. We can use that to create relationships, but we should challenge the jokes and banter – especially where it results in discrimination or harmful attitudes.

It also effective to create and use resources, games, and high-energy activities to reach boys. Research shows that boys often respond better and find it easier to talk when counseling (or other assistance) is combined with activities.

Good Practice – Breaking the Stereotypes

Redefine masculine stereotypes and tackle the "boys don't do this" attitude by offering new opportunities. Redefine the act of asking for help as a sign of strength rather than weakness. After all, it takes strength and courage to ask for help.

Good Practice – Teach Important Survival Skills

Boys like to be good at things! Harness this desire to teach them to be considerate and responsible. Important topics include relationship skills, attitudes and values (including those related to "masculine ideals") and the nature and value of relationships. Use games, drama and role play to develop social skills such as listening, negotiating and decision making. Help boys explore ways to resist being pressured by peers. Build self-esteem, positive attitudes and respect for others.

Good Practice – Keep It Focused on Boys' Needs Not Adults' Perceptions

Education about sex and relationships should be based on their needs, not adults' perceptions. Keep a journal of what works and what is useful when working with boys. Research the needs of boys, including those with "special needs." Ensure that boys and men are not presented as the "bad guys." Try to avoid distancing boys by over-emphasizing girls' needs and ignoring the needs of boys.

Good Practice – Evaluate What You Do and Share Positive Practice

Develop action-learning styles of evaluation that involve boys. Share those findings with others and make a commitment to building lessons learned into your policy and program development.

Good Practice – Words of Wisdom from a Cambodian Social Worker
Working with Vulnerable Boys

"It is difficult ... but if you want to get boys involved, make efforts to meet with them where they live and where they spend their time.... Explain what you do, but leave the choice up to them.... Do not disturb what they do, and show them respect ... treat them as equals ... many street children are afraid of adults ... and don't make promises that you can't keep."

Conclusion

Many of the expectations placed on boys lead to unhelpful attitudes towards them. Boys often get blamed, criticized or misunderstood. People often complain not only when boys are tough and aggressive, but also when they are considered gentle, soft or "too feminine." If we want boys to change, then we need to as well!

In summary, here are some important steps we can take:

1. No matter what they say or do, remember the "whole person." Try not to label them as bad or "just boys" or reinforce stereotypes by saying "boys will be boys."
2. Remember that boys are also individuals – they are not all the same.
3. Listen to and learn from boys about what it is like to be a boy/young man.

4. Find ways to talk to boys about masculinity and the expectations of gender and how society influences and shapes these ideas.
5. Challenge homophobia and other forms of discrimination that limit our approaches and also force boys into living up to harmful expectations of masculinity.
6. Recognize the important role that sports and activities play in boys' lives and use them to get your ideas and messages across.
7. Do not underestimate the media (TV, magazines, etc.) and the key role it plays in shaping attitudes about boys, men and masculinity.
8. Help them develop social skills and other ways of expressing their thoughts, feelings and attitudes.
9. Show them that you respect them.
10. Remember not to focus only on the negative where boys are concerned.

Advice from Practitioners, by Jonathan W. Hancock

I was seated at my office desk early one morning. It was quiet around Emmaus Ministries, so I could go throughew my to-do lists before more staff and "the guys" arrived. There is always so much to do in running this twenty-year-old ministry that serves men who turn to the streets of Chicago to survive. That's where they sell their bodies to male customers. Our guys simply don't think they are worth more than that transaction.

If I am in early and the phone rings, I never know who might be on the other end. This call was from Willie.[5] He has been a client for over fifteen years. Never too happy to talk to me, he has his favorites and I am not high on that list. So he is always asking for someone else, but as I was alone, he settled for me.

Willie was calling from a residential program we had helped him get into. Willie wanted me to call his dad and see if he could send him $20. I hesitated, but said I would try. After our short conversation, I called his dad and reached him right away. I conveyed the message and he said "sure I'll do that, I always love hearing from my kids."

I relayed this to a co-worker an hour later. She said, "Well that's interesting. It was his father who sold him in prostitution to begin with." When Willie was fourteen his dad brought him down to the city and sold Willie for a quick trick in order to feed his father's drug addiction. While Willie's deep brokenness didn't begin there, that was a whole new level of abuse than he had known before.

There is very little in my life experience that allows me to relate to a story like that. And Willie's story, in one form or another, can be repeated over and over by men who turn to the streets. They have been taught and have come to believe that they simply aren't worth any more than that.

---

[5] Not his real name.

If those closest to you – whom you loved and trusted – had treated you like Willie's father did, and at such a vulnerable age, how would it have gone for you in life? Then add to that no steady home or school, no money, poor education, abuse from neighbors and cousins, and a lousy diet. Top it off with there being no one in your life who really believes in you, no one who pours hope into you for your future.

This was the foundation of Willie's life. He didn't have what we call the safety net; the support that helps most of us to make it. If you have people who love you, good health and education, quality food, a faith, role models, people who love you and believe in you, you have been richly blessed. When you make poor choices or bad things happen in your life, that safety net of blessings are what will catch you, and me. Willie and the men of Emmaus have never had such a safety net. We know it is the streets that catch them.

Willie and the other men once had dreams just like regular people. They wanted to be basketball players, or firemen, or musicians. They didn't grow up wanting to prostitute themselves on the street, having other men "pleasure" themselves for a few dollars. But no one nurtured their dreams. Instead, repeatedly through the abuse they experienced, the lack of support, and the lack of people to invest in them, they came to believe that they were not worthy of more. Many of our men think they were just made to do this; that this is simply their lot in life.

Do these boys and men make wrong and sinful choices? Do they make these bad decisions repeatedly? Are their behaviors beyond the comprehension of most of us? Would most of us not even want to consider that such behavior goes on in every city on this planet?

But have boys and men like Willie really had the same set of choices that you and I have had in life? Do they have any other hope for themselves in life; a vision for something so much better? Do they believe they are of real worth and have anything to give besides their body to a stranger?

These men and these boys are made in God's image just like you and me. They sin and hurt God deeply, also like you and me. They need the love and acceptance of Christ in the same way as all the other inhabitants of this fragile planet do. They need hope and forgiveness. They need others to listen to them and love them.

Practical Advice

So how can we, as individuals or as the church, get over the hurdles that keep us from engaging with such men as these? How can we realistically provide support and love for those so wounded, demonstrating "they will indeed know we are Christians by our love"? How are we to have compassion and take time to attend to such wounded people?

In my work with Emmaus Ministries, we have had to ask and wrestle with these questions over the years. The following are some ideas of how we – and you – can more effectively work with men and boys in a non-judgmental and supportive way.

1. Picture that person as your own daughter or son, brother or sister.
When an issue becomes a person and even more so, a person we know, then we
are much more likely to have compassion. *In my work at Emmaus, and in my
interactions with the guys we serve, am I willing to think of them as a family
member, as my own child?*

2. Imagine you are helping Jesus when you help them. In Matthew 25
Jesus tells us that when we gave food to the hungry, water for the thirsty,
clothing to the naked, and visited and cared for the sick and the prisoner, we
did it to him. Put the face of Jesus on them – he did. *When we visit our guys in
prison or share food or clothing with them each week, am I able to take Jesus
at his word in Matthew 25 and believe that we do this as unto him?*

3. Learn about their area of brokenness through reading about it.
Understand the complexity of the issues they have dealt with and the power of
those issues. Don't take a simplistic or minimalist approach. If you really want
to reach out to those who have been in prostitution, then care enough to learn
some about the struggle and the journey of people in those shoes. *At Emmaus
we work with guys with very specialized needs and situations. We are a
ministry set apart for men in prostitution because they are safer here and can
be more open and honest knowing that they share a big part of their story with
every other guy here.*

4. Learn through listening. Listen with openness and care to their story and
pain. Simply listening to others is a very tangible form of caring, and can be a
huge gift to them. *The men we serve at Emmaus have few places that they can
go, few relationships that they can engage in where people actually sit down to
listen to them and simply give them the gift of time. Can I take time to listen to
their pains and joys? Am I too busy wanting to do for others that I rarely stop
to listen?*

5. Pray for wisdom in how to respond to their needs. Don't presume you
know all about them or understand their situation. Ask them what their needs
are. Undoubtedly as an individual or as a church you can't meet all the needs
they have, nor should you. But ask them. Maybe you can meet one of their
needs. *We want to bring practical help to the men but we want to do this while
in relationship. They need practical investment in them now, and so a meal or
clothing goes hand in hand with that attentive and patient ear.*

6. Pray for your heart to reflect the heart of God. Pray for a softening and
a tenderness of your own heart. Pray that you would see that "those people" are
really no different, no worse, no more sinful than you are. Pray that you would
see them the way that God sees them. *We set a day aside each month for
prayer as a staff. While never enough, it's an important part of what we do and
how we invite God into the fullness of all that happens here. The staff and
volunteers at know they are not all that different from the guys we serve.*

As my family of four, including two adolescent daughters, has gone to be
with the guys the last several Christmases, we have found friends. We play
group games and board games and cards. We talk together and laugh and eat a
lot. We sing, pray together, and talk about the story of Christmas. We share
about our Christmas memories. My daughters know what brings the men to

Emmaus. Yes, what they have done on the streets is part of why they come. But my daughters also know that they come because they find a place of warmth and love. They find a place where there are people who know what they have done and yet accept them. They find a place where people want more for them and are going to fight alongside them for that. They find a place that is a simple group of people, each made in the image of God.

Discussion Questions

1. As you read this essay, what emotions does it bring about for you? Why do you think these emotions emerge? How can you invite Jesus in to help you feel more fully the pain and hurt that surrounds us all?
2. How are you intentional about bringing people into your life who are significantly different than you as far as lifestyle, values, economics, etc.?
3. What can you do to more greatly reflect Christ's heart in the relationships you intentionally pursue?

Chapter 23: How Should Christians and the Church Engage with Boys and Men?

Advice from Practitioners, by Doug Van Ramshorst

Now that we have taken a look at the problems facing men involved in sexual exploitation, let's address the obvious questions. So now what? How does a ministry that works with women open their services up to men? How does a new ministry to men start its work?

The answers to these questions begin with starting small and being consistent. If you have an existing outreach team, I would suggest devoting one night a week to seeking men in the areas of your city where prostitution among men occurs (if you live in a medium or large city, I guarantee there is an area or two where this takes place).

Hang out where the men hang out. Build a presence. Build trust. Cover your work in prayer, but don't wait around for God to give you a sign from the sky. Take this article as your sign: *They need help... go to them.*

Be cautious, but don't let discomfort and fear keep you from the work. Keep showing up. I tell my volunteers consistency is more important than frequency. If you are able to have teams out every night... great! If you can devote one night a month to this outreach... great! Regardless, just keep going! The more consistent the better, and eventually increase your frequency, as you are able.

Right up there with consistency is the gift of listening. If you are not a good listener, then this probably isn't the right line of work for you. Often times our guys just need to talk. Give them the opportunity. In listening, we can also find out what their needs are. By assessing and meeting these felt needs you will give them a reason to come to you.

Advice from Practitioners, by Jane Beal

In order to effectively work with boys and men who have been sexually exploited, Christians must have a heart of compassion – the ability to empathize with and to care about men. They also need to develop a deeper understanding and awareness of the physical, psychological, social, spiritual and relational challenges facing men who are sexually exploited. Healthy, Christian mentorship of men by men can also be truly transformative.

There are various places where men who are sexually victimized, exploited or prostituted can be reached: in prisons, on the streets and in churches. Groups like Prison Fellowship effectively disciple men in prisons. Others like Emmaus Ministries effectively assist men on the streets of Chicago. Similar programs are needed in cities across the U.S. and around the world.

The men themselves not only need love and support, but also healthy, Christian models to imitate. They also need accountability for their actions. Many need treatment for addictions to alcohol, drugs and/or sex. The work of Patrick Carnes is extremely relevant to helping men break the cycle of addiction.[1]

The church must become willing to address issues of sexual brokenness from the pulpit and in small groups, in children's church, youth groups and adult groups. Every church needs to come to a place of authentic vulnerability and honesty as well. Unfortunately many men in the church have abused their positions of power and used them to exploit boys and girls sexually. This makes it difficult for abused people to trust church leadership. Great integrity, patience, and gentleness is therefore necessary in church leaders who would minister to boys and men.

Discussion Questions

1. What would a good role model look like for men who have been sexually exploited, bearing in mind their understandable lack of trust?
2. How can we be brave enough to go to places others dare not go but be prepared to be more vulnerable so men open up to us?
3. Even if you currently only work with women, how and where could you start to do outreach to men in your neighborhood?

Case Study, by Derek Collard

Many people in our modern society have drawn a lot of attention to the issues of human trafficking and sexual exploitation. Most of this attention has been given to the abuse and exploitation of women and young girls. As much of the exploitation does happen to girls and women, this is understandable, but if we as the church are going to have any effect in this area we must open our eyes to the reality that human trafficking and sexual exploitation is not a one gender issue.

While boys can also be abused and exploited, until a few years ago there was little understanding of this topic. For years, both religious and secular organizations have been avoiding this issue because they either did not want to appear homophobic or they didn't want to appear to agree with homosexuality. For some, the idea of boys and men being exploited and abused does not make sense. Some people think that men and boys ought to be able to defend themselves so they ignore it. Others have thought that men and boys enjoy sex

---

[1] E.g. *Out of the Shadows: Understanding Sexual Addiction* (Center City, MI: Hazelden, 2001).

so it is not so abusive as it is with girls. These are some of the myths and common misconceptions.

As people of faith, we can no longer allow our decisions to be made on biases that have flourished in a homophobic church culture. Instead, we must learn to love these men and boys where they are and for who they are. Jesus loves all people right where they are at and as followers of Christ, we must be willing to do the same. What Jesus did for us on the cross was not just for any specific type of person, but the love shown there was for all the world to see. These men and boys desperately need to know that love. For many of them, they have come to understand their worth and value simply in terms of services they can provide and dollar amounts that they can generate. The beauty of the gospel for this group is that they are inherently valuable and God loved them so much that He came to earth to show them His love.

In Cambodia, there are many different ways that the sexual exploitation of men and boys occurs. There are many cases of boys who have been exploited by foreign pedophiles, but there are also many cases of Cambodian men seeking out young boys for sex. Along with that, there is a growing number of all-male massage parlors and spas which front as brothels. In these places the men who are in prostitution are given a number and they are asked to stand behind windows while clients come and look at them deciding who they desire. It is not too dissimilar to a meat market and effectively dehumanizes the men there. Both the men and the boys are being robbed of something very important: their dignity. It is hard to hold your head up high when you are being used day after day and night after night.

As the body of Christ, we must not just stand by and let this happen. In Matthew 25:31-46, Jesus talks about the final judgment of all of the world. In this section he describes some of the criteria for judgment. These things might not be what you would expect. It does not mention sins as much as it mentions the people's lack of care for one another. He talks about feeding the hungry and clothing the naked. I think we need to understand that our care for the broken and the poor is something that Jesus cared about a lot.

In December 2010 and January 2011, Love 146 and The Hard Places Community conducted a survey in six different all-male massage parlors in Phnom Penh, Cambodia.[2] They interviewed fifty young men who worked in those establishments. One of the questions asked what kind of service an organization could offer that would be helpful to them. Respondents replied that free English classes would be helpful to them. In response, in April 2011 we at The Hard Places Community began to go into the massage parlors to begin teaching.

In June of 2011 I had my first experience working with these men in person. I was leading a team from the church that I worked at and my co-leader and I had been given the special task of going three days a week into the massage parlor to teach. While we were there one day, we were having fun playing

---

[2] Glenn Miles and Heather Blanch, *What About Boys? An Initial Exploration of Sexually Exploited Boys in Cambodia* (2011). http://love146.org/research/

hangman to review the words we had taught, when all of a sudden the mood changed and they started to rush us out. I looked to our translator, who had been there many times, and asked him what was happening. He told me that a client had just come in and we needed to leave. As I was putting on my shoes I overheard the client make a comment about the men. He said that none of them were unique or special and he sounded unimpressed. This made me furious. I could not believe that this man would say that about these men whom I had gotten to know. These guys had become friends to me and I had been given the chance to see beyond the facade that they put up so often with their work in prostitution. I knew in that moment that I could never forget this and I needed to do something about it.

In January 2012 we started the Punlok Thmey Tours training program. We have been working with these men for the past two years and have seen amazing growth in their lives. Currently, we have four men who are full-time tour guides with us and we have six new guys who just began the training process with us. We have had the chance to be the hands and feet of Christ to these men and show the love of God to them on a daily basis in practical ways. Through job creation we have seen lives transformed and hope renewed and I believe that transformation is what Jesus was all about. The church needs to engage the imagination that God has given us to create solutions to the problems that exist in the world and find ways to live that out.

Discussion Questions

1. What are the needs of boys and men in your area?
2. How are those needs hidden?
3. What are some barriers to meeting those needs?
4. Is anyone meeting those needs? Who should be responsible for meeting them?
5. How can Christians/the church in your area begin to meet those needs?

CHAPTER 24: HOW DO WE DEAL WITH BEING CONSIDERED "PRO-GAY" FOR WORKING WITH MEN INVOLVED IN COMMERCIAL SEX AND BEING CONSIDERED "ANTI-GAY" BECAUSE OF OUR FAITH?

Key Issues, by Wendy Gritter

The intersection of faith and sexuality can be a very complex landscape to navigate. This challenge is exacerbated by the anxiety carried into such conversations. It is important, therefore, to articulate common-ground realities and core values before we attempt to answer this question.

The First Reality: Difference Happens

The first reality is simply that in every context one will find individual persons who do not fit the majority experience of gender or sexual identity. But beyond the labels, is the reality that individuals may, *by no conscious choice of their own*, find themselves intrinsically knowing that they are different than most of their peers. For most, this will be a scary and confusing discovery. Many individuals will do whatever they can think of to "make this go away." Many will try to hide this reality from those around them. Shame, fear and self-loathing cross cultural boundaries for such individuals.

The corresponding core value to this reality is that *each individual is of inestimable worth and value*. A gender or sexual minority may not feel connected with this truth. Therefore, it is of great importance that such individuals find themselves in an environment of acceptance and love. Acceptance and agreement are not synonymous. Regardless of one's beliefs and values regarding appropriate behavior, it is critical that a minority individual is accepted as he or she is in that moment as an intrinsically-valued human being whom God loves.

It would be simpler if gender and sexual identity were cut and dried and there were simply two binary categories. One: those who fit the majority group where biological sex and internal sense of gender match and where relational and sexual attractions are directed towards the opposite sex. And two: those who fit a minority group where sex and gender do not neatly match and where attractions are to the same or both genders. The reality is that such black and white categories fail to take into account the complex combination of factors that may contribute to the dissonance one experiences in gender or sexual identity. In particular, when working among populations where the experience of trauma, exploitation and abuse is high, it can greatly muddy the waters in seeking to discern how to support those who have minority experiences.

No one can with certainty point to simplistic, deterministic causation of minority gender or sexual identity. The idea that one day one particular gene will be isolated, or one particular environmental factor will be identified, is disconnected from the chaotic interplay of predisposing factors of both the nature and nurture variety. *The truth is we don't precisely know what causes people to feel they are gay or transgender.* What we do know is that environmental experiences like trauma or abuse can complicate a person's experience of sexual identity. What we do know is that it is very normal during puberty and adolescence for individuals to feel uncertainty and confusion about their sexual identity. What we do know is that, particularly for women, sexuality can seem somewhat fluid and malleable. But what we also know is that for some individuals, the experience of a same-sex orientation seems to be quite hard-wired and attempts to shift such an orientation can prove to be not only unsuccessful, but also harmful to spiritual, emotional, and mental well-being. Similarly, while we know of individuals who previously experienced dissonance between their biological sex and sense of gender who have eventually seemed to return to a more integrated sense of self, we also know that to force someone to live as their biological sex when the sense of disconnection is both strong and consistent can wreak incredible havoc in a person's life. Many of the transgender people I have come to know went through periods of deep depression and being suicidal prior to finally beginning the transition process. It is important, however, that people do have access to professionals trained in gender issues prior to pursuing any kind of reassignment surgery. Such professionals can ensure that any underlying mental health issues can be addressed prior to full-time transition.

Such complexity leaves us with inevitable questions: "What then does the transforming work of Christ look like for such individuals? How does the good news of the gospel compel us to respond?"

Our response shouldn't look very different than our response to any vulnerable person. Personal needs for safety, provision and care will be addressed. Trauma and abuse will be addressed. *The critical factor is that such intervention not be driven by a reparative agenda.* If an individual's gender or sexual identity is viewed as a project, the overall result will be dehumanizing rather than nurturing. The good news of Christ is that individuals are loved and enfolded into the redemptive embrace of God, *as they are*. Transformation comes as individuals are able to receive God's grace to flourish. It means they move out of a place of shame, fear and self-loathing and into a place of humble confidence that they are restored to God. It means they are able to maturely and autonomously make decisions about the beliefs and values they hold and then choose to conduct themselves in a manner that is congruent with them. It means they develop in character and integrity and live honest, authentic lives. Their minority gender or sexual identity may not shift, but *their primary identity is found in being a Beloved child of God.*

The Second Reality: Perspectives Differ

The second reality to acknowledge is that people of faith come to divergent perspectives on the question of what faithful discipleship for a gender or sexual minority looks like. Some people view same-sex attraction as rebellion against God's created order. Such a view considers the appropriate response to be repentance. Others view same-sex attraction as a susceptibility to moral weakness, similar to the experience of the alcoholic. In this view, the response is abstinence. Still others view same-sex attraction as brokenness as a result of the original fall into sin. The appropriate response is to experience an accommodation of grace that can be found either in celibacy or in covenanted same-sex relationships. And then some will view same-sex attraction as a natural variant in creation. The response is to celebrate one's sexual orientation as an expression of God's love of diversity.

It is quickly apparent that there are significant differences across this spectrum of views. It is not uncommon for people to have very strong reactions to the views that seem most different from their own. However, these views are held by different people who all confess love for and faith in Christ and who hold a high regard for the Scriptures. This can create tremendous tension and judgment of one another. Acknowledging this diversity does not mean that one must consider all views equally valid. What such acknowledgment does demand, however, is the embodiment of a *posture of humility.*

Answering The Question

The question posed to guide this essay asks, *"How do we deal with concerns about being anti-gay by secular colleagues and pro-gay concerns of Christian colleagues?"* The question seems to assume that it will be secular colleagues who will be concerned about Christian organizations being anti-gay and that it will be Christian colleagues who critique organizations that seem too progressive and accepting as being pro-gay. The current global reality, however, is that those whose radar is up for language, attitudes and actions that could be interpreted as anti-gay are both those inside and outside of the Christian community. Similarly, those who vigilantly watch for any signs of succumbing to what is perceived as a "gay agenda" may also come from both groups.

We are still faced with the challenge of how to navigate such terrain. We must first acknowledge that this is difficult and can feel like a distraction. In a world where we are all connected by a few clicks on our computer, the intensity of this polarity is a reality we must learn to accept. Such polarity presents an opportunity to be a peacemaker and promoter of unity in the midst of a diverse constituency.

Consider the following principles drawn from the example of Jesus:

- Jesus' ministry was inclusive and he specifically enfolded those on the social margins of his day. *We should value inclusivity in our work and choose to not discriminate against gender and sexual minorities.*

- Jesus' ministry was not coercive but always invitational. *We should honor the autonomy of individuals as they shape their beliefs, values and decisions.*
- Jesus prayed that we would be one. *We should have a "big tent" mentality in our constituency despite differing views on the appropriate conduct for gender or sexual minority individuals.*
- Jesus trusted unlikely candidates with his message (e.g. the eunuch, the tenth leper, the demoniac, etc.). *We should invite all to serve in our work regardless of gender, race or sexual orientation and our codes of conduct should be consistent for all.*
- Jesus focused on what the Father entrusted him to do and didn't respond to the orthodoxy tests of the religious leaders. *We should focus on the mission and vision of our organizations in the protection and care of the vulnerable, we should advocate for the value and dignity of all persons, and we should acknowledge our diversity on secondary matters.*

When our ministry began to engage a more diverse constituency, I was worried that it could seem like I was talking out of both sides of my mouth as I tried to build bridges with people coming from very different perspectives on LGBT (lesbian, gay, bisexual, transgender) questions. My sense was that God encouraged me to be committed to three practices: never get defensive, be as gracious and patient as possible, and wherever possible point unapologetically to Jesus. This has served me very well, whether I am speaking to post-Christian people, fundamentalist conservative people, cynical people, hurting people, or highly political people. When we call people to remember our interconnectedness, our shared humanity, we can often soften the harsh polarity that typically marks these discussions. I find myself often referring to Desmond Tutu's phrase, "If I diminish you, I diminish myself."[1]

The criticisms from either anti-gay or pro-gay perspectives can take our time, zap our energy, and leave us feeling like it's a lose-lose situation. Calling people to a common mission, focused on shared values, allows all of us to put first things first: living out God's requirement of us to *"do justice, love mercy, and walk humbly with your God."*

Discussion Questions

1. Miroslav Volf has said, "The harder we pursue justice, the blinder we become to the injustice we ourselves perpetuate."[2] How might such a statement challenge us in our response to sexual and gender minority persons?

---

[1] Desmond Tutu, *Believe: The Words and Inspiration of Desmond Tutu* (Boulder, CO: Blue Mountain Arts Inc., 2007).

[2] Miroslav Volf, *Exclusion and Embrace: A Theological Exploration of Identity, Otherness, and Reconciliation* (Nashville: Abingdon Press, 1996).

2. What core values regarding gender and sexuality will help you to keep integrity in your messaging when communicating with different groups?

3. How can you open dialogue within your agency regarding these matters of gender and sexuality so that people will feel safe to ask hard questions and wrestle with diverse perspectives?

4. How can you create opportunities to share stories of sexual and gender minority persons with your support community?

5. When confronted with a closed-ended question about your position on homosexuality or transgender realities, how might you transform this into an opportunity for education and awareness about the individuals you are serving?

Case Study, by Paul Goodell

The answer to this question that Emmaus has employed for the past twenty years is simple, but not at all easy. It is to genuinely love people who are gay without affirming them in their lifestyle.

At a dinner honoring her work with the poor, Mother Teresa condemned the Clinton administration's support for abortion rights while President Clinton was in the room. After the event was over, President Clinton was asked by a reporter about his response to Mother Teresa's address. The President simply said, "It's hard to argue with a life so beautifully lived." President Clinton's response captures the central truth at the heart of Emmaus Ministry's answer to this question: positions and points of view can be argued with, but genuinely loving actions committed consistently over many years cannot be.

As Mother Teresa's years of serving the poorest of the poor in Calcutta's slums has given her the credibility to speak on issues of life and death, Emmaus's years of serving the forgotten poor among Chicago's hustlers has earned us the respect of Chicago's gay community. Even as America's gay subculture has become increasingly aggressive, even militant, about being accepted over the past decade, and even though Emmaus Ministries refuses to affirm the homosexual lifestyle, we have nevertheless maintained a positive relationship with Chicago's gay community.

But this is only the case because of our actions over the past twenty years. There just is no short cut to successfully answering the question presented. People who would otherwise call us anti-gay bigots because of our position on sexuality look at the witness of our actions and find nothing bigoted about them. We reach out to any man who is prostituting; we help them as long as they are serious about getting their lives together – and even if they aren't, we still maintain a relationship with them; we don't hand out tracts or walk the streets with a bullhorn condemning their actions; we feed them, clothe them and give them a measure of dignity. No one who takes the time to look at our actions can draw any conclusion other than that we genuinely love the men we work with and are trying to help them.

As for people who are inclined to think Emmaus pro-gay, they can only do so as long as they don't learn too much about us. If they see our statement on sexuality or if they look at our policies that affirm (small "o") orthodox Christian doctrine on sexuality – such as requiring our guests to come to the Ministry Center dressed as men, regardless of whether they cross-dress on the streets – they will see that we don't affirm the homosexual lifestyle. But we are clear that sin is sin, and that homosexual sin, while wrong and repeatedly condemned in scripture, is no less damning than jealousy, lust or unrighteous anger.

But again, this answer is only effective over the course of years as an unassailable witness of love. Only such a witness can answer objections about our motives. Any verbal response to the question presented, if it's not backed up by that witness, risks being interpreted as glib or hateful or worse, and being rejected.

CHAPTER 25: SHOULD CHRISTIANS AND THE CHURCH WORK WITH THE LGBT COMMUNITY AND IF SO HOW?

Key Issues, by Carl Jylland-Halverson

One need only turn on the television or open a popular magazine to find stark examples of the clash between "Christians" and members of the Lesbian, Gay, Bisexual and Transgender (LGBT) communities. Signs declaring "God Hates Fags" or photographs of members of the LGBT community participating in hedonistic activities are viewed as objective presentations of the communities by the opposing groups. For those of us who are Christian and working in the areas of human trafficking, abuse or HIV/AIDS prevention, such unchallenged stereotypes have dire consequences.

Christians ministering to people who are at risk of human trafficking limit their own entry into communities of people who need their help when they exclude members of the LGBT community from assisting in these efforts. Members of the LGBT community forfeit potential allies in serving street children, exploited women and men, and people living with AIDS when they assume all Christians will harshly judge them instead of embrace and love them.

Both communities have legitimate concerns about maintaining their values and integrity while working with one another. It is important for Christians to consider what their faith teaches about sexuality, identity and sin. It is important for members of the LGBT community to expect respect and to be treated with dignity and not as second-class citizens when working with faith communities.

Fortunately these are not exclusionary positions. Christians are familiar with viewing humanity as broken. This refers not only to communities or behaviors, it refers to all of us. We are broken. We are all called to forgive, to care for and to love our neighbors. For us, everyone is our neighbor.

The LGBT community is not a monolithic community. The needs of lesbians, gay men and transgendered people are not always the same. The result is a long history of dialog and cooperating in the areas of shared goals. This LGBT history of cooperation and the Christian model of loving one's neighbor makes working together a very real possibility.

Perspectives

The author did his field study requirements for his Masters in Theology at Emmaus Ministries in Chicago. He then went on to serve his sabbatical as a clinical psychologist at Emmaus. Emmaus Ministries is an ecumenical urban ministry that works with homeless males who participate in prostitution. The ministry clearly articulates its position on homosexuality, which is stated below. At the same time there are clear expectations of how employees and volunteers are to treat the men they serve.

Training for potential employees or volunteers includes providing clear guidelines related to sexuality and interacting with clients. The Emmaus Ministries Position on Homosexuality states, "God created man in his image; in the divine image he created him; male and female he created them."[1] Further, trainees are informed that "God's creative intent provides for sexual intimacy only in the context of heterosexual, monogamous, lifelong marriage, and thus excludes adultery, homosexuality, promiscuity, pornography, lust, etc."[2] This is a clear statement about values and sexuality.

The position paper also addresses how members of the ministry are expected to interact with homosexuals. The paper states that "all persons are created in the image of God and must therefore be treated with love and respect. These persons have the freedom to make their own choices. While we may not agree with these choices, we will not judge the individual but will seek to walk with them on their journey." The hoped for result is that "we will strive to become vehicles of God's grace among those we meet, recognizing that God is the one who effects change, and that transformation is an experience between God and an individual."[3]

Treating our brothers and sisters with respect and maintaining a humble stance toward others is important. Issues of sexuality are rarely as clear-cut as one would prefer. In a number of studies males who participated in prostitution self-identified as heterosexual or bisexual.[4] The people we minister to are often dealing with multiple issues that result in their experiencing marginalization or harassment. Runaway youth are at increased risk to being introduced to prostitution.[5] They are more likely to experience on-going abuse[6] and are at risk of exposure to STDs. What they need from us is support, advocacy and care. That does not include enabling by providing vague values. It does include being very clear that one of those values is unconditional acceptance of the person we are ministering to.

---

[1] Genesis 1:27 (New American Bible).

[2] Emmaus Ministries, "Emmaus Ministries Position on Homosexuality," in *Training Manual,* 3d ed. (Chicago: Emmaus Ministries, 2010).

[3] Emmaus Ministries, "Emmaus Ministries Position on Homosexuality," in *Training Manual,* 3d ed. (Chicago: Emmaus Ministries, 2010), 11.

[4] See, for example, Manue Fernandex-Alemay, "Comparative Studies on Male Sex Work in the Era of HIV/AIDS," *The Journal of Sex Research* 37, no. 2 (2000): 187-90; Robin Lin Miller, David Klot and Haftan M. Eckholdt, "HIV Prevention with Male Prostitutes and Patrons of Hustler Bars: Replication of an HIV Preventive Intervention," *American Journal of Community Psychology* 26, no. 1 (1998): 97-131.

[5] Lisa Smith Wagner et al., "A Snapshot of Homeless Youth in Seattle: Their Characteristics, Behaviors and Beliefs About HIV Protective Strategies," *Journal of Community Health* 26, no. 3 (2001): 219-32.

[6] Angela J. Stewart et al., "Victimization and Posttraumatic Stress Disorder among Homeless Adolescents," *Journal of the American Academy of Child and Adolescent Psychiatry* 43, no. 3 (2004): 325-31.

There are times when direct cooperation with self-identified homosexual persons for the purpose of helping others is mutually beneficial. Gay activists may have a more trusting relationship with street children or males involved in prostitution. They may know of or have access to communities that require our services. Many of the people we want to help are people who have also felt rejected by their own faith tradition. Working alongside the gay activists may help bridge that distrust the potential client may feel for us.

The gay activist may in fact need our assistance. Members of the above-mentioned communities may want to reconnect with the church. If we have a positive established relationship with members of the LGBT community they may be able to recommend us as Christians who are there to help and not judge.

Bridge Building

Bridge building (described by Andrew Marin as the conscious choice to find commonality between Christian and LGBT communities[7]) is essential if we are to serve our brothers and sisters. One need only work outreach in a red-light district or a city with an active night community to experience the residual anger of people who have felt rejected by their own churches. It is not unusual for people to search out outreach workers from faith-based organizations only to verbally abuse them for being "Christians." If the outreach worker is blessed with patience and simply listens, a story of rejection and/or abuse sometimes emerges based on being gay and Christian. This painful story is often described in the context of a "Christian, church" experience. If we are not willing to work the streets, if we are not willing to work with members of the LGBT community, then how will healing dialog occur?

One need only attend a service at a LGBT welcoming/affirming church to grasp the depth of desire of some members of the LGBT community to again be part of the Church. Affirming churches are hardly the most radical response gay Christians can have to their history of rejection. Exclusive LGBT churches that are either founded on LGBT-Theology or churches founded on Queer Theology may institutionalize the divide that is in part the result of rejection their members experienced in their churches of origin.

Working effectively with members of the LGBT community while remaining faithful to one's theology requires discipline. Just as inter-faith dialog becomes meaningless when one fails to recognize very real differences between faiths, one can lose ones values when uncritically accepting all aspects of a person in an attempt to unconditionally love. Additionally unconditional love and limitless forgiveness requires clear boundaries so that this does not translate into "everything is acceptable." It should be noted that these would be the same guidelines a Christian would apply in all of his or her relationships.

---

[7] Andrew Marin, *Love is an Orientation: Elevating the Conversation with the Gay Community* (Nottingham: InterVarsity Press, 2009), 187.

My experience at Emmaus Ministries again served me well. When we worked outreach we never worked alone. Not only did this keep us safe while on the streets it also provided us with feedback about our interactions. There was always someone around to identify when we were becoming ambiguous in the name of love.

We also provided clear boundaries for us and for our men. When we worked outreach we were entering their world. If the men wore dresses, if they referred to one another as "girl," if they had women's names we did not comment. We were after all guests in their world. When the men came to the Ministry Center they were given an orientation to the culture of the Ministry Center. They were told that to participate in the activities of the Ministry Center they must wear men's clothes and be addressed by their male names. Because we did not demand this behavior on the streets we were not viewed as rigid or judgmental but rather as being consistent with our values.

Effective Partnership

So, what would an effective partnership between a Christian ministry and a member of the LGBT community or LGBT agency look like? Hopefully it would look like a Christian ministry working with any other agency. The Christian ministry would first and foremost take care of its own spiritual needs and focus on the Triune God first, the ministry next and then issues of self. The members would routinely practice self-care. The ministry would be grounded in prayer and Scripture.

Members of the ministry would need to be open to honest feedback about how they present to members of the LGBT community. That includes a willingness to change offensive vocabulary and perhaps considering living the Gospel more than preaching it with words.

It would be important to avoid tee shirts and posters that talk about "Loving the Sinner but Hating the Sin." While this might be theologically correct, it may in fact be interpersonally offensive. For the individual who has experienced rejection from their church of origin all they may focus on is the word "Hate."

It would be helpful to schedule a safe time for members of the two groups to get together and review their interactions openly and honestly. While this is potentially painful it also can lead to a deeper relationship. When possible it would be beneficial to have time where both groups could worship together.

Such a collaborative relationship could have wide-ranging ramifications. First, we are called on to love our neighbors. Second, in finding Christ in others we learn to be humble which is always important for people involved in ministries. Third, it may truly help us be more effective in our ministers to others.

Case Study, by Carl Jylland-Halverson

Emmaus Ministries

When I was doing my field placement at Emmaus Ministries I encountered a man who was an employee of an agency that provided services for people living with HIV. He would visit Emmaus Ministries weekly to provide counseling, group sessions and HIV services. The man was openly gay. Initially neither he nor the staff of the Ministry Center appeared comfortable with one another. I suspect the staff was concerned that he would make it appear the ministry had a less than clear position on sexuality. I suspect he was waiting for the staff to discriminate against him.

I was at the Ministry Center two years later during my sabbatical. The gentleman was moving on to a new job. The Ministry Staff had a party for him. Our guys (clients) were sad to see him leaving, our staff even sadder. The gentleman was moved and expressed his desire to visit often and possibly to volunteer. The Ministry Center staff encouraged this and expressed their love for this man and their gratitude for his sustained commitment to the men they both served. Tears were shed that evening.

Both sides had learned a lot from one another. The gentleman learned that a Christian can hold a view about homosexuality that he disagrees with and yet the same Christians can authentically care for people who identify as gay. He learned that Christian love can be unconditional and that Christians can see the whole person and not one aspect of the person. The staff learned that he was more than a "gay man." They learned that cooperation and trust were possible. The clients of Emmaus Ministries clearly benefitted from this experience.

I suspect this was not a new learning for any of the people involved. I suspect the gentleman who worked with diverse groups had learned to look beyond labels. I know Emmaus Ministries staff routinely looked beyond labels when dealing with the men or when working outreach.

Love146 and Sambhavana Society

Developing a cooperative and compassionate relationship between Christian communities and the LGBT communities has the potential of benefitting both communities. Glenn Miles, a Christian who is Love146 Director of Prevention in Asia, had developed a working relationship with Jasmir Thakur, a gay activist who is the CEO of the Sambhavana Society in Mumbai, India. The Society works with men who are at risk for contracting HIV/AIDS, including men who participate in prostitution and transgendered men.

These two men were able to work together despite different faith traditions, different motivations and different orientations because they respected one another's commitment to care for exploited men. In one instance, Miles presented Thakur's research on "Baseline Survey with Masseur Boys in

Mumbai"[8] at the University of Nebraska's Second Annual Interdisciplinary Conference on Human Trafficking in 2010. Another result of this relationship is that Miles invited Thakur to assist in identifying males involved in prostitution in Cambodia. While Miles was unaware of such sites, Thakur identified six male masseur parlors in one weekend. The willingness of a Christian and a gay activist to work together had benefitted the very men both cared about.

Discussion Questions

1. You decide to work with a LGBT organization to provide services for homeless youth. Members of your congregation accuse you of leaving your faith to be politically correct. How do you respond?
2. You approach a LGBT group about possible collaboration to work with victims of human trafficking. The members of the group accuse you of being homophobic and of distorting religion and Scripture to feel superior to sexual minorities and to deny them social equality. How do you respond?
3. What does Scripture and your faith tradition tell you about how you should interact with people you identify as living "outside of the law" or out of line with the teachings of the church?
4. What are your biggest concerns/fears about working with the LGBT community? What might you do to turn those concerns into guideposts for effective interactions as opposed to barriers to collaboration?

---

[8] Glenn Miles and Jasmir Thakur, "Baseline Survey with Masseur Boys in Mumbai" (PowerPoint Presentation, 2010). http://digitalcommons.unl.edu/humtrafconf2/14/

PART 5

HOW CAN WE BETTER WORK WITH TRANSGENDER PEOPLE?

Introduction, by Glenn Miles

When many people see Thai ladyboys, Indian *hijira* or other transgender people they experience a deep sense of distrust or revulsion. But is that how Jesus sees them? Even more than boys and men, transgender people have been neglected by the faith-based community.

One notable exception is Intermission Cares (IMCARES)[1] who introduced me to the transgender community in Mumbai, India. I was deeply impressed to watch IMCARES as they reached out to the *hijira* living on the edge of a slum community who had contracted HIV and were rejected even by their own. As we arrived they greeted us with excitement and smiles, revealing just how deeply grateful they were to feel that someone genuinely cared about them.

IMCARES went on to develop a docu-drama called "ASHU: Behind the Smile"[2] to challenge the church to wake up and see this community that they cannot fail to see every day on the streets, but which have ironically become "invisible." I also developed a short documentary at the same time entitled "Accepted or Rejected"[3] that shares the testimonies of several *hijira* and their journey to faith.

Focusing on their appearance of transgender people is unhelpful. But it is their appearance that marginalizes them and pushes them to the edges of society. With so few opportunities open to them this group of *hijira* consider working in the sex trade as their only option. As we have sought to reach out to transgender people in Cambodia we have seen a similar pattern. Viewing them instead as people whose options are much broader than those defined by others may be one way forward.

Sadly, apart from those who exploit them, the few people who seem to be interested in this marginalized group are those who like studying, writing about and filming exotic groups or those who see them as an at-risk population for HIV in need of services.

But transgender people are not just subjects. They are primarily people made in the image of God who can experience God's love the same as everyone else.

So how can we better work with transgender people? This chapter explores four key questions:

- What is a Biblical approach to the transgender community?
- How can we work more effectively with transgender people who are sexually exploited?
- How can the church effectively minister to transgender people who are sexually exploited?
- Why does the church ignore transgender people and how can we bridge the gap?

---

[1] www.imcares.org

[2] http://m.youtube.com/watch?v=A2m3uz0lhPg# and http://m.youtube.com/watch?v=FmZBZoYmrf4#

[3] Available through http://www.imcares.org

Eric Mason begins with the assertion that "we have neutered the Bible. Specifically, we have unsexed the eunuch." He goes on to explore what the Bible says about the eunuch in both the Old and New Testaments. It is a fascinating hermeneutic in a context where castration was sometimes used as a weapon of war. Mason suggests that we no longer understand how eunuchs once challenged cultural understandings of male and female. As a result, we miss what a passage like Matthew 19:1-12 might really have to say regarding transgendered individuals. Mason radically suggests that "the contempt and repudiation that Jewish males had for eunuchs is akin to the aversion many individuals today feel towards transgender people." When we understand this, we realize that Jesus' words about eunuchs in Matthew 19:12 stood in contrast to the culture around him, and he had compassion for people who fell outside the paradigm of male and female. Mason invites us to follow the example of Jesus, having compassion for and aligning with eunuchs so that we might better proclaim and manifest the kingdom of heaven to them.

Next **Jarrett Davis and Glenn Miles** discuss how we can work more effectively with the transgender community based on research they conducted among self-identified transgender sex workers in Phnom Penh, Cambodia. The purpose of the research was in part to help improve services for transgender people desiring an alternative to the sex industry. To that end Davis and Miles conducted research into their needs and found that they had high vulnerability for physical abuse and sexual violence as well as strong stigma and discrimination from family members and peers. Davis and Miles make practical recommendations for meeting these and other needs. In addition, the research revealed that common beliefs about fatalism and self-identity negatively affected transgender peoples' perception of alternative employment and other self-development options for the future. Davis and Miles recommend that we should not allow ourselves, others or even transgender people themselves to obtain their identity only from their sexuality and therefore job creation and training programs should reflect this value. Finally, Davis and Miles share how this research led them to begin a ministry to transgender people, and they invite others to reach out to this unreached people group as well.

Celeste McGee explains some reasons why the church has been reluctant to reach out to and meet the needs of transgender people. She also provides advice for how churches can begin to respond effectively, based in part on her experience leading one of the few faith-based organizations working with transgender people in the sex industry. McGee challenges us that we are all misfits who need God. She encourages us to avoid being pharisaical and instead reach out to those we deem unlovely. Superficial friendliness just isn't enough. We need to avoid labels, which distance us, and be courageous enough to care. McGee encourages us to look at the research and see the facts of just how marginalized and discriminated these people are and how this can lead to self-hatred and suicidal ideation. McGee also shares positive examples of transgender people experiencing love from Christians and the church. But she warns that there is no "step-by-step guide" to reaching out to transgender people. Every individual needs individual love and care.

Finally, **Duncan Craig** also explains why the church has tended to ignore transgender people. One reason is there are few bridges of compassion between those in the transgender community and those outside of it due to lack of understanding and fear of exposure. In a deeply personal and moving account Craig shares his own experience in an attempt to bridge the gap. Another reason Craig offers for why the church ignores transgender people is because churches on one side of the spectrum may be so orthodox as to exclude them while other churches may be so liberal as to ignore their needs through weak discipleship. Instead, Craig suggests that we should have an "open-set" view of discipleship that clearly defines boundaries for salvation but allows more flexibility in discipleship. This will allow the church to bridge the gap. He encourages us that "The more space for grace we have, the stronger the bridges of compassion become allowing God's unconditional love to flow through us to reach and disciple transgenders."

CHAPTER 26: WHAT IS A BIBLICAL APPROACH TO THE TRANSGENDER COMMUNITY?

Key Issues, by Eric Mason

We have neutered the Bible. Specifically, we have unsexed the eunuch. We have lost familiarity with how this differently-gendered being was perceived in the ancient world, and so we no longer hear how the Biblical passages regarding eunuchs might speak to our contemporary conversations around gender and sexuality. In the current European or American context, the eunuch is understood to have been an asexual man whose testicles had been removed for some higher purpose, such as loyally guarding the harem or selflessly attending to the affairs of state. We no longer see how eunuchs upset gender norms.

Eunuchs in the ancient world were victims of violence, sexual exploitation and social condemnation.[1] Castration is violating; it assaults masculinity. Ancient Greek or Latin speakers had various words to differentiate whether a male's testicles had been crushed or pounded, torn from the body or cut out of it.[2] This was often done to degrade men who had been conquered in war. 2 Kings 20:18 and Isaiah 39:7 recount how King Hezekiah's sons were captured, castrated and enslaved. The intent was to humiliate a weak Israelite king and establish Babylonian dominance.[3]

The sexual exploitation of eunuchs is widely depicted in the ancient literature. Powerful men used eunuchs for their sexual gratification.[4] Aristocratic women would sometimes wait until after puberty to have a male slave castrated "so they could be sexually useful without worry about pregnancy."[5] Alternatively, boy victims of pederasty were often castrated prior

---

[1] See J. David Hester, "Eunuchs and the Postgender Jesus: Matthew 19:12 and Transgressive Sexualities," *Journal for the Study of the New Testament* 28, no. 1 (2005): 13-40; Rick Talbot, "Imagining the Matthean Eunuch Community: Kyriarchy on the Chopping Block," *Journal of Feminist Studies in Religion* 22, no. 1 (2006): 21-43; Faris Malik, "Born Eunuchs: Homosexual Identity in the Ancient World," Born Eunuchs Homepage and Library. http://www.well.com/user/aquarius/contents.htm.

[2] Hester, 21.

[3] The irony in 2 Kings 20:19 or Isaiah 39:8 should be noted. Hezekiah proclaims the prophecy of Babylonian captivity to be "good." The end of the Davidic line, the loss of Judah's wealth, and the violence done to his own sons seems a just exchange for his own "peace and security." Hezekiah's character is being called into question. See Walter Bruggemann, *Isaiah 1-39* (Louisvile, KY: Westminster John Knox Press, 1998), 312-13.

[4] Hester, 22-23.

[5] Hester, 23, n.43. To clarify, many eunuchs in the ancient world had penises. In Greek and Roman contexts, castration just involved removal of the testicles. The penis was left

to puberty in order to preserve their desirability.[6] Rather than being asexual or celibate, eunuchs were often sex slaves.

Not all eunuchs were made that way by the aggression of men. Some were natural born eunuchs, either due to some deformity of the genitals, or because they had no desire for sexual intercourse with females. They did not follow gender norms like other males.[7] Church Father Clement of Alexandria (c. 150-215AD) said of natural eunuchs: "Some men, from their birth, have a natural sense of repulsion from a woman; and those who are naturally so constituted do well not to marry."[8] Whether eunuchs were that way from birth or made that way by others, eunuchs were generally victims of social censure. Seen as emasculated, un-manned men, they are regularly depicted as being effeminate, weak, deceitful, sexually transgressive, and incapable of virtue.[9] Their gender status was ambiguous, and they are often seen as a third gender, violating the norms of male or female.[10] For example, Philo (20BC-50AD), in explaining why some individuals would be excluded from Jewish sacred assemblies (per Deuteronomy 23:1) says of eunuchs:

> (T)hey belie their sex and are affected with effemination, [they] debase the currency of nature and violate it by assuming the passions and the outward form of licentious women. For [the Law] expels those whose generative organs are fractured or mutilated....[11]

Philo's perspective is an indication of how Jewish men may have viewed eunuchs during Jesus' lifetime. Josephus (37-100AD), another Jewish male of the first century, echoes the same contempt:

> Shun eunuchs and flee all dealings with those who have deprived themselves of their virility and those fruits of generation...For plainly it is by reason of the effeminacy of their soul that they changed the sex of their body also. [They are] deemed a monstrosity....[12]

---

intact, and apparently was still capable of an erection. The reasons for castrating slaves had more to do with making slaves docile rather than concern for sexual chastity.

[6] Seneca said, "Lust castrates scads of boys" (*On Anger, I 21.*) For other examples see Faris Malik, "Castration is a Product of Male Lust and Mistrust," Born Eunuchs Homepage and Library, http://www.well.com/user/aquarius/contents.htm.

[7] In the *Babylonian Talmud, Tractate Yebamoth, VIII 79b-80b*, the rabbis have a very curious discussion about what criteria to use to discern a natural-born eunuch from a gender normative male: Does he have smooth skin, silky hair, watery semen and a high-pitched voice? Genital deformity is not in the list. See also Malik, "Ancient Roman and Talmudic Definition of Natural Eunuchs."

[8] Clement of Alexandria, "Stromota 3.1.1," trans. by John Ernest Leonard Oulton and Henry Chadwick in *Alexandrian Christianity: Selected Translations of Clement and Origen*, Philadelphia, 1954. Referenced by Malik, "Ancient Roman and Talmudic Definition of Natural Eunuchs."

[9] Hester, 21-22.

[10] Hester, 20.

[11] Philo, Special Laws, I. 325.

[12] Josephus, *Jewish Antiquities* 4.292(4.8.40).

These Jewish perspectives of eunuchs as ambiguously-gendered, sexually-transgressive, effeminate beings who are incapable of virtue are at odds with how eunuchs came to be remembered later in the Christian tradition. The shift in how eunuchs are perceived occurs in the West during the fourth century as celibacy gains spiritual respectability.[13] The details cannot be elaborated here. But as celibacy is championed as being spiritually superior to marriage in Latin Christianity, Matthew 19:12,[14] one of two significant New Testament passages on eunuchs, becomes a foundational text to support the idea that Jesus taught celibacy as a spiritual calling. This becomes the dominant Catholic interpretation, and it undergirds Catholicism's justification for the institution of clerical celibacy.[15] Protestant interpreters have continued to interpret Matthew 19:12 in terms of abstinence in singleness.[16] This is done to support the view that sexuality should not be expressed outside of marriage.[17]

The misperception of eunuchs persists in the contemporary situation, such that the word "eunuch" continues to be interpreted as referring to asexuality and celibacy. We no longer understand how eunuchs once challenged cultural understandings of male and female. As a result, we miss what a passage like Matthew 19:1-12 might have to say regarding transgendered individuals.

When read with the ancient perspectives of eunuchs in mind, Matthew 19:1-12 confronts our contempt and repudiation of individuals who are seen to transgress gender. A re-reading of that passage is in order:

> **19:1** When Jesus had finished saying these things, he left Galilee and went into the region of Judea to the other side of the Jordan. **2** Large crowds followed him, and he healed them there.
>
> **3** Some Pharisees came to him to test him. They asked, "Is it lawful for a man to divorce his wife for any and every reason?"
>
> **4** "Haven't you read," he replied, "that at the beginning the Creator 'made them male and female,' **5** and said, 'For this reason a man will leave his father and

---

[13] See David G. Hunter, *Marriage, Celibacy, and Heresy in Ancient Christianity: The Jovinianist Controversy* (Oxford: Oxford University Press, 2007); Mathew Kuefler, *The Manly Eunuch: Masculinity, Gender Ambiguity, and Christian Ideology in Late Antiquity* (Chicago: University of Chicago Press, 2001).

[14] "For there are eunuchs who were born that way, and there are eunuchs who have been made eunuchs by others – and there are those who choose to live like eunuchs for the sake of the kingdom of heaven. The one who can accept this should accept it." (NIV).

[15] Ulrich Luz, *Matthew 8-20,* Hermenia Minneapolics (MN: Fortress Press, 2001), 498-499.

[16] This even though they have greater skepticism about the virtue or possibility of living celibately. Luther, who himself took a vow of celibacy, remarked on those who have the gift of abstinence: "They are a scarce people. One will not find one in a thousand," *Luther 2.651* (Luz, 498, n. 98). Calvin warned against facile vows of celibacy, *Calvin 2.248-9; Inst. 4.13.17* (Luz, 498, n. 99). Zwingli even suggested that Jesus' call to sexual abstinence was primarily meant for the apostle's themselves, as there was so much work to do in establishing the early church (Luz, 498, n. 100).

[17] Luz, 503. See also R. T. France, *The Gospel of Matthew,* NICNT (Grand Rapids, MI: Eerdmans, 2007), 725-26; Donald A. Hagner, *Word Biblical Commentary, Vol: 33b: Matthew 14-28* (Nashville, TN: Thomas Nelson, 1995), 550; Craig S. Keener, *A Commentary on the Gospel of Matthew* (Grand Rapids, MI: Eerdmans, 1999), 469-70.

mother and be united to his wife, and the two will become one flesh'? **6** So they are no longer two, but one flesh. Therefore what God has joined together, let no one separate."

7 "Why then," they asked, "did Moses command that a man give his wife a certificate of divorce and send her away?"

8 Jesus replied, "Moses permitted you to divorce your wives because your hearts were hard. But it was not this way from the beginning. **9** I tell you that anyone who divorces his wife, except for sexual immorality, and marries another woman commits adultery."

10 The disciples said to him, "If this is the situation between a husband and wife, it is better not to marry."

11 Jesus replied, "Not everyone can accept this word, but only those to whom it has been given. **12** For there are eunuchs who were born that way, and there are eunuchs who have been made eunuchs by others – and there are those who choose to live like eunuchs for the sake of the kingdom of heaven. The one who can accept this should accept it."[18]

In the predominant interpretation of this passage, the text is read as if Jesus' intent is to tighten the regulations around marriage so as to preclude unwarranted divorce. Jesus is seen as doing so either because he is reestablishing ethical requirements of the kingdom of heaven,[19] and/or because he is protecting women in a context where they have no legal protection.[20] But in merely reading this way, the commentators fall in step with the Pharisees. They focus on the law and under what conditions divorce is acceptable. Thus, among contemporary Christians, this text (along with Mark 10:1-12) is widely known and debated primarily for what Jesus has to say about divorce in relation to marriage. This is just what the Pharisees were asking for.

The Pharisees' question, "Is it lawful for a man to divorce his wife for any cause?" arises out of the rabbinic commentary on Deuteronomy 24:1-4 and the debate between the schools of Shammai and Hillel.[21] Jesus responds by quoting the story of creation: "Have you not read that at the beginning the Creator 'made them male and female'?"[22] and "For this reason a man will leave his father and mother and be united to his wife, and the two will become one flesh."[23] Commentators differ on the degree to which they interpret sexual

---

[18] Matthew 19:1-12 (NIV).

[19] R. T. France, *The Gospel of Matthew,* NICNT (Grand Rapids, MI: Eerdmans, 2007); Donald A. Hagner, *Word Biblical Commentary, Vol: 33b: Matthew 14-28* (Nashville, TN: Thomas Nelson, 1995); Ulrich Luz, *Matthew 8-20,* Hermeneia (Minneapolis, MN: Fortress Press, 2001).

[20] Craig S. Keener, *A Commentary on the Gospel of Matthew* (Grand Rapids, MI: Eerdmans, 1999); John Nolland, *The Gospel of Matthew,* NIGTC (Grand Rapids, MI: Eerdmans, 2005).

[21] Hagner, 547; Luz 488, France, 207. Hillel permitted divorce on the grounds of mere dissatisfaction with one's wife. Shammai permitted it only in the case of adultery. Most Jewish men preferred Hillel's view.

[22] Genesis 1:27.

[23] Genesis 2:24.

union as having importance here,[24] but they agree that Jesus' intent is expressed in verse 6: "Therefore what God has joined let no one separate." This is interpreted as being Jesus' ethical verdict, which is seen as being reiterated and amended in verse 9.[25]

I suggest that if we read these verses with healing in mind (see 19:2), our perspective shifts. The Pharisees approach Jesus wanting to talk about divorce. But Jesus doesn't seem particularly motivated to talk about it; he does so only as a concession. He is in the midst of healing people. That is what is dear to his heart. Is it possible that when the Pharisees want to talk about divorce, Jesus hears them asking about broken sexual relationships and the loss of desire? As a healer, Jesus knew of the need for the redemption of the marriages of these Jewish men. So instead of responding directly to their question, Jesus prompts the Pharisees to think about Eden and the goodness of God's creation: "Don't you know, God created them male and female." It's a reference to Genesis 1, and an evocation of the refrain of creation, "God saw that it was good."[26] In calling Eden to mind, Jesus affirms the blessing of being male and female. The two became one flesh; they were naked and knew no shame.

This focus on sex and gender is significant in light of what Jesus will say later in the passage about eunuchs.

The Pharisees interrupt Jesus' work of healing by wanting to talk about divorce. Jesus responds by saying, in effect, "Don't you remember the goodness of being male and female with each other? Of the joy that comes with becoming one flesh? This is why you left your father and mother and became a man. God desires to give you good, why then do you try to divide what God has joined?"

The phrase, "Therefore what God has joined together, let no one separate" (v. 6), can be read both as a conclusion about the goodness of sexual union and a caution about protecting ourselves sexually. Jesus could be saying, "There is goodness for you when God puts you together with someone. Don't harm yourself by destroying that." This is a different tone than the one Jesus uses in verse 9, where Jesus clearly does establish an absolute ethical limit: "I say to you, whoever divorces his wife, except for unchastity, and marries another commits adultery." The tone shifts because the Pharisees are "hard-hearted." They don't want to talk about the goodness of sexuality or the redemption of their marriages. They want a way out; they want justification by law. So Jesus,

---

[24] Nolland, 772, downplays sexual union: "(A) larger psychosexual unity is intended. One flesh is seen as a persistent state, not something localized in the act of copulation." Hagner, 548, favors "mysterious union" over sexual intercourse. Keener, 463, does not mention sexual intimacy and instead focuses on "marital harmony." Luz, 789, in contrast holds that "one flesh . . . expresses the unity of man and woman that is experienced in sexual activity." France, 717, in my opinion, does the best job of understanding "one flesh" as an integration of sexual intimacy leading to a greater bonding or joining together.

[25] Hagner, 549, specifically notes Jesus' "absolutism" in v. 6, which he then views as being watered down by the exception made in v. 9. See also Keener, 466.

[26] I make this argument in contraposition to Hester and Talbot who interpret what Jesus says about eunuchs as undermining normative gender categories.

like Moses, makes a concession. He gives them a clearly delineated ethical norm that surpasses the teachings of either Shammai or Hillel.[27] Because of their hard-heartedness, Jesus gives them more than they asked for and more than they can handle. He uses the law to put them in a bind. But that was not his desire when the conversation started.

In verse 10, Matthew gives us a sense of how Jesus' most sympathetic listeners, the disciples, received the bind. Their response is incredulity.[28] They get reactive. They propose what no self-respecting Jewish male would entertain, "Well, if such is the case of a man with his wife, it is better not to marry." For Jewish males, marriage and fathering children was seen as a religious duty.[29] There was no honor in remaining single or celibate, and in fact, failing to marry or father children brought on social censure.[30] Males who did not procreate were sterile, un-manned men, lacking virility.[31] The disciples are suggesting a startling renunciation of both their sexuality and a core expectation of their faith. In effect, the disciples are saying, "It is better to be emasculated. It's better to be a eunuch." But their suggestion is facetious; they don't mean it. In their reactivity, *their* hard-heartedness is exposed. They re-enact the stubborn-resistance of the Pharisees.

This hard-heartedness manifests as contempt for those who transgress gender norms. It is the same contempt that Philo and Josephus exhibit; a cultural reprehension for males who are engendered differently, who don't marry or sire children. Ironically, the disciples do so in protest of the stringent application of the bounds of marriage toward themselves. They don't want to be good husbands, and in their protest, they reveal their ambivalence about manhood. Deep down, they are afraid of being eunuchs, of not being man enough. Jesus discerns this and so talks explicitly about eunuchs in verse 12. His desire is that his disciples would become the kind of men who could proclaim and manifest the kingdom of heaven. Yet the disciples' insecurity, ambivalence and contempt are an impediment in that mission. Jesus thus confronts the disciple's hard-heartedness and refuses to let them out of their bind.[32] He counters their contempt with an invitation to become like that which

---

[27] Though Jesus' position is close to that of Shammai, various interpreters see Jesus as being more proscriptive than Shammai. France, 721, notes that Jesus narrows the offense to "sexual unfaithfulness" rather than Shammai's criteria of having done "something shameful." Hagner, 549, tends to think that the "absolute statements" in Matthew 19:6, Mark 10:11 and Luke 16:18 are Jesus' view, whereas the exception "except for unchastity" is uniquely Matthean. Luz, 494, focuses on the proscription against "marrying another." Shammai would have been more lenient.

[28] Both France, 722, and Hagner, 549, pick up on the incredulity. Keener, 471, simply sees the disciples as "concerned about the danger of marrying without an escape clause."

[29] France, 722; Nolland, 777. The religious command derives from Genesis 1:28, "Be fruitful and multiply." Even though Jesus quotes the verses around this, he does not reference this specifically, as if he is mindful of those who are non-procreative.

[30] France, 715, 722-23; Hagner, 550; Luz, 500-1.

[31] Josephus, *Antiquitates Judaicae*, 4.290-91.

[32] Though Nolland, 781, does not share my interpretation, he does agree that Jesus is creating a bind here. "(T)he imagery of becoming a eunuch is chosen precisely because

they despise. He says, "Not everyone can accept this word, but only those to whom it has been given. For there are eunuchs who were born that way, and there are eunuchs who have been made eunuchs by others – and there are those who choose to live like eunuchs for the sake of the kingdom of heaven. The one who can accept this should accept it."

The invitation to become like that which they despise, to act counter to the cultural construction of their masculinity, is present throughout Matthew 18-20:28, where the disciples are being educated and reformed in the "revolutionary values of the kingdom of heaven."[33] When the disciples jockey for position and ask, "Who is the greatest?", Jesus challenges them to "become like little children" (Matthew 18:3), to humble themselves. They are taught that the "first will be last . . . and the last first" (Matthew 19:30), and that if they want to be great, they must become a slave (Matthew 20 26-7). In each case, Jesus is encouraging his male disciples to go against the pride that undergirds how their masculine identity has been culturally constructed.[34] In challenging them to be "last" and become like children, eunuchs and slaves, Jesus calls the disciples to a radical humility that seems at odds with their sense of masculinity. Paradoxically, Jesus invites the disciples to align with eunuchs specifically because the healing and restoration of their own ambivalent, impotent masculinity is bound up in letting go of their contempt and pride. Jesus is offering his disciples freedom from the insecurity that they are not man enough.

What Should Our Response Be?

So how does the Bible speak here to our contemporary conversations around gender and sexuality? Why should Christians work with the transgendered community? The contempt and repudiation that Jewish males had for eunuchs is akin to the aversion many individuals today feel towards transgender people. When we read Matthew 19:1-12 with this in mind, we can hear the gospel anew. Jesus affirms the goodness of male and female and the blessing of procreative sexuality within marriage. But Jesus understood that there were those who didn't fit the paradigm of male and female, who stood outside it. Unlike the culture around him, Jesus had compassion for such individuals. We are invited to follow Jesus, have compassion and align with eunuchs so that we might better proclaim and manifest the kingdom of heaven. The softening of

---

it takes up and intensifies the negative feelings engendered in a Jewish context by the notion that one should abstain from marriage and subsequent sexual expression within marriage."

[33] France, 710. France breaks it up into two parts: (a) Matthew 18:1-19:2 where the focus is on discipleship training and (b) Matthew 19:3-20:28 which is "re-education for the disciples" because it did not stick the first time around.

[34] Keener, 447, observes that Jesus' "radical consideration of humility in Matthew 18 challenges his hearer's sense of social power structures."

our hearts and the healing of our own gender and sexuality depend upon it.[35] This is a hard teaching. Let anyone accept this who can.

Discussion Questions

1. What has been your perception of eunuchs in the Bible? How was that passed on to you?
2. What descriptive heading does your Bible give to Matthew 19:1-12? In most Bibles the editor has written a heading such as "Teaching on Divorce." How has that influenced your reading of the text?
3. How has this essay impacted you? How has it blessed you? How does it make you wrestle and question?
4. What is your understanding of the connection between working with transgender individuals and the restoration and healing of your own gender and sexuality?
5. Deuteronomy 23:1 forbids eunuchs from entering into the worship life of Israel. Read Isaiah 56:3-8. How might the Isaiah passage have presented a prophetic challenge to ancient Israel? How is it a prophetic challenge for us today?
6. Read Acts 8:26-40. How does understanding the ancient contempt for eunuchs inform how you might now read this passage? How is this story an example of a Jewish man becoming a eunuch for the sake of the kingdom of heaven?

---

[35] I suggest that the story of Philip and the Ethiopian Eunuch (Acts 8:26-40) is an example of this. It is a story of how Philip becomes a eunuch for the sake of the kingdom of heaven. Despite cultural and religious prohibitions, he listens to the Spirit and aligns with the eunuch, such that the kingdom of heaven is gloriously made manifest. By tradition the eunuch founds the church in Ethiopia, while Philip's ministry seems to go into high gear (see Acts 8:40). Philip is a more potent evangelist as a result.

CHAPTER 27: HOW CAN WE WORK MORE EFFECTIVELY WITH TRANSGENDER PEOPLE WHO ARE SEXUALLY EXPLOITED?

Key Issues, by Jarrett Davis and Glenn Miles

Transgender people are a familiar sight on the streets of many cities across Southeast Asia. In recent years, there has been a gradual understanding among a few organizations that members of this group are vulnerable to being sexually exploited. Love146 is a part of a small, collaborative movement of interested organizations who have both recognized – and acted upon – the neglect of males and sexual minorities, particularly transgender persons involved in the sex industry.

This essay will examine the question of how we can more effectively work with transgender people who are sexually exploited. While this essay focuses on our research and experiences in Cambodia, it is hoped that lessons learned will be applicable in other contexts as well.

The Hidden Problem

While the vulnerability of women and girls has continued to be the subject of much research and a growing concern among social service providers and non-governmental organizations, few attempts have been made to understand the vulnerabilities and lived experiences of transgender people in the sex industry in Cambodia. Among the minimal studies that have been conducted, nearly all have solely focused on sexual health and the likelihood of transgender people to contract or spread HIV/AIDS, while often ignoring the existence of other potential vulnerabilities.

Love146 has therefore attempted to provide a baseline of data to better understand the lives of transgender persons in the Cambodian sex trade industry. This baseline of data was intended to be used as a resource for social service providers and future researchers who hope to provide useful and informed intervention strategies for transgender people who desire an alternative to the sex industry. We began this endeavor with the understanding that we cannot work effectively with people if we don't first understand their backgrounds, contexts and the depth of their stories, both individually and collectively. After all, they are the best experts of their own lives.

The Research

Research was conducted in 2013 among fifty self-identified "transgender sex workers" in or near Phnom Penh, Cambodia. The findings of the research are published in a report entitled "More than Gender."[1] The study utilized both quantitative and qualitative research methodologies and merged careful fieldwork with extensive, one-on-one structured interviews.

The research found a particularly high vulnerability for physical abuse and sexual violence among transgender sex workers in Phnom Penh, as well as strong stigma and discrimination coming from family members and peers. In analysis of the gathered data, the study also discussed a seemingly inherent fatalism that was commonly observed within social identity of transgender sex workers and the impact that this fatalism may have on their perception of alternative employment and other self-development options for the future. Additionally, the study attempted to unpack some of the ways in which exploitation can be derived from self-identity, and how the formation and adoption of exploitive self-identities can make transgender groups within the Cambodia (and perhaps broader Southeast Asian) cultural context uniquely vulnerable.

We wanted to provide a broad baseline of data that was descriptive of the holistic needs and vulnerabilities of transgender people in the sex industry in Phnom Penh. It was hoped that such a survey would allow for a deeper understanding of such groups, including their trajectory into the sex industry and potential alternatives. Additionally, we wanted the study to aid in the development of programming and social services that meets the needs of such groups holistically, looking beyond their gender expressions and social identities to address the deeper human needs and vulnerabilities that may often go overlooked.

The Needs Revealed

Sexual exploitation research within the anti-trafficking-in-persons movement has almost exclusively focused on young girls and some women. Young men and transgender people need a higher profile in this conversation. While males and transgender people are not commonly seen as vulnerable or objects of sexual abuse and violence, data in this study clearly revealed that transgender people in fact experience high levels of physical, verbal and sexual abuse, including gang rape and other forms of dehumanizing violence. It is important that greater efforts be made to underscore the vulnerability of all persons – regardless of what gender identity, gender expression or social group they may fall into.

It is important that both government and non-government sectors work together towards the development of policy and programs that recognize and affirm the holistic, human needs and vulnerabilities of transgender persons, beyond merely sexual health. This should include the creation of legal, social and health services that address the broader developmental needs of persons

---

[1] Jarrett Davis and Glenn Miles, "More Than Gender: A Baseline Study of Transgendered Males in the Sex Industry in Phnom Penh, Cambodia" (Phnom Penh: Love 146, October 2013).

who are marginalized and exploited, rather than merely catering to the needs of females and children.

It is important that all NGOs receive education and support in how to treat transgender persons with dignity and respect. Sex worker unions and legal support organizations also need to consider how they can provide legal help when transgender people experience violence and discrimination. Police, legal, health and social workers need education as to the specific needs of transgender people so that they can better understand such groups and ensure that they are acting in supportive ways, rather than in discriminatory ways. Additionally, faith-based groups have often been key in advocating for the needs and vulnerabilities of numerous marginalized groups in society, including sexually exploited females, but it is also important that they begin to recognize the needs and vulnerabilities of males and transgender persons as well, and work towards a healthy and non-discriminatory way of addressing the developmental needs of such groups.

Alternative job opportunities should be made available to transgender persons who are seeking to leave the sex industry, while also working to develop a greater diversity of employment options for individuals from such groups. Through our research, we have observed that the range of perceived work options that transgender people understand to be available for themselves is often limited to a very narrow collection of job sectors, mainly in the beauty and fashion industry. While the creation of jobs or training opportunities in this sector would be welcome, it might also be helpful to explore other possibilities in different sectors of the employment market. This could be accompanied by mentoring or coaching for transgender people to help them to discover their "hidden potential" and to develop a wider perception of who they are and what they can do. Being very optimistic, this could lead into the creation of new jobs in sectors that might not be yet developed in places like Cambodia. In addition to this, free or low-cost vocational and life skills training programs provided by NGOs, governments, corporations or local churches could be greatly beneficial for young males and transgender persons seeking to leave the sex industry.

Additionally, it is important that MSM and transgender people are not grouped into the same category, but are defined as separate people groups with unique needs and vulnerabilities. Non-government organizations should work with the government in the creation of community centers or "safe spaces" that are able to cater to the development needs of LGBT people, especially transgenders. It is important that private and public social services address the development of such groups as whole, integrated persons. This requires more than simply providing condoms and STI checks, but rather recognizing transgender persons as multi-faceted individuals who are more than just a gender identity or sexual orientation.

Concluding Thoughts

While our field research team understood there to be many potential respondents for the study, finding transgender sex workers to interview was a challenging task to undertake. Researchers quickly discovered that, due to the levels of violence and discrimination experienced by members of this group, it was common that respondents could only be found in the very early hours of the morning. However, despite their perhaps intentional difficultly to be found, our research team discovered many of the respondents in the study to be greatly appreciative to be able to speak with people who were genuinely interested in them as persons who deserve dignity and respect. In fact, once interviewing had begun, it became common for respondents to invite other transgender friends to come and speak to us, due to it being so unusual for them to find friendly strangers who were genuinely concerned about their lives and experiences. Further, a couple of respondents even expressed a strong interest in meeting with and exploring alternative employment with one particular faith-based organization in Cambodia, Sons of Cambodia,[2] which works to provide livelihood and vocational skills to transgender persons coming from the sex industry.

On completion of the research we felt uncomfortable just leaving this population when so few other organizations had made any attempts to connect with such groups. Thus, we decided to continue to do outreach on the streets in a few of the locations in which we had conducted the study. This has now evolved into a ministry called "Bridge to Life," which is a part of the ministry of "The Message Parlour."[3] The purpose of this project is to befriend transgender people and build relationships with them, providing them with access to valuable resources such as potential alternative work as well as health and legal services. A partner organization, Open Arms Cambodia,[4] has since opened up a beauty salon geared towards transgender persons as a means of building relationships.

While there has been little precedence of the faith-based community reaching out to the dynamic individuals within this highly marginalized people group, we must reach out to them. In the life and ministry of Jesus, he was notorious for hanging out and sharing meals with the overlooked and marginalized groups of his society – a habit that often made the religious leaders of his day quite uncomfortable. Perhaps it is important for us to ask ourselves: "In our present society and context where would Jesus be? Who would he be joining with at the dinner table?" It is our foundational belief that he would be – and indeed is – right there with us as we connect with one of the most marginalized and invisible groups of Cambodian society, who are yet his children.

Discussion Questions

1. What are the reasons that we have tended to ignore transgender people? Is it because we don't know where to start? Is it fear of

---

[2] http://daughtersofcambodia.org/sons

[3] www.themessageparlour.org

[4] www.openarmscambodia.org

working with this group who are sometimes confrontational? Is it lack of donor support? Is it because traditionally your organizational focus has been females because they are seen to be more vulnerable?

2. What could you do to start engaging with this population?
3. Does the Bible say that people need to change before we work with them? What would it look like for a sexually exploited transgender person to become more whole, in a way that is truly Biblical and not merely based on our own culture, assumptions and/or prejudices?

CHAPTER 28: HOW CAN THE CHURCH EFFECTIVELY MINISTER TO TRANSGENDER PEOPLE WHO ARE SEXUALLY EXPLOITED?

Key Issues, by Celeste McGee

How the church should interact with transgender people is complicated with numerous complex answers depending on the perspective of the person responding, whether they are exploring a theological understanding and/or if they are involved in current political debate and the concerns around possible repercussions. There is little research in this area either.[1] How can the church effectively minister? How is the word "effective" even defined or measured here? Most individuals would have various opinions and expectations so when asked to write about this topic, I hesitated due to all of these bombarding thoughts. I started with quoting counselors, articles and current research and facts but then it came to me that the answer is really not that complicated.

A Simple Answer That Requires Much

It may not be complicated but it does require much from the church. It involves asking believers to step out of their comfortable surroundings and choose to enter a deep friendship with someone who may seem so strikingly unique in the beginning – to connect with a transgender person and not be afraid of the unknowns. The church needs to remember whom they are, how Jesus interacted with others, and then live out these two concepts when encountering a transgender. He or she is simply another human being. On first contact a transgender person can appear to be so extremely different than a "normal" person. This first impression both isolates the transgender but also prevents the church from believing that a believer can relate to him or her. It's unhelpful that something so simple provides a barrier but seems to happen by many Christians over and over again.

To clarify, and give some background for saying this, I work specifically with Thai "ladyboys" that are at risk of entering the sex industry or already work in Bangkok's red light districts.[2] Thai believers are less than 2% of the

---

[1] In order to increase the body of research our organization, Dton Naam Ministries, partnered with Love146 in 2013 to conduct a study entitled "Beyond Gender: A Baseline Study on the Vulnerability of Transgender Sex Workers in Bangkok, Thailand" (Love 146/Dton Naam, October 2013).

[2] Dton Naam Ministries, which the author founded in Bangkok, Thailand in 2009. Dton Naam focuses specifically on transgender individuals working in the sex industry, offering them alternative jobs, job training, counseling and classes in order to help them rebuild their lives in a healthy way. www.dtonnaam.org

entire population.[3] Several studies and NGOs show there are more Thai prostitutes (male, female and transgender) than there are Thai believers.[4] However, there is little evidence that the Thai church is ministering to Thai transgender people, whether they are involved in the sex industry or not.

God's path for me has included the privilege of getting to know some of these transgender since the summer of 2005. I also do not consider myself "effective" yet, because there is still so much to learn. Almost all of the ladyboys I know discuss feeling "feminine" before the age of five, despite their male anatomy. I have not met a ladyboy that was born with ambiguous genitals yet. Whether they were pressured, raised, teased, or simply felt more comfortable playing with the girls, there has been some level of acceptance by family or society to become a ladyboy.

Thai ladyboys have unique cultural factors that are different from the transgendered in the US. People from all over the world travel to Thailand for sex reassignment surgeries. In nine years, I've personally only known three stories of where a ladyboy slowly walked into masculinity. In our experience it is not helpful to push transgender people into living physically as a certain gender, but to start with their needs and longings and begin reaching out to that part of their being. Although some believers may naturally try to do this with coworkers, friends and strangers, it often becomes uncomfortable, unknown and awkward to reach out to a transgender person.

Responding to Needs Effectively

If we are to respond to the needs of transgender people, how can we do so effectively? This section will offer suggestions based on Biblical principles and practical experience.

Remember, We're All Just Misfits

First, the church needs to remember that believers are also all a bunch of misfits! It started back with the first group following Jesus around to various cities and desert places, seeing numerous miracles performed, but often lacking faith. Many were poor, uneducated fishermen and/or money hoarders. Most failed horribly and ran away when things became heated. Then, the Holy Spirit came. Different languages, cultures, ethnicities and backgrounds were immediately slammed together. Believers started living in community, growing in number daily and learning together. Persecution spread them to surrounding areas. There were discussions, disputes and "Councils" about what traditions to keep, what food was allowed, baptism, cultural and moral issues, how to confront each other and more. Misfits from everywhere and their sins were listed out bluntly, such as fornicators, adulterers, etc. Paul tells them, "such

---

[3] "Thailand" Joshua Project Website.

[4] See, for example, Randy Wollf, "Reaching Thailand in this Generation: The Thai Church's National Plan" (World Evangelical Alliance Website, May 12, 2010), 3.

were some of you" but you were sanctified and forgiven through Christ.[5] That definitely does not sound like a safe, protective bubble like many Western churches seem to crave for their children and congregation.

Believers today are similar: declared new creations in an instant, but sometimes the walking out of addictions, deception, idolatry, gluttony and other impurities take years. Believers are not perfect and should not pretend to have their lives all wrapped up in a nice, pretty bubble. They are declared holy, children of the King who should likewise show mercy, compassion and truth to every other human being on the planet. Believers should never forget they are only declared righteous because of what Jesus did for them. Believers need to exude grace, patience and compassion when building a connection with a ladyboy/transgender. Churches with discipleship and healing programs already as part of their weekly fabric will be more effective. They are already aware of needs related to grief, divorce, trauma, addictions, and substance abuse. There is the possibility of a support system and solid relationships.

Learn to Truly Love Each Other

Second, the church must learn to love misfits. Remember Jesus, the one and only Savior, who interacted with misfits on a daily basis? He would continually say profound phrases such as, "Love one another. Love your enemies. Love your neighbor as yourself." He lived it out. He loved and called the misfits "friends." He even loved the one that betrayed him to the very end.[6] Paul followed suit and said, "Let love be without hypocrisy; give preference to one another in honor. Love does no wrong to a neighbor."[7] Somehow, however, one phrase seems to have slowly replaced all these powerful ideas: "Treat others as you want to be treated."[8] Parents use it constantly. Bible teachers seem to quote it more than the others. The concept is there, but has slowly become more about outward behavior, about keeping people polite. But, love is so much deeper and connected. It's abundantly more than a smile or a gesture. It's also not based on a personal perspective, painful wounds, or a personality type. Love is based on Jesus – rooted in his love for mankind. This is just one reason why it's the "kindness" of God that leads people to repentance.[9] It is this simple: if the church wants to be effective, they need to deeply love. Do not treat the transgender with superficial friendliness while keeping him at arm's length. Love. It's the greatest thing.[10] Everyone needs it.

One idea to lovingly start walking alongside a transgender person is for the church to drop the labels. Churches occasionally use labels to try to fit something unfamiliar into something that can be defined and then pushed into a mold. Labels like "drag queen," "transvestite," and "transsexual" become

---

[5] I Corinthians 6:9-11.
[6] Matthew 5; John 13:1.
[7] Romans 12:9-10; Romans 13:10.
[8] Luke 6:31.
[9] Romans 2:4.
[10] I Corinthians 13:13.

congruent with "freak" and are then used negatively against the person. Instead, we must look past the label and see the individual standing before us as a person who is created in the image of God, no matter how distorted or tainted or wounded this person seems to be.

Seek to Learn More

Third, we must not fear certain political agendas but learn what is happening medically, scientifically and culturally. For example, transgender people have high rates of suicide attempts:

> "In a national survey of 7,000 transgender who were asked 'have you ever attempted suicide?' 41% answered yes. 'I knew that the magnitude would be high, but I did not think the suicide attempt numbers would be that high,' said clinical psychologist Gail Knudson... The percentage is corroborated by another source that says among transgender people ages 18-44, the suicide attempt rate was 45%."[11]

The knowledge that such a high percentage of transgender people attempt suicide should wake the church's senses to the question, "Why isn't the church reaching out more?"

Other research can provide helpful information about the complicated lives of transgender people: XY chromosomes, ambiguous genitals, DNA, low testosterone and hormonal levels. We can learn about how some transgender experience botched surgeries, sexual diseases, substance abuse and the long-term serious side effects of the hormones and silicone often injected into their bodies. We need to engage with these issues and show concern. Depression, abuse, trauma and family dynamics also need to be considered.

However, the transgender person does not want the believer to discuss research, stats and scenarios in hopes that he can magically be put into a box and then fixed, just like a person who recently went through a difficult divorce does not want another to assume that the "three top reasons people divorce today" necessarily relates to him. The divorcee needs a friend, a support system, time to heal, time to move forward. In the same way, the church needs to provide transgender people with someone who is there on the good days and on the really rough ones. Fifty strangers shouldn't be weekly telling a transgender of all the possible risks out there. Each individual is unique. Every story has beauty and despair. The church has to be willing to enter a story and walk alongside each person, no matter how long it takes – which again, can make people uncomfortable. I've met only a few people who have been willing to do this. In the next section I will introduce you to them.

---

[11] Walt Heyer, *Paper Genders: Pulling the Mask Off the Transgender Phenomenon* (Sacramento: Make Waves Publishing, 2011), 44 (citing Jaime M. Grant et al., "National Transgender Discrimination Survey Report on Health and Health Care/ Findings of a Study by the National Center for Transgender Equality and the National Gay and Lesbian Task Force," October 2010 and Clara Moskowitz, "High Suicide Risk, Prejudice Plague Transgender People," Live Science Website, November 19, 2010).

Examples in Effectiveness

One couple, Dr. Roy and his wife Bonita befriended Walt Heyer for years as he lived as a woman and then returned to living as a man. As Dr. Roy shares,

> Thus began a journey that turned "a few days" into nine months and nine months into twelve more years with visits lasting months at a time. We had no precedent for this situation in other relationships, nor did we find any specific Scripture to act as a road map through this minefield. We did know that we had a responsibility to love her. About this, Scriptures were clear. [12]

Dr. Roy and Bonita, with masters and doctoral degrees in education, psychology and theology, openly admit they were not prepared or knew what Walt was facing and experiencing, but their friendship and love was effective. Walt openly shares his story online and has authored several books. He has actively been helping others for years, specifically sharing his own story with the transgender community.

Sy Rogers is another amazing guy with an unusual story. He planned and was working toward the sex reassignment surgery when he remembered a childhood song "Jesus Loves Me." It brought him to tears and Jesus. Sy writes,

> Three days later, I heard a report on the morning news that would change my life: Johns Hopkins Hospital announced they would no longer be performing sex "reassignment" surgery. They were closing their program, suspending the waiting list of patients seeking the operation, and saying this surgical treatment wasn't the answer for the vast majority of transsexuals. [13]

Sy travels and speaks to churches. It is important for churches to collectively agree to learn stories such as Walt's and absorb Sy's insight to help shift the church into a loving and healthy response.

How Should Our Church Begin?

If a church recognizes there are transgender people in its city and believers are crossing paths with them, there are so many ways for a church to help the believers prepare to connect in healthy ways. Resources from Sy and Walt and others are easily accessible. There should not be a completed, formulated step-by-step guide though because God is so much bigger than that. Every journey is different and a transformational process. Each believer should remember his or her own personal journey with God. He does tend to reveal himself at a deep level, let each person respond and heal and then he does it again in another area. He doesn't convict and reveal all the horrible things in a person's life at once. Hearts couldn't take it. Again, it is God's love and kindness.

Sadly, there are also many ways the church can injure and cause horrible spiritual abuse. The Westboro Church is a sad example of causing horrendous injury to individuals as well as attempting to ruin the church's reputation in general. Of course, most churches are nothing like Westboro but could still

---

[12] Walt Heyer, *Trading My Sorrows: A True Story of Betrayals, Bad Choices, Love, and the Journey Home* (Salem: Xulon Press, 2006), 81.

[13] Sy Rogers, "The Man in the Mirror" (Last Days Ministries Website, March 27, 2012).

cause harm to a transgender person by "pushing truth and a preemptive healing" onto him. There are so many individuals, transgender or not, who long for supernatural, immediate healing of their internal wrestling. But Western churches, in particular, tend to project that fast-food-line mentality onto deep layers of healing that need time. People want things to change quickly and clearly. Some think that if one prayer to cast out an unclean spirit does not "work" it must be because the transgender lacks faith. But incredible damage will result from such assumptions. Jesus did not enforce dress codes or "no make up policies" the first day a person believed. Why do some feel compelled to do this? Why is it only connected to certain physical appearances? Do these same places have the same requirement for instant transformation when it comes to morality, healthy eating habits and lifestyles?

I know of one Thai ladyboy who became a Christian but remained living as a woman for at least twelve years. Many believers thought he should become a man again and tried to force it at times, often hurting this person. He had walked through so much healing internally, but his physical appearance made some believers uncomfortable. But, he kept following Jesus and finally the Holy Spirit revealed a deep layer of identity to him. It undid him but due to the years of intimacy with Jesus, he courageously responded to what Jesus revealed. He cut his hair and is now embracing masculinity. It wasn't forced.

Dig deep into Scripture too. Ask Jesus to speak. Is it possible to find some truths about eunuchs to which transgender people can relate? There are different speculations but in Acts 8, there is nothing clearly stated to why the Ethiopian eunuch was a eunuch or how he became one. Jesus told Philip to leave the crowds where healings occurred and travel far to meet this one man. This eunuch mattered to Christ and he quickly became a believer. What if the church is simply willing to be there, to speak truth, teach Scripture (not push it) and let the Holy Spirit do the rest? Does that seem too messy still?

There's also a beautiful passage in Isaiah: "Nor let the eunuch say, 'Behold, I am a dry tree.' For thus says the Lord, 'To the eunuchs who keep My Sabbaths, and choose what pleases Me, and hold fast My covenant, to them I will give in My house… a memorial, and a name better than that of sons and daughters; I will give them an everlasting name which will not be cut off.'"[14] This misfit is definitely happy to be considered a daughter of the King, but there is a promise to give eunuchs something better! Doesn't this show how incredible God's mercy, love and plans are for individuals who may have lost reproductive organs due to war, slavery or choice? So, the starting question does involve asking a large percentage of believers to step out of their comfort zones and choose to enter a deep friendship with a transgender person, without fear.

Can the church be effective? Absolutely. But to do so, we need to remember who we are and not be distracted by politics or legalism. We need to always love deeply and be willing to walk out own journey as we walk next to a transgender person.

---

[14] Isaiah 56:4-5, (NASB).

Discussion Questions

1. Is the church offering or failing to offer support to those in the transgender community? In what ways?
2. In what practical ways can the church start reaching out to the transgender community?
3. How did Jesus approach people who were considered on the margin of society?
4. Are you willing to allow God to transform your mindset in regards to this topic?

CHAPTER 29
WHY DOES THE CHURCH IGNORE TRANSGENDER PEOPLE AND HOW CAN WE BRIDGE THE GAP?

Key Issues, by Duncan Craig

Why Do We Ignore Transgender People?

Bridges of Compassion

When building a bridge, both ends must span the chasm of separation. It is similar when building bridges of compassion. We understand the suffering brought by natural disasters or war and build bridges of compassion when we reach out to help those in greater need than us. However, when something like the HIV/AIDS pandemic first appeared there was little understanding and sufferers were ignored and rejected. In time though, through greater understanding, bridges of compassion have been built.

Few outside the transgender community understand what it is like to live a transgender identity. Likewise, transgenders often live in secrecy. There is very little to begin building bridges of compassion. This paper is one small brick in that bridge.

Polarization

"We" the church encompasses a spectrum which can be summarized below:

◀   ▶

Orthodox   Liberal

On the orthodox wing, theological positions are tightly defined with a high moral entry level, requiring outsiders to embark on a significant journey of transformation before they are fully accepted as an insider. Transgenders can be ignored as the journey of transformation may be perceived so great; preferring instead people already closer to their moral landscape.

Whereas on the liberal wing, theological positions are more fluid with lower moral entry levels; leaving outsiders with less reason to embark on a journey of transformation. Transgenders are more likely to be accepted but could have their needs ignored if liberal discipleship is weak.

Theology of Conformity

Society groups people through conformity of gender, linguistics, political allegiances, social spheres, ethnicity or demographics. Across the spectrum many churches are possibly shaped more by social conformity rather than by a theology of conformity to Christ.[1] It takes a radically brave church to include people who could destabilize their comfortable status quo. We see this frequently in Scripture where the Pharisees are aghast when Jesus associates with "notorious sinners."

Perception

How we perceive transgenders shapes how we receive them. According to one study, approximately one to three percent of the UK population struggles with transgender identity and seeks resolution through cross-dressing, hormone treatment or gender reassignment surgery (GRS).[2] Many live with their transgender identity hidden from public view as a result of fear, prejudice or ignorance. In fact, that fear is not misplaced. In a recent study in Cambodia, 78 percent of those who revealed their transgender identity have suffered discrimination.[3]

The hidden transgender's voice is rarely heard. But here is a tiny whisper: from me.

A Hidden Voice

Since earliest childhood I have struggled with transgender identity. I was deeply ashamed of my feelings and expressions of those feelings, so kept them secret. I have always lived in isolation, unable to discuss with parents, family, friends or church leaders. My transgendered identity is the only place of comfort I know.

When my transgender identity was first revealed it resulted in divorce and homelessness. Those closest to me chose to reject me rather than help me. Thankfully a counselor[4] helped me understand and express my inner feelings. Despite accepting Christ as my savior, my transgender desires persist. It is a daily battle of conformity to Christ. I constantly struggle with very low self worth as I reconcile my inner identity at variance with my outer identity. I recently wrote:

---

[1] Paul S. Chung, "A Theology of Justification and God's Mission," *Currents in Theology and Mission* 34, no. 2 (April 2007): 117-27. http://www. thefreelibrary.com/A+Theology+of+justification+and+God's+mission.-a0162834381

[2] Evangelical Alliance, *Transsexuality: A Report by the Evangelical Alliance Policy Commission* (London: Evangelical Alliance, 2000), 12.

[3] Jarrett Davis and Glenn Miles, "More Than Gender: A Baseline Study of Transgendered Males in the Sex Industry in Phnom Penh, Cambodia" (Phnom Penh: Love 146, October 2013).

[4] www.transformationinchrist.org

I just don't want to be me, forced to live as others expect.
The pain in my heart forces me to live between worlds.
I journey away from myself with anticipation;
returning to me with guilt and self-loathing.
But if I did not return, I'd no longer have a journey of escape.
Trapped into being me, whoever I really am.
So I live this secret life;
the tide of identity flowing back and forth,
slowly washing my character away,
until I become eroded into no one.

Many transgenders are hidden and scared to come out; those who do dare, find a reception of hostility and rejection.

So how can the church respond instead?

How Should the Church Engage?

Love God, Love Your Neighbor

Firstly, we must get our relationship with God right through Jesus, allowing his love to flow through us to reach others. Jesus revealed "I am the vine; you are the branches. Those who remain in me and I in them, will produce much fruit."[5] The fruit produced is "love, joy, peace, patience, kindness, goodness, faithfulness, gentleness and self-control."[6] These fruits reveal our inner conformity to Christ. By growing these fruits, we the church will reveal outward conformity to Christ by unconditionally loving transgenders.

Discipleship Pathways

Secondly, each of us is unique in our spiritual gifts, what we enjoy doing, abilities, personality and life experiences.[7] It is inconceivable that any two people will have exactly the same discipleship journey as our starting points are different. There are two generic discipleship journeys for transgenders: those who will seek to revert back to their birth gender; and those who will remain a transgender. Each journey will have differing complexities: extent of cross-dressing, sexual activities, hormone treatment, GRS, marital status, sex trade activities, etc. The Holy Spirit will guide each transgenders' discipleship journey – which will be lengthy and complex – to yield transformation in Christ without necessarily transformation in appearance.

We are called to "run with endurance the race that God has set before us, by fixing our eyes on Jesus."[8] Possibly the church does not like running alongside

---

[5] John 15:5 (NLT).

[6] Galatians 5:22 (NLT).

[7] "You Were Shaped for Serving God," Saddleback Church Website. http://www. saddleback.com/aboutsaddleback/livingonpurpose/shapedforservinggod/

[8] Hebrews 12:1b-2a.

someone they are not comfortable with. And yet, the church's role is to help, encourage and support each transgender along the pathway set by God.

An "Open-Set" Church

Thirdly, while salvation has clear boundaries of either being "in Christ" or "out of Christ," discipleship is a journey whose pathways vary for each person depending on starting points.[9] We can see how this works using Booker and Ireland's illustration of the "Closed-Set" and "Open-Set" church.[10] A closed-set church tends to have clearly defined boundaries for salvation *and* for discipleship, whereas an open-set church has a clearly defined boundary for salvation but more flexibility in discipleship.

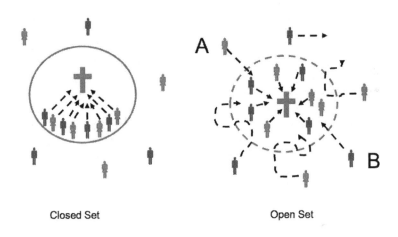

Closed Set   Open Set

As seen above, persons A and B appear to be on totally opposite discipleship journeys, whereas in reality, both are journeying *towards* Christ.[11] The more open we are to differing discipleship journeys, the more welcome transgender people will be.

Conclusion

The more space for grace we have, the stronger the bridges of compassion become allowing God's unconditional love to flow through us to reach and disciple transgenders. We need to affirm and support the Holy Spirit's unique

---

[9] Dave Andrews, *Christi-Anarchy: Discovering a Radical Spirituality of Compassion* (Oxford: Lion Publishing, 1999), 86-87.

[10] Adapted from Mike Booker and Mark Ireland, *Evangelism - Which Way Now? An Evaluation of Alpha, Emmaus, Cell Church and Other Contemporary Strategies for Evangelism* (London: Church Publishing House, 2003), 17.

[11] Adapted from Mike Booker and Mark Ireland, *Evangelism - Which Way Now?*, 17.

discipleship pathways for each transgender, adopting an open approach towards discipleship whilst still maintaining core Biblical teaching on salvation. Organizations that listen to and do research with transgenders can facilitate discipleship with them through helping us listen to the whispered voice of many transgenders.

Case Study, by Duncan Craig

Since the age of five, I have grappled with the confusion of gender identity. As a child, I found comfort in wearing items of my mother's such as her necklaces or bangles. It was during my teens that I had to face my sexual identity. I never had a girlfriend until my mid-twenties, preferring to repeatedly switch gender identity in private. I was always awkward as a man, but found solace as I cross-dressed.

I have always felt a profound sense of shame and went to great lengths to conceal my inner self. I never discussed it with anyone. By my twenties, it was an increasing part of my private life. A broken marriage forced me to "come out," but the horrendous hostility I faced (resulting in being forced out of my own home to become homeless), ensured that I kept my inner self secret.

Whilst I have had a life-transforming encounter with Jesus Christ that is radically changing every aspect of my life, I still grapple with gender identity daily. I have chosen to live externally as a man, but have had to accept the tension this causes me internally. I describe my sexuality as "celibate" as this avoids complicated "labels." My self-worth is virtually non-existent as a result of these choices.

My desire is for society and in particular the church to embrace the struggles of transgender people so that the private agony of many can be lovingly shared in a supportive environment. Perhaps writing these lines will allow that journey to begin in those who read them.

Discussion Questions

1. What gender is your soul?
2. What is gender identity that defines masculinity or femininity across different cultures?
3. Is the act of cross-dressing a betrayal of celibacy ethos?

PART 6

HOW SHOULD WE COLLABORATE?

Introduction, Tania DoCarmo

Most of us recognize the need for collaboration. We understand that no organization, agency or individual could possibly address the complexity of human trafficking on its own, and most of us (ideally) belong to a network of some sort to ensure we "stay connected" to others in our field. Discussion surrounding the need for collaboration to address social problems is nothing new. Collaboration has many benefits, including the opportunity to focus on one's own core competencies while gaining from the competencies of others; the opportunity to learn from the experiences of others; and the opportunity to combine and share valuable resources.

And yet, somehow, regardless of this seemingly unanimous sentiment that collaboration is vital to our work, many of us (maybe even *most* of us) seem to treat networking and collaboration as a sort of "side project" – one that we participate in when we have the time, when it suits our needs, and/or when it's most convenient.

The Bible is clear about the benefits of teamwork (e.g. Ecclesiastes 4:9, Proverbs 27:17, 1 Corinthians 12:20, Ephesians 4:16). Stories from throughout the Old and New Testament reflect ways in which God's people worked together, sometimes well and sometimes not-so-well (and sometimes with outsiders) toward a common purpose (e.g. Exodus 18:17-24, Nehemiah 2-6).

Do many of us claim to understand the importance of collaboration? Yes. But do we often plan, organize and implement our projects with collaboration as a priority? Perhaps not.

According to Kania and Kramer, while the social sector may collectively recognize that collaboration is beneficial and may be filled with examples of partnerships, networks and other types of joint efforts, the nonprofit sector most frequently operates out of "isolated impact" – an approach oriented toward finding and funding a solution embodied within a single organization. As a result, nearly 1.4 million nonprofits in the United States alone "try to invent independent solutions to major social problems, often working at odds with each other and exponentially increasing the perceived resources required to make meaningful progress." [1] This dynamic of isolated impact is unfortunately also the case with the global response to sexual exploitation and trafficking.

This chapter explores ways to improve collaboration by addressing four key questions:
- Why is networking important?
- What are some existing models of collaboration? How did they develop? What are some of the challenges?
- How can technology and the Internet be used to enhance collaboration?

---

[1] John Kania and Mark Kramer, "Collective Impact," *Stanford Social Innovation Review* (Winter 2011), 38.

- What are the challenges of partnership? How do we work with people/organizations who may seem controversial or who may not espouse similar Christian values (without compromising)?

First, **Brian Wilkinson** addresses the importance of networking. While there may be many individuals, unsung heroes and "saints" doing miraculous individual work, perhaps we need to dare to ask the "bigger" questions as to whether we are truly contributing to change on a grand scale. He challenges us to ask the important question: If we continue to focus solely on individual, isolated efforts, will society ever change? Wilkinson also challenges us to ask ourselves how well networking is going and offers a vision drawn from Revelation 19 of how organizations can come together as the Bride of Christ for greater effectiveness.

Next, this chapter explores what networking looks like in action. Case studies by **Lauran Bethell** of International Christian Alliance on Prostitution (ICAP) and **Tania DoCarmo** of Freedom Registry describe the process of how their networks were formed, including some of the challenges faced along the way. The case studies also illustrate in detail the benefits gained by prioritizing and persevering in working together.

This look at in-person networks is followed by an exploration of how technology and the Internet can be harnessed to link people globally. **Christa Foster Crawford** discusses the ways in which outdated tools fail to meet the need for better connectivity and introduces us to some innovative tools that enable us to connect better for freedom. These tools are explored in greater detail in the case studies that follow. In the first, **Tania DoCarmo** explains the key features of Freedom Collaborative, which is a unique online resource that seeks to increase collaboration and networking among anti-trafficking practitioners, organizations and academics. Then **Ané Auret** of Counter Child Trafficking Global Online Conference (CCTC) describes how the first ever global online conference on child trafficking created learning and connection opportunities.

Finally, the difficulties and challenges of partnership are explored in the final two essays. **Helen Sworn** suggests that it is often our own preferences, prejudices and inherent attitudes that prevent us from collaborating with others, especially when faced with working with organizations or individual who hold a different faith or theological tradition. Most of us would rather stay within our comfort zones than expose our prejudices, especially when collaboration may put us in a situation where our own beliefs are challenged. In order to overcome challenging prejudices, Sworn argues we must make a point of practicing respect (regardless of perceived differences), and seeking common ground, regardless of how miniscule it may seem. By looking at the bigger picture of how our ministry, organization and beneficiaries can benefit from partnership with others, we will begin to recognize greater potential toward achieving our goals.

Jennifer Roemhildt Tunehag also discusses how we can collaborate with individuals or organizations that may seem controversial (and/or do not espouse Christian values) without compromising our own beliefs or principles. Using various examples, including her own ministry's collaboration with transgender individuals involved in prostitution in Greece, Tunehag explains how working with such groups has only provided them with additional opportunities to demonstrate God's grace and reach additional beneficiaries. She recommends five principles to partnership: be clear about your identity, keep shared objectives in mind, acknowledge differences, form limited partnerships when needed and practice ongoing communication.

CHAPTER 30: WHY IS NETWORKING IMPORTANT?

Key Issues, by Brian Wilkinson

The word networking has lost its value in recent times. If you ask someone about networking they are likely to respond, "Everyone does it all the time, don't they?" But just because networking is a familiar concept and a term that is frequently used does not mean that networking is happening often enough, or even well enough. This is true in the world in general, and unfortunately it is also true for those working to end exploitation and trafficking, even among Christians.

Why Is Networking Important?

Networking, partnerships, collaborations or indeed collective action are all terms to describe working together to achieve something more than we could have achieved on our own. To understand the importance of networking let us use the example of working to help children at risk.

Imagine that a single organization invests its efforts in one or even ten individual children at risk projects, what is the result? We may well see improvements in the quality of care provided over time, and we may even see an increase in the scale of operation or number of children reached. But will we really be changing the situation or tackling the root issues? When one organization seeks to address a complex and pervasive problem alone, it can sometimes feel more like trying to dam a flowing river or stop the tide from coming in.

Instead imagine this scenario: That single organization joins a network of 100 local organisations. Working together these organizations directly reach at least 10,000 children. Collectively these organizations will be the largest provider of care for children in the city, giving them the right to be at the table with significant decision-makers. Now imagine that these organizations are joined by more than 30 church congregations consisting of approximately 15,000 motivated and envisioned people, living and working across all areas of the city. Unite them under the banner of a strong and visionary network designed to create, communicate and manage collective action. Give them relevant ideas from local experienced people, expertise from development specialists, opportunities with local and national media, money from interested partners and potentially government sources – and that is just the beginning! Surely this approach has the extraordinary potential for changing the situation of the children in that city. Beyond that, if such a network existed within the four or five largest cities in that country there would be ground-up, united action on a national scale.

While this vision may seem grand, it is not just a fantasy illusion. Rather it is a perspective that we all must have. When we consider the magnitude of addressing issues such as trafficking and exploitation, it will surely require concerted and coordinated action such as this at every level of society if we are to see positive change.

How Well Is Networking Going?

Over the past ten years, more and more Christians have responded to the needs of children at risk out of a heart of compassion and a call from God. Each in their own way is doing good – maybe even great – work in touching and changing lives one at a time. You may have met some of the amazing men and women who sacrificially give their time, money and lives to help the abandoned, traumatised, unwanted and lost. These are the unsung heroes and heroines of the Christian faith, the best examples of what the Bible refers to as "saints."

Despite this, however, if we dare to ask big questions such as "Are we winning?" and "Is the situation of children at risk changing for the better?" the answer is not so clear. Cities are getting larger and the gap between rich and poor is more apparent, even when living in increasingly close proximity. Children continue to be the bottom of many people's value chain, and abuse and trafficking appears to be more common. The word transformation is used quite regularly these days, but are we honestly seeing it on a wider scale? We want to believe and earnestly pray that God will help us influence the communities that make up the cities or rural landscape and that we will see more of his transformation there. This requires us to ask another question: "If we carry on doing what we are doing, will we see societal trends change *or* does it require something to happen on a much bigger scale?"

Imagine looking down on a city and seeing the lights of the Christian response to children at risk – how encouraging it is to see the numbers now playing their part. Churches, organisations and individuals are busy doing good work. However, the reality is it would not take long before we realised few were really talking or cooperating with one another. To some it may look too disconnected, dispersed and small scale – strange for a people who believe and want the same things! As Christians we have a clear biblical mandate from Jesus' prayer to work together.[1] We know this and agree with it in principle, but bad experiences often set us back and we settle for doing what we can in the circumstances. Surely there needs to be a paradigm shift in the way we work if we are to really succeed in making a difference.

Coming Together

In Revelations 19:7-8, we are given an image to aspire to:

---

[1] John 17: 21-23.

Let us rejoice and be glad and give him glory! For the wedding of the Lamb has come, and his bride has made herself ready. Fine linen, bright and clean, was given her to wear.[2]

The fine linen in this passage represents the righteous acts of the saints. As ones seeking to act righteously in addressing exploitation and trafficking, we realize that the Bride of Christ – the body of believers – needs to be coming together and getting in better shape! The clothing needs to be looking its best, and the whole package ready for the return of the Bridegroom. Is that not the type of Christian response we want to see?

It reminds me of when I was in school and they showed us the power of magnets. Iron filings were randomly spread across a piece of card but when the magnet was placed underneath they all magically came into line in a planned order. Perhaps that's what the shape of the Bride should look like. If the united force of the Bride can work together and deliver collective influence on top of our existing individual work, that would bring about "acts of righteousness" on an even greater scale, and might even look like the right style of clothing for a Bride!

But like iron filings, we don't come together naturally on our own. Formal networks can help draw us together. One such network, Viva, was founded in 1996 in response to the fragmentation that was evident in the Christian response to children at risk. Since then Viva has championed working together, connecting children at risk organizations globally as well as inspiring the establishment of dozens of other networks.

Viva currently partners with 35 networks worldwide, helping them grow and develop in scope and scale, and inspiring lasting change in the lives of almost one million children who are being reached through 3,000 churches and organisations working together. In Nepal, for example, the network CarNet is working with 350 churches that speak into their local communities about the issue of child exploitation and trafficking in order to change traditional mindsets and values about these issues. In Kampala, Uganda, the CRANE network has over 170 groups working together to create a safe city for working children. They work with the children on how to protect themselves, and advocate to change commonly abusive behaviours of adults. In Bolivia there are eight city-wide networks working toward the common goal of no more street children. This network is working collectively on a national campaign for "good treatment" of these children, involving schools, businesses and churches with the support of government and media. These are only a few examples of Christians and others coming together for effective change.

Conclusion

Individuals, projects and local churches located in vulnerable communities are the flickering candle flames that can be helped to burn brightly, especially as they connect together to the resources and expertise they need. Christians and churches are already located in cities all around the world. They do not need to

---

[2] (NIV).

be sent but rather encouraged, envisioned and equipped to better respond to vulnerable people by working together. Collaboration is the lifeline to an effective response. Let us remember the importance of networking and come together as the Bride for even greater acts of righteousness.

Discussion Questions

1. In your own words explain why networking and other forms of collaboration are important. Can you think of examples in your own work when you have been more effective by working together with others?
2. How well is networking going for you personally? How well is networking going in your community? What is working? What needs to be improved?
3. Honestly ask yourself the question posed: "If we carry on doing what we are doing, will we see societal trends change or does it require something to happen on a much bigger scale?" Find a group of people who are also working in your area and ask the question together.
4. How can you come together with other individuals, organizations and churches in responding to exploitation and trafficking? What things are drawing you together? Are there any things that are keeping you apart? What things must you and others do to prepare yourselves to work together? Are there networking or other resources available to help? If not, how can you identify or create what is lacking?

CHAPTER 31: WHAT ARE SOME EXISTING MODELS OF COLLABORATION? HOW DID THEY DEVELOP? WHAT ARE SOME OF THE CHALLENGES?

Case Study, by Lauran Bethell

International Christian Alliance On Prostitution (ICAP)

The International Christian Alliance on Prostitution (ICAP)[1] is an international partnership that seeks to unite, equip and empower practitioners and advocates who are involved in compassionately challenging injustice and offering freedom to people exploited by prostitution, including sex trafficking. This case study describes ICAP's development, challenges and opportunities.

Development

I began working with women and girls in prostitution in 1986 in Bangkok, Thailand. At that time, I could find only one Protestant Christian organization working to address the enormous issues in the country – a small group home for approximately ten children who had been taken out of brothels. That was it. But God's Spirit was moving, and within five years, there were five groups, spread around the country. We leaders of the groups became friends and met together for prayer, nurture and support – because we needed each other. We prayed that God's Spirit would continue to move, and that more and more individuals and groups would be called into ministry throughout Thailand and the world.

We watched in awe and amazement as the Movement grew. Each one of us "pioneers" spent hours of our time mentoring and sharing information with folks who were profoundly being called into ministry in the darkest corners of the world – where God's precious souls were being bought and sold. By 2000, God clearly called me to leave my project – the New Life Center located in Chiang Mai, Thailand – and spend my time encouraging the development of these new, rapidly multiplying endeavors. I had the privilege of visiting numerous organizations all over the world – grassroots ministries meeting victims of human trafficking and prostitution in the places where they worked. They were offering help and hope and healing in the name of Jesus.

But they were isolated from each other. In some countries there was only one group. In other countries, there may have been just one, two or three groups, separated by provincial borders. Often they didn't know about each other. They expressed loneliness and the desire to meet others who deeply

---

[1] www.icapglobal.org

understood the issues with which they were grappling. Many were on the edge of "burn-out" from participating in the lives of so many who were severely traumatized. They wanted to learn new strategies for coping and more effective ways of addressing the needs they saw.

In late 2001, I heard about a network of Christian organizations addressing prostitution issues in the UK that met yearly to network, support and learn from each other. I arrived at the National Christian Alliance on Prostitution (NCAP) annual conference, meeting near London, to find an amazing group of more than 60 Christians from all corners of the UK who were walking the streets and ministering in Christ's name to people in prostitution. But what was most remarkable was finding seven other women from all over the globe, most of them founders of grassroots organizations ministering with people in prostitution, and – like me – looking for a network. During those three days, the eight of us "stuck together like glue," sharing our passions and dreams, and fervently praying that somehow, somewhere, we could get more of us together. We stayed in touch by e-mail and continued to hold our dream of an international network up to God in prayer. We expected that we would begin by holding a conference in some urban location noted for prostitution, like Bangkok or Amsterdam. But God had other plans!

In early 2003, the President of the Green Lake Conference Center (GLCC), Ken Giacoletto, and his wife Peggy visited my home in Prague. Over tea in my living room, Ken asked if there was any kind of conference I'd ever wanted to organize. Without hesitation, I told him about our vision for a network and a conference. Ken offered the use of the GLCC and pledged to find funding to make it happen! We put together an organizing committee of ministry leaders and those who had experience in conference planning and began preparations.

There were lots of questions about why this conference would be held in the middle of "dairy country," when our ministries were primarily in urban areas. But as people began to arrive in August 2004, the answer became clear: the fresh air, the quiet, the beauty, the space for reflection and prayer....it became an event which was as much about "caring for the caregiver" as it was for information sharing and networking. We provided professional counselors whom attendees could meet with individually or as couples. Worship was at the center of all we did, and prayer surrounded everything.

The participants were so enthusiastic about the first conference that we immediately decided a second conference would be held two years later. When we came together in April 2006, it was decided that we should form an organization, and our name became ICAP – the International Christian Alliance on Prostitution.

As we attempted to "organize" ourselves, divergent thoughts surfaced about what we would become. What we did agree on was the vision: "Networking for Transformation and Hope" and the mission: "Through conferencing and consultation, the International Christian Alliance on Prostitution (ICAP) unites, equips and empowers practitioners who compassionately challenge injustice and offer freedom to people exploited by prostitution, including sex trafficking. The ICAP Leadership Team represents founders and visionaries of grass-roots organizations from Africa, Asia, Central Asia, Europe, Latin America and North America."

Challenges

Multi-cultural communication, varieties of management styles and theological diversity presented major challenges as we began navigating "organization." There were moments when I thought we weren't going to make it – and along the way we did (painfully) lose some of those who had the original vision. At one point, we were able to hire an executive director who was with us for nearly a year. However, the economic crisis did away with the funding and we returned to being a fully volunteer organization.

Facing Change and Challenge with God's Guidance

Yet despite these challenges, we recognized the importance of networking. At one critical point, the leadership team met and assessed the resources that we did have:

- The leadership team consists of committed representatives from all our regions – primarily indigenous founders of grassroots organizations with a passion for sharing their wisdom and experience as widely as possible.
- We have talented, high-profile individuals (especially in field of counseling and trauma care) who are committed to our vision and are willing to volunteer and raise their own funding to do trainings, speak at conferences or serve in multiple ways.
- Practitioners who are faithful attendees to our conferences provide a wealth of information, wisdom and encouragement through their leadership in seminars and workshops – and informal conversations.
- The GLCC Board is committed to underwriting our global conferences, meaning that we are able to provide a quality venue that serves great purpose for a very low price.
- The leadership of the GLCC provides administrative help, including non-profit status registration and maintenance as well as banking/accounting services. They also provide a part-time administrative assistant for the coordinator, who takes responsibility for inquiries through our website and registrations for our conferences.

We realize that though we have virtually no funding and no full-time staff, we have a treasure-chest of resources. What has evolved is a fully-volunteer, loosely-organized network. The regional leadership is committed to sponsoring culturally relevant trainings, consultations and/or conferences for practitioners in each of their regions during the years between the triennial Global Conference. The leadership team meets annually, and spends a major part of the time in profound worship and prayer, sharing their hearts and hurts, taking care of each other, and planning for how they feel they can best serve practitioners around the world. When we meet, we model the organization we want to be – caring and serving in Jesus' name.

A couple of our participants have summarized our purpose beautifully:

"ICAP provided me with a place to connect with others with the same passion for women and Jesus. It was a time of much needed respite, refueling and restoration for me to continue doing what I was already doing. It also provided me with a chance to network and connect with other organizations doing similar work to facilitate new ideas and growth in my own ministry."

"ICAP is a place to be equipped, connect and rest. The contacts and information have been invaluable for mobilization and the rest essential for inspiration and restoration. The location is beautiful in Wisconsin. The closing ceremonies are a glimpse of what must be in store in heaven---the beauty of diversity, common love and united hearts in committed service."

With God's guidance, may it continue to be so!

Case Study, by Tania DoCarmo

Freedom Registry

Freedom Registry [2] is a one-of-a-kind registry of vetted counter-human trafficking organizations that began in the United States and has since expanded to other nations. Freedom Registry seeks to improve collaboration though improving connectivity. This case study describes the need for and development of Freedom Registry, including some of the challenges faced along the way, and a glimpse of how Freedom Registry has expanded into a global platform for connection.

The Need

Chab Dai has been involved in coalition building, advocacy and research in Cambodia since 2005. In 2008, when we were establishing Chab Dai USA (our first international office outside of Cambodia) we weren't exactly sure what our US-based projects would look like. We had a strong reputation for coalition-building among anti-trafficking stakeholders in Cambodia, and had already worked with partners in other regions who had approached us for assistance in these areas, so we knew what our core competencies were. However, because it was our first time officially contextualizing our expertise in a new location, we planned to spend the first several months (if not longer) observing and learning what others were already doing, what was being done well, what the gap areas were, and where we could fit in.

Due to existing relationships with US-based organizations through our work in Cambodia, I was appointed by one of our partners to conduct trainings for caregivers around the United States. By conducting these trainings in various cities, states and regions, I soon discovered it was the perfect opportunity to observe and talk with attendees about their work, their perceptions of the

---

[2] www.freedomregistry.org

national counter trafficking movement, and – perhaps most relevant to Chab Dai – how (or whether) they collaborated with others in their work.

What I found surprised me. Because so many of the projects in Cambodia were often funded or otherwise supported by Western efforts, I had made the assumption that efforts in the United States would be similarly informed and/or coordinated. I quickly realized, however, that perhaps Cambodia's anti-trafficking efforts were more advanced than I had thought. While working in Cambodia I had certainly witnessed challenges in collaboration, the need for training and capacity building among stakeholders, and situations where stakeholders were not well informed or resourced about good practices; I had unknowingly grown accustomed to being part of an anti-trafficking community that engaged with one another much more deeply, and with much more accountability, than what I was perceiving to be the case in the United States.

The organizations, practitioners and others I encountered during my first year in the U.S. were often unaware of other anti-trafficking efforts – often even in their own city – and many claimed to be one-of-a-kind and/or the "only" group doing awareness, aftercare, etc. in their region. Many project leaders had joined the cause out of mere urgency in hearing about human trafficking at their church, on the news, or some other source. I often found that while most leaders and practitioners had "big plans" (and maybe even funding) for their projects, many were struggling with how to move from planning and fundraising onto the next steps of implementation. They came to the training seeking information about how to move forward, and were usually very disconnected from resources where they could receive qualified assistance. I was surprised that even though I had only been back in the United States a short time, I was continuously providing numerous organizations, donors and even government agencies with the necessary US-based resources, contacts and referrals to assist them in their efforts.

The coalition efforts I encountered – some established by local government, some established through grassroots efforts – were usually either very exclusive or very loose in nature, with few activities and often limited accountability. Many project leaders spoke of the need for collaboration and networking, but admitted to either not knowing how to collaborate, or not having the time to initiate or participate in collaborative activities. Coalition-building was practically seen as something an organization does "on the side." The concept of a "backbone support organization"[3] dedicated specifically to the intentional coordination of efforts toward "collective impact" (Chab Dai's core organizational purpose) was a novel, almost "dubious" concept.

I'll never forget my experience during one meeting with a prominent state government agency who insistently requested Chab Dai become involved in setting up an aftercare shelter for trafficked teens. When I explained that our core competency was coalition-building, coordinating efforts and increasing collaboration among stakeholders (and not setting up or managing direct aftercare programs), they were confused. *Chab Dai helps anti-trafficking*

---

[3] John Kania and Mark Kramer, "Collective Impact," *Stanford Social Innovation Review* (Winter 2011): 36-41.

organizations collaborate. That's great. But what else do you do? Don't you provide direct services? It was difficult for them to understand how an organization like ours could solely focus our time and efforts on coalition-building. But as Kania and Kramer (2011) point out, "coordination takes time ... the expectation that collaboration can occur without a supporting infrastructure is one of the most frequent reasons it fails."[4]

Despite the challenges mentioned above, it was clear that a major movement was being formed by churches, government agencies, victim advocates, social service providers, students, and others deeply concerned and committed to addressing human trafficking, abuse and exploitation in their communities. What was *lacking* was a system in which these stakeholders could find and be accountable to one another, seek reputable resources and share their expertise.

Development and Challenges

In 2009, approximately eight months after establishing Chab Dai USA, we began initial project plans for what would eventually become Freedom Registry. The original intention of Freedom Registry was to develop an online, comprehensive and sustainable database of anti-trafficking stakeholders in the United States. Little did we know that the project would eventually evolve into an all-encompassing, international web application to assist stakeholders to connect with one another not only locally, but also regionally and internationally.

Because the intent of the initial Freedom Registry project was to encourage and increase *collaboration*, it was only natural that the project be designed and implemented in partnership with others. We knew that projects done in collaboration with a wide range of stakeholders in various sectors had greater potential not only in being successful, but also in gaining "buy-in" from others down the road. Thus, after developing our initial concept paper for the project in 2009, our next step was to establish a national steering committee made up of experienced and well-respected individuals engaged in various aspects of anti-trafficking across the country. We reached out to various stakeholders to discuss the project, invited organizations to join the project, and in 2010 we held our first committee meeting, made up of individuals representing seven distinct organizations (including at least one social service provider, academic, legal advocate, community activist, and member of law enforcement).

Because members of the steering committee represented a wide variety of interests, agendas, concerns, and preferences, the planning process for Freedom Registry took a considerable amount of time. While we were all interested in developing an accessible database where stakeholders involved in addressing trafficking could find one another and initiate coordination of efforts, members of the committee did not agree on issues such as participation (can any organization be listed), criteria (if only some organizations are allowed to be listed, what is the criteria), data (what data should we collect for each

---

[4] John Kania and Mark Kramer, "Collective Impact," 40.

registrant), transparency (how can we and/or the users of the registry be sure organizations are accurately representing themselves), accessibility (who would have access to the database), and so on. While the committee had no interest in "rating" organizations, there was significant concern about ensuring those on the registry were legitimate. After almost a year of meetings, lengthy discussions and debate surrounding questions like these, the committee agreed on functionality of the site, and was ready to move forward with development.

After conducting a small pilot with organizations willing to participate in Freedom Registry while we still worked out some of the "kinks" in the system, the application was launched to the public in March 2012. While the launch, promotion and eventual "buy-in" of Freedom Registry perhaps didn't occur as seamlessly as we'd hoped (we are still working on ways to recruit more US organizations to participate and submit their data), the project has nonetheless been successful in providing data on the current state of the national movement (researchers have used registry data for research on anti-trafficking organizations), reflecting the need for visibility and accountability among stakeholders (many registered organizations have expressed a need for assistance in implementing good practices), and providing organizations with information on other trafficking efforts in their region.

Expansion

Within days of Freedom Registry's public launch, Chab Dai began receiving inquiries from stakeholders in other countries asking if the site would eventually go international – they wanted Freedom Registry in *their* country too. A process was developed whereby countries interested in expanding Freedom Registry to their region are able to establish their own national steering committee and contextualize the registry to the needs and circumstances of their country. This process is currently underway in countries such as Cambodia, Costa Rica, Canada and South Africa.

Not only did Freedom Registry expand in geographic reach, it also evolved to become an expanded scope of services called Freedom Collaborative.[5] Freedom Collaborative is an online platform that links the entire counter-trafficking movement through a number of integrated collaboration tools and resources that will be described in more detail later in this chapter.

---

[5] www.freedomcollaborative.org

CHAPTER 32: HOW CAN TECHNOLOGY AND THE INTERNET BE USED TO ENHANCE COLLABORATION?

Key Issues, by Christa Foster Crawford

"Organized criminal groups and networks, better equipped with new information and communication technologies, are becoming diversified and connected in their illicit operations."

United Nations Security Council, Statement by the President[1]

Human traffickers are well connected for the sake of exploitation. How much more then should we be connected for the sake of freedom. This essay will look at how far we as a movement have come in leveraging technology for connection – and how far we still have yet to go.

The Need for Better Connectivity

I remember when I was first learning about human trafficking in Thailand. It was the late 1990s and while the Internet had already been invented, it wasn't yet possible to "just Google it" to find information. I had first heard the term "human trafficking" from reading Kevin Bales' *Disposable People*[2] (in hard copy, the only kind of reading possible in that era) and felt that God was calling me to respond. But where could I go for more information? As a lawyer, I had access to LexisNexis – the old version that used strict Boolean searches, meaning that if you searched for "human trafficking" instead of "trafficking in humans" it was likely that your results would turn out different. But even assuming the search terms were right, there wasn't much information out there. Instead of returning results of anti-trafficking organization websites (because websites didn't yet exist), I got a list of law review articles and legislation. This was fine for the academic research I was conducting, but did nothing to prepare me for the exploratory trip I was about to make to Thailand to see how God was already at work there.

It was also the early days of email, and somehow we were able to track down a missionary in Thailand who referred us to someone he knew who was doing work with trafficked girls. We got on the plane with that single contact in hand and prayers that God would somehow show us who else to talk to once we arrived. Miraculously we were able to make a few ad hoc connections but we discovered that there was no comprehensive directory of organizations in Thailand – electronic or otherwise. While this was inconvenient for me, it was a gigantic gap for the people on the ground who had been doing the faithful

---

[1] 25 April 2012, S/PRST/2012/16.
[2] Berkeley: University of California Press, 1999.

work of helping exploited people for more than a decade before the term "human trafficking" became popularized. These missionaries – who were overworked, under-resourced and physically isolated – were only connected with one another if they had existing relationships (such as denominational affiliations), but they had no way to easily find out who else was doing similar work and how they could support each other.

Fast forward more than fifteen years to 2014. After living in Thailand working against trafficking and exploitation for more than a decade, I was now the one at the other end of the email: "Do you know of anyone in Thailand who is doing aftercare?" I get several emails like that a month. Many are from explorers like I once was, but many others are from the numerous organizations who have come to Thailand in the last several years in response to the growing awareness of trafficking through the now-exploding Internet. Google searches. Facebook posts. Twitter feeds. Interactive websites. Trendy media campaigns. Online tools and emerging technology have been successfully harnessed to increase awareness of the issues and prompt an outpouring of response. It is a world of difference what you can find out about human trafficking on the Internet now compared to the early days. But sadly, there is one thing that is still not available, electronically or otherwise: A comprehensive, up-to-date directory of organizations who are doing the actual work. While a decade of advances in Internet and communications technology have helped create a globally integrated world, for the most part connections among organizations working toward freedom continue to happen on an accidental and ad hoc basis.

The Wrong Tool For the Right Task

Why is this? It's not for lack of trying; in fact over the years there have been several well meaning but ultimately lacking attempts to develop nationwide referral databases. The problem is that every time we try we keep using old-fashioned methods that will never be effective. We're reinventing the wheel, and we're doing a bad job of it in the process!

Over the years I have been to countless conferences on human trafficking and prostitution. Each time, I am asked to write my contact information down on a piece of paper. The hope is that that list will help us maintain connections and share resources after the conference is over. However, I can only think of a handful of times in which the basic contact information was actually shared or the promised PowerPoint slides were successfully disbursed. As one who has herself been responsible for that failing, I know that there are a number of barriers to this "old-school" method of information sharing.

First, we are using the wrong model. It is inefficient to try to create a comprehensive directory by relying on a single individual to input handwritten information. The process is time consuming and prone to error. Even under the best of circumstances, organizations that are busy with their "real" work cannot devote personnel to data entry much less the on-going chore of keeping it up to date. It is no wonder that information gets "stuck" at the very organization that had the highest hopes of seeing it disseminated. Yet in recent years, the Internet and communications technology have innovated ways to eliminate this hurdle.

Social networks like Facebook and LinkedIn do not rely on a single individual or organization to input millions of entries. Instead, users are empowered to input – and update – their own entries, ensuring that they are kept accurate and current without overburdening a single organization with this herculean task. Why is it then that until recently, we lacked a dedicated, self-maintaining registry for the anti-human trafficking movement?

Second, we are using the wrong tools. When someone asks me "Who is doing outreach work with teenage boys in Chiang Mai?" Excel-based participant lists are unable to tell me. I do in fact know how to answer, but it is only because my network of relationships and knowledge is not divided into stagnant, one-dimensional ledger columns but are instead interconnected, multi-layered circles that are constantly evolving. So how can we better keep track of such important information about who is doing what? Thankfully Apps like Apple's Address Book have allowed me to "tag" entries with unlimited fields, expanding my search capacity, but they still fall short when it comes to producing results in a shareable format.

More importantly, the information in my directories is still limited by my own personal sphere of connection. I can't tell others about organizations that I don't know exist. And like that first trip to Thailand fifteen years ago, I still find that most connections I make continue to take place accidentally and ad hoc. For instance, I'm amazed how frequently I get requests like this one: "I want to get involved in anti-trafficking work in Minnesota, who should I contact?" I've never worked in Minnesota and my expertise is Thailand and Southeast Asia. Why are they asking me? Amazingly, I actually do happen to know of a few organizations in Minnesota – only because I randomly had lunch with a group of Midwestern organizations at a conference several years back.

But connecting people and resources for the kingdom of God shouldn't be a matter of happenstance! Surely, God is able to do better than this. And so should we. The traffickers are certainly better able to be connected. Internet and communications technology is increasingly better able to help us be connected. So why aren't we able to get beyond our outdated models and tools?

Building Better Connection

Thankfully innovative solutions to these perennial barriers already exist and are constantly being developed – both by commercial services like Facebook, which have made a fortune in creating global connection, as well as by innovators within the freedom movement who are creating dedicated tools and resources to help us work together better. For instance, online networking tools like the Freedom Collaborative[3] provide an indispensible platform to better connect us with each other and with the resources we need for success. In addition, Freedom Registry[4] offers a self-updating, global directory to finally liberate us from our antiquated approaches to information sharing.

---

[3] www.freedomcollaborative.org (case study follows).

[4] www.freedomregistry.org (case study follows).

Advances in communications technology also allow us to make important "in person" connections without the usual limitations of time, space and money. Virtual conferencing services are being used by the Counter Trafficking Global Online Conference[5] and Freedom Dialogues[6] to connect people beyond geographical and temporal boundaries, and to keep the conversation going even when participants are not all in the same place. Similarly, online education like the course I teach for Fuller Seminary[7] offers grassroots workers the opportunity to learn more about fundamental frameworks and explore cutting-edge solutions. These online services provide more efficient and cost-effective ways of getting vital information to the people on the field who most need it, without requiring them to purchase expensive plane tickets to attend a conference or take time away from their ongoing work to pursue education. However, there is much more to that still needs to be done to develop resources that are appropriate for a variety of levels, learning styles and languages.

Conclusion

We must connect better for freedom. The good news is that technology and the Internet have already made what was once an insurmountable goal a very achievable task – if only we are willing to pick up a new set of tools.

Let's move beyond the old ways of information sharing, networking and learning and into the emerging new world where information and resources are generated and shared organically, dynamically, virally and continuously.

Let's harness the power that is already out there and create solutions that have never been imagined before. If Facebook can innovate for profits, and human traffickers can use new media for exploitation, let's leverage technology and the Internet in even greater measure so that more and more people can be set free!

Discussion Questions

1. What are gaps that you see in sharing information and resources? How do you see technology helping?
2. Have you heard of the resources discussed in this essay and in the related case studies? Take some time to check them out and share them with others in your circle.
3. Are there tools out on the Internet that you wish were available to the freedom movement? Are there tools that don't yet exist that you wish the freedom movement had? What resources do you have in

---

[5] www.counterchildtrafficking.org (case study follows).

[6] www.freedomcollaborative.org

[7] MD544 Ministry with Sexually Exploited and Trafficked Children.

your network of friends and colleagues who may be able to help develop such tools?

4. Do you know of someone who thinks: "I wish there was something I could do about human trafficking, but I'm 'just' a computer guy/gal." Show them this essay. Get them involved.

Case Study, by Tania DoCarmo

Freedom Collaborative

Freedom Collaborative[8] is a comprehensive online platform that links the entire counter-trafficking movement through a number of integrated collaboration tools and resources. This case study describes how Freedom Collaborative leverages the Internet and technology to enhance collaboration globally.

About Freedom Collaborative

It is clear that no organization can address the complexity of abuse, trafficking and exploitation on their own. Yet while true change can only be achieved through collective impact, to date there are few mechanisms available to facilitate coordination on a grand scale. The aim of Freedom Collaborative is to enable organizations to contribute to and draw from their collective knowledge base, in order that we might multiply each others' efforts. It accomplishes this through the innovative tools and resources described below.

Freedom Registry

Freedom Registry is an online database of vetted organizations, agencies and institutions working to address abuse, exploitation and human trafficking. Its aim is to enable the continued formalization of referral networks, help advance best practices and allow the community to objectively identify gaps in services.

Organizations register themselves. After information is vetted, organization owners are able to self-update program information, resources, members and volunteer opportunities on an ongoing, real-time basis. Users can search for organizations by location, demographic reached, services offered and a number of other fields.

Freedom Library

Freedom Library empowers the community to create and collaborate in real time. No one individual or organization owns or curates the content – books, articles, research, videos and tools are added by any member of the community.

---

[8] www.freedomcollaborative.org

Items are then classified, updated and rated by the community to ensure that the most relevant items rise to the top.

API

In addition to these tools, Freedom Collaborative seeks to encourage the development of new tools and resources by offering an application programming interface (API). The importance of this feature is explained by the following quote from The Programmable Web:

> "What if you wanted to tackle a really big issue. How about freeing the 27 million people caught in 'modern day slavery'? Would you: A) Figure out the answer and build the biggest organization you could to solve the problem by yourself, or, B) Work with other organizations already working on this issue because cooperation is essential to solving this, or C) Build an API so the smart people who chose B could have an even bigger impact? Freedom Registry, founded by a group called Chab Dai (which stands for "joining hands" in Khmer) is already doing B, has just chosen C."[9]

The API enables *anyone* to build new tools that can be used by the community. It allows other large systems (such as hotlines) to augment their systems to keep real-time up-to-date records on regional services. It also gives academics the capacity to pull the data and run analysis on it.

Other Features

Freedom Collaborative offers a number of other features that are constantly improving and expanding. An Interactive Map allows users to navigate Freedom Collaborative and find resources available in their region through data visualization. Freedom Dialogues allows users to listen in on video conversations between two human trafficking experts about important topics. Users can respond, discuss and ask questions through threaded comments. Freedom Collaborative also offers a forum for collaboration on special projects or to pilot new ideas.

The possibilities for collaboration are endless!

Case Study, by Ané Auret

Counter Child Trafficking Global Online Conference (CCTC)

> "By having an online conference we are able to collaborate much more globally. We connect people from around the world... and [participants]connect and formulate relationships. Connections are like a web that I believe human traffickers will get stuck in."

---

[9] Greg Bates, "The Freedom Registry API: Fighting the Good Fight Against Human Trafficking," The Programmable Web Blog (July 26, 2013).

Participant, Counter Child Trafficking Global Online Conference 2013

The Counter Child Trafficking Conference (CCTC)[10] seeks to use modern technology and social media to facilitate and connect the global counter trafficking community on a scale that has not been done before, where participants can network, share learning and resources, good practice, innovation, research and ideas. This case study describes how online conferencing tools can effectively build real-world connections and facilitate collaboration across countries and continents.

Background

The first ever free, global online conference bringing together frontline practitioners and experts, including survivors, took place on 16-18 October 2013. The Counter Child Trafficking Global Online Conference 2013 (CCTC13) had nearly 600 participants from 72 countries taking part in the event, which was held exclusively online using a customized version of the Adobe Connect virtual meeting platform.

Founded on the notion that when adults speak and listen to each other, children are generally safer, the organizers of the conference looked for a way to facilitate connectivity and connection between the many organizations and individuals that form the global counter child trafficking community. Aware of the fact that so many are not in a position to afford travel and accommodation costs to access conferences and training organizers felt that modern technology and the use of social media could help to bridge this gap. The conference format allowed many individuals and organizations without the financial means to attend in-person conferences to participate, significantly expanding the conference's audience and reach.

About the Conference

In order to strengthen the global response to child trafficking, the conference organizers focused on achieving two important goals:
- To share resources and information, providing participants with practical information and tools that they could integrate into their own work; and
- To encourage networking by promoting and supporting the work of the many organizations and individuals involved in the field.

To successfully reach these goals, the conference offered 44 webinar sessions presented by 56 speakers covering 6 major themes. The diversity of speakers and subject areas covered helped to deliver practical information and practice points to participants from a broad range of organizations and specializations, whether child protection workers, law enforcement or border protection officials, academic researchers, legal professionals, health care professionals, counselors, volunteers and many others.

---

[10] www.counterchildtrafficking.org

While the conference took place across several time zones, because it was synchronous participants were able to interact in "real time" with speakers and with each other, enhancing both learning and connections. They could do this in the virtual Networking Area that was open for online discussion threads during each webinar and for a short period preceding and following the session. The open discussion format allowed for greater participation than might occur at an in-person conference because all of the participants were present in the same place at the same time and could follow discussion threads even if they were themselves not part of the conversation. Many key connections were able to be made in the Networking Area that would not have happened outside the conference, and participants could exchange contact information to continue conversations and connections initiated online.

Another way for participants to connect was through social media, both during and after the event. The conference developed a live Twitter feed (@NoChildHarmed) for participants and others to follow along with conference events. The conference also hosts a YouTube channel, NoChildHarmed, which was visited over 2,200 times during the CCTC's three days of operation. The YouTube is also a platform for post-conference learning to continue. For any who were unable to attend CCTC13, most of the conference's webinars are available on the YouTube channel, representing a rich, sustainable source of counter-trafficking information and best practices.

An additional key component of the event was the number of trafficking survivors who took part in the online discussions and shared their experiences and views as part of the counter trafficking community. To this effect the event was ended by a session delivered by eight survivors who are currently working as leaders in the counter trafficking field. This session solidified messages of hope and inspiration, of resilience, and the importance of working alongside survivors as partners.

Going Forward

Conference participants indicated overwhelmingly that they were interested in continuing to be part of a global child protection/counter-trafficking network. Out of 285 conference participants who answered this poll question, 283 agreed with this statement.

The CCTC represents a major first step in the creation of a global community of practice in the counter child trafficking field. Discussions between participants in the conference's Networking Area reinforced the consensus that a global response is needed to confront what has become a global problem. One participant emphasized the significant good will in the counter-trafficking sector, arguing that there is real sincerity in people's collaborative sentiment and willingness to work together.

The significance of this finding should be emphasized. It suggests that the crucial limiting factors in terms of global networking and collaboration are most often time, cost, and distance, rather than a lack of interest in forging collective responses on the part of organizations in the field. The challenges in establishing global networks using conventional means were summed up well by one participant:

> "I attend a lot of great in-person conferences, make great connections, start good collaborations and then we all go off to our separate parts of the world and nothing happens, until two years and thousands of dollars in plane tickets later when we start from scratch all over again."

These experiences explain why many conference participants expressed a desire to maintain online networking opportunities once the conference concluded. Online conferences and collaboration are powerful tools that enable conversations and connections to continue without being limited by geographical and financial barriers.

This event's lasting impact will depend on participants' ability to translate relationships developed online into practical collaboration and information sharing in the field. It is too early to measure the CCTC's impact in this respect; however, the volume of email addresses exchanged, resources shared and plans for collaboration made in the event's Networking Area indicate that the event generated real connections in the field. As an annual event, the CCTC has the potential to become the premiere networking event for professionals working in this field around the globe.

CHAPTER 33
WHAT ARE THE CHALLENGES OF PARTNERSHIP?
HOW DO WE WORK WITH PEOPLE/ORGANIZATIONS
WHO MAY SEEM CONTROVERSIAL OR
WHO MAY NOT ESPOUSE SIMILAR CHRISTIAN VALUES
(WITHOUT COMPROMISING)?

Key Issues, by Helen Sworn

Words such as partnership and collaboration have become part of our daily language in multiple sectors of our lives. Whether we work in church ministry, non-profit organizations, corporate sector companies, or are involved in our local community activities or school committees; we talk about increasing our impact by working together. Regardless of how easily these words roll off our tongues, however, it is not as easy in practice to develop partnerships with those who we do not naturally align to within our religious, cultural or personal preferences.

So, is this chapter a guide to developing partnerships in 10 easy steps? Unfortunately, no. Sorry to disappoint you! The reality is that before we consider any type of partnership, we need to explore ourselves, our own preferences, and if we are honest, our own prejudices. Each of us has prejudices whether we readily admit to them, or push them under the veneer of false acceptance.

Protected by Our Personal Prejudices and Preferences

All of us, for example, have a historical and cultural context of growing up, a way in which we developed moral and ethical frameworks for viewing and assessing the world around us. These deep-rooted values become part of who we are, help establish our character, and often affect our on-going behavior. It is always easy to judge another's prejudices and preferences, but never easy to receive criticism for our own. In the midst of criticism from others, each of us has developed a stream of justifications as to why we believe and behave as we do. This in itself creates division and polarizes us from those we feel challenged by, and by association, can often compromise our reputation and/or character.

As we look at the life of Jesus, we cannot help but be shocked by those he chose to associate himself with. It seems that over the last two thousand years, we have tried to sterilize and romanticize stories of the Bible in order to not make them as socially and religiously unacceptable as they actually were. Yet

Jesus smashed through moral, cultural and religious norms to show that we not only needed him, but that we also need one another.

While our own values may be subjective, they make up the essence of our character and behavior. Most of us would much rather stay within our comfort zones than expose ourselves, our prejudices and our preferences by working with others in an environment where they may be challenged.

Spiritual Synergy or Separation

Unfortunately, theological differences can be the most divisive, and are often used as an excuse for working alone. It seems we often find ourselves in conflict not just with individuals or organizations that have no Christian affiliation, but also with other Christians and Christian organizations who may differ from us in their theological standpoint.

Until trust is established (which takes time and may seem too distant a process), we need to start from a point of practicing *respect*. Respect does not mean we just give up our beliefs and compromise our faith. Respect simply means we listen without judgment, show regard and consideration without criticism, and recognize opportunities for learning before jumping to our own responses and conclusions.

Spiritual diversity does not need to be a ground for argument and criticism (whether verbal or passive) but it is an opportunity for us to model grace. Surely there is nothing compromising about that.

Moving Beyond Our Wall of Protection

Do we opt out or cooperate with those we disagree with? We get to choose. Being salt and light surely means we have been mandated to be in the world, not *of* the world, and to model our faith in deeds and practice. But it does not require us to separate ourselves from the world by putting a wall of protection around us.

There are, of course, as many different examples of this wall of protection as there are characteristics of personalities. The wall of protection is different for each of us. When facing disagreements and challenges some of us respond in a passive-aggressive manner. On the surface we may be smiling, but underneath there is aggression and tension that will eventually work its way to the top when the stress begins to show. Others use aggressive behavior as a form of defense and protection. Either way, we avoid the real tension in front of us, and often avoid seeking a solution that favors both parties.

It is important for us to begin from a point of honesty and self-reflection. If we are ever going to develop partnerships and truly collaborate, we need to face our own prejudices in order to find *common ground,* even and *especially* in the most unlikely of partnerships.

Finding the Common Ground

In order to find common ground for partnership and working together, we need to stand back to look for the opportunities and not just the roadblocks. A realistic evaluation of the partnership situation and what both are expecting out of working together is a starting point. *Facts first*, not feelings. Keep focused on the facts, rather than how they are presented. Don't allow your own assumptions to break down the opportunities or possibilities that could result from working together.

Partnerships are built on relationships, but this doesn't mean you either need to become best friends or have no partnership at all! We need to be wise in developing appropriate and strategic partnerships and/or working relationships within the framework of our common ground and purpose.

For example, driving in the city of Phnom Penh, Cambodia tries the patience of the best of us. Roadblocks are a common predicament and it is impossible to see the big picture of the situation from the middle of the traffic jam. If I could just be in a helicopter, I would be able to see where the problem is, and more importantly, how to get to the easiest exit route! Metaphorically, this is what we need to do with partnerships. We need to know where we are heading, what the big picture of the challenge or issue is, and where the possible exits or partnerships could be.

Sometimes the common ground may seem too small in comparison to the problem. Nevertheless, however small it may seem to us, it is a *starting point* for building toward partnership. We need to keep this common ground or goal in mind as we begin building the partnership relationship. Our own perceptions and preferences quickly and easily cloud the issues and/or our responses which can easily build or destroy the way forward.

Handling Conflict and Controversy

As I outlined at the beginning of this essay, partnership and collaboration are not easy! Of course there will be times of conflict and controversy. But do we see these as an "exit" or as an opportunity?

The old adage says: "If at first you don't succeed, try, try again!" It may seem cliché and out of date but the essence still stands. Partnership is a process not an event. It requires patience and purpose, as does any relationship in life.

Partnership needs to go beyond our personal preferences and back to the vision and common goal. The second of Stephen Covey's seven habits is "Begin with the end in mind."[1] In order for partnership to work, we need to know what the big picture and/or goal is so we can stay focused on where we are going in the midst of the process – especially when we hit the roadblocks of conflict and controversy. Positive results and greater impact often come out of resolved conflicts and controversy, and in fact might not have emerged from partnerships where there is little challenge and where complacency is more likely to result.

---

[1] Stephen Covey, *The 7 Habits of Highly Effective People* (New York: Free Press, 1989).

Appropriately handing conflict doesn't mean we have to apologize for our theology or renounce our faith. However, we do need to be aware that spiritual and theological superiority complexes can certainly build high walls and burn bridges. It is important to respond to issues of controversy respectfully, with evidence and facts, and be open to seeing it as a learning opportunity for all parties concerned.

The Way Forward

Once we've considered our personal prejudices and committed to finding common ground with potential partners, the next step to collaboration is to consider the existing partnerships we have, and how these fit into the framework, vision and purpose we wish to achieve. A strategic yet practical way to do this is to develop a partnership analysis.

Look at your goal and key objectives. First think of your internal staff and how their work is helping to achieve your goal. Then consider a wider circle of partnerships. Perhaps these are with individuals or organizations you already have common ground with, and those who espouse to similar faith and practice.

Next draw a wider circle, this time considering the other organizations or individuals that you know have a similar goal but who may have a different faith or way of working. Begin to look at who within this circle could be strategic partners at some capacity in order to help achieve the greater goal. A ranking process could also be helpful in seeing which potential partners have more influence or skills than others.

A SWOT analysis (strengths, weaknesses, opportunities and threats) or similar tool can be useful in carrying out a risk assessment, and in seeing potential for opportunities in partnering. When doing a SWOT analysis I personally prefer looking at weaknesses first, then examining strengths at the same as threats/roadblocks in order to evaluate how I might turn them into opportunities.

Once you see the completed picture, you will begin to recognize potential partnership opportunities, including how you may best approach them to achieve your greater goal.

Conclusion

We all have a choice. We can move alone and avoid the hazards of working with others who have differing values or behaviors than ours, or we can be purposeful in developing partnerships and working deliberately to find common ground in order to achieve a greater purpose and vision.

Case Study, by Helen Sworn

Considering the Greater Purpose

Recently I met with someone who fits the challenge of this question exactly. Everyone who knew her warned me that she was verbally aggressive, dominant, uncooperative and almost impossible to work with, let alone develop external partnerships with.

However, this individual was working on similar issues to my own organization, and developing a partnership would enable us both to be more effective in achieving our purpose.

I kept the first conversations very professional and factual. During one conversation, she made controversial comments about the lack of ability for my organization to build relationships with others due to our Christian ethos. I respectfully pointed out that I did not agree with her perspective and that I had much evidence in our history of successfully working with organizations and others who did not assume a Christian faith. I stated clearly and deliberately that I made no apology for my faith, but that I believe everyone has a choice of faith and I respected that right.

I verbally acknowledged that although we did not share the same faith standpoint, we did share the same standpoint regarding the issues of trafficking and sexual abuse, and I suggested we should focus on a possible way forward in that regard. It was clear to me that there had been a negative history between this individual and Christians who were more interested in personal agenda than partnership building. By the end of the conversation we had not only moved beyond these points of contention, but were also able to see some key partnership opportunities that benefitted both of our organizations.

I often find that the challenging partnerships we have to work hardest to secure are those that have greater impact. There are many similar cases I could cite. Some of these more challenging partnerships have taken many meetings to solidify, and it has taken perseverance and humility to keep pursuing partnership for the greater good of those we are seeking to serve.

Discussion Questions

1. What experiences do you have working with individuals and/or organizations who hold different positions or opinions than you do? If you do have experience, how did it go? If you don't have many experiences doing so, why not?
2. Do you tend to opt-out or cooperate with those you disagree with?
3. Are there individuals or organizations you would like to work with but are hesitant to do so due to differences in opinion? Are there ways in which you may be able to find common ground?

4. Is there any difference you feel you could not overlook in partnership? Why or why not?
5. As suggested by the author, consider organizations you are not working with now who may have a similar goal but have a different faith or way of working. Begin to consider who may be strategic partners to help achieve your common, greater goal. Do a SWOT analysis to consider risks, strengths and/or weaknesses in working with each potential partner.

Key Issues, by Jennifer Roemhildt Tunehag

What do a Christian mission organization, the LGBT community, the communist party of Greece and a sex worker's union have in common? (This isn't a joke.) The answer: Concern for people who are being harmed in prostitution.

We will never be able to address the harms of prostitution and human trafficking on our own. One organization alone will never be able to remediate the suffering of those who are exploited or address the issues that caused their vulnerability. Finding partners is essential to accomplishing these goals.

Our ministry works among several groups of people involved in prostitution in Athens: Greek nationals (both women and men), women in prostitution from Eastern Europe (most of whom are trafficked), and women who are trafficked from Africa. It was our work among transgender people involved in prostitution that drew the attention of the local LGBT community.

"Could you host a booth at the Gay Pride Festival in two weeks?" a colleague was asked. Flabbergasted, she hesitated. "You understand our ministry doesn't approve of homosexual behavior, right?" she asked. "We know," came the response, "but we know that you love us, and we think that you should be there."

Jesus had drawn near to these men, and they wanted more. How amazing to be invited into their community as a "bridge" to relationship with God! How astonishing to work together – at the request of the organizing committee – to reach people with the Good News of God's love.

How to partner with dissimilar or controversial organizations is, in some respects, the second question. The first must be, *Why*? When Christians talk about partnership, it is generally assumed that we will choose others who ascribe to a similar or "good" faith. Why should we consider working with partners of good will?

Why Work with Others?

Common Grace

Nicholas Kristof and Sheryl WuDunn's book *Half the Sky*[2] recalls an old Chinese proverb: "Women hold up half the sky." The authors take a hard look at the problems of maternal mortality, human trafficking and gender-based violence, and suggest that these, and other social ills (including poverty), could be addressed if societies would begin to harness the contribution of women.

Women across the world care about peace … clean water … and economic viability because they care about the future of their children. It makes sense to engage them in solving these problems! They have a vital contribution to make.

God cares about *his* children, too...women, men and children who are trapped or forced into prostitution, labor and other forms of exploitation. *It makes sense to understand who else is committed to their future!* The goals of our partners will not always be identical to our own. But in this case, it is the *Church* that risks being marginalized.

Our understanding of common grace comes into question here. Do we believe that God is able to accomplish His purposes through non-believers? Is God's activity in the world limited to the Church, or *by* it?

Repudiating Fear of Man

Will others understand why we have a booth at Gay Pride? What do they think of our work in bars and brothels, and our friendships with desperately broken people? Will our friends be welcome in their worship services and homes? Will *we*?

To work among people in prostitution, we have already faced the "fear of man." Yet it often returns to burden us with ungodly expectations. The question we must ask is not what will *others* think, but what does *God* think?

It is very good news for us and for the people that we serve that Jesus was not afraid of controversy! Jesus scandalized the religious establishment regularly in his efforts to restore, to destroy the works of the devil, and to seek and save lost ones. He is the one whom we follow, love and serve! In the Gospels, Jesus is rebuked for being a "friend of sinners." More of us should be such friends.

In our efforts to avoid the "appearance of evil,"[3] we sometimes distance ourselves from the very people that God is calling us to. Is it possible that this desire to be "good" can cause us to miss the heart of God and his purposes in the world? The Apostle Paul's answer to his accusers is relevant: "To those not having the law I became like one not having the law (though I am not free from God's law but am under Christ's law), so as to win those not having the law.

---

[2] Nicholas Kristof and Sheryl WuDunn, *Half the Sky: Turning Oppression into Opportunity for Women Worldwide* (New York: Alfred A. Knopf, 2009).
[3] 1 Thessalonians 5:22.

To the weak I became weak, to win the weak. I have become all things to all men so that by all possible means I might save some."[4]

Glory of God

The media has often expressed interest in our work. Why do we leave warm, safe homes at night to offer kindness and coffee to women on the streets? What could possibly compel us to commit to the restoration of women who have been victimized in unthinkable ways?

What wonderful opportunities to give a public answer for the hope that we have! The Good News about who God is and whom he loves is not *only* good news to women and men on the street. It is good news to the Church. It is good news to Communists and activists, to homosexuals and academics. We have the opportunity to bear the news of God's love to all of the people in this arena!

"You are the light of the world...let your light shine before men, that they may see your good deeds and glorify your Father in heaven."[5]

How (And When) Do We Work With Others?

Along with a decision to work with controversial partners must come an understanding of when and how to do so. "Blessed is the man who does not condemn himself by what he approves," Romans 14:22[6] tells us. A clear understanding of these parameters allows us to be salt and light in the broader community.

So what principles should guide our partnerships?

Be Clear about Your Identity

My husband worked for many years in partnership development and often used an activity to illustrate this point. He would dump a child's puzzle on the table, ask each group member to take a piece, and then challenge the group to assemble it correctly. It was a doable task...as long as each member showed the others the pattern, shape and size of his piece.

To be a good partner, others must understand where you "fit" in the overall scheme. You must define for yourself and others your contribution (the scope, character and skills of your organization). Your decisions and actions will be strongly influenced by your faith perspective, and it is legitimate and often necessary to define yourself in terms of this motivation. Hiding your motivations diminishes trust.

It is impossible to assemble a puzzle with pieces made of jelly! Good partners understand their unique contribution and help others to understand it.

---

[4] 1 Corinthians 9:21-22 (NIV).
[5] Matthew 5:14-16 (NIV).
[6] (NIV).

Keep Shared Objectives in Mind

As we consider working with controversial partners, we need to have our goal – and the people that we are serving – clearly in mind. Our mission organization shares little in common with many of the groups mentioned, but *the vision for assisting women and men who are suffering is enough.*

Focus on what you have in common. Although you have some things in common, there are other issues on which you will not agree. It is important to remember the purpose behind the partnership!

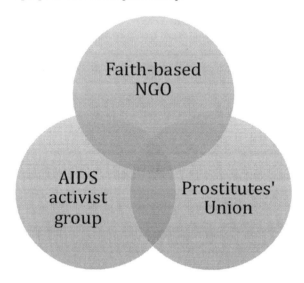

I was invited to chair a consultation under the auspices of the European Union. Our goal was to offer recommendations on a legal framework that would help women in prostitution in the region. Academics, abolitionists, feminists, sex workers and evangelical Christians assembled for the job! There was much that could have divided us, but our task – serving the needs of women – as too important to allow those distractions.

We recognized that a report from a team as diverse as ours would be taken far more seriously than an "agenda driven" report from any one of our member agencies, and we worked to extend grace to those with different opinions even as we maintained our unique perspectives on the issue and the debate.

Acknowledge Differences

Acknowledge differences...but don't be afraid of them! I started our consultation with these words: "I am an evangelical Christian missionary. For some of you, those words as are scary as 'feminist' or 'sex worker' or 'abolitionist.'"

Never say, "Let's just forget about our differences." Instead, recognize that they can offer an advantage when we work together! Be proactive about identifying problems that may be created by those differences, and seeking resolution.

Form Limited Partnerships

Could the World Evangelical Alliance (WEA) ever work with Muslims? Absolutely – if the opportunity allows us to achieve common goals and demonstrate the character of Christ. Could we work together on everything? Probably not.

Know *when* to work with others to accomplish common goals and work until those goals are met. Effective partnerships stay focused on the ultimate vision for which they were formed. "What are we trying to accomplish?" is a key question. Knowing *whom* to work with is also important. CARE International, a UK-based charity, suggests that we should always ask, "Which stakeholders are working for change in ways that we believe are constructive?"

Obviously, we are not able to work with those who actively oppose our goals. The WEA may work with the Muslim community on disaster relief, but would not be able to cooperate in evangelistic outreach. Understand the specific objectives in line with your shared purpose, and also decide on the limits and boundaries that will inform your cooperation.

Communicate

Practice your cross-cultural communication skills and choose language that your partners will understand. Christian jargon is a part of church sub-culture. Leave it behind! References to sin, Satan, and "the blood of the Lamb" will be lost on – or worse, alienate – partners who also need to know Jesus. There is plenty of room for misunderstanding in a group with different motivations and ideals. Be clear in sharing your motivations and values, as well as your objectives and actions.

Build trust with your partners by devoting time and energy to relationship building, clear communication, and mutual understanding.

Benefits of Partnership

There are many blessings to partnership, not least the ability to serve our clients better and to do things that we could not accomplish on our own.

Enjoy the benefits of partnership:
- good stewardship of limited resources,
- broader impact, and
- ability to focus on your specific areas of calling and gifting (as partners take on complimentary tasks).

The medium *is* the message. As we serve people in prostitution and victims of human trafficking with faith, hope and love (and a commitment to professionalism and integrity!), we also win the opportunity to make the message and character of Christ known to a new audience…our partners.

Case Study, by Jennifer Roemhildt Tunehag

The networking efforts of our ministry caught the attention of a doctor from ACT Up, an AIDS activist group. Patients with HIV/AIDS in Athens are referred to one hospital. On the ward, they receive medical care and the drug cocktails that will prolong their lives, yet quality of life can be elusive. "We can provide for the medical needs of our patients," the doctor told me, "but we don't have the time to sit and hold their hands. Do you know anyone who might be willing to do that?" A match made in heaven! No need for a professional degree, just a heart for people: a call went out immediately for volunteers from the local church.

Prostitution is a taboo subject in Ukrainian culture, and local churches have historically been blind to the issue of trafficking. The results are tragic. Over the past ten years, more than 300,000 women have been trafficked within Ukraine and across its borders to Western Europe. Recently, the church has become aware of the issue...and concerned for the women who are victimized.

A local NGO is responding. Its members are not Christians, and its methods are not always edifying. (One of the group's initiatives involves regular lingerie "parades" down a central Kyiv boulevard, holding placards with the message "Ukraine is not a brothel"!) However, this courageous group has also taken on a creative anti-pornography campaign that directs anyone surfing the Web for pornography to a warning page describing the damage that porn does to women and men before they can proceed.

How should the church respond? It is certainly tempting to judge. But imagine what could happen if the church were to bless the efforts of these young women to curb the consumption of pornography in their country – a task which neither group is likely to accomplish on their own. Taking advantage of the Orthodox Easter holiday, our Athens ministry team assembled gifts (a *lambada* (Easter candle) and a copy of the Jesus film) to bring to women working in the brothels and streets of Athens.

Inside one dimly-lit brothel, we met members of the sex workers' union who were collecting dues, and offered them gifts as well. "Candy," a transgendered person who serves as president of the union accepted the film. "I've been working in prostitution for over 25 years and this is the kindest thing I have ever seen." Although the goal of the union is to help individuals stay in prostitution, and our ministry's aim is to help them leave, we agree on one thing: neither of us wants to see those involved in prostitution suffer! Candy agreed to refer exploited women to our organization for assistance.

Discussion Questions

1. Why should we consider working with partners who do not share our faith?

2. Can you think of other "blessings" of partnership not named in this chapter? List some.
3. Do you believe that God is able to accomplish his purposes through non-believers? What Scriptures come to mind?
4. What are some possible problems with partnership? What are some proactive solutions to those challenges?
5. What needs are you currently unable to meet or address on your own? Make a list of other organizations working on these issues in your community or country. How well do you know them and their priorities? Are any of these groups responding to the needs you listed?
6. What unique contribution do you bring to the table in terms of skills and experience?
7. Does your organization have a vision/mission statement? A good mission statement will solidify your identity and also inform your actions.
8. What are your organization's values? These foundations are important for you and others as you work in partnership. Can you communicate your vision and values without using religious language? (Give it a try!)

RECOMMENDED RESOURCES AND WORKS CITED

FOREWORD

Faith Alliance Against Slavery and Trafficking. *Hands that Heal: International Curriculum to Train Caregivers of Trafficking Survivors.* Shared Hope International/FAAST, 2007.

Phyllis Kilbourn and Marjorie McDermid, eds. *Sexually Exploited Children: Working to Protect and Heal.* Monrovia, CA: MARC, 1998.

PART 1

Recommended Resources

1. Is it naive to think slavery and exploitation will ever come to an end?

BOOKS AND ARTICLES

Bales, Kevin. *Disposable People: New Slavery in the Global Economy.* Berkeley: University of California Press, 1999, 2000, 2004, 2012.

Bales, Kevin. *Ending Slavery: How We Free Today's Slaves.* Berkeley: University of California Press, 2007.

Bales, Kevin with Monti Narayan Datta. "Slavery in Europe: Part 1, Estimating the Dark Figure." *Human Rights Quarterly* 35, no. 4 (Nov 2013): 817-29. doi: 10.1353/hrq.2013.0051.

Blackmon, Douglas A. *Slavery by Another Name: The Re-Enslavement of Black Americans from the Civil War to World War 2.* Anchor Press, 2009.

Cadet, Jean-Robert. *Restavec: From Haitian Slave Child to Middle-Class American.* Austin: University of Texas Press, 1998.

Datta, Monti Narayan and Kevin Bales. "Slavery is Bad for Business: Analyzing the Impact of Slavery on National Economies." *The Brown Journal of World Affairs* 19, no. 11 (2013): 205-224.

Hochschild, Adam. *King Leopold's Ghost.* Boston: Houghton Mifflin, 1999.

Hochschild, Adam. *Bury the Chains: Prophets and Rebels in the Fight to Free an Empire's Slaves.* London: Macmillan, 2005.

Miers, Suzanne. *Slavery in the Twentieth Century: The Evolution of a Global Problem.* New York: Altamira, 2003.

OTHER

Bellagio-Harvard Guidelines on the Legal Parameters of Slavery (2012) available from http://www.qub.ac.uk/schools/SchoolofLaw/Research/HumanRightsCentre/Resources/Bellagio-HarvardGuidelinesontheLegalParametersofSlavery/

WEBSITES

Free the Slaves Website (including informational videos) http://www.freetheslaves.net
Walk Free Website http://www.walkfree.org
End Slavery Now Website http://www.endslaverynow.com

2. How can donors positively engage in the anti-trafficking movement?

BOOKS AND ARTICLES

Crutchfield, Leslie, John Kania and Mark Kramer. *Do More Than Give: The Six Practices of Donors Who Change the World.* San Francisco: Jossey-Bass, 2011.

Derks, Annuska, Roger Henke and Ly Vanna. *Review of a Decade of Research on Trafficking in Persons, Cambodia.* The Asia Foundation, 2006. http://asiafoundation.org/resources/pdfs/CBTIPreview.pdf.

Frumkin, Peter. *The Essence of Strategic Giving: A Practical Guide for Donors and Fundraisers* . Chicago: University of Chicago Press, 2010.

Tierney, Thomas and Joel Fleishmann. *Give Smart: Philanthropy That Gets Results.* New York: Public Affairs, 2011.

Works Cited

KEY ISSUES (FLOYD)

Crutchfield, Leslie, John Kania and Mark Kramer. *Do More Than Give: The Six Practices of Donors Who Change the World.* San Francisco: Jossey-Bass, 2011.

Frumkin, Peter. *The Essence of Strategic Giving: A Practical Guide for Donors and Fundraisers.* Chicago: University of Chicago Press, 2010.

The Asia Foundation. *Review of a Decade of Research on Trafficking in Persons, Cambodia.* The Asia Foundation, 2006. http://asiafoundation.org/resources/pdfs/CBTIPreview.pdf

Tierney, Thomas and Joel Fleishmann. *Give Smart: Philanthropy That Gets Results.* New York: Public Affairs, 2011.

PART 2

Recommended Resources

3. What does the Bible say about being involved in justice for the sexually exploited?

BOOKS AND ARTICLES

Bunge, Marcia J., Terence Fretheim, and Beverly Roberts Gaventa, eds. *The Child in the Bible.* Grand Rapids: Eerdmans, 2008.

Kilbourn, Phyllis, ed. *Shaping The Future: Girls And Our Destiny.* Pasadena: William Carey Library, 2008.

McConnell, Douglas, Jennifer Orona and Paul Stockley, eds. *Understanding God's Heart for Children: Toward a Biblical Framework.* Carlisle: Authentic Media, 2007.

OTHER

For Biblical insight on children and childhood (but not focused on abuse itself), there is a very helpful list at the end of this page: http://www.elca.org/Growing-In-Faith/Vocation/Lutheran-Partners/Complete-Issue/090708/090708_04.aspx.

4. How should the church be involved in responding to sexual exploitation?

BOOKS AND ARTICLES (JUSTICE AND THEOLOGY)

Bonhoeffer, Dietrich. *Ethics.* Simon & Schuster, 1995.

Bonhoeffer, Dietrich. *Letters and Papers from Prison.* Simon & Schuster, 1997.

(It is recommended that the two selections by Bonhoeffer be read together for comprehension.)

Haugen, Gary A. *Good News About Injustice: A Witness of Courage in a Hurting World (Tenth Anniversary Edition).* InterVarsity Press, 2009.

Haugen, Gary A. *Just Courage: God's Great Expedition for the Restless Christian.* InterVarsity Press, 2008.

Labberton, Mark. *The Dangerous Act of Worship: Living God's Call to Justice.* InterVarsity Press, 2007.

Lewis, C.S. *God in the Dock.* William. B. Eerdmans Publishing Company, 1994.

BOOKS AND ARTICLES (TRAFFICKING, SLAVERY AND GENERAL HUMAN RIGHTS)

Bales, Kevin. *Disposable People: New Slavery in the Global Economy.* University of California Press, 2004.

Batstone, David. *Not for Sale: The Return of the Global Slave Trade – and How We Can Fight It.* HarperCollins Publishers, 2007.

Kristof , Nicholas D. and Sheryl WuDunn. *Half the Sky: Turning Oppression into Opportunity for Women Worldwide.* Alfred A. Knopf, 2009.

Dallaire, Roméo. *Shake Hands with the Devil: The Failure of Humanity in Rwanda.* Da Capo Press, 2004.

Hochschild, Adam. *Bury the Chains: Prophets and Rebels in the Fight to Free an Empire's Slaves.* Houghton Mifflin Harcourt, 2006.

Hochschild, Adam. *King Leopold's Ghost: A Story of Greed, Terror and Heroism in Colonial Africa.* Mariner Books, 1999.

Human Rights Watch. *Human Rights Watch World Report.* (published annually)

Kara, Siddharth. *Sex Trafficking: Inside the Business of Modern Slavery.* Columbia University Press, 2008.

Kidder, Tracy. *Mountains Beyond Mountains: The Quest of Dr. Paul Farmer, A Man Who Would Cure the World.* Random House Inc., 2004.

Paton, Alan. *Cry the Beloved Country.* Simon & Schuster, 2003.

Perkins, John. *Let Justice Roll Down.* Regal Books, 2006.

Power, Samantha. *A Problem from Hell: America and the Age of Genocide.* Harper Perennial, 2007.

United States Department of State. *Trafficking in Persons Report.* (published annually)

Wiesel, Elie. *Night.* Farrar, Straus and Giroux, 2006.

5. Does sex matter to God? Why should it matter to us as Christians??

BOOKS AND ARTICLES

Freitas, Donna. *Sex and the Soul: Juggling Sexuality, Spirituality, Romance, and Religion on America's College Campuses.* Oxford: Oxford University Press, 2008.

Longman III, Tremper. *Song of Songs (New International Commentary on the Old Testament).* Grand Rapids, MI: Wm. B. Eerdmans Publishing Co., 2001.

Moalem, Sharon. *How Sex Works: Why We Look, Smell, Taste, Feel and Act the Way We Do.* New York: Harper, 2008.

West, Christopher. *Fill These Hearts: God, Sex, and The Universal Longing.* New York: Image, 2012.

6. How have we messed up sex?

BOOKS AND ARTICLES

Dines, Gail. *Pornland: How Porn Has Hijacked Our Sexuality.* Boston, MA: Beacon Press, 2010.

Ferder, Fran and John Heagle. *Tender Fires: The Spiritual Promise of Sexuality.* New York: The Crossroad Publishing Company, 2002.

Ferree, Marnie C. *No Stones: Women Redeemed from Sexual Addiction.* Downers Grove, IL: InterVarsity Press, 2010.

Heath, Elaine A. *We Were the Least of These: Reading the Bible with Survivors of Sexual Abuse.* Grand Rapids, MI: Brazos Press, 2011.

West, Christopher. *Theology of The Body for Beginners: A Basic Introduction to Pope John Paul II's Sexual Revolution.* West Chester, PA: Ascension Press, 2004.

MEDIA

"Somebody's Daughter" Documentary www.shessomebodysdaughter.com/somebodys-daughter-dvd

WEBSITES

Candeo Behavior Change Website www.candeobehaviorchange.com
Morality in Media Porn Harms Website www.pornharms.com
Brushfires Website www.brushfiresfoundation.org
She's Somebody's Daughter Website www.shessomebodysdaughter.org
The Social Costs of Pornography Website www.socialcostsofpornography.com
Christopher West Website www.christopherwest.com

7. Where is God when sex gets messy?

BOOKS AND ARTICLES

Ash, Christopher. *Marriage: Sex in the Service of God.* Leicester, UK: IVP, 2003.

Biddle, Mark E. *Missing the Mark: Sin and Its Consequences in Biblical Theology.* Nashville, TN: Abingdon, 2005.

Schmutzer, Andrew J., ed.. *The Long Journey Home: Understanding and Ministering to the Sexually Abused.* Eugene, OR: Wipf and Stock, 2011.

Schmutzer, Andrew J. "Spiritual Formation and Sexual Abuse: Embodiment, Community, and Healing." *Journal of Spiritual Formation and Soul Care* 2 (2009): 67–86.

Volf, Miroslav. *The End of Memory: Remembering Rightly in a Violent World.* Grand Rapids, MI: Eerdmans, 2006.

8. How can we survive in the midst of the mess?

BOOKS AND ARTICLES

Ajulu, Deborah. *Holism in Development.* Monrovia, CA.: MARC (World Vision), 2001.

Byworth, Justin. "World Vision's Approach to Transformational Development: Frame, Policy and Indicators," *Transformation* 20, no. 2 (April – June 2003): 99-111.

Bosch, David. *Transforming Mission: Paradigm Shifts in Theology.* Maryknoll, NY: Orbis Books, 1992.

Chester, Tim. *Awakening to a World of Need: The Recovery of Evangelical Social Concern.* Leicester: IVP, 1993.

Chester, Tim. *Justice, Mercy and Humility: Integral Mission and the Poor.* Carlisle: Paternoster, 2002.

Chester, Tim. *Good News to the Poor: Sharing the Gospel through Social Involvement.* Leicester: IVP, 2004.

Evans, David and Mike Fearon. *From Strangers to Neighbours: How You Can Make the Difference in Your Community.* London: Hodder and Stoughton, 1998.

Gordon, Graham. *What If I Got Involved? Taking a Stand against Social Injustice.* Carlisle: Paternoster, 2003.

Grant, Peter. *Poor No More: Be Part of a Miracle.* Oxford: Monarch, 2008. (especially the first section)

Hoek, Marijke and Justin Thacker. *Micah's Challenge: The Church's Responsibility to the Global Poor.* Carlisle: Paternoster, 2008.

Hollow, Mike. *A Future and a Hope: The Story of Tearfund.* Oxford: Monarch, 2008.

Hughes, Dewi. *God of the Poor.* Carlisle: OM, 1997.

Myers, Bryant. *Walking with the Poor: Principles and Practice of Transformational Development Theory.* Maryknoll, NY: Orbis Books, 1999.

Nicholls, Bruce and Beulah Wood. *Sharing the Good News with the Poor.* Carlisle: Paternoster, 1996.

Samuel, Vinay and Chris Sugden, eds. *The Church in Response to Human Need.* Oxford: Regnum, 1987. (especially God's intention for the world)

Sider, Ronald. *Evangelism and Social Action.* London: Hodder and Stoughton, 1993.

Sider, Ronald. *Rich Christians in a World of Hunger.* London: Hodder and Stoughton, 1997.

So, Damon W.K. "The Missionary Journey of the Son of God into the Far Country: A Paradigm of the Holistic Gospel Developed from the Theology of Karl Barth." *Transformation* 23, no. 3 (2006):130-42.

Stott, John. *Christian Mission in the Modern World.* London: Church Pastoral Aid Society, 1977.

Symonds, Melanie. *Love in Action: Celebrating 25 Years of Tearfund.* Guildford: Eagle, 1993.

Tizon, Al. *Transformation after Lausanne: Radical Evangelical Mission in Global-Local Perspective.* Oxford: Regnum, 2008.

Wallis, Jim. *God's Politics: Why the Right Gets It Wrong and the Left Doesn't Get It.* Oxford: Lion, 2005.

Wallis, Jim. *Seven Ways to Change the World: Reviving Faith and Politics.* Oxford: Lion, 2008.

9. How can we get from hostility to hospitality when dealing with transgender and other sexual minorities?

BOOKS AND ARTICLES

Volf, Miroslav. *Exclusion and Embrace: A Theological Exploration of Identity, Otherness, and Reconciliation.* Nashville: Abington Press, 1996.

Works Cited

BIBLICAL MANDATE (DE VILLIERS)

Grant, Beth. "A Theology of the Value of the Girl Child." Faith Alliance Against Slavery and Trafficking website. http://storage.cloversites.com/ faithallianceagainstslaveryandtrafficking/documents/A%20Theology%20of%20the% 20value%20of%20the%20girl%20child_2.pdf

Schmutzer, Andrew J. "A Theology of Sexual Abuse: A Reflection on Creation and Devastation." *Journal of the Evangelical Theological Society* 51, no. 4 (December 2008): 785-812. http://www.etsjets.org/files/JETS-PDFs/21/21-4/JETS%2051-4%20785-812%20Schmutzer.pdf.

Williams, Rowan. *Christ on Trial: How the Gospel Unsettles Our Judgment.* Grand Rapids, MI: Wm. B. Eerdmans Publishing Co., 2003.

KEY ISSUES (MARTIN)

The content of this essay has been expanded into a full-length book: Martin, Jim. *The Just Church: Becoming a Risk-Taking, Justice-Seeking, Disciple-Making Congregation*. Carol Stream, IL: Tyndale Momentum, 2012. http://www.thejustchurch.com/

Ferris, Elizabeth. "Faith-Based and Secular Humanitarian Organizations." *International Review of the Red Cross* 87, No. 858 (June 2005): 311-25.

Wright, Christopher J.H. *The Mission of God: Unlocking the Bible's Grand Narrative* (Downers Grove, IL: InterVarsity Press, 2006).

THEOLOGICAL REFLECTION (ALLENDER)

Allender, Dan B. *To Be Told: Know Your Story, Shape Your Future*. Colorado Springs: WaterBrook Press, 2005.

THEOLOGICAL REFLECTION (THOMPSON)

Balswick, Judith K. and Jack O. Balswick. *Authentic Human Sexuality: An Integrated Christian Approach*. Downers Grove, IL: InterVarsity Press, 2008.

Buechner, Frederick. *Wishful Thinking: A Seeker's ABC*. New York: HarperCollins, 1993.

Freed, Wendy. "From Duty to Despair: Brothel Prostitution in Cambodia." In *Prostitution, Trafficking, and Traumatic Stress,* edited by Melissa Farley, 133-146. Binghamton, New York: The Haworth Maltreatment & Trauma Press, 2003.

Moore, Russell D. "Love, Sex and Mammon: Hard Times, Hard Truths, and the Economics of the Christian Family." In *Touchstone* (March 2009). http://www.touchstonemag.com/archives/article.php?id=22-02-003-e

Strauss, Lehman. *"Man A Trinity (Spirit, Soul, Body)."* Bible.org Website (June 14, 2004). https://bible.org/seriespage/man-trinity-spirit-soul-body.

West, Christopher. *Theology of the Body for Beginners: A Basic Introduction to Pope John Paul II's Sexual Revolution*. West Chester, PA: Ascension Press, 2004.

THEOLOGICAL REFLECTION (SCHMUTZER)

Biddle, Mark E. *Missing the Mark: Sin and Its Consequences in Biblical Theology*. Nashville, TN: Abingdon, 2005.

Brueggemann, Walter. *Reverberations of Faith: A Theological Handbook of Theological Themes*. Louisville, KY: Westminster John Knox, 2002.

Kapic, Kelly M. "Christian Existence and the Incarnation: Humiliation of the Name." Plenary Address to the Evangelical Theological Society. San Francisco, 2011.

Moltmann, Jürgen. *God in Creation: An Ecological Doctrine of Creation*. London: SCM Press, 1985.

Mounce, Robert H. *The Book of Revelation*. Grand Rapids, MI: Eerdmans, 1977.

Oswalt, John N. *The Bible Among the Myths: Unique Revelation or Just Ancient Literature*. Grand Rapids, MI: Zondervan, 2009.

Plantinga, Jr., Cornelius. *Not the Way It's Supposed to Be: A Breviary of Sin*. Grand Rapids, MI: Eerdmans, 1995.

Schmutzer, Andrew J. "A Theology of Sexuality and its Abuse: Creation, Evil, and the Relational Ecosystem." In *The Long Journey Home: Understanding and Ministering to the Sexually Abused*, edited by Andrew J. Schmutzer, 105-135. Eugene, OR: Wipf and Stock, 2011.

THEOLOGICAL REFLECTION (PREVETTE)

Barth, Karl. *The Epistle to the Romans*. Translated by E. C. Hoskyns. 6th ed. Oxford: Oxford University Press, 1968.

Brueggemann, Walter. *The Prophetic Imagination.* 2nd ed. Minneapolis, MN: Fortress Press, 2001.

Brueggemann, Walter. "Nineteen Theses: Overcoming the Dominant Script of our Age." Paper presented at the Emergent Church and Theology, Minneapolis, MN, 2005.

Fernando, Ajith. "To Serve Is to Suffer." *The Global Conversation (blog), Christianity Today.* August 2010. http://www.christianitytoday.com/ globalconversation/august2010/.

Rohr, Richard. *Everything Belongs: The Gift of Contemplative Prayer.* New York: Crossroad Publishing Company, 2003.

Simon, Ulrich E. *A Theology of Auschwitz: The Christian Faith and the Problem of Evil.* Atlanta: John Knox Press, 1979.

Willmer, Haddon. Review of *Mission as Transformation: A Theology of the Whole Gospel,* by Vinay Samuel and Chris Sugden, eds. *Transformation* 18, no. 3 (July 2001): 194-96.

Yancy, Philip and Paul Brand. *Pain: The Gift Nobody Wants.* New York: Harper Collins, 1999.

THEOLOGICAL REFLECTION (LIPPMANN)

Davis, Jarrett and Glenn Miles. "More Than Gender: A Baseline Study of Transgendered Males in the Sex Industry in Phnom Penh, Cambodia." Phnom Penh: Love 146, October 2013. http://gmmiles.co.uk/wp-content/uploads/2013/07/More-than-Gender-ISWC-2013.pdf and www.Love146.org/research.

Greshake, Gisbert. *Der dreieine Gott – Eine trinitarische Theologie.* Freiburg: Herder, 2007.

Pannenberg, Wolfhart. *Systematische Theologie Band 2.* Goettingen: Vandenhoeck & Ruprecht, 1991.

Volf, Miroslav. *Exclusion and Embrace: A Theological Exploration of Identity, Otherness, and Reconciliation.* Nashville: Abington Press, 1996.

PART 3

Recommended Resources

10. Why is demand important to tackle and what can the church do about it?

BOOKS AND ARTICLES

Bianchi, Gabriel, Miroslav Popper, and Ivan Lukšík. *Between Demand and Supply: Regional Analysis of the Supply and Demand for Sex Services and Trafficking in Hungary, Poland, Slovakia and Slovenia.* Budapest, Hungary: International Organization for Migration, 2007.

Brewer, Devon D., John J. Potterat, Stephen Q. Muth, and John M. Roberts, Jr. "A Large Specific Deterrent Effect of Arrest for Patronizing a Prostitute."*PLoS ONE* 1, no.1 (2006). doi:10.1371/journal.pone.0000060.

Coy, Maddy, Miranda Horvath, and Liz Kelly. *It's Just Like Going to the Supermarket: Men Buying Sex in East London.* London: Child and Woman Abuse Studies Unit, London Metropolitan University, 2007.

Dines, Gail. *Pornland: How Porn Has Hijacked Our Sexuality.* Boston: Beacon Press, 2010.

Dworkin, Andrea. "Prostitution and Male Supremacy." Lecture presented at the symposium "Prostitution: From Academia to Activism," University of Michigan Law School, October 31, 1992.

European Baptist Federation Anti-Trafficking Working Group. *EBF Anti-Trafficking Resource Book 3: Demand.* Hungarian Baptist Aid, 2009. http://www.ebf.org/failid/File/resources/ebf-anti-trafficking-resource-book-no-3.pdf.

Giobbe, Evelina. "A Comparison of Pimps and Batterers." 1998. http://ressourcesfeministes.files.wordpress.com/2012/09/a-comparison-of-pimps-and-batterers.pdf.

Joe-Cannon, Ilvi and Coalition Against Trafficking in Women. *Primer on the Male Demand for Prostitution.* North Amherst, MA: Coalition Against Trafficking in Women, 2006. http://action.web.ca/home/catw/attach/PRIMER.pdf.

Macleod, Jan, Melissa Farley, Lynn Anderson, and Jacqueline Golding. *Challenging Men's Demand for Prostitution in Scotland: A Research Report Based on Interviews with 110 Men Who Bought Women in Prostitution.* Glasgow, Scotland: Women's Support Project, 2008. http://www.prostitutionresearch.com/ChallengingDemandScotland.pdf.

Malarek, Victor. *The Johns: Sex for Sale and the Men Who Buy It.* New York: Arcade Publishing, 2009.

Nelson, Vednita. "Prostitution: Where Racism and Sexism Intersect." *Michigan Journal of Gender & Law* 1 (1993): 81-89.

Raymond, Janice G. "Prostitution on Demand." *Violence Against Women* 10, no. 10 (2004): 1156-1186. doi: 10.1177/1077801204268609.

Rice, Kim and Ross Wantland. "Put Away Your Wallet: Money, Sex and the Demand for Prostitution." *Doin' It Well Blog.* August 30, 2007. http://doinitwell.blog.com/2007/08/30/put-away-your-wallet-money-sex-the-demand-for-prostitution/.

WEBSITES

Publications by Donna M. Hughes on Trafficking, Slavery, and Sexual Exploitation http://www.uri.edu/artsci/wms/hughes/pubtrf.htm

Prostitution Research & Education Website www.prostitutionresearch.com

11. Where are the men of the church in addressing demand?

BOOKS AND ARTICLES

Sheerattan-Bisnauth, Patricia and Philip Vinod Peacock, eds. *Created in God's Image: From Hegemony to Partnership.* Geneva: World Communion of Reformed Churches, 2010. http://wcrc.ch/wp-content/uploads/2013/09/PositiveMasculinitiesGenderManual_0.pdf

WEBSITES

First Man Standing Website www.restoredrelationships.org/firstmanstanding

Restored Website www.restoredrelationships.org

12. How can we stop the demand for child sex tourism and instead create a demand for child safe tourism?

BOOKS AND ARTICLES

Bales, Kevin. *Disposable People: New Slavery in the Global Economy.* Berkeley and Los Angeles, University of California Press, 2000.

Batstone, David. *Not For Sale: The Return of the Global Slave Trade – And How We Can Fight It.* New York: HarperOne, 2007.

Haugen, Gary. *Good News About Injustice: A Witness of Courage in a Hurting World.* Downers Grove, IL: InterVarsity Press, 2009.

Skinner, Benjamin. *A Crime So Monstrous: Face-to-Face with Modern-Day Slavery.* New York: Free Press, 2008.

US State Department, *Trafficking in Persons Report* (published annually). http://www.state.gov/j/tip/rls/tiprpt/

WEBSITES

World Vision Advocate Network Website http://www.worldvision.org/get-involved/advocate

Child Safe Tourism Website http://www.childsafetourism.org

The Code Website http://www.thecode.org

13. Isn't it time we see the links between pornography, prostitution and sex trafficking?

BOOKS AND ARTICLES

Farley, Melissa, Julie Bindel, and Jacqueline M. Golding. *Men Who Buy Sex, Who They Buy and What They Know.* London: Eaves, 2009. http://www.eaves4women. co.uk/Documents/Recent_Reports/Men%20Who%20Buy%20Sex.pdf

Macleod, Jan, Melissa Farley, Lynn Anderson, and Jacqueline Golding. *Challenging Men's Demand for Prostitution in Scotland: A Research Report Based on Interviews with 110 Men Who Bought Women in Prostitution.* Glasgow, Scotland: Women's Support Project, 2008. http://www.prostitutionresearch.com/ ChallengingDemandScotland.pdf

Tewksbury, Richard, and Seana Golder. "Why Do Johns Use Pornography? Predicting Consumption of Pornography by Clients of Street Level Prostitutes." *The Southwest Journal of Criminal Justice* 2, no. 2 (2005): 101-118. http://g.virbcdn.com/_f/files/df/FileItem-149965-Tewksbury.pdf.

WEBSITES

Prostitution Research & Education Website www.prostitutionresearch.com

Pornography and Sex Trafficking Website http://stoptraffickingdemand.com/

14. How can we encourage men in the church to challenge the use of pornography?

WEBSITES

She's Somebody's Daughter Website www.shessomebodysdaughter.org

Enough is Enough Website www.enough.org

WEBSITES (HELP FOR PEOPLE STRUGGLING WITH PORNOGRAPHY)

Restoring the Soul Website www.restoringthesoul.com

Bethesda Workshops Website www.bethesdaworkshops.org

Hope and Freedom Counseling Website www.hopeandfreedom.com

Pure Desire Ministries International Website www.puredesire.org

15. Why is addressing access of youth to pornography so important to tackling demand?

BOOKS AND ARTICLES

Bennett, Morgan. "The New Narcotic." *Public Discourse*. The Witherspoon Institute, October 9, 2013. http://www.thepublicdiscourse.com/2013/10/10846/

PRWeb. "Study: Porn Addiction Increasing as Technology Proliferates Access." PR Web Press Release, February 1, 2013. http://www.prweb.com/releases/2013/2/prweb10382447.htm

WEBSITE (RESOURCES ABOUT KEY ISSUES)

Porn Harms: Research Website www.pornharmsresearch.com

WEBSITES (RESOURCES FOR TEACHING AND PROTECTING CHILDREN)

Good Touch, Bad Touch (downloadable prevention tool) www.good-touch-bad-touch-asia.org

Stairway Foundation (animations on preventing child sexual abuse and exploitation) http://www.stairwayfoundation.org/stairway/index.php/Resources/animation-film-toolkits.html

Tell Your Friends (prevention curriculum) http://www.fairgirls.org/page/tell-your-friends

My Life My Choice (prevention) http://jri.org/services/behavioral-health-and-trauma-services/community-based-behavioral-health-services/my-life-my-choice

NCMEC Resources for Families (links to online safety resources) http://www.missingkids.com/Families

Stay Smart Online (links to online safety resources) https://www.staysmartonline.gov.au/kids_and_teens

GetNetWise (links to online safety resources) http://kids.getnetwise.org

ThinkUKnow (links to online safety resources) www.thinkuknow.co.uk

16. What is our responsibility towards pornographers? Are they outside of God's redemption?

BOOKS AND ARTICLES

Gross, Craig with Adam Palmer. *Open: What Happens When You Get Real, Get Honest, and Get Accountable*. Nashville: Thomas Nelson, 2013.

Gross, Craig and Jason Harper. *Jesus Loves You, This I Know*. Grand Rapids, MI: Baker Books, 2009.

Gross, Craig. *The Gutter: Where Life Is Meant to Be Lived*. Relevant Books, 2005.

Gross, Craig with Jason Harper. *Eyes of Integrity: The Porn Pandemic and How It Affects You*. Grand Rapids, MI: Baker Books, 2010.

MEDIA

"The Porn Kills Tour" (digital download available at XXXchurch.com)

"Starving Jesus: 40 Days of Nothing Tour" DVD (Available from XXXchurch.com website)

"Starving Jesus: 4 Short Films" DVD (Available from XXXchurch.com website)

"Porn and Pancakes" DVD (Available from XXXchurch.com website)

WEBSITES

XXX Church Website www.XXXchurch.com

X3 Watch Website www.X3watch.com

X3 Pure Website www.X3pure.com

X3 Groups Website www.X3groups.com
Strip Church Website www.StripChurch.com
Open: What Happens When You Get Real, Get Honest, and Get Accountable Book
   Website www.GetOpen.com
Jesus Loves You, This I Know Book Website www.JesusLovesYou.net

17. What is our responsibility towards pimps and pedophiles? Are they outside of God's redemption?

BOOKS AND ARTICLES

Spencer Jr., Jimmy. *Love Without Agenda: Moving Our Spiritual Goalposts from Heaven and Hell to Wholeness.* ebook, 2011. http://www.lovewithoutagenda.com
Perkins, John M. *Beyond Charity: The Call to Christian Community Development.* Grand Rapids, MI: Baker Books, 1993.
Perkins, John M., ed. *Restoring At-Risk Communities: Doing It Together and Doing It Right.* Grand Rapids, MI: Baker Books, 1995.
Keller, Timothy. *Generous Justice: How God's Grace Makes Us Just.* New York: Riverhead Books, 2010.

18. Is there hope for men who visit red-light districts?

WEBSITE

MST Project Website http://www.mstproject.com

Works Cited

KEY ISSUES (HUGHE)

Office of the Press Secretary, The White House. "Trafficking in Persons National Security Presidential Directive." February 25, 2003.

KEY ISSUES (LIDÉN)

Parts of this essay have been adapted from Lidén, Sven-Gunnar. "DEMAND From a Sociological Point of View." In *EBF Anti-Trafficking Resource Book 3: Demand.* European Baptist Federation Anti-Trafficking Working Group. Hungarian Baptist Aid, 2009. http://www.ebf.org/failid/File/resources/ebf-anti-trafficking-resource-book-no-3.pdf.
Coy, Maddy, Miranda Horvath, and Liz Kelly. *It's Just Like Going to the Supermarket: Men Buying Sex in East London.* London: Child and Woman Abuse Studies Unit, London Metropolitan University, 2007.
Groom, T.M. and R. Nandwani. "Characteristics of Men Who Pay for Sex: A UK Sexual Health Clinic Survey." *Sexually Transmitted Infections* 82, no. 5 (2006): 364-367. doi:10.1136/sti.2006.020537.
Kuosmanen, Jari. Tio år med lagen. Om förhållningssätt till och erfarenheter av prostitution i Sverige [Study of prostitution in Sweden]. In *Prostitutionen i Norden – Forskningsrapport*, edited by Charlotta Holmström and May-Len Skilbrei, 357-81. Denmark: TemaNord, 2008.
Macleod, Jan, Melissa Farley, Lynn Anderson, and Jacqueline Golding. *Challenging Men's Demand for Prostitution in Scotland: A Research Report Based on Interviews with 110 Men Who Bought Women in Prostitution.* Glasgow, Scotland: Women's Support Project, 2008. http://www.prostitutionresearch.com/ ChallengingDemandScotland.pdf.

Ohlsson, Emma, Susanne Sterba, and Annika Ulff. *Uppbrottsprocessen – en dragkamp.* En studie om män som har slutat köpa sexuella tjänster [The Breakup Process - A Tug of War. A Study of Men Who Have Stopped Buying Sexual Services]. Gothenburg, Sweden: University of Gothenburg, 2008.

United Nations. United Nations Convention against Transnational Organized Crime, Protocol to Prevent, Suppress and Punish Trafficking in Persons, Especially Women and Children. General Assembly resolution 55/25. Entered into force on December 25, 2003. http://www.unodc.org/documents/treaties/UNTOC/ Publications/TOC%20Convention/TOCebook-e.pdf

KEY ISSUES (EAVES AND HØILAND)

Beaulieu, Catherine. "Extraterritorial Laws: Why They Are Not Working and How They Can Be Strengthened." In *Creating A United Front Against Child Exploitation*, ECPAT International. Bangkok: ECPAT International, June 2009.

Bousquette, Jessica and Jesse Eaves. "We Are Working With Our Bare Hands: Strengthening USAID's Response to Human Trafficking" Washington D.C.: World Vision US, December 2012.

Davidson, Julia O'Connell. "Child Sex Tourism: An Anomalous Form of Movement?" *Journal of Contemporary European Studies* 12, no.1 (April 2004).

ECPAT. "CSEC Terminology." ECPAT Website. http://www.ecpat.com/EI/Csec_cst.asp

International Labour Office, Special Action Programme to Combat Forced Labour. *ILO Global Estimate of Forced Labor: Results and Methodology.* Geneva: ILO, 2012. http://www.ilo.org/wcmsp5/groups/public/---ed_norm/--- declaration/documents/publication/wcms_182004.pdf

Matthews, Arnie. *The Child Safe Traveller.* Sydney: World Vision Australia, University of Western Sydney, November 2013.

Roche, Christine. "High Rates of HIV Infection Documented Among Young Nepalese Girls Sex-Trafficked to India: Infection Rate Exceeded 60 Percent in Girls Forced into Prostitution Prior to Age 15." *Harvard Science.* Harvard School of Public Health, October 14, 2007. http://www.harvardscience.harvard.edu/medicine-health/articles/high-rates-hiv-infection-documented-among-young-nepalese-girls-sex-traffick?view=print

Skinner, Benjamin. *A Crime So Monstrous: Face-to-Face with Modern-Day Slavery.* New York: Free Press, 2008.

The Protection Project. *International Child Sex Tourism: Scope of the Problem and Comparative Case Studies.* The Protection Project, Johns Hopkins University, January 2007.

The Seattle Times. "Haitian Migrants Exploited, Forced to Beg," *The Seattle Times,* February 23, 2011. http://seattletimes.com/html/nationworld/2014312783 _apcbdominicanhaitihumantrafficking.html

UNICEF. "Child Protection from Violence, Exploitation and Abuse: Data and Evaluations." UNICEF Website. http://www.unicef.org/protection/57929_57979.html

US State Department, Office to Combat and Monitor Trafficking in Persons. *Trafficking in Persons Report.* Washington D.C.: US State Department, June 2008 and June 2010.

US Immigration and Customs Enforcement. "Operation Predator: Targeting Child Exploitation and Sexual Crimes" Fact Sheet. US ICE, November 20, 2008. http://www.ice.gov/doclib/pi/news/factsheets/operationpredator.pdf

World Vision US, *Child Sex Tourism Prevention Project: Final Report.* Washington D.C.: World Vision US, February 2007.

KEY ISSUES (GARCIA AND CRAWFORD)

Carnes, Patrick J. *Don't Call It Love: Recovery from Sexual Addiction.* New York: Bantam Books, 1992.

Cline, Victor B. "Pornography's Effects on Adults and Children." New York: Morality in Media, 2001. http:// www.scribd.com/bluptr/d/20282510-Dr-Victor-Cline-Pornography-s-Effects-on-Adults-and-Children

Doidge, Norman. *The Brain That Changes Itself: Stories of Personal Triumph from the Frontiers of Brain Science.* New York: Penguin Group, 2007.

Eberstadt, Mary, and Mary Ann Layden. *The Social Costs of Pornography: A Statement of Findings and Recommendations.* Princeton, NJ: The Witherspoon Institute, 2010.

Farley, Melissa, Ann Cotton, Jacqueline Lynne, Sybille Zumbeck, Frida Spiwak, Maria E. Reyes, Dinorah Alvarez, and Ufuk Sezgin. "Prostitution and Trafficking in 9 Countries: Update on Violence and Posttraumatic Stress Disorder." *Journal of Trauma Practice* 2, no. 3/4 (2003): 33-74. http://www.prostitutionresearch.com/ pdf/Prostitutionin9Countries.pdf.

Farley, Melissa. "'Renting an Organ for Ten Minutes': What Tricks Tell Us about Prostitution, Pornography and Trafficking." In *Pornography: Driving the Demand in International Sex Trafficking,* edited by David E. Guinn and Julie DiCaro. Bloomington, IN: Xlibris, 2007.

Farley, Melissa, Julie Bindel, and Jacqueline M. Golding. *Men Who Buy Sex, Who They Buy and What They Know.* London: Eaves, 2009. http://www.eaves4women. co.uk/Documents/Recent_Reports/Men%20Who%20Buy%20Sex.pdf

Hughes, Donna M. *The Demand for Victims of Sex Trafficking.* 2005. http://www.uri.edu/artsci/wms/hughes/demand_for_victims.pdf

Macleod, Jan, Melissa Farley, Lynn Anderson, and Jacqueline Golding. *Challenging Men's Demand for Prostitution in Scotland: A Research Report Based on Interviews with 110 Men Who Bought Women in Prostitution.* Glasgow, Scotland: Women's Support Project, 2008. http://www.prostitutionresearch.com/ ChallengingDemandScotland.pdf

Malarek, Victor. *The Johns: Sex for Sale and the Men Who Buy It.* New York: Arcade Publishing, 2009.

Monto, Martin A. and Nick McRee. "A Comparison of Male Customers of Female Street Prostitutes with National Samples of Men." *International Journal of Offender Therapy and Comparative Criminology* 49, no. 5 (2005): 1-25. doi:10.1177/0306624X04272975.

Peters, Robert W., Laura J. Lederer and Shane Kelly. "The Slave and the Porn Star: Sexual Trafficking and Pornography." *The Protection Project Journal of Human Rights and Civil Society* 5 (Fall 1012): 1-22. http://www.protectionproject.org/wp-content/uploads/2012/11/TPP-J-HR-Civ-Socy_Vol-5_2012-w-cover1.pdf

Stack, Steven, Ira Wasserman, and Roger Kern. "Adult Social Bonds and Use of Internet Pornography." *Social Science Quarterly* 85, no. 1 (2004): 75-88. doi: 10.1111/j.0038-4941.2004.08501006.x.

Taylor, Max, Ethel Quayle, and Gemma Holland. "Child Pornography: The Internet and Offending." *Isuma-Canadian Journal of Policy Research* 2, no. 2 (2001): 94-100.

Tewksbury, Richard, and Seana Golder. "Why Do Johns Use Pornography? Predicting Consumption of Pornography by Clients of Street Level Prostitutes." *The Southwest Journal of Criminal Justice* 2, no. 2 (2005): 101-118. http://g.virbcdn.com/_f/files/df/FileItem-149965-Tewksbury.pdf.

KEY ISSUES (SILER AND STAUFFER)

Cusick, Michael John. *Surfing for God: Discovering the Divine Desire Beneath Sexual Struggle.* Nashville, TN: Thomas Nelson, 2012.

KEY ISSUES (CRAWFORD AND MILES)

Bennett, Morgan. "The New Narcotic." *Public Discourse.* The Witherspoon Institute, October 9, 2013. http://www.thepublicdiscourse.com/2013/10/10846/

Brooks, Gary R. *The Centerfold Syndrome: How Men Can Overcome Objectification and Achieve Intimacy with Women.* San Francisco: Jossey-Bass, 1995.

Fordham, Graham. *"Wise" Before Their Time: Young People, Gender-Based Violence and Pornography in Kandal Stung District.* Phnom Penh: World Vision Cambodia, 2005. http://www.childtrafficking.com/Docs/wvi_violence_ pornography_070402.pdf

O'Shea, Deirdre. *A Preliminary Study into the Accessibility by Minors of Pornography in Cambodia: Briefing Paper No. 1.* Phnom Penh: Child Welfare Group, 2003. http://www.licadho-cambodia.org/reports/files/ 38Pornography%20Report%20Final%20English1.pdf

KEY ISSUES (TAYLOR, MILES AND AINSWORTH)

Amen, Daniel G. *Healing the Hardware of the Soul: How Making the Brain-Soul Connection Can Optimize Your Life, Love, and Spiritual Growth.* New York: Free Press, 2002.

Barbera, Donald R. *The 80% Solution: Christians Doing the Right Thing.* Bloomington: Xlibris Corporation. 2012.

Barna Group. "Young Adults and Liberals Struggle with Morality." August 25, 2008. http://www.barna.org/barna-update/teens-nextgen/25-young-adults-and-liberals- struggle-with-morality#.UunLzMbxvIU

Barna Group. "New Research Explores the Changing Shape of Temptation." January 4, 2013. http://www.barna.org/barna-update/culture/600-new-years-resolutions- temptations-and-americas-favorite-sins#.Uun8hMbxvIU

Bergin, Mark. "Porn Again." *World Magazine,* April 23, 2005. http://www.worldmag.com/2005/04/porn_again/page1

Carnes, Patrick. *Facing the Shadow.* Carefree: Gentle Path Press, 2005.

Carnes, Patrick J., Bradley A. Green, Lisa J. Merlo, Alexis Polles, Stefanie Carnes and Mark S. Gold. "PATHOS: A Brief Screening Application for Assessing Sexual Addiction." *Journal of Addiction Medicine* 6, no. 1 (2012): 29-34.

ChristiaNet, Inc. "ChristiaNet Poll Finds That Evangelicals Are Addicted to Porn." *Market Wired* August 7, 2006. http://www.marketwired.com/press- release/christianet-poll-finds-that-evangelicals-are-addicted-to-porn-703951.htm

Christianity Today. "The Leadership Survey on Pastors and Internet Pornography." *Leadership Journal,* 22(1), Winter 2001. http://www.christianitytoday.com/ le/2001/winter/12.89.html

Christianity Today. "Christians and Sex Leadership Journal Survey." March 2005.

Laudet, Alexandre B. "Attitudes and Beliefs About 12-Step Groups Among Addiction Treatment Clients and Clinicians: Toward Identifying Obstacles to Participation." *Substance Use Misuse* 38, no. 14 (2003): 2017-2047.

Taylor, Kenneth R. and Glenn Miles. "Survey of Expatriate Christian Men Living in Cambodia Regarding Views and Practices of Pornography, Erotic Massage, and Prostitution," *Social Work & Christianity: An International Journal* , forthcoming. Available through www.nacsw.org

Weiss, Daniel. "All Men Look at Pornography, Right?" ROCK Website, April 3, 2011. http://www.myrocktoday.org/default.asp?q_areaprimaryid=7&q_ areasecondaryid=74&q_areatertiaryid=0&q_articleid=859

PART 4

Recommended Resources

21. What are the unique challenges of working with boys and young men and how can we effectively meet their needs?

BOOKS AND ARTICLES

Davis, Jarrett, Elliot Glotfelty and Glenn Miles. *Boys for Baht? An Exploratory Study On the Vulnerability of Male Entertainment Workers in Chiang Mai, Thailand.* Love146 and Urban Light, 2013. http://d2mlf3dkzjfjn9.cloudfront.net/wp-content/uploads/2013/06/CMMEW_Baseline_Final.pdf. Also available from http://love146.org/research/.

ECPAT-USA. "And Boys Too: An ECPAT-USA Discussion Paper about the Lack of Recognition of the Commercial Sexual Exploitation of Boys in the United States." ECPAT-USA, 2013. http://ecpatusa.org/wp/wp-content/uploads/2013/08/AndBoysToo_FINAL_single-pages.pdf

Grieger, Matthew T. "Challenging Conventional Wisdom: Sex Work, Exploitation, and Labor Among Young Akha Men in Thailand." Master's thesis, George Washington University, 2012.

WEBSITE

Urban Light Website www.urban-light.org

22. How can we effectively work with boys and men in a non-judgmental and supportive way?

BOOKS AND ARTICLES

Green, John. *Streetwalking with Jesus: Reaching Out in Justice and Mercy.* Huntington, Indiana: Our Sunday Visitor, 2011.

Hilficker, David. *Not All of Us Are Saints: A Doctor's Journey with the Poor.* New York: Hill and Wang, 1994.

Sutter, Arloa. *The Invisible: What the Church Can Do to Find and Serve the Least of These.* Indianapolis: Wesleyan Publishing House, 2010.

BOOKS AND ARTICLES (ABUSE AND EXPLOITATION OF MALES)

Crowder, Adrienne. *Opening the Door: A Treatment Model for Therapy with Male Survivors of Sexual Abuse.* New York: Brunner/Mazel, 1995.

Durham, Andrew. *Young Men Surviving Child Sexual Abuse: Research Stories and Lessons for Therapeutic Practice.* Chichester: NSPCC/Wiley, 2003.

Etherington, Kim. *Narrative Approaches to Working with Adult Male Survivors of Child Sexual Abuse: The Clients', the Counsellor's and the Researchers' Story.* London: Jessica Kingsley, 2000.

Ford, Hannah. *Women Who Sexually Abuse Children.* Chichester: NSPCC/Wiley, 2006.

Hilton, Alastair, et al. *"I Thought It Could Never Happen to Boys" The Sexual Abuse and Exploitation of Boys in Cambodia: An Exploratory Study.* Phnom Penh: World Vision, Hagar and Social Services of Cambodia, 2008.

Lew, Mike. *Victims No Longer: The Classic Guide for Men Recovering from Child Sexual Abuse.* 2nd ed. New York: Harper Collins, 2004.

Mezey, Gillian and Michael King, eds. *Male Victims of Sexual Assault,* 2nd ed. Oxford: Oxford University Press, 2000.

BOOKS AND ARTICLES (GENDER)

Bannon, Ian and Maria. C. Correa, eds. *The Other Half of Gender: Men's Issues in Development.* Washington, D.C.: The World Bank, 2006.

Biddulph, Steve, *Raising Boys.* Berkeley: Celestial Arts, 2008.

Cohen, Simon Baron. *The Essential Difference.* London: Penguin, 2004.

Gurian, Michael. *The Purpose of Boys.* San Francisco: Jossey-Bass, 2005.

Gurian, Michael and Kathy Stevens. *The Minds of Boys: Saving Our Sons from Falling Behind in School and Life.* San Francisco: Wiley, 2005.

Gurian, Michael with Kathy Stevens. *Boys and Girls Learn Differently: A Guide for Teachers and Parents.* San Francisco: Jossey-Bass, 2011.

Neall, Lucinda. *Bringing the Best Out In Boys.* Stroud, Gloucestershire: Hawthorne Press, 2002. http://www.workingwithmen.org http://www.workingwithmen.org http://www.first-step-cambodia.org http://www.first-step-cambodia.org

WEBSITES

Database on Male Abuse (Dr. Jim Hopper is a lecturer at Harvard Medical School; his database is both authoritative and academically robust) www.jimhopper.com/male-ab

Sexual Violence Research Initiative (A new international research forum and database project based in South Africa) www.svri.org

Male Survivor (US-based male survivor support organization with a substantial research library) www.malesurvivor.org/library.html

Directory and Book Services (DABS) (Specialist sexual violence and abuse book seller (UK-Based) for male and female victims and survivors) www.dabsbooks.co.uk

The Survivors Trust (The largest association of specialist sexual violence services in Europe) www.thesurvivorstrust.org

Working with Men (Excellent UK-based organization with over twenty years experience of developing work with men and boys. The ethos of Working with Men is to develop and implement support projects that benefit the development of men and boys; it also seeks to raise awareness of issues impacting upon men and boys in addition to trying to gain a greater understanding of the underlying issues behind male behavior. The website has a useful resource section and links to training and development programs.) http://www.workingwithmen.org

23. How should Christians and the church engage with boys and men?

BOOKS AND ARTICLES

Allender, Dan. *The Wounded Heart: Hope for Adult Victims of Childhood Sexual Abuse.* Rev. ed. Colorado Springs, CO: NavPress, 2008.

Carnes, Patrick. *Out of the Shadows: Understanding Sexual Addiction.* 3rd ed. Center City, MI: Hazelden, 2001.

Henslin, Earl. *This is Your Brain on Joy.* Nashville, TN: Thomas Nelson, 2008.

Jewell, Dawn Herzog. *Escaping the Devil's Bedroom: Sex Trafficking, Global Prostitution, and the Gospel's Transforming Power* (Chapter 4 "Men in Prostitution: Equal Opportunity, Equal Despair") Toronto: Monarch Books, 2008.

Schumtzer, Andrew, ed. *The Long Journey Home: Understanding and Ministering to the Sexually Abused.* Eugene, OR: Wipf & Stock, 2011.

WEBSITES

Emmaus Ministries Website www.streets.org
Exodus International Website www.exodus-international.org
Focus on the Family Website www.lovewonout.com
Healing for the Soul Website www.healingforthesoul.org

Male Survivor: Overcoming Victimization of Boys & Men Website
   http://www.MaleSurvivor.org/myths.html
Prison Fellowship Website www.prisonfellowship.org
Redeemed Lives Website
   http://www.redeemedlives.org/PastoralCourses.asp#Redeemed

24. How do we deal with being considered "pro-gay" for working with men involved in commercial sex and being considered "anti-gay" because of our faith?

BOOKS AND ARTICLES

Gritter, Wendy. *Generous Spaciousness: Responding to Gay Christians in the Church*. Grand Rapids: Brazos Press, 2014.

Marin, Andrew. *Love is an Orientation: Elevating the Conversation with the Gay Community*. Downers Grove, IL: IVP Books, 2009.

Lee, Justin. *Torn: Rescuing the Gospel from the Gays-vs.-Christians Debate*. Nashville: Jericho Books, 2013.

25. Should Christians and the church work with the LGBT community and if so how?

The following is a brief resource list. The list is not meant to be exhaustive. It is likely that any list on the topic of ministering or working with the LGBTQ community risks alienating either the Christian community, the LGBTQ community, or both. It is recommended that the reader begin their research by looking for resources in the archives of their home denomination and then begin to expand outward.

BOOKS AND ARTICLES

Episcopal Commission for Doctrine, Canadian Conference of Catholic Bishops, "Pastoral Ministry to Young People with Same Sex Attraction." 2011. http://www.calgm.org/sites/default/files/CanadianCatholicBishops.pdf

Green, John. *Streetwalking with Jesus: Reaching Out in Justice and Mercy*. Huntington, Indiana: Our Sunday Visitor, 2011.

Harvey, John F. *Homosexuality and the Catholic Church: Clear Answers to Difficult Questions*. Necadah, WI: Ascension Press, 2007.

United States Conference of Catholic Bishops. "Ministry to Persons with a Homosexual Inclination: Guidelines for Pastoral Care." 2006. http://www.usccb.org/issues-and-action/human-life-and-dignity/homosexuality/upload/minstry-persons-homosexual-inclination-2006.pdf

MEDIA

New Direction Videos. "Tony Campolo's Story of a Gay Son" http://www.youtube.com/watch?v=gWYtkn_8D-g

Works Cited

KEY ISSUES (HILTON)

Crowder, Adrienne. *Opening the Door: A Treatment Model for Therapy with Male Survivors of Sexual Abuse*. New York: Brunner/Mazel, 1995.

Jejeebhoy, Shireen J. and Sarah Bott. "Non-Consensual Sexual Experiences of Young People in Developing Countries: An Overview." In *Sex without Consent: Young People in Developing Countries,* edited by Jejeebhoy, Shireen J., Iqbal Shah and Shyam Thapa. London-New York: Zed Books, 2005.

World Health Organization. *World Report on Violence and Health.* Geneva: World
    Health Organization, 2002.
Mathews, Frederick. "Implications." In *A View From Inside The Box III: "Invisible
    Boys."* Survivors West Yorkshire, 2009. http://www.napac.org.uk/
    DOWNLOADS/view_from_box_III.pdf
Lew, Mike. *Victims No Longer: The Classic Guide for Men Recovering from Child
    Sexual Abuse.* 2nd ed. New York: Harper Collins, 2004.
Mendel, Matthew Parynik. *The Male Survivor: The Impact of Sexual Abuse.* Thousand
    Oaks: Sage Publications, 1995.
Pinheiro, Paulo Sergio. *United Nations Study on Global Violence.* Geneva: United
    Nations, 2006.
Save the Children Norway. *10 Essential Learning Points: Listen and Speak Out against
    Sexual Abuse of Girls and Boys.* Save the Children Norway, 2005.
Spiegel, Josef. *Sexual Abuse of Males: The SAM Model of Theory and Practice.* New
    York: Brunner-Routledge, 2003.

KEY ISSUES (RUSSELL)

Davis, Jarrett, Elliot Glotfelty and Glenn Miles. *Boys for Baht? An Exploratory Study
    On the Vulnerability of Male Entertainment Workers in Chiang Mai, Thailand.*
    Love146 and Urban Light, 2013. http://d2mlf3dkzjfjn9.cloudfront.net/wp-
    content/uploads/2013/06/CMMEW_Baseline_Final.pdf. Also available from
    http://love146.org/research/.
ECPAT-USA. "And Boys Too: An ECPAT-USA Discussion Paper about the Lack of
    Recognition of the Commercial Sexual Exploitation of Boys in the United States."
    ECPAT-USA, 2013. http://ecpatusa.org/wp/wp-
    content/uploads/2013/08/AndBoysToo_FINAL_single-pages.pdf
Grieger, Matthew T. "Challenging Conventional Wisdom: Sex Work, Exploitation, and
    Labor Among Young Akha Men in Thailand." Master's thesis, George Washington
    University, 2012.
Hunter, Mic. *Abused Boys: The Neglected Victims of Sexual Abuse.* New York: Fawcett
    Columbine, 1990.
Jackson, Peter A. and Gerard Sullivan, eds. *Lady Boys, Tom Boys, Rent Boys: Male and
    Female Homosexualities in Contemporary Thailand.* Binghamton, NY: Haworth
    Press, Inc., 1999.
US State Department, Office to Combat and Monitor Trafficking in Persons. *Trafficking
    in Persons Report.* Washington D.C.: US State Department, June 2013.

KEY ISSUES (HILTON)

Hilton, Alastair, et al. *"I Thought It Could Never Happen to Boys."* The Sexual Abuse
    and Exploitation of Boys in Cambodia: An Exploratory Study. Phnom Penh: World
    Vision, Hagar and Social Services of Cambodia, 2008.
Spiegel, Josef. *Sexual Abuse of Males: The SAM Model of Theory and Practice.* New
    York: Brunner-Routledge, 2003.

ADVICE FROM PRACTITIONERS (BEAL)

Carnes, Patrick. *Out of the Shadows: Understanding Sexual Addiction.* Center City, MI:
    Hazelden, 2001.

CASE STUDY (COLLARD)

Miles, Glenn and Heather Blanch. *What About Boys? An Initial Exploration of Sexually
    Exploited Boys in Cambodia.* 2011. http://love146.org/research/

KEY ISSUES (GRITTER)

Tutu, Desmond. *Believe: The Words and Inspiration of Desmond Tutu.* Boulder, CO: Blue Mountain Arts Inc., 2007.

Volf, Miroslav. *Exclusion and Embrace: A Theological Exploration of Identity, Otherness, and Reconciliation.* Nashville: Abingdon Press, 1996.

KEY ISSUES (JYLLAND-HALVERSON)

Emmaus Ministries. "Emmaus Ministries Position on Homosexuality." In *Training Manual* 3d edition (Chicago: Emmaus Ministries, 2010).

Manue, Fernandex-Alemay. "Comparative Studies on Male Sex Work in the Era of HIV/AIDS." *The Journal of Sex Research* 37, no. 2 (2000): 187-90.

Marin, Andrew. *Love is an Orientation: Elevating the Conversation with the Gay Community.* Nottingham: InterVarsity Press, 2009.

Miles, Glenn and Jasmir Thakur. "Baseline Survey with Masseur Boys in Mumbai." PowerPoint Presentation, 2010. http://digitalcommons.unl.edu/humtrafconf2/14/. Since published as Miles, Glenn, Jasmir Thakur, Kathryn M. Davis, Kiran Khambe and Jayalakshmi Ganapathy. *The Exploitation of Boys/Youth in the Massage Trade: A Comparative Study of 79 Masseur and 79 Escort Young Men in Mumbai, India.* Mumbai, India: Love146 and Samabhavana Society, 2013. http://www.love146.org/wp-content/uploads/2013/06/Exploitation-of-Boys_Youth-in-the-Massage-Trade-Mumbai-India.pdf

Miller, Robin Lin, David Klot and Haftan M. Eckholdt. "HIV Prevention with Male Prostitutes and Patrons of Hustler Bars: Replication of an HIV Preventive Intervention." *American Journal of Community Psychology* 26, no. 1 (1998): 97-131.

Stewart, Angela J., Mandy Steiman, Ana Mari Cauce, Bryan N. Cochron, Les B. Whitbeck, and Dan R. Hoyt. "Victimization and Posttraumatic Stress Disorder among Homeless Adolescents." *Journal of the American Academy of Child and Adolescent Psychiatry* 43, no. 3 (2004): 325-31.

Wagner, Lisa Smith, Linda Carlin, Ana Mari Cauce and Adam Tenner. "A Snapshot of Homeless Youth in Seattle: Their Characteristics, Behaviors and Beliefs About HIV Protective Strategies." *Journal of Community Health* 26, no. 3 (2001): 219-32.

PART 5

Recommended Resources

26. What is a Biblical approach to the transgender community?

BOOKS AND ARTICLES

Brown Mildred L. and Chloe Ann Rounsley, *True Selves: Understanding Transsexualism – For Families, Friends, Coworkers, and Helping Professionals.* Jossey-Bass, 2003. http://ca.wiley.com/WileyCDA/WileyTitle/productCd-0787967025.html

MEDIA

"Prodigal Sons" Film http://www.prodigalsonsfilm.com

"TransAmerica" Film http://en.wikipedia.org/wiki/Transamerica_%28film%29

"Transgeneration" Film http://en.wikipedia.org/wiki/TransGeneration

"Two Families Grapple with Sons' Gender Preferences" NPR, "All Things Considered" May 7, 2008 (First part of two-part series examining how two families took different approaches with their transgender sons; one chose a path of trying to "fix" the child's

gender identity, one chose acceptance) http://www.npr.
org/2008/05/07/90247842/two-families-grapple-with-sons-gender-preferences
"Parents Consider Treatment to Delay Son's Puberty" NPR, "All Things Considered"
May 7, 2008 (Second in the series about the perceived advantages of delaying
puberty with hormone blockers for kids who might be
transgender) http://www.npr.org/templates/story/story.php?storyId=90273278

27. How can we work more effectively with transgender people who are sexually exploited??

BOOKS AND ARTICLES

Aldous, Susan and Pornchai Sereemongkonpool. *Ladyboys: The Secret World of Thailand's Third Gender*. Bangkok, Thailand: Maverick House, 2008.

Bose, Brinda and Subhabrata Bhattacharyya. *The Phobic and the Erotic: The Politics of Sexualities in Contemporary India*. Oxford/New York: Seagull Books, 2007.

Davis, Jarrett, Elizabeth Isaac, Heike Lippman and Glenn Miles. "More Than Gender: A Baseline Study of Transgendered Males in the Sex Industry in Phnom Penh, Cambodia." Phnom Penh: Love 146, October 2013. http://gmmiles.co.uk/wp-content/uploads/2013/07/More-than-Gender-ISWC-2013.pdf. Also available from www.love146/research.

Gaddis, Jayson. "The Single Biggest Obstacle Facing Boys and Men Today." The Good Men Project Website. June 13, 2012. http://goodmenproject.com/featured-content/the-single-biggest-obstacle-facing-boys-and-men-today/

Jackson, Peter A. *Lady Boys, Tom Boys, Rent Boys: Male and Female Homosexualities in Contemporary Thailand*. Chiang Mai, Thailand: Haworth Press/Silkworm Books, 1999.

Marin, Andrew. *Love is an Orientation: Elevating the Conversation with the Gay Community*. Nottingham: InterVarsity Press, 2009.

Paris, Jenell Williams. *The End of Sexual Identity: Why Sex is Too Important to Define Who We Are*. Downers Grove, IL: InterVarsity Press, 2011.

Totman, Richard. *The Third Sex: Kathoey – Thailand's Ladyboys*. Bangkok, Thailand: Silkworm Books, 2003.

28. How can the church effectively minister to transgender people who are sexually exploited?

BOOKS AND ARTICLES

Allender, Dan. *The Wounded Heart: Hope for Adult Victims of Childhood Sexual Abuse*. NavPress, 2008.

Davis, Jarrett, Tesia Geyer and Glenn Miles. "Beyond Gender: A Baseline Study on the Vulnerability of Transgender Sex Workers in Bangkok, Thailand." Love 146/Dton Naam, October 2013.

Dhejne, Cecilia, Paul Lichtenstein, et al. "Long-Term Follow-up of Transsexual Persons Undergoing Sex Reassignment Surgery: Cohort Study in Sweden." *PLoS ONE* 6, no. 2 (2011). doi: 10.1371/journal.pone.0016885.

Heyer, Walt. *Paper Genders: Pulling the Mask Off the Transgender Phenomenon*. Sacramento: Make Waves Publishing, 2011.

Heyer, Walt. *Trading My Sorrows: A True Story of Betrayals, Bad Choices, Love, and the Journey Home*. Salem: Xulon Press, 2006.

Jackson, Peter A. and Gerard Sullivan *Lady Boys, Tom Boys, Rent Boys: Male and Female Homosexualities in Contemporary Thailand*. Chiang Mai, Thailand: Silkworm Books, 1999.

Moskowitz, Clara. "Transgender Americans Face High Suicide Risk." NBC News Website, November 19, 2010. http://www.nbcnews.com/id/40279043/ns/health-health_care/#.Uw2Uj6XEi5Z

Paulk, John. *Not Afraid to Change: The Remarkable Story of How One Man Overcame Homosexuality.* Mukilteo: WinePress Publishing, 1998.

Stevenson, Michael R. "Public Policy, Homosexuality, and the Sexual Coercion of Children" *Journal of Psychology & Human Sexuality* 12, no.4 (2000).

Worthen, Anita and Bob Davies, *Someone I Love is Gay, How Family and Friends Can Respond.* Downers Grove, IL: InterVarsity Press, 1996.

WEBSITES

Dton Naam Ministries Website www.dtonnaam.org

Sy Rogers Website www.syrogers.com

Sex Change Regret Website www.sexchangeregret.com

29. Why does the church ignore transgender people and how can we bridge the gap?

BOOKS AND ARTICLES

Borrowdale, Anne. *Distorted Images: Christian Attitudes to Women, Men and Sex.* London: SPCK, 1991.

Evangelical Alliance. *Transsexuality: A Report by the Evangelical Alliance Policy Commission.* London: Evangelical Alliance, 2000.

Gender Identity Research and Education Society (GIRES). "Atypical Gender Development", Symposium in London assisted by BCC Trans Group and the Kings Fund, London 2003. http://www.gires.org.uk/genderdev.php

Gillon, Ewan. "Gender Difference in Help Seeking." *Therapy Today* 18, no. 10 (December 2007). http://www.therapytoday.net/article/search/author/EwanGillon/

Horton, David. *Changing Channels? A Christian Response to the Transvestite and Transsexual.* Nottingham: Grove Books, 1994.

Lockwood, Craig. *Falling Forward: The Pursuit of Sexual Purity.* Anaheim: Desert Stream Press, 2000.

O'Donovan, Oliver. *Transsexualism: Issues and Argument.* Cambridge: Grove Books, 2007.

Reddy, Gayatri. *With Respect to Sex: Negotiating Hijra Identity in South India.* Chicago: The University of Chicago Press, 2005.

WEBSITES

Beaumont Society Website www.beaumontsociety.org.uk

Gender Identity Research and Education Society Website www.gires.org.uk

New Direction Ministries Website www.newdirection.ca

Stonewall Website www.stonewall.org.uk

Transformation in Christ Website www.transformationinchrist.org

True Freedom Trust Website www.truefreedomtrust.co.uk

Works Cited

KEY ISSUES (MASON)

Babylonian Talmud, Tractate Yebamoth, VIII 79b-80b

Bruggemann, Walter. *Isaiah 1-39.* Louisville, KY: Westminster John Knox Press, 1998.

Clement of Alexandria, "Stromota 3.1.1." Translated by John Ernest Leonard Oulton and Henry Chadwick in *Alexandrian Christianity: Selected Translations of Clement and Origen.* Philadelphia, 1954.

France, R.T. *The Gospel of Matthew.* The New International Commentary of the New Testament. Grand Rapids, MI: Eerdmans, 2007.

Hagner, Donald A. *Word Biblical Commentary, Vol: 33b: Matthew 14-28.* Nashville, TN: Thomas Nelson, 1995.

Hester, J. David. "Eunuchs and the Postgender Jesus: Matthew 19:12 and Transgressive Sexualities." *Journal for the Study of the New Testament* 28, no. 1 (2005): 13-40.

Josephus. *Jewish Antiquities* 4.292(4.8.40).

Hunter, David G. *Marriage, Celibacy, and Heresy in Ancient Christianity: The Jovinianist Controversy.* Oxford: Oxford University Press, 2007.

Keener, Craig S. *A Commentary on the Gospel of Matthew.* Grand Rapids, MI: Eerdmans, 1999.

Kuefler, Mathew. *The Manly Eunuch: Masculinity, Gender Ambiguity, and Christian Ideology in Late Antiquity* (Chicago: University of Chicago Press, 2001

Luz, Ulrich. *Matthew 8-20.* Hermeneia. Minneapolis, MN: Fortress Press, 2001.

Malik, Faris. "Ancient Roman and Talmudic Definition of Natural Eunuchs." Born Eunuchs Homepage and Library. http://www.well.com/user/aquarius/cardiff.htm.

Malik, Faris. "Born Eunuchs: Homosexual Identity in the Ancient World." Born Eunuchs Homepage and Library. http://www.well.com/user/aquarius/contents.htm.

Nolland, John. *The Gospel of Matthew.* The New International Greek Testament Commentary. Grand Rapids, MI: Eerdmans, 2005.

Philo. *Special Laws* 3:37-42. In *Works of Philo,* trans. Charles Duke Yonge. London: H.G. Bohn, 1854/55, http://cornerstonepublications.org/Philo/Philo_The_Special_Laws_III.html.

Talbot, Rick. "Imagining the Matthean Eunuch Community: Kyriarchy on the Chopping Block." *Journal of Feminist Studies in Religion* 22, no. 1, (2006): 21-43.

KEY ISSUES (DAVIS AND MILES)

Davis, Jarrett and Glenn Miles. "More Than Gender: A Baseline Study of Transgendered Males in the Sex Industry in Phnom Penh, Cambodia." Phnom Penh: Love 146, October 2013. http://gmmiles.co.uk/wp-content/uploads/ 2013/07/More-than-Gender-ISWC-2013.pdf. Also available from www.love146/research.

KEY ISSUES (MCGEE)

Davis, Jarrett, Tesia Geyer and Glenn Miles. "Beyond Gender: A Baseline Study on the Vulnerability of Transgender Sex Workers in Bangkok, Thailand." Love 146/Dton Naam, October 2013.

Heyer, Walt. *Paper Genders: Pulling the Mask Off the Transgender Phenomenon.* Sacramento: Make Waves Publishing, 2011.

Heyer, Walt. *Trading My Sorrows: A True Story of Betrayals, Bad Choices, Love, and the Journey Home.* Salem: Xulon Press, 2006.

Joshua Project. "Thailand." Joshua Project Website. http://www.joshuaproject.net/countries.php?rog3=TH

Rogers, Sy. "The Man in the Mirror." Last Days Ministries Website, March 27, 2012. http://www.lastdaysministries.com/Groups/1000087900/Last_Days_Ministries/Articl es/Other_Authors/The_Man_in/The_Man_in.aspx

Wollf, Randy. "Reaching Thailand in this Generation: The Thai Church's National Plan." World Evangelical Alliance Website, May 12, 2010. http://www.worldevangelicals.org/pdf/2010_0512_Reaching_Thailand_in_this_Gene ration.pdf

KEY ISSUES (CRAIG)

Andrews, Dave. *Christi-Anarchy: Discovering a Radical Spirituality of Compassion.* Oxford: Lion Publishing, 1999.

Booker, Mike and Mark Ireland. *Evangelism - Which Way Now? An Evaluation of Alpha, Emmaus, Cell Church and Other Contemporary Strategies for Evangelism.* London: Church Publishing House, 2003.

Chung, Paul S. "A Theology of Justification and God's Mission." *Currents in Theology and Mission* 34, no. 2 (April 2007): 117-27. http://www.thefreelibrary. com/A+Theology+of+justification+and+God's+mission.-a0162834381

Davis, Jarrett and Glenn Miles. "More Than Gender: A Baseline Study of Transgendered Males in the Sex Industry in Phnom Penh, Cambodia." Phnom Penh: Love 146, October 2013. http://gmmiles.co.uk/wp-content/uploads/ 2013/07/More-than-Gender-ISWC-2013.pdf. Also available from http://love146.org/research/.

Evangelical Alliance. *Transsexuality: A Report by the Evangelical Alliance Policy Commission.* London: Evangelical Alliance, 2000.

Saddleback Church. "You Were Shaped for Serving God." Saddleback Church Website. http://www.saddleback.com/aboutsaddleback/livingonpurpose/ shapedforservinggod/

PART 6

Recommended Resources

30. Why is networking important?

WEBSITES

Viva Website www.viva.org

Micah Network Website www.micahnetwork.org

International Christian Alliance on Prostitution Website (ICAP)
http://www.icapglobal.org

Chab Dai Website www.chabdai.org

United Nations Inter-Agency Project on Human Trafficking (UNIAP) Website www.no-trafficking.org

31. What are some existing models of collaboration? How did they develop? What are some of the challenges?

BOOKS AND ARTICLES

Foot, Kirsten. "Actors & Activities in the Anti-Human Trafficking Movement." In *The Dark Side of Globalization,* edited by Ramesh Thakur and Jorge Heine. United Nations Press, 2010.

Hanleybrown, Fay, John Kania and Mark Kramer. "Channeling Change: Making Collective Impact Work." *Stanford Social Innovation Review* (January 2012). http://www.ssireview.org/blog/entry/channeling_change_making_collective_impact_work

Kania, John and Mark Kramer. "Embracing Emergence: How Collective Impact Addresses Complexity." *Stanford Social Innovation Review* (January 2013). http://www.ssireview.org/blog/entry/embracing_emergence_how_collective_impact_addresses_complexity

Stoll, Jennifer, Kirsten Foot and W. Keith Edwards. "Between Us and Them: Building Connectedness Within Civic Networks." *Proceedings of the ACM 2012 conference on Computer Supported Cooperative Work* (2012): 237-240. http://dl.acm.org/citation.cfm?id=2145240.

WEBSITES

International Christian Alliance on Prostitution (ICAP Website) www.icapglobal.org
Information about ICAP Conferences http://www.icapglobal.org/events.html
Freedom Registry Website www.freedomregistry.org
Freedom Collaborative Website www.freedomcollaborative.org
Chab Dai Website (with links to national websites) http://www.chabdai.org

32. How can technology and the Internet be used to enhance collaboration?

WEBSITES

Freedom Registry Website www.freedomregistry.org
Freedom Collaborative Website www.freedomcollaborative.org
Counter Child Trafficking Global Online Conference Website
www.counterchildtrafficking.org

OTHER

MD544 "Ministry with Sexually Exploited and Trafficked Children." Graduate course offered by Fuller Theological Seminary, School of Intercultural Studies, Children at Risk program. http://www.fuller.edu/childrenatrisk/

33. What are the challenges of partnership? How do we work with people/organizations who may seem controversial or who may not espouse similar Christian values (without compromising)?

BOOKS AND ARTICLES

Addicott, Ernie. *Body Matters: A Guide to Partnership in Christian Mission*. Edmonds, WA: Interdev Partnership Associates, 2005.

Butler, Phill. *Well Connected: Releasing Power and Restoring Hope Through Kingdom Partnerships*. Federal Way, WA: Authentic, 2005

Carter, Doug. *Partnership: Accomplishing Big Dreams Together*. Duluth, GA: Equip.

Doz, Yves L. and Gary Hamel. *Alliance Advantage: The Art of Creating Value through Partnering*. Boston, MA: Harvard Business School Press, 1998.

Himmelman, Arthur. T. "Collaboration for a Change: Definitions, Decision-Making Models, Roles, and Collaboration Process Guide." Himmelman Consulting, 2007. Available from http://depts.washington.edu/ccph/pdf_files/4achange.pdf

Holmen, Hans. *NGOs, Networking, and Problems of Representation*. Linköping, Sweden: Linköping University, 2002.

Innovations for Scaling Impact and Keystone Accountability for Social Change. "Next Generation Network Evaluation." Innovations for Scaling Impact and Keystone Accountability for Social Change, 2010. http://www.scalingimpact.net/files/IDRC_Network_IPARL_Paper_Final_0.pdf

Kania, John and Mark Kramer. "Collective Impact: Large-Scale Social Change Requires Broad Cross-Sector Coordination, Yet the Social Sector Remains Focused on the Isolated Intervention of Individual Organizations." *Stanford Social Innovation Review* (Winter 2011): 36-41.

Kellar-Guenther, Yvonne and Bill Betts. *Come Together Now: Measuring the Level of Collaboration*. ARA Annual Conference. San Antonio, TX, 2010.

Liebler, Claudia and Marisa Ferri. *NGO Networks: Building Capacity in a Changing World*. A Study Supported by Bureau for Democracy, Conflict and Humanitarian Assistance, Office of Private and Voluntary Cooperation, 2004. http://pdf.usaid.gov/pdf_docs/pnadb767.pdf

Lipnack, Jessica and Jeffrey Stamps. *The Age of the Network: Organizing Principles for the 21st Century*. New York: John Wiley and Sons, Inc., 1994.

Mattessich, Paul W. *Collaboration: What Makes It Work*. 2nd ed. Saint Paul, MN: Amherst H. Wilder Foundation, 2001.

Reichel, Phillip L. *Cross-National Collaboration To Combat Human Trafficking: Learning From The Experience of Others*. U.S. Department of Justice, 2008.

Wolff, Tom. *The Power of Collaborative Solutions: Six Principles and Effective Tools for Building Healthy Communities*. San Francisco, Jossey-Bass, 2010.

WEBSITES

Coalition Building for Healthy Communities. Tom Wolff and Associates Website
www.tomwolff.com

Nonprofit Collaboration Resources. Foundation Center Website
http://foundationcenter.org/gainknowledge/collaboration/

Resources for Coalition Leaders. Healthy Wisconsin Leadership Institute Website
http://hwli.org/leadership-library/resources-for-coalition-leaders/

US AID principles for government/NGO cooperation www.usaid.gov

Partnership principles for Christian groups www.powerofconnecting.net

Works Cited

INTRODUCTION (DOCARMO)

Kania, John and Mark Kramer. "Collective Impact." *Stanford Social Innovation Review* (Winter 2011): 36-41.

CASE STUDY (DOCARMO)

Kania, John and Mark Kramer. "Collective Impact: Large-Scale Social Change Requires Broad Cross-Sector Coordination, Yet the Social Sector Remains Focused on the Isolated Intervention of Individual Organizations." *Stanford Social Innovation Review* (Winter 2011): 36-41.

KEY ISSUES (CRAWFORD)

Bales, Kevin. *Disposable People: New Slavery in the Global Economy*. Berkeley: University of California Press, 1999, 2000, 2004, 2012.

Fuller Theological Seminary, MD544 "Ministry with Sexually Exploited and Trafficked Children." Graduate course offered by Fuller Theological Seminary, School of Intercultural Studies, Children at Risk program. http://www.fuller.edu/childrenatrisk/

United Nations Security Council. "Statement by the President of the Security Council." 25 April 2012, S/PRST/2012/16.
http://www.securitycouncilreport.org/atf/cf/%7B65BFCF9B-6D27-4E9C-8CD3-CF6E4FF96FF9%7D/IPS%20S%202012%2016.pdf

CASE STUDY (DOCARMO)

This Case Study is adapted from "Freedom Collaborative Vision Overview-2012" (Leaflet) and Freedom Collaborative Website.

Bates, Greg. "The Freedom Registry API: Fighting the Good Fight Against Human Trafficking." The Programmable Web Blog (July 26, 2013).
http://blog.programmableweb.com/2013/07/26/the-freedom-registry-api-fighting-the-good-fight-against-human-trafficking/

Freedom Collaborative. "Freedom Collaborative Vision Overview-2012." Leaflet. 2012.

KEY ISSUES (SWORN)

Covey, Stephen. *The 7 Habits of Highly Effective People: Powerful Lessons in Personal Change*. New York: Free Press, 1989.

KEY ISSUES (TUNEHAG)

Kristof, Nicholas and Sheryl WuDunn. *Half the Sky: Turning Oppression into Opportunity for Women Worldwide.* New York: Alfred A. Knopf, 2009.

CONTRIBUTORS

Editors

Glenn Miles, Ph.D.

Glenn is the Asia Capacity Building Director for Love146 in Cambodia. He has been involved in mentoring, training, research and advocacy for children and vulnerable people in Asia for over twenty years. He has a special concern for marginalized sexual minorities and is conducting research on boys and transgender sex workers, and male clients. He has developed the *Celebrating Children* training curriculum and teaches up to post-graduate level at various seminaries. He has been involved in developing resources such as the Tearfund karaoke video series and the *Good Touch Bad Touch* flipchart. He has helped to pioneer several NGOs and collaborative projects including the Message Parlour. He is married, has three daughters and lives in Phnom Penh, Cambodia. Please visit

www.gmmiles.co.uk, www.love146.org, www.themessageparlour.org, www.tearfund.org, www.agstalliance.org, www.celebratingchildrentraining.info, www.good-touch-bad-touch-asia.org, and www.kone-kmeng.org.

Christa Foster Crawford, J.D.

Christa is an international consultant providing resources and expert advice on ending human trafficking and sexual exploitation in Thailand and the Greater Mekong Subregion. Since 2001, Christa has lived in Thailand working to end exploitation at both the grassroots and policy levels with the United Nations, International Justice Mission and as co-founder of The Garden of Hope. She currently serves as an Adjunct Assistant Professor of Children at Risk at Fuller Theological Seminary and an Instructor for GoED Mekong, teaching courses about human trafficking and sexual exploitation. Christa has also authored and edited numerous books, chapters and articles on ministering to trafficked and sexually exploited children and women. She holds a J.D. from Harvard Law School, a B.A. in Philosophy and Public Affairs from Claremont McKenna College, and is also completing a Master's of Arts in Holistic Child Development from Malaysia Baptist Theological Seminary. Please visit www.traffickingresourceconnection.wordpress.com.

Tania DoCarmo, M.S.

Tania is the Program Director for Chab Dai International, an organization which addresses trafficking and exploitation by building collaboration among multi-sector stakeholders through increased knowledge-sharing and evidence-based practice. Previously, she also worked as Teaching Assistant in the Anthropology department of the University of North Texas, as an Instructor on trafficking survivor care with FAAST International, and as Overseas Associate and ESL Teacher with World Horizons in Cambodia, Wales, South Korea and Brazil. Tania has an M.S. in Anthropology and a B.A. in Social Science. She has published, presented and lectured extensively on the importance of collaboration to fight trafficking and exploitation. Please visit www.chabdai.org and www.freedomcollaborative.org.

Gundelina Velazco, Ph.D.
Gundelina is the CEO of Love146 Philippines and the Love146 Asia Director of Aftercare. She conceptualized, designed and established the Love146 girls' safehome (the Round Home) in 2007 and the boys' safehome in 2013. She also started the urban community development project among street families of trafficked children in 2012. Love146 Philippines recently won the "Best NGO" award given by the Department of Social Welfare and Development. Gundelina has taught, conducted training, and presented papers in numerous countries worldwide. She was a university professor, having obtained her training and specializations in the Philippines, US and UK in the fields of nursing, education, psychology, test development and drug abuse rehabilitation. Please visit www.love146.org.

Contributors

Mark Ainsworth, M.Eng.
Mark has been involved in a wide range of activities from working for an inventor to working with the homeless in York. There, Mark worked with Arc Light, a homeless hostel, and helped set up Restore, which houses homeless men and women. He recently started Boroh La-or Pit, a ministry in Cambodia that seeks to see Khmer men disciple and reach out to other Khmer men. While in Cambodia, Mark also worked with the MST Project, a ministry that works with expatriate men in red light districts. He currently works with the Boaz Trust in Manchester, serving asylum seekers and refugees. Mark is married to Jen and they live in northern England with their daughter. Please visit
www.york-arclight.co.uk, www.facebook.com/borohlaorpit,
www.mstproject.com and www.boaztrust.org.uk.

Dan B. Allender, M.Div., Ph.D.
Dan Allender holds a Ph.D. in Counseling Psychology. He taught in the Biblical Counseling Department of Grace Theological Seminary for seven years, before working as professor in the Master of Arts in Biblical Counseling program at Colorado Christian University. Currently, he serves as Professor of Counseling at The Seattle School of Theology & Psychology and was the founding President. He travels and speaks extensively to present his unique perspective on sexual abuse recovery, love and forgiveness, worship, and other related topics. Dr. Allender is the author of *The Wounded Heart* and *The Healing Path* and co-author of *Intimate Allies, The Cry of the Soul, Bold Love,* and *Bold Purpose.* He and his wife Rebecca and their three children live on Bainbridge Island, Washington. Please visit
www.theseattleschool.edu/Academics/faculty/dan-allender.

Ané Auret, M.A.

Ané is a Child Protection Social Worker, Trainer and Consultant who works with individual practitioners, teams, and voluntary and statutory organizations to develop and strengthen frontline practice, systems and programs. She has obtained a B.A. in Social Work, an M.A. in International Social Work, and is an accredited Emotional Intelligence Coach who holds a strong belief in the importance of social and emotional intelligence in child protection work. She is the principal author of the *Child Protection and Welfare Practice Handbook* and co-founder of the Counter Child Trafficking Global Online Conference. Please visit

www.counterchildtrafficking.org and www.touchpointcp.com.

Kevin Bales

Kevin is Professor of Contemporary Slavery at the Wilberforce Institute for the Study of Slavery and Emancipation, University of Hull, and Lead Author on the Global Slavery Index. He was co-founder of Free the Slaves. He is also the author of the award-winning books *Disposable People: New Slavery in the Global Economy* and *Ending Slavery: How We Free Today's Slaves* and co-writer of the award-winning documentary *Slavery: A Global Investigation.* Since then, Kevin has co-authored *To Plead Our Own Cause: Personal Stories by Today's Slaves* and *The Slave Next Door: Human Trafficking and Slavery in America Today.* He is currently writing on the relationship between slavery and environmental destruction. Please visit

www.freetheslaves.net and www.kevinbales.net.

Jane Beal, Ph.D.

Jane is a writer who received her Ph.D. from University of California Davis in English literature and has worked as a professor at Wheaton College and Colorado Christian University. From 2007-2009, she volunteered with a variety of Christian ministries involved in human trafficking prevention, intervention and redemption efforts and worked on-site with students and programs in Moldova, Eastern Europe and Ghana, West Africa. Since 2010, she has been involved in serving women in childbirth, most recently in Uganda, East Africa. To learn more about her life's work, see

sanctuarypoet.net and christianmidwife.org.

Lauran D. Bethell, M.Div., D.D.

Lauran has been involved with the issues of human trafficking since 1987 when she helped to start and became the first director of The New Life Center in Chiang Mai, Thailand. The Center offers an education and vocational training in order to prevent young vulnerable women from the hill tribes of Northern Thailand from labor and sexual exploitation. It also facilitated rescue and reintegration from exploitive situations to girls and women. In 2001, she relocated to Europe and has since worked as an international consultant, helping to raise awareness about human trafficking and facilitate the development of grass-roots endeavors addressing the issues worldwide. She is one of the founders of the International Christian Alliance on Prostitution and its Leadership Team Coordinator. Please visit www.newlifecenterfoundation.org and www.icapglobal.org.

Donald J. Brewster, M.Div.
Don is the Founder and CEO of Agape International Missions which fights child sex trafficking. Following a successful business career and a charge as pastor of a large church, he felt called to missions and social justice issues full time. Don and his wife Bridget moved to Cambodia in 2005 after learning about child sex slavery there. In the years that followed, they established the AIM ministries including Agape Restoration Center, The Lord's Gym, and Rahab's House, which includes a community church and school. They are also offering sustainable employment opportunities for restored girls through AIM Employment Centers and plan to expand outreach efforts to other areas affected by sex trafficking. They have four children and twelve grandchildren. Please visit www.agapewebsite.org/projects/.

Derek Collard, B.A.A.
Derek is on staff with The Hard Places Community in Cambodia and has been working with them since 2009. For the past two years, he has worked as Spiritual Advisor with their Punlok Thmey Tours training program. During this time, he has had the opportunity to develop some very strong relationships with the men that he works with and has seen immense growth in them. Derek also conducts speaking and fund-raising tours in America to present the work these ministries are doing. Please visit www.hardplaces-community.org.

Duncan Craig, B.A.
Duncan studied at All Nations Christian College between 2010 and 2013. He worked as an intern with Love146 in 2011, working with Ladyboys in Cambodia and Hijra in India. Duncan has personally grappled with the confusion of gender identity. His desire is for society, and in particular the church, to embrace the struggles of transgender people so that the private agony of many can be lovingly shared in a supportive environment. Please visit duncan.craig@live.com, www.allnations.ac.uk, and www.love146.org.

Jarrett Davis, M.A.
Jarrett is a social researcher working with Love146. His work over the past two years has focused on building an understanding of vulnerable people groups that are often overlooked in research, policy and social development programming. As a part of this, Jarrett has led and conducted numerous studies on sexually-exploited males and transgender persons within various sites in the Philippines, Cambodia and Thailand. Jarrett completed his M.A. degree at Asia-Pacific Nazarene Theological Seminary in Taytay, Rizal, Philippines where his thesis focused on social identity and identity development within a marginalized people group on the outskirts of Metro-Manila. Please visit www.love146.org.

Ian de Villiers, M.A.

Ian is currently working with World Vision as Local Partnering Advisor, leading and coordinating the development of partnership with others for child well-being. This includes research, training and staff development, organizational development, and church engagement. He was previously the Asia Coordinator for Viva Network, supporting networks to build collaborative responses to children at risk issues in South and South-East Asia, with particular focuses on abuse and trafficking and gender discrimination. Please visit www.wvi.org and www.viva.org.

Jesse Eaves, M.A.

Jesse Eaves is the Senior Policy Advisor for Child Protection at World Vision in Washington D.C. World Vision is a relief, development, and advocacy organization in nearly 100 countries that works with children, their families, and communities to tackle the root causes of poverty and injustice. Based in Washington D.C., Jesse coordinates the advocacy portfolio for child protection issues that include child soldiers, exploitative child labor, child trafficking, and child sexual exploitation. Through his advocacy efforts, Jesse works to empower Americans to take a stand for social justice and child protection and attempts to ensure that U.S. policymakers know how they can work to protect vulnerable children around the world. Please visit www.worldvision.org.

Jeremy Floyd, M.Div.

Jeremy is a Program Officer for Equitas Group in Knoxville, Tennessee, a philanthropic organization seeking justice for the vulnerable and oppressed and encouraging holistic and responsive thinking toward that end. Equitas focuses the majority of its efforts on two issues: child domestic servitude in Haiti and child trafficking and exploitation in Southeast Asia. Jeremy has overseen Equitas' Southeast Asia directive since 2008. Previously, he was a research assistant at ProVision Foundation. He is currently completing a Master of Public Administration. Please visit www.equitasgroup.org.

Nicole Garcia, M.Ed.

Nicole has a Master's of Education in Community Development and Action from Vanderbilt University's Peabody College and a Bachelor of Arts in International Studies from Pepperdine University. She currently resides in Nashville, Tennessee and does case management with at-risk youth. Please visit www.nicolegarcia.net.

Paul Goodell, M.P.P.

Paul does fundraising and development work for Emmaus Ministries in Chicago. He holds degrees from Wheaton College in Illinois and The George Washington University. He began work with Emmaus Ministries through an 18-month internship from 2003-2004, and came back to work in his current capacity in 2009. His experience working with sexually broken men at Emmaus has profoundly impacted his life, teaching him much about the depths of God's mercy and grace. In his spare time, he writes articles about his other passions, which include sports, politics, theology, and real estate investing. He and his wife Aubrey live in Chicago. Visit www.streets.org to learn more.

Peter Grant, M.A.

Peter is the Co-Director of Restored, an international Christian alliance working with churches to transform relationships and end violence against women. Peter founded First Man Standing, Restored's men's campaign which calls for men to respect women, challenge each other and pledge to end violence against women. Peter was previously International Director for Tearfund, a UK-based development agency, and for the UK Government's Department for International Development. Peter holds an M.A. in Economics from University of Cambridge. He is married, has two grown-up children and lives in London. Please visit www.restoredrelationships.org and www.tearfund.org.

Wendy Gritter, M.Div., D.Min.

Wendy is the Executive Director at New Direction Ministries, an organization committed to nurturing generous spaciousness where gender and sexual minorities can explore and grow in faith in Jesus Christ. She is an internationally recognized contributor to the conversations at the intersection of faith and sexuality and the author of *Generous Spaciousness: Responding to Gay Christians in the Church*. Please visit www.newdirection.ca.

Craig Gross

Craig is an author, speaker, pastor and revolutionary. In 2002, he founded the website www.XXXchurch.com as a response to the hurting he saw both in those addicted to pornography and those employed in the industry. Craig also spearheaded the development of X3watch, an internet accountability system that is used by over 1 million people. He is the author of nine books, has been featured in renowned publications and has appeared on national news channels and talk shows. He currently resides in Los Angeles with his wife Jeanette and their two children. His most recent book is called *OPEN - What Happens When You Get Real, Get Honest and Get Accountable*. Please visit www.craiggross.com/bio for a list of his published work.

Jonathan W. Hancock, M.Div.

Jonathan is a past Executive Director of Emmaus Ministries in Chicago. He has a B.A. from Wheaton College and M.Div. from Trinity Evangelical Divinity School. He has worked in urban ministry in Chicago since 1986. He is also a former pastor and ministry director at LaSalle Street Church and a church planter with the Evangelical Covenant Church of America. Jonathan was a founding Board member of Emmaus, was on the board for 10 years, and joined the staff in 2005, serving for eight years. He and his wife Beverly have two daughters and live on Chicago's near west side. He enjoys vacations, hiking, the environment, movies, exercise and chocolate. For more about Emmaus, please visit www.streets.org.

Alastair Hilton

Originally hailing from the UK, Alastair has a thirty year career in social work and lead the team which carried out the very first in-depth study in Cambodia to focus on the sexual abuse of males, entitled "I Thought It Could Never Happen to Boys: The Sexual Abuse and Exploitation of Boys in Cambodia" (2008). He was a founding member, and is now technical advisor of First Step Cambodia, a specialist NGO working with male survivors of sexual abuse and their supporters. Please visit www.first-step-cambodia.org.

Tim Høiland, M.A.

Tim is Editor of Flourish PHX, an online storytelling platform focused on metro Phoenix. He is also Co-director of Communications for Lemonade International, a community development organization working in La Limonada, the largest urban slum in Central America. Previously, he worked in communications and media relations at World Vision and in the Cuban/Haitian refugee resettlement program of Church World Service. Tim received an M.A. in International Development from Eastern University. He also writes for a number of magazines on issues of faith, integral mission, international development, and social justice. The son of linguists, Tim was born and raised in Guatemala. He lives in Tempe, Arizona with his wife Katie. Please visit www.tjhoiland.com.

Donna M. Hughes, Ph.D.

Donna is a leading international researcher on human trafficking. She has completed research on the trafficking of women and girls for sexual exploitation in the United States, Russia and Ukraine. She has also worked on issues related to women, science and technology, particularly on how new information technologies are used for the sex trafficking of women and girls. She is frequently consulted by governments and NGOs on policy related to women's human rights, particularly on trafficking of women and girls for sexual exploitation. She has testified before the U.S. House International Relations Committee, the Senate Foreign Relations Committee, the Moscow Duma, and the Czech Parliament. Her research has received wide support from governmental, academic and civil society entities both nationally and abroad. Please visit www.uri.edu/artsci/wms/hughes.

Carl W. Jylland-Halverson, Ph.D.

Dr. Jylland-Halverson is the Director of the Mental Health Counseling program and the Pastoral Counseling postgraduate programs at the University of Saint Francis. He is a Professor at USF and an adjunct instructor for the Adler School of Professional Psychology in Chicago. He is also a licensed clinical psychologist. Dr. Jylland-Halverson did field work and sabbatical in Chicago where he worked with Emmaus Ministries, an urban ministry for homeless males who participate in prostitution. He has provided training in basic counseling skills and self-care to agencies that work with survivors of human trafficking in Nepal, Thailand, Malaysia and India. He has presented on exploited males, disaster mental health and trafficking to national and international conferences. Please visit www.sf.edu and www.streets.org.

Christian Lenty
Christian is the founder and director of the MST Project, a ministry which seeks to mentor men into a pursuit of greater purity and sexual wholeness. The MST Project engages in ministry to men who visit red-light districts in Thailand and in pursuing follow-up meetings and long-term discipleship with these men when possible. They also run a purity course for Christian men dealing with addictions and struggles through one-on-one mentoring and group sessions, as well as partner with the local expatriate church in Thailand in running Real Men Pursuing Purity events and conferences. Christian has lived and worked in Thailand for over 13 years and resides in Bangkok with his wife, Nui. Please visit www.mstproject.com.

Sven-Gunnar Lidén, M.S.S.
Rev. Lidén is the pastor of a Baptist Church in Kungsör, Sweden, that runs a second-hand shop, an exhibition about trafficking, and an aid program in Eastern Europe in cooperation with local churches and social government. He is currently pursuing a Doctorate in Sociology of Religion at Åbo Akademi, Finland. Rev. Lidén is also the Coordinator of the work against human trafficking for Equmenia Church, a merged denomination of Baptists, Methodists and Covenant churches, as well as the Coordinator for the European Baptist Anti-Trafficking Network. He has a nice family with Maria, three grown children and two dogs. Please visit www.ebf-atwg.org.

Heike Lippmann, B.A.
Heike has worked for Operation Mobilization in Europe since 2004 as a Training and Member Care Facilitator and Co-leader of an urban ministry team in Zurich, Switzerland. She obtained a B.A. in Theology in Switzerland and conducted her postgraduate studies in the UK. In 2013, she spent six months in Asia to work alongside people who combat human trafficking and sexual exploitation. After her return to Europe she joined the core team of the European Freedom Network as part of her mandate with OM. Her role includes speaking at church and mission events, strategic planning, networking and theological reflection. Please visit
www.europeanfreedomnetwork.org and www.om.org.

Jim Martin, B.A.
Jim is the author of *The Just Church* and the Vice President of Spiritual Formation for International Justice Mission. In this role, he supports the spiritual development of IJM's global leaders and their staff and speaks about IJM's work at churches and conferences to help build the justice movement. Jim recently served as IJM's Vice President of Church Mobilization, where he lead a team working to move churches to a deeper level of understanding of God's heart for justice. Before joining IJM, he was a pastor at The River

Church in San Jose, California. Over the years, Jim has spoken at church and mission events and provided training for pastors and lay leaders around the world. He received a B.A. in Education from the University of Massachusetts. He lives with his wife Jenna and three children in Washington, DC. The material in his essay is adapted from *The Just Church: Becoming a Risk-Taking, Justice-Seeking, Disciple-Making Congregation* by Jim Martin (Tyndale Momentum, 2012). Please visit www.thejustchurch.com and www.ijm.org.

Eric Mason, M.Div., M.A.
Rev. Eric Mason serves as an Episcopal priest and psychotherapist in the Seattle area. He holds a M.Div. from Yale University and a M.A. in Counseling Psychology from the Seattle School of Theology and Psychology. As a priest and therapist, he works with individuals in integrating faith, gender and sexuality. He continues to be inspired by the profundity of the Gospel. Please visit http://www.gracehere.org and http://ericmason.org.

Celeste McGee, M.A.
Celeste is originally from Oklahoma. She did her undergraduate studies in Family Psychology and then spent two years teaching in South Korea before beginning her Masters in Marriage and Family counseling in Texas. Celeste counseled female survivors of sexual trauma and also worked with men struggling with various forms of addiction in Oklahoma and Texas from 2001-2006. Celeste began traveling to Thailand between 2004 and 2006 before moving there permanently in 2007 to work at The Well in Bangkok. The Well helps Thai females and their families get away from prostitution. During this time, Celeste also started spending time with transgender sex workers. The men and transgender working in the sex industry are often overlooked and ignored by groups wanting to help "victims of human trafficking." In 2009, Celeste started a non-profit called Dton Naam. Today, Dton Naam focuses specifically on transgender individuals working in the sex industry, offering them alternative jobs, job training, counseling and classes in order to help them rebuild their lives in a healthy way. Please visit www.dtonnaam.org.

Bill Prevette, Ph.D.
Bill is the Admissions Tutor at the Oxford Centre for Mission Studies. His research focuses on youth and children at risk in the developing world. He also conducts studies on human trafficking and interventions, urban research, community development, and Pentecostalism in global mission. Bill is currently a board member for the Child Theology Movement in the UK and an appointed missionary to Europe and internationally with the Assemblies of God World Mission, as well as member of several other boards and technical advisor to faith-based organizations in Romania, Moldova, Cambodia and Africa. He further conducts semi-annual academic seminars and lectureships and is a member of the adjunct faculty in the School of Behavioral Sciences at Northwest University. Please visit www.ocms.ac.uk.

Alezandra Russell, B.A.
Alezandra is the founder of Urban Light, one of the only organizations providing tailored services and support to a severely overlooked and neglected group of young male victims of sex trafficking and child prostitution working in the red light districts of Chiang Mai, Thailand. She is committed to offering them realistic opportunities, services and programs for a life outside the grasp of the lucrative sex trade. Alezandra also works closely with U.S. policy-makers to implement and pass legislation surrounding the prevention of trafficking and exploitation. She has spoken to thousands of college students through her campus tours creating an entry point for youth involvement in combating sex trafficking. Please visit www.urban-light.org.

Andrew J. Schmutzer, Ph.D.
Andrew is Professor of Biblical Studies at Moody Bible Institute in Chicago. He devotes some of his research to theological issues involved in sexual abuse, including the nature of systemic evil, collective grief, the suffering of God, and transgenerational sexual abuse. He is the editor and contributor to *The Long Journey Home: Understanding and Ministering to the Sexually Abused.* Andrew is presently collaborating with other professionals to develop a curriculum on abuse prevention that graduate programs can use. He lives with his wife and three children in West Chicago. Please visit
www.moody.academia.edu/AndrewSchmutzer and
www.academia.edu/1033723/The_Long_Journey_Home_Understanding_and _Ministering_to_the_Sexually_Abused.

Steven Siler
Steven, founder of Music for the Soul, is executive producer of the six-time award-winning documentary film "Somebody's Daughter: A Journey to Freedom from Pornography," a proven resource for helping others understand the issue. He envisions an ongoing dialog about the realities of pornography, restoring dignity in the daughters and women of our culture. Steven hopes that by equipping people with the facts, the cultural tide can begin to see a shift. Please visit www.shessomebodysdaughter.org and www.musicforthesoul.org.

Tammy Stauffer
Tammy, Director of "She's Somebody's Daughter," is a dedicated advocate helping to raise awareness about sex trafficking and sexual exploitation. Understanding the harms our over-sexualized culture is causing in our young girls and women, her vision is to be a voice, helping others understand the connection of pornography in driving the demand for sexual exploitation, empowering others to create the kind of culture that honors all women. Please visit www.shessomebodysdaughter.org.

Helen Sworn, M.A.
Helen founded Chab Dai in 2005 and is now the International Director. In 2010, she completed a succession plan in handing Chab Dai Coalition

Cambodia to national Cambodian directors. Since then, she has been responsible for the international strategy and planning for Chab Dai, developing collaborative and learning coalitions in more than 18 countries. Helen has been working in the field of counter-trafficking and abuse since arriving in Cambodia in 1999, having assisted in the establishment of an aftercare home, reintegration program, prevention programs, field research and NGO support. Previously, she attended business school, worked in the corporate sector, attended Bible college and earned a Master's in Leadership, Innovation and Change. Helen lives in Cambodia with her husband Trevor and their two children. Please visit www.chabdai.org.

Kenneth R. Taylor, LCSW, CSAT

Ken is a mental health professional from the United States serving the mental health needs of expatriates in Southeast Asia. He specializes in the treatment of sex addiction and marital therapy. He has experience in treating adolescents and adults in both inpatient and outpatient settings. Ken was a counselor in a private practice clinic in Wheaton, Illinois for 25 years. He also was the director of an adolescent unit at a mental hospital in the Chicago area. He is a member of the International Institute for Trauma and Addiction Professionals, through which he received direct training from the renowned addictionologist Patrick Carnes. He and his wife Ruth live in Phnom Penh, Cambodia. They have four grown children and seven grandchildren. Please visit www.kenandruthtaylor.org.

Lisa L. Thompson, B.A., M.A.

Lisa is the Director of Anti-Trafficking for World Hope International, where she manages anti-trafficking and sexual violence recovery responses in Azerbaijan, Cambodia and Sierra Leone, as well as guides the development of new anti-trafficking related programs. Previously, she was the Liaison for the Abolition of Sexual Trafficking for The Salvation Army USA National Headquarters for more than 12 years. She chaired The Salvation Army's North American Anti-Trafficking Council and directed its Initiative Against Sexual Trafficking. Prior to this, Lisa was the Policy Representative for the National Association of Evangelicals' Office for Governmental Affairs in Washington, DC, where she was heavily involved in efforts seeking passage of legislation now known as the Trafficking Victims Protection Act of 2000. Please visit www.worldhope.org and www.iast.net.

Jennifer Roemhildt Tunehag, B.A.

Jennifer founded Nea Zoi, a ministry to exploited people in Athens, Greece, in 1998. She is also a founder and core team member of the European Freedom Network, a network of faith-based NGOs working to build a bridge to freedom across Europe. Jennifer serves on the Human Trafficking Task Force of the World Evangelical Alliance. Please visit
www.preventrestore.wordpress.com and www.europeanfreedomnetwork.org.

John Douglas Van Ramshorst
Doug comes from the glorious state of Indiana. Doug started with Emmaus Ministries as an intern in early 2005. After a few months he joined the staff and eventually began serving as Emmaus' Outreach Coordinator. He is now Outreach Director. When he is not walking the streets of Chicago late at night, he enjoys cycling, coffee, punk rock and hanging out with his wife Mary. Please visit www.streets.org.

Brian Wilkinson
Brian is the Head of Network Development at Viva. After a degree in Civil Engineering, ten years with John Laing Construction, and five years as a Director within Laing Homes, Brian brought his strategic outlook and management experience to the running of Viva. He has travelled extensively to all continents, developing the scope of the networks to design and implement initiatives that make a sustainable difference for vulnerable children. He has a passion to see the quality of Christian response to children at risk improved and find ways of developing greater collective action through Viva's partner networks. Brian and his wife live in Oxford with two daughters and have been registered foster carers with the local authority for over 15 years. Please visit www.viva.org.

David A. Kerr, Kenneth R. Ross (Eds)
Mission Then and Now
2009 / 978-1-870345-73-6 / 343pp (paperback)
2009 / 978-1-870345-76-7 / 343pp (hardback)

No one can hope to fully understand the modern Christian missionary movement without engaging substantially with the World Missionary Conference, held at Edinburgh in 1910. This book is the first to systematically examine the eight Commissions which reported to Edinburgh 1910 and gave the conference much of its substance and enduring value. It will deepen and extend the reflection being stimulated by the upcoming centenary and will kindle the missionary imagination for 2010 and beyond.

Daryl M. Balia, Kirsteen Kim (Eds)
Witnessing to Christ Today
2010 / 978-1-870345-77-4 / 301pp (hardback)

This volume, the second in the Edinburgh 2010 series, includes reports of the nine main study groups working on different themes for the celebration of the centenary of the World Missionary Conference, Edinburgh 1910. Their collaborative work brings together perspectives that are as inclusive as possible of contemporary world Christianity and helps readers to grasp what it means in different contexts to be 'witnessing to Christ today'.

Claudia Währisch-Oblau, Fidon Mwombeki (Eds)
Mission Continues
Global Impulses for the 21st Century
2010 / 978-1-870345-82-8 / 271pp (hardback)

In May 2009, 35 theologians from Asia, Africa and Europe met in Wuppertal, Germany, for a consultation on mission theology organized by the United Evangelical Mission: Communion of 35 Churches in Three Continents. The aim was to participate in the 100th anniversary of the Edinburgh conference through a study process and reflect on the challenges for mission in the 21st century. This book brings together these papers written by experienced practitioners from around the world.

Brian Woolnough and Wonsuk Ma (Eds)
Holistic Mission
God's Plan for God's People
2010 / 978-1-870345-85-9 / 268pp (hardback)

Holistic mission, or integral mission, implies God is concerned with the whole person, the whole community, body, mind and spirit. This book discusses the meaning of the holistic gospel, how it has developed, and implications for the church. It takes a global, eclectic approach, with 19 writers, all of whom have much experience in, and commitment to, holistic mission. It addresses critically and honestly one of the most exciting, and challenging, issues facing the church today. To be part of God's plan for God's people, the church must take holistic mission to the world.

Kirsteen Kim and Andrew Anderson (Eds)
Mission Today and Tomorrow
2010 / 978-1-870345-91-0 / 450pp (hardback)

There are moments in our lives when we come to realise that we are participating in the triune God's mission. If we believe the church to be as sign and symbol of the reign of God in the world, then we are called to witness to Christ today by sharing in God's mission of love through the transforming power of the Holy Spirit. We can all participate in God's transforming and reconciling mission of love to the whole creation.

Tormod Engelsviken, Erling Lundeby and Dagfinn Solheim (Eds)
The Church Going Glocal
Mission and Globalisation
2011 / 978-1-870345-93-4 / 262pp (hardback)

The New Testament church is… universal and local at the same time. The universal, one and holy apostolic church appears in local manifestations. Missiologically speaking… the church can take courage as she faces the increasing impact of globalisation on local communities today. Being universal and concrete, the church is geared for the simultaneous challenges of the glocal and local.

Marina Ngurusangzeli Behera (Ed)
Interfaith Relations after One Hundred Years
Christian Mission among Other Faiths
2011 / 978-1-870345-96-5 / 338pp (hardback)

The essays of this book reflect not only the acceptance and celebration of pluralism within India but also by extension an acceptance as well as a need for unity among Indian Christians of different denominations. The essays were presented and studied at a preparatory consultation on Study Theme II: Christian Mission Among Other Faiths at the United Theological College, India July 2009.

Lalsangkima Pachuau and Knud Jørgensen (Eds)
Witnessing to Christ in a Pluralistic Age
Christian Mission among Other Faiths
2011 / 978-1-870345-95-8 / 277pp (hardback)

In a world where plurality of faiths is increasingly becoming a norm of life, insights on the theology of religious plurality are needed to strengthen our understanding of our own faith and the faith of others. Even though religious diversity is not new, we are seeing an upsurge in interest on the theologies of religion among all Christian confessional traditions. It can be claimed that no other issue in Christian mission is more important and more difficult than the theologies of religions.

Beth Snodderly and A Scott Moreau (Eds)
Evangelical Frontier Mission
Perspectives on the Global Progress of the Gospel
2011 / 978-1-870345-98-9 / 312pp (hardback)

This important volume demonstrates that 100 years after the World Missionary Conference in Edinburgh, Evangelism has become truly global. Twenty-first-century Evangelism continues to focus on frontier mission, but significantly, and in the spirit of Edinburgh 1910, it also has re-engaged social action.

Rolv Olsen (Ed)
Mission and Postmodernities
2011 / 978-1-870345-97-2 / 279pp (hardback)

This volume takes on meaning because its authors honestly struggle with and debate how we should relate to postmodernities. Should our response be accommodation, relativizing or counter-culture? How do we strike a balance between listening and understanding, and at the same time exploring how postmodernities influence the interpretation and application of the Bible as the normative story of God's mission in the world?

Cathy Ross (Ed)
Life-Widening Mission
2012 / 978-1-908355-00-3 / 163pp (hardback)

It is clear from the essays collected here that the experience of the 2010 World Mission Conference in Edinburgh was both affirming and frustrating for those taking part - affirming because of its recognition of how the centre of gravity has moved in global Christianity; frustrating because of the relative slowness of so many global Christian bodies to catch up with this and to embody it in the way they do business and in the way they represent themselves. These reflections will - or should - provide plenty of food for thought in the various councils of the Communion in the coming years.

Beate Fagerli, Knud Jørgensen, Rolv Olsen, Kari Storstein Haug and
Knut Tveitereid (Eds)
A Learning Missional Church
Reflections from Young Missiologists
2012 / 978-1-908355-01-0 / 218pp (hardback)

Cross-cultural mission has always been a primary learning experience for the church. It pulls us out of a mono-cultural understanding and helps us discover a legitimate theological pluralism which opens up for new perspectives in the Gospel. Translating the Gospel into new languages and cultures is a human and divine means of making us learn new 'incarnations' of the Good News.

Emma Wild-Wood & Peniel Rajkumar (Eds)
Foundations for Mission
2012 / 978-1-908355-12-6 / 309pp (hardback)

This volume provides an important resource for those wishing to gain an overview of significant issues in contemporary missiology whilst understanding how they are applied in particular contexts.

Wonsuk Ma & Kenneth R Ross (Eds)
Mission Spirituality and Authentic Discipleship
2013 / 978-1-908355-24-9 / 248pp (hardback)

This book argues for the primacy of spirituality in the practice of mission. Since God is the primary agent of mission and God works through the power of the Holy Spirit, it is through openness to the Spirit that mission finds its true character and has its authentic impact.

Stephen B Bevans (Ed)
A Century of Catholic Mission
2013 / 978-1-908355-14-0 / 337pp (hardback)

A Century of Catholic Mission surveys the complex and rich history and theology of Roman Catholic Mission in the one hundred years since the 1910 Edinburgh World Mission Conference. Essays written by an international team of Catholic mission scholars focus on Catholic Mission in every region of the world, summarize church teaching on mission before and after the watershed event of the Second Vatican Council, and reflect on a wide variety of theological issues.

Robert Schreiter & Knud Jørgensen (Eds)
Mission as Ministry of Reconcilation
2013 / 978-1-908355-26-3 / 382pp (hardback)

There is hope – even if it is "Hope in a Fragile World", as the concluding chapter of Mission as Ministry of Reconciliation puts it. At the very heart of the gospel of Jesus Christ is a message of hope and reconciliation. Nothing could be more relevant and more necessary in a broken world than this Christian message of hope and reconciliation. ... I would like to congratulate the editors of Mission as Ministry of Reconciliation, for they listened carefully and planned with farsightedness. ... This rich book offers a valuable elucidation of the importance and the understanding of mission as ministry of reconciliation.

Petros Vassiliadis, Editor
Orthodox Perspectives on Mission
2013 / 978-1908355-25-6 / 262pp (hardback)
Orthodox Perspectives on Mission is both a humble tribute to some great Orthodox theologians, who in the past have provided substantial contribution to contemporary missiological and ecumenical discussions, and an Orthodox input to the upcoming 2013 Busan WCC General Assembly. The collected volume is divided into two parts: Part I: The Orthodox Heritage consists of Orthodox missiological contributions of the past, whereas Part II includes all the papers presented in the Plenary of the recent Edinburgh 2010 conference, as well as the short studies and contributions prepared, during the Edinburgh 2010 on going study process.

Pauline Hoggarth, Fergus MacDonald,
Bill Mitchell & Knud Jørgensen, Editors
Bible in Mission
2013 / 978-1908355-42-3 / 317pp (hardback)
To the authors of Bible in Mission, the Bible is the book of life, and mission is life in the Word. This core reality cuts across the diversity of contexts and hermeneutical strategies represented in these essays. The authors are committed to the boundary-crossings that characterize contemporary mission – and each sees the Bible as foundational to the missio Dei, to God's work in the world.

Wonsuk Ma, Veli-Matti Kärkkäinen
& J Kwabena Asamoah
Pentecostal Mission and Global Christianity
2014 / 978-1908355-43-0 / 397pp (hardback)
Although Pentecostalism worldwide represent the most rapidly growing missionary movement in Christian history, only recently scholars from within and outside the movement have begun academic reflection on the mission. This volume represents the coming of age of emerging scholarship of various aspects of the Pentecostal mission, including theological, historical, strategic, and practical aspects.

Afe Adogame, Janice McLean & Anderson Jeremiah, Editors
Engaging the World
Christian Communities in Contemporary Global Societies
2014 / 978-1908355-21-8 / 235pp (hardback)
Engaging the World deals with the lived experiences and expressions of Christians in diverse communities across the globe. Christian communities do not live in a vacuum but in complex, diverse social-cultural contexts; within wider communities of different faith and social realities. Power, identity and community are key issues in considering Christian communities in contemporary contexts.

Peniel Jesudason Rufus Rajkumar, Joseph Prabhakar Dayam
& IP Asheervadham, Editors
Mission At and From the Margins
Patterns, Protagonists and Perspectives
*2014 / 978-1908355-13-3 / 283pp (*hardback)

Mission At and From the Margins: Patterns, Protagonists and Perspectives revisits the 'hi-stories' of Mission from the 'bottom up' paying critical attention to people, perspectives and patterns that have often been elided in the construction of mission history. Focusing on the mission story of Christian churches in the South Indian state of Abdhra Pradesh this collection of essays ushers its readers to re-shape their understanding of the landscape of mission history by drawing their attention to the silences and absences within pre-dominant historical accounts.

REGNUM STUDIES IN GLOBAL CHRISTIANITY

David Emmanuel Singh (Ed)
Jesus and the Cross
Reflections of Christians from Islamic Contexts
2008 / 978-1-870345-65-1 / 226pp

The Cross reminds us that the sins of the world are not borne through the exercise of power but through Jesus Christ's submission to the will of the Father. The papers in this volume are organised in three parts: scriptural, contextual and theological. The central question being addressed is: how do Christians living in contexts, where Islam is a majority or minority religion, experience, express or think of the Cross?

Sung-wook Hong
Naming God in Korea
The Case of Protestant Christianity
2008 / 978-1-870345-66-8 / 170pp (hardback)

Since Christianity was introduced to Korea more than a century ago, one of the most controversial issues has been the Korean term for the Christian 'God'. This issue is not merely about naming the Christian God in Korean language, but it relates to the question of theological contextualization - the relationship between the gospel and culture - and the question of Korean Christian identity. This book demonstrates the nature of the gospel in relation to cultures, i.e., the universality of the gospel expressed in all human cultures.

Hubert van Beek (Ed)
Revisioning Christian Unity
The Global Christian Forum
2009 / 978-1-870345-74-3 / 288pp (hardback)

This book contains the records of the Global Christian Forum gathering held in Limuru near Nairobi, Kenya, on 6 – 9 November 2007 as well as the papers presented at that historic event. Also included are a summary of the Global Christian Forum process from its inception until the 2007 gathering and the reports of the evaluation of the process that was carried out in 2008.

Young-hoon Lee
The Holy Spirit Movement in Korea
Its Historical and Theological Development
2009 / 978-1-870345-67-5 / 174pp (hardback)

This book traces the historical and theological development of the Holy Spirit Movement in Korea through six successive periods (from 1900 to the present time). These periods are characterized by repentance and revival (1900-20), persecution and suffering under Japanese occupation (1920-40), confusion and division (1940-60), explosive revival in which the Pentecostal movement played a major role in the rapid growth of Korean churches (1960-80), the movement reaching out to all denominations (1980-2000), and the new context demanding the Holy Spirit movement to open new horizons in its mission engagement (2000-).

Paul Hang-Sik Cho
Eschatology and Ecology
Experiences of the Korean Church
2010 / 978-1-870345-75-0 / 260pp (hardback)

This book raises the question of why Korean people, and Korean Protestant Christians in particular, pay so little attention to ecological issues. The author argues that there is an important connection (or elective affinity) between this lack of attention and the other-worldly eschatology that is so dominant within Korean Protestant Christianity.

Dietrich Werner, David Esterline, Namsoon Kang, Joshva Raja (Eds)
The Handbook of Theological Education in World Christianity
Theological Perspectives, Ecumenical Trends, Regional Surveys
2010 / 978-1-870345-80-0 / 759pp

This major reference work is the first ever comprehensive study of Theological Education in Christianity of its kind. With contributions from over 90 international scholars and church leaders, it aims to be easily accessible across denominational, cultural, educational, and geographic boundaries. The Handbook will aid international dialogue and networking among theological educators, institutions, and agencies.

David Emmanuel Singh & Bernard C Farr (Eds)
Christianity and Education
Shaping of Christian Context in Thinking
2010 / 978-1-870345-81-1 / 374pp

Christianity and Education is a collection of papers published in *Transformation: An International Journal of Holistic Mission Studies* over a period of 15 years. The articles represent a spectrum of Christian thinking addressing issues of institutional development for theological education, theological studies in the context of global mission, contextually aware/informed education, and academies which deliver such education, methodologies and personal reflections.

J.Andrew Kirk
Civilisations in Conflict?
Islam, the West and Christian Faith
2011 / 978-1-870345-87-3 / 205pp

Samuel Huntington's thesis, which argues that there appear to be aspects of Islam that could be on a collision course with the politics and values of Western societies, has provoked much controversy. The purpose of this study is to offer a particular response to Huntington's thesis by making a comparison between the origins of Islam and Christianity.

David Emmanuel Singh (Ed)
Jesus and the Incarnation
Reflections of Christians from Islamic Contexts
2011 / 978-1-870345-90-3 / 245pp

In the dialogues of Christians with Muslims nothing is more fundamental than the Cross, the Incarnation and the Resurrection of Jesus. Building on the *Jesus and the Cross*, this book contains voices of Christians living in various 'Islamic contexts' and reflecting on the Incarnation of Jesus. The aim and hope of these reflections is that the papers weaved around the notion of 'the Word' will not only promote dialogue among Christians on the roles of the Person and the Book but, also, create a positive environment for their conversations with Muslim neighbours.

Ivan M Satyavrata
God Has Not left Himself Without Witness
2011 / 978-1-870345-79-8 / 264pp

Since its earliest inception the Christian Church has had to address the question of what common ground exits between Christian faiths and other religions. This issue is not merely of academic interest but one with critical existential and socio-political consequences. This study presents a case for the revitalization of the fulfillment tradition based on a recovery and assessment of the fulfillment approaches of Indian Christian converts in the pre-independence period.

Bal Krishna Sharma
From this World to the Next
Christian Identity and Funerary Rites in Nepal
2013 / 978-1-908355-08-9 / 238pp

This book explores and analyses funerary rite struggles in a nation where Christianity is a comparatively recent phenomenon, and many families have multi-faith, who go through traumatic experiences at the death of their family members. The author has used an applied theological approach to explore and analyse the findings in order to address the issue of funerary rites with which the Nepalese church is struggling.

J Kwabena Asamoah-Gyada
Contemporary Pentecostal Christianity
Interpretations from an African Context
2013 / 978-1-908355-07-2 / 194pp

Pentecostalism is the fastest growing stream of Christianity in the world. The real evidence for the significance of Pentecostalism lies in the actual churches they have built and the numbers they attract. This work interprets key theological and missiological themes in African Pentecostalism by using material from the live experiences of the movement itself.

David Emmanuel Singh and Bernard C Farr (Eds)
The Bible and Christian Ethics
2013 / 978-1-908355-20-1 / 217pp

This book contains papers from the Oxford Centre for Mission Studies' quarterly journal, Transformation, on the topic of Christian Ethics. Here, Mission Studies is understood in its widest sense to also encompass Christian Ethics. At the very hearts of it lies the Family as the basic unit of society. All the papers together seek to contribute to understanding how Christian thought is shaped in contexts each of which poses its own challenge to Christian living in family and in broader society.

Martin Allaby
Inequality, Corruption and the Church
Challenges & Opportunities in the Global Church
2013 / 978-1-908355-16-4 / 228pp

Why are economic inequalities greatest in the southern countries where most people are Christians? This book teases out the influences that have created this situation, and concludes that Christians could help reduce economic inequalities by opposing corruption. Interviews in the Philippines, Kenya, Zambia and Peru reveal opportunities and challenges for Christians as they face up to corruption.

Paul Alexander and Al Tizon (Eds)
Following Jesus
Journeys in Radical Discipleship – Essays in Honor of Ronald J Sider
2013 / 978-1-908355-27-0 / 228pp

Ronald J. Sider and the organization that he founded, *Evangelicals for Social Action*, are most respected for their pioneering work in the area of evangelical social concern. However, Sider's great contribution to social justice is but a part of a larger vision – namely, biblical discipleship. His works, which span more than four decades, have guided the faithful to be authentic gospel-bearers in ecclesial, cultural and political arenas. This book honors Ron Sider, by bringing together a group of scholar-activists, old and young, to reflect upon the gospel and its radical implications for the 21st century.

Cawley Bolt
Reluctant or Radical Revolutionaries?
Evangelical Missionaries and Afro-Jamaican Character, 1834-1870
2013 / 978-1-908355-18-8 / 287pp

This study is based on extensive research that challenges traditional ways of understanding some evangelical missionaries of nineteenth century Jamaica and calls for revision of those views. It highlights the strength and character of persons facing various challenges of life in their effort to be faithful to the guiding principles of their existence.

Isabel Apawo Phiri & Dietrich Werner (Eds)
Handbook of Theological Education in Africa
2013 / 978-1-908355-45-4 / 1110pp

The *Handbook of Theological Education in Africa* is a wake-up call for African churches to give proper prominence to theological education institutions and their programmes which serve them. It is unique, comprehensive and ambitious in its aim and scope.

Hope Antone, Wati Longchar, Hyunju Bae, Huang Po Ho, Dietrich Werner (Eds)
Asian Handbook for Theological Education and Ecumenism
2013 / 978-1-908355-30-0 / 675pp (hardback)

This impressive and comprehensive book focuses on key resources for teaching Christian unity and common witness in Asian contexts. It is a collection of articles that reflects the ongoing 'double wrestle' with the texts of biblical tradition as well as with contemporary contexts. It signals an investment towards the future of the ecumenical movement in Asia.

Bernhard Reitsma
The God of My Enemy
The Middle East and the Nature of God
2014 / 978-1-908355-50-8 / 206pp

The establishment of the State of Israel in 1948 for the Church in the West has been the starting point of a rediscovery of its own roots. In the Middle East the effect has been exactly the opposite: Christians have become estranged from their Old Testament roots, because they have been expelled from their land exactly because of an appeal to the Old Testament. The concept of Israel changed from a nation in the Bible, with which they could associate, to an economic, political and military power that was against them

REGNUM STUDIES IN MISSION

Kwame Bediako
Theology and Identity
The Impact of Culture upon Christian Thought in the Second Century and in Modern Africa
1992 / 978-1870345-10-1 / 507pp

The author examines the question of Christian identity in the context of the Graeco–Roman culture of the early Roman Empire. He then addresses the modern African predicament of quests for identity and integration.

Christopher Sugden
Seeking the Asian Face of Jesus
The Practice and Theology of Christian Social Witness
in Indonesia and India 1974–1996
1997 / 1-870345-26-6 / 496pp

This study focuses on contemporary holistic mission with the poor in India and Indonesia combined with the call to transformation of all life in Christ with micro-credit enterprise schemes. 'The literature on contextual theology now has a new standard to rise to' – Lamin Sanneh (Yale University, USA).

Hwa Yung
Mangoes or Bananas?
The Quest for an Authentic Asian Christian Theology
1997 / 1-870345-25-5 / 274pp

Asian Christian thought remains largely captive to Greek dualism and Enlightenment rationalism because of the overwhelming dominance of Western culture. Authentic contextual Christian theologies will emerge within Asian Christianity with a dual recovery of confidence in culture and the gospel.

Keith E. Eitel
Paradigm Wars
The Southern Baptist International Mission Board Faces the Third Millennium
1999 / 1-870345-12-6 / 140pp

The International Mission Board of the Southern Baptist Convention is the largest denominational mission agency in North America. This volume chronicles the historic and contemporary forces that led to the IMB's recent extensive reorganization, providing the most comprehensive case study to date of a historic mission agency restructuring to continue its mission purpose into the twenty-first century more effectively.

Samuel Jayakumar

Dalit Consciousness and Christian Conversion

Historical Resources for a Contemporary Debate

1999 / 81-7214-497-0 / 434pp

(Published jointly with ISPCK)

The main focus of this historical study is social change and transformation among the Dalit Christian communities in India. Historiography tests the evidence in the light of the conclusions of the modern Dalit liberation theologians.

Vinay Samuel and Christopher Sugden (Eds)

Mission as Transformation

A Theology of the Whole Gospel

1999 / 978-18703455-13-2 / 522pp

This book brings together in one volume twenty five years of biblical reflection on mission practice with the poor from around the world. This volume helps anyone understand how evangelicals, struggling to unite evangelism and social action, found their way in the last twenty five years to the biblical view of mission in which God calls all human beings to love God and their neighbour; never creating a separation between the two.

Christopher Sugden

Gospel, Culture and Transformation

2000 / 1-870345-32-3 / 152pp

A Reprint, with a New Introduction,

of Part Two of Seeking the Asian Face of Jesus

Gospel, Culture and Transformation explores the practice of mission especially in relation to transforming cultures and communities. - 'Transformation is to enable God's vision of society to be actualised in all relationships: social, economic and spiritual, so that God's will may be reflected in human society and his love experienced by all communities, especially the poor.'

Bernhard Ott

Beyond Fragmentation: Integrating Mission and Theological Education

A Critical Assessment of some Recent Developments

in Evangelical Theological Education

2001 / 1-870345-14-9 / 382pp

Beyond Fragmentation is an enquiry into the development of Mission Studies in evangelical theological education in Germany and German-speaking Switzerland between 1960 and 1995. The author undertakes a detailed examination of the paradigm shifts which have taken place in recent years in both the theology of mission and the understanding of theological education.

Gideon Githiga

The Church as the Bulwark against Authoritarianism

Development of Church and State Relations in Kenya, with Particular Reference to the Years

after Political Independence 1963-1992

2002 / 1-870345-38-x / 218pp

'All who care for love, peace and unity in Kenyan society will want to read this careful history by Bishop Githiga of how Kenyan Christians, drawing on the Bible, have sought to share the love of God, bring his peace and build up the unity of the nation, often in the face of great difficulties and opposition.' Canon Dr Chris Sugden, Oxford Centre for Mission Studies.

Myung Sung-Hoon, Hong Young-Gi (Eds)
Charis and Charisma
David Yonggi Cho and the Growth of Yoido Full Gospel Church
2003 / 978-1870345-45-3 / 218pp

This book discusses the factors responsible for the growth of the world's largest church. It expounds the role of the Holy Spirit, the leadership, prayer, preaching, cell groups and creativity in promoting church growth. It focuses on God's grace (charis) and inspiring leadership (charisma) as the two essential factors and the book's purpose is to present a model for church growth worldwide.

Samuel Jayakumar
Mission Reader
Historical Models for Wholistic Mission in the Indian Context
2003 / 1-870345-42-8 / 250pp
(Published jointly with ISPCK)

This book is written from an evangelical point of view revalidating and reaffirming the Christian commitment to wholistic mission. The roots of the 'wholistic mission' combining 'evangelism and social concerns' are to be located in the history and tradition of Christian evangelism in the past; and the civilizing purpose of evangelism is compatible with modernity as an instrument in nation building.

Bob Robinson
Christians Meeting Hindus
An Analysis and Theological Critique of the Hindu-Christian Encounter in India
2004 / 987-1870345-39-2 / 392pp

This book focuses on the Hindu-Christian encounter, especially the intentional meeting called dialogue, mainly during the last four decades of the twentieth century, and specifically in India itself.

Gene Early
Leadership Expectations
How Executive Expectations are Created and Used in a Non-Profit Setting
2005 / 1-870345-30-9 / 276pp

The author creates an Expectation Enactment Analysis to study the role of the Chancellor of the University of the Nations-Kona, Hawaii. This study is grounded in the field of managerial work, jobs, and behaviour and draws on symbolic interactionism, role theory, role identity theory and enactment theory. The result is a conceptual framework for developing an understanding of managerial roles.

Tharcisse Gatwa
The Churches and Ethnic Ideology in the Rwandan Crises 1900-1994
2005 / 978-1870345-24-8 / 300pp
(Reprinted 2011)

Since the early years of the twentieth century Christianity has become a new factor in Rwandan society. This book investigates the role Christian churches played in the formulation and development of the racial ideology that culminated in the 1994 genocide.

Julie Ma
Mission Possible
Biblical Strategies for Reaching the Lost
2005 / 978-1870345-37-8 / 142pp

This is a missiology book for the church which liberates missiology from the specialists for the benefit of every believer. It also serves as a textbook that is simple and friendly, and yet solid in biblical interpretation. This book links the biblical teaching to the actual and contemporary missiological settings with examples, making the Bible come alive to the reader.

I. Mark Beaumont
Christology in Dialogue with Muslims
A Critical Analysis of Christian Presentations of Christ for Muslims
from the Ninth and Twentieth Centuries
2005 / 978-1870345-46-0 / 227pp

This book analyses Christian presentations of Christ for Muslims in the most creative periods of Christian-Muslim dialogue, the first half of the ninth century and the second half of the twentieth century. In these two periods, Christians made serious attempts to present their faith in Christ in terms that take into account Muslim perceptions of him, with a view to bridging the gap between Muslim and Christian convictions.

Thomas Czövek,
Three Seasons of Charismatic Leadership
A Literary-Critical and Theological Interpretation of the Narrative of
Saul, David and Solomon
2006 / 978-1870345-48-4 / 272pp

This book investigates the charismatic leadership of Saul, David and Solomon. It suggests that charismatic leaders emerge in crisis situations in order to resolve the crisis by the charisma granted by God. Czovek argues that Saul proved himself as a charismatic leader as long as he acted resolutely and independently from his mentor Samuel. In the author's eyes, Saul's failure to establish himself as a charismatic leader is caused by his inability to step out from Samuel's shadow.

Richard Burgess
Nigeria's Christian Revolution
The Civil War Revival and Its Pentecostal Progeny (1967-2006)
2008 / 978-1-870345-63-7 / 347pp

This book describes the revival that occurred among the Igbo people of Eastern Nigeria and the new Pentecostal churches it generated, and documents the changes that have occurred as the movement has responded to global flows and local demands. As such, it explores the nature of revivalist and Pentecostal experience, but does so against the backdrop of local socio-political and economic developments, such as decolonisation and civil war, as well as broader processes, such as modernisation and globalisation.

David Emmanuel Singh & Bernard C Farr (Eds)
Christianity and Cultures
Shaping Christian Thinking in Context
2008 / 978-1-870345-69-9 / 271pp

This volume marks an important milestone, the 25th anniversary of the Oxford Centre for Mission Studies (OCMS). The papers here have been exclusively sourced from Transformation, a quarterly journal of OCMS, and seek to provide a tripartite view of

Christianity's engagement with cultures by focusing on the question: how is Christian thinking being formed or reformed through its interaction with the varied contexts it encounters? The subject matters include different strands of theological-missiological thinking, socio-political engagements and forms of family relationships in interaction with the host cultures.

Tormod Engelsviken, Ernst Harbakk, Rolv Olsen, Thor Strandenæs (Eds)
Mission to the World
Communicating the Gospel in the 21st Century:
Essays in Honour of Knud Jørgensen
2008 / 978-1-870345-64-4 / 472pp (hardback)

Knud Jørgensen is Director of Areopagos and Associate Professor of Missiology at MF Norwegian School of Theology. This book reflects on the main areas of Jørgensen's commitment to mission. At the same time it focuses on the main frontier of mission, the world, the content of mission, the Gospel, the fact that the Gospel has to be communicated, and the context of contemporary mission in the 21st century.

Al Tizon
Transformation after Lausanne
Radical Evangelical Mission in Global-Local Perspective
2008 / 978-1-870345-68-2 / 281pp

After Lausanne '74, a worldwide network of radical evangelical mission theologians and practitioners use the notion of "Mission as Transformation" to integrate evangelism and social concern together, thus lifting theological voices from the Two Thirds World to places of prominence. This book documents the definitive gatherings, theological tensions, and social forces within and without evangelicalism that led up to Mission as Transformation. And it does so through a global-local grid that points the way toward greater holistic mission in the 21st century.

Bambang Budijanto
Values and Participation
Development in Rural Indonesia
2009 / 978-1-870345-70-4 / 237pp

Socio-religious values and socio-economic development are inter-dependant, inter-related and are constantly changing in the context of macro political structures, economic policy, religious organizations and globalization; and micro influences such as local affinities, identity, politics, leadership and beliefs. The book argues that the comprehensive approach in understanding the socio-religious values of each of the three local Lopait communities in Central Java is essential to accurately describing their respective identity.

Alan R. Johnson
Leadership in a Slum
A Bangkok Case Study
2009 / 978-1-870345-71-2 / 238pp

This book looks at leadership in the social context of a slum in Bangkok from a different perspective than traditional studies which measure well educated Thais on leadership scales derived in the West. Using both systematic data collection and participant observation, it develops a culturally preferred model as well as a set of models based in Thai concepts that reflect on-the-ground realities. It concludes by looking at the implications of the anthropological approach for those who are involved in leadership training in Thai settings and beyond.

Titre Ande
Leadership and Authority
Bula Matari and Life - Community Ecclesiology in Congo
2010 / 978-1-870345-72-9 / 189pp

Christian theology in Africa can make significant development if a critical understanding of the socio-political context in contemporary Africa is taken seriously, particularly as Africa's post-colonial Christian leadership based its understanding and use of authority on the Bula Matari model. This has caused many problems and Titre proposes a Life-Community ecclesiology for liberating authority, here leadership is a function, not a status, and 'apostolic succession' belongs to all people of God.

Frank Kwesi Adams
Odwira and the Gospel
A Study of the Asante Odwira Festival and its Significance for Christianity in Ghana
2010 /978-1-870345-59-0 / 232pp

The study of the Odwira festival is the key to the understanding of Asante religious and political life in Ghana. The book explores the nature of the Odwira festival longitudinally - in pre-colonial, colonial and post-independence Ghana - and examines the Odwira ideology and its implications for understanding the Asante self-identity. Also discussed is how some elements of faith portrayed in the Odwira festival can provide a framework for Christianity to engage with Asante culture at a greater depth.

Bruce Carlton
Strategy Coordinator
Changing the Course of Southern Baptist Missions
2010 / 978-1-870345-78-1 / 273pp

This is an outstanding, one-of-a-kind work addressing the influence of the non-residential missionary/strategy coordinator's role in Southern Baptist missions. This scholarly text examines the twentieth century global missiological currents that influenced the leadership of the International Mission Board, resulting in a new paradigm to assist in taking the gospel to the nations.

Julie Ma & Wonsuk Ma
Mission in the Spirit:
Towards a Pentecostal/Charismatic Missiology
2010 / 978-1-870345-84-2 / 312pp

The book explores the unique contribution of Pentecostal/Charismatic mission from the beginning of the twentieth century. The first part considers the theological basis of Pentecostal/Charismatic mission thinking and practice. Special attention is paid to the Old Testament, which has been regularly overlooked by the modern Pentecostal/Charismatic movements. The second part discusses major mission topics with contributions and challenges unique to Pentecostal/Charismatic mission. The book concludes with a reflection on the future of this powerful missionary movement. As the authors served as Korean missionaries in Asia, often their missionary experiences in Asia are reflected in their discussions.

Allan Anderson, Edmond Tang (Eds)
Asian and Pentecostal
The Charismatic Face of Christianity in Asia
2011 / 978-1870345-94-1 / 500pp
(Revised Edition)

This book provides a thematic discussion and pioneering case studies on the history and development of Pentecostal and Charismatic churches in the countries of South Asia, South East Asia and East Asia.

S. Hun Kim & Wonsuk Ma (Eds)
Korean Diaspora and Christian Mission
2011 / 978-1-870345-89-7 / 301pp (hardback)

As a 'divine conspiracy' for Missio Dei, the global phenomenon of people on the move has shown itself to be invaluable. In 2004 two significant documents concerning Diaspora were introduced, one by the Filipino International Network and the other by the Lausanne Committee for World Evangelization. These have created awareness of the importance of people on the move for Christian mission. Since then, Korean Diaspora has conducted similar research among Korean missions, resulting in this book

Jin Huat Tan
Planting an Indigenous Church
The Case of the Borneo Evangelical Mission
2011 / 978-1-870345-99-6 / 343pp

Dr Jin Huat Tan has written a pioneering study of the origins and development of Malaysia's most significant indigenous church. This is an amazing story of revival, renewal and transformation of the entire region chronicling the powerful effect of it evident to date! What can we learn from this extensive and careful study of the Borneo Revival, so the global Christianity will become ever more dynamic?

Bill Prevette
Child, Church and Compassion
Towards Child Theology in Romania
2012 / 978-1-908355-03-4 / 382pp

Bill Prevett comments that "children are like 'canaries in a mine shaft'; they provide a focal point for discovery and encounter of perilous aspects of our world that are often ignored." True, but miners also carried a lamp to see into the subterranean darkness. This book is such a lamp. It lights up the subterranean world of children and youth in danger of exploitation, and as it does so travels deep into their lives and also into the activities of those who seek to help them.

Samuel Cyuma
Picking up the Pieces
The Church and Conflict Resolution in South Africa and Rwanda
2012 / 978-1-908355-02-7 / 373pp

In the last ten years of the 20th century, the world was twice confronted with unbelievable news from Africa. First, there was the end of Apartheid in South Africa, without bloodshed, due to responsible political and Church leaders. The second was the mass killings in Rwanda, which soon escalated into real genocide. Political and Church leaders had been unable to prevents this crime against humanity. In this book, the question is raised: can we compare the situation in South Africa with that in Rwanda? Can Rwandan leaders draw lessons from the peace process in South Africa?

Peter Rowan
Proclaiming the Peacemaker
The Malaysian Church as an Agent of Reconciliation in a Multicultural Society
2012 / 978-1-908355-05-8 / 268pp

With a history of racial violence and in recent years, low-level ethnic tensions, the themes of peaceful coexistence and social harmony are recurring ones in the discourse of Malaysian society. In such a context, this book looks at the role of the church as a reconciling agent, arguing that a reconciling presence within a divided society necessitates an ethos of peacemaking.

Edward Ontita
Resources and Opportunity
The Architecture of Livelihoods in Rural Kenya
2012 / 978-1-908355-04-1 / 328pp

Poor people in most rural areas of developing countries often improvise resources in unique ways to enable them make a living. Resources and Opportunity takes the view that resources are dynamic and fluid, arguing that villagers co-produce them through redefinition and renaming in everyday practice and use them in diverse ways. The book focuses on ordinary social activities to bring out people's creativity in locating, redesigning and embracing livelihood opportunities in processes.

Kathryn Kraft
Searching for Heaven in the Real World
A Sociological Discussion of Conversion in the Arab World
2012 / 978-1-908355-15-7 / 142pp

Kathryn Kraft explores the breadth of psychological and social issues faced by Arab Muslims after making a decision to adopt a faith in Christ or Christianity, investigating some of the most surprising and significant challenges new believers face.

Wessley Lukose
Contextual Missiology of the Spirit
Pentecostalism in Rajasthan, India
2013 / 978-1-908355-09-6 / 256pp

This book explores the identity, context and features of Pentecostalism in Rajasthan, India as well as the internal and external issues facing Pentecostals. It aims to suggest 'a contextual missiology of the Spirit,' as a new model of contextual missiology from a Pentecostal perspective. It is presented as a glocal, ecumenical, transformational, and public missiology.

Paul M Miller
Evangelical Mission in Co-operation with Catholics
A Study of Evangelical Tensions
2013 / 978-1-908355-17-1 / 291pp

This book brings the first thorough examination of the discussions going on within Evangelicalism about the viability of a good conscience dialogue with Roman Catholics. Those who are interested in evangelical world missions and Roman Catholic views of world missions will find this informative.

Alemayehu Mekonnen
Culture Change in Ethiopia
An Evangelical Perspective
2013 / 978-1-908355-39-3 / 199pp

This book addresses the causes and consequences of culture change in Ethiopia, from Haile Selassie to the present, based on thorough academic research. Although written from an evangelical perspective, this book invites Ethiopians from all religions, ideological, and ethnic backgrounds to reflect on their past, to analyse their present and to engage in unity with diversity to face the future.

Godwin Lekundayo
The Cosmic Christ
Towards Effective Mission Among the Maasai
2013 / 978-1-908355-28- 7 / 259 pp

This book reveals a complex interaction between the Christian gospel brought by western missionaries and the nomadic Massai culture of Tanzania ... an important insider's voice courageously questioning the approach to condemn some critical Maasai practices, particularly polygamy, and its missionary consequences. This is a rare study from a Maasai Christian leader.

Philippe Ouedraogo
Female Education and Mission
A Burkina Faso Experience
2014 / 978-1-908355-11-9 / 263pp

This volume is the result of six years research in 'Overcoming Obstacles to Female Education in Burkina Faso'. It narrates how Christians and religious groups can speed up female education and contribute to the socio-economic growth of Burkina Faso. Religious culture and traditions were seen as a problem to female education. However, the evidence from this research shows that Christianity is also part of the solution to a quality female education, thus a key factor of socio economic growth
of the country.

Haw Yung
Mangoes or Bananas?
The Quest for an Authentic Asian Christian Theology
(Second Edition)
2014 / 978-1-908355-47-8 / 232pp

Over the past few decades there has been a growing awareness of the need for contextual theologies throughout Asia. But how genuinely contextual are these? Based on the premise that theology and mission are inseparable, the author applies four missiological criteria to representative examples of Protestant Asian writings to assess their adequacy or otherwise as contextual theologies.

Daniel Taichoul Yang
Called Out for Witness
The Missionary Journey of Grace Korean Church
2014 / 978-1-908355-49-2 / 167pp

This book investigates the theological motivation for GKC's missions: Reformed theology, Presbyterian theology, and mission theology. The book also shows the extent of the church's mission engagement by continents. Finally, the book turns its attention to the future with an evaluation of the church's missionary journey.

REGNUM RESOURCES FOR MISSION

Knud Jørgensen
Equipping for Service
Christian Leadership in Church and Society
2012 / 978-1-908355-06-5 / 150pp

This book is written out of decades of experience of leading churches and missions in Ethiopia, Geneva, Norway and Hong Kong. Combining the teaching of Scripture with the insights of contemporary management philosophy, Jørgensen writes in a way which is practical and applicable to anyone in Christian service. "The intention has been to challenge towards a leadership relevant for work in church and mission, and in public and civil society, with special attention to leadership in Church and organisation."

Mary Miller
What does Love have to do with Leadership?
2013 / 978-1-908355-10-2 / 100pp

Leadership is a performing art, not a science. It is the art of influencing others, not just to accomplish something together, but to want to accomplish great things together. Mary Miller captures the art of servant leadership in her powerful book. She understands that servant leaders challenge existing processes without manipulating or overpowering people.

Mary Miller (Ed)
Faces of Holistic Mission
Stories of the OCMS Family
2013 / 978-1-908355-32-4 / 104pp

There is a popular worship song that begins with the refrain, 'look what the Lord has done, look what the Lord has done'. This book does exactly that; it seeks to show what the Lord has done. Fifteen authors from five different continents identify what the Lord has indeed been doing, and continues to do, in their lives. These are their stories.

David Cranston and Ruth Padilla DeBorst (Eds)
Mission as Transformation
Learning from Catalysts
2013 / 978-1-908355-34-8 / 77pp

This book is the product of the first Stott-Bediako Forum, held in 2012 with the title *Portraits of Catalysts*. Its aim was to learn from the stories of Christian leaders whose lives and work have served as catalysts for transformation as each, in his or her particular way, facilitated the intersection between the Good News of Jesus Christ and the context in which they lived, in particular amongst people who are suffering.

Brian Woolnough (Ed)
Good News from Africa
Community Transformation Through the Church
2013 / 978-1-908355-33-1 / 123pp

This book discusses how sustainable, holistic, community development can be, and is being, achieved through the work of the local church. Leading African development practitioners describe different aspects of development through their own experience.

Makonen Getu (Ed)
Transforming Microfinance
A Christian Approach
2013 / 978-1-908355-31-7 / 264pp

"This book highlights the important role that Christian-based organisations bring to the delivery of financial services for the poor. It is times, significant and important and deserves a wide circulation".

Lord Carey of Clifton, former Archbishop of Canterbury

Jonathan Ingleby, Tan Kand San, Tan Loun Ling, (Eds)
Contextualisation & Mission Training
Engaging Asia's Religious Worlds
2013 / 978-1-908355-40-9 / 109pp

Contextualisation & Mission Training, offers "contextual frameworks" and "explorations" in order to enhance deeper engagement with the complexity of Asian social, cultural and religious systems.

On Eagle's Wings
Models in Mentoring
2013 / 978-1-908355-46-1 / 105pp

David Cranston writes unashamedly as a Christian for whom no account of mentoring would be complete without placing it in the biggest context of all – that of the relationship between humans and God.

John Lennox, Professor of Mathematics, University of Oxford
Fellow in Mathematics and Philosophy of Science

GENERAL REGNUM TITLES

Vinay Samuel, Chris Sugden (Eds)
The Church in Response to Human Need
1987 / 1870345045 / xii+268pp

Philip Sampson, Vinay Samuel, Chris Sugden (Eds)
Faith and Modernity
Essays in modernity and post-modernity
1994 / 1870345177 / 352pp

Klaus Fiedler
The Story of Faith Missions
1994 / 0745926878 / 428pp

Douglas Peterson
Not by Might nor by Power
A Pentecostal Theology of Social Concern in Latin America
1996 / 1870345207 / xvi+260pp

David Gitari
In Season and Out of Season
Sermons to a Nation
1996 / 1870345118 / 155pp

David. W. Virtue
A Vision of Hope
The Story of Samuel Habib
1996 / 1870345169 / xiv+137pp

Everett A Wilson
Strategy of the Spirit

J.Philip Hogan and the Growth of the Assemblies of God Worldwide, 1960 - 1990
1997 /1870345231/214

Murray Dempster, Byron Klaus, Douglas Petersen (Eds)
The Globalization of Pentecostalism
A Religion Made to Travel
1999 / 1870345290 / xvii+406pp

Peter Johnson, Chris Sugden (Eds)
Markets, Fair Trade and the Kingdom of God
Essays to Celebrate Traidcraft's 21st Birthday
2001 / 1870345193 / xii+155pp

Robert Hillman, Coral Chamberlain, Linda Harding
Healing & Wholeness
Reflections on the Healing Ministry
2002 / 978-1- 870345-35- 4 / xvii+283pp

David Bussau, Russell Mask
Christian Microenterprise Development
An Introduction
2003 / 1870345282 / xiii+142pp

David Singh
Sainthood and Revelatory Discourse
An Examination of the Basis for the Authority of Bayan in Mahdawi Islam
2003 / 8172147285 / xxiv+485pp

REGNUM AFRICA TITLES

Kwame Bediako
Jesus in Africa, The Christian Gospel in African History and Experience
(2000) (Theological Reflections from the South series)
SECOND EDITION FORTHCOMING 2013

Mercy Amba Oduyoye
Beads and Strands, Reflections of an African Woman on Christianity in Africa
(Theological Reflections from the South series)
2002 / 1-870345-41-X / 114pp

Kä Mana
Christians and Churches of Africa Envisioning the Future, Salvation in Christ and the Building of a new African Society
(Theological Reflections from the South series)
2002 / 1-870345-27-4 / 119pp

Ype Schaaf
On Their Way Rejoicing, The History and Role of the Bible in Africa
2002 / 1-870345-35-9 / 252pp

E.A.W. Engmann
Kpawo-Kpawo Toi Kpawo – Vol. 1, Adesai, Oboade, Lalai, Ajenui ke Shwemoi
(Folklore of the Ga People)
(Gbotsui Series - Indigenous Sources of Knowledge in Ghanaian Languages)
2009 / 978-9988-1-2296-6 / 70pp

Philip Tetteh Laryea
Yesu Homowo Nuntso (Jesus, Lord of Homowo)
(Nyamedua series in Mother-tongue Theology)
(reprinted 2011) / 1-870345-54-1 / 176pp

E.A.W. Engmann
Kpawo-Kpawo Toi Kpawo – Vol. 2, Kusumii (Folklore of the Ga People)
(Gbotsui Series - Indigenous Sources of Knowledge in Ghanaian Languages)
2012 / 978-9988-1-2294-2, 186pp

Philip T. Laryea
Ephraim Amu: Nationalist, Poet and Theologian (1899–1995)
2012 / 978-9988-1-2293-5, 425pp

Jon P. Kirby
The Power and the Glory, Popular Christianity in Northern Ghana
(Trends in African Christianity Series)
2012 / 978-9988-1-2295-9, 350pp

For the up-to-date listing of the Regnum books visit www.ocms.ac.uk/regnum

Regnum Books International
Regnum is an Imprint of The Oxford Centre for Mission Studies
St. Philip and St. James Church
Woodstock Road
Oxford, OX2 6HR

regnum

40220117R00202

Made in the USA
San Bernardino, CA
14 October 2016